WE'LL HAVE
MANHATTAN

WE'LL HAVE MANHATTAN

The Early Work
of Rodgers and Hart

DOMINIC SYMONDS

OXFORD
UNIVERSITY PRESS

OXFORD
UNIVERSITY PRESS

Oxford University Press is a department of the
University of Oxford. It furthers the University's objective
of excellence in research, scholarship, and education
by publishing worldwide.

Oxford   New York

Auckland   Cape Town   Dar es Salaam   Hong Kong   Karachi
Kuala Lumpur   Madrid   Melbourne   Mexico City   Nairobi
New Delhi   Shanghai   Taipei   Toronto

With offices in

Argentina   Austria   Brazil   Chile   Czech Republic   France   Greece
Guatemala   Hungary   Italy   Japan   Poland   Portugal   Singapore
South Korea   Switzerland   Thailand   Turkey   Ukraine   Vietnam

Oxford is a registered trade mark of Oxford University Press
in the UK and certain other countries.

Published in the United States of America by
Oxford University Press
198 Madison Avenue, New York, NY 10016

Library of Congress Cataloging-in-Publication Data
Symonds, Dominic, author.
We'll have Manhattan: the early work of Rodgers and Hart, 1919–1931
/Dominic Symonds.
pages   cm.—(The Broadway legacies series)
ISBN 978-0-19-992948-1 (hardback)
1. Rodgers, Richard, 1902–1979—Criticism and interpretation.
2. Hart, Lorenz, 1895–1943—Criticism and interpretation.
3. Musicals—United States–20th century—History and criticism.   I. Title.
ML410.R6315S96   2015
782.1'40922—dc23   2014016376

1 3 5 7 9 8 6 4 2
Printed in the United States of America
on acid-free paper

For KAREN, VERITÉ, EVELYN, *and* MAX, *with love*

(And because there's a song about everything)

CONTENTS

● ● ●

ILLUSTRATIONS

* * *

FOREWORD

• • •

A 1938 *Time* magazine cover story boldly proclaimed that "nobody ever fused words and music more effectively than Rodgers and Hart." The twenty-six Broadway shows the pair created between their first meeting in 1919 and Hart's death in 1943 contain a vast legacy of timeless songs, at least one or two in each show (see the accompanying footnote for a representative list of fine songs first appearing in the shows that are explored in the present volume).* But while the songs are glorious and rightfully revered, the shows that introduced them are far less well known and less appreciated. This is a shame. From the beginning of their career, the "boys from Columbia [i.e., Columbia University]" worked hard to use songs to tell stories in new ways and often achieved this goal. The result was a succession of innovative musicals that broke new dramatic ground and a long list of swell and witty, sweet and grand, and often wicked, beautifully crafted, sophisticated, memorable, and seldom formulaic songs.

Despite their relatively low profile—with some exceptions later in their career such as *On Your Toes* (1936), *Babes in Arms* (1937), *The Boys from Syracuse* (1938), and the widely acclaimed pioneering classic *Pal Joey* (1940)—the Rodgers and Hart shows, especially those from the early years, deserve to be better known and understood. This is where the author of *We'll Have Manhattan: The Early Work of Rodgers and Hart, 1919–1943* comes to the rescue. Symonds, Reader in Drama at the University of Lincoln, author of the forthcoming *Broadway Rhythm: Imaging the City in Song* (University of Michigan Press), co-editor (with George Burrows) of the journal *Studies in Musical Theatre,* and co-founder of the international conference *Song, Stage and Screen,* has meticulously but engagingly examined the early work of Rodgers and Hart with special attention to the two *Garrick Gaieties* (1925 and 1926), *Dearest Enemy*

---

* "Manhattan" (*Garrick Gaieties*, 1925); "Here in My Arms" (*Dearest Enemy*, 1925); "Mountain Greenery" (*Garrick Gaieties*, 1926); "Blue Room" and "The Girl Friend" (*The Girl Friend,* 1926); "A Tree in the Park" and "Where's That Rainbow?" (*Peggy-Ann*, 1926); "My Heart Stood Still," "Thou Swell," and "On a Desert Isle with Thee" (*A Connecticut Yankee,* 1927); "You Took Advantage of Me" (*Present Arms,* 1928); "Yours Sincerely" and "With a Song in My Heart" (*Spring Is Here,* 1929); "A Ship without a Sail" (*Heads Up!,* 1929); "Ten Cents a Dance" (*Simple Simon,* 1930); "Dancing on the Ceiling" (*Ever Green,* 1930); "I've Got Five Dollars" (*America's Sweetheart,* 1931).

(1925), *The Girl Friend* and *Peggy-Ann* (1926), *A Connecticut Yankee* (1927), *Chee-Chee* (1928), and the three shows the team wrote for the London stage, *Lido Lady* (1926), *One Dam Thing after Another* (1927), and *Ever Green* (1930, on which the 1934 film *Evergreen* is based). Symonds also offers a chapter on the team's frustrating, mostly amateur years between 1919 and 1925, during which they struggled to find a place in the commercial marketplace. They finally took Manhattan by storm with the song "Manhattan" in the Theatre Guild fundraiser, the *Garrick Gaieties* of 1925. Another chapter, on their less successful Broadway efforts that followed the stock market crash of 1929, illuminates a series of lesser successes that prompted the pair to seek their fortune in Hollywood (a story to be continued in Symonds's second volume).

In his introduction, Symonds reveals "three main influences that weave through each of the chapters": (1) "Rodgers and Hart's continued exploration of how song works dramatically within a narrative"; (2) "how the business of theater, guided by influences from the media, audiences, economics, and technologies, affected their aesthetic and creative output": and (3) "the significance of identity." In *"We'll Have Manhattan,"* readers will learn more about the impressive but largely unrecognized work by this innovative team and in the bargain also gain a new appreciation for a largely unsung collaborator, their talented librettist Herbert Fields. Fields contributed well-crafted and stylish (and sometimes blue) books for nearly all the Rodgers and Hart successes in the 1920s and was conspicuously absent for some of the less successful shows of this period.

Symonds's story of *Chee-Chee* stands out as particularly gripping. Although their greatest disappointment at thirty-one performances, this musical about "castration," as Rodgers characterized the show in his autobiography *Musical Stages* (1975), was especially daring artistically as well as in subject matter. Rodgers wrote that *Chee-Chee* was the first musical that gave the pair the opportunity to put into practice their theories on how to achieve their desired goal of "unity of song and story," and he described their use in it of song fragments rather than longer, traditional (i.e., 32-bar) song forms. In fact, despite an unusually abundant score, only six full-length songs are given in most song lists for the show. Rodgers includes the program note that explains why this is the case: "The musical numbers, some of them very short, are so interwoven with the story, that it would be confusing for the audience to peruse a complete list." It is clear from interviews and letters that Rodgers and Hart took great pride in this innovative show. Its also clear in retrospect that the show's painful failure was a turning point in their career, especially evident in the artistic retrenchment in the shows that followed, a move that arguably postponed their next wave of dramatic innovation until their return to Broadway in the late 1930s after their Hollywood diaspora. In his generous chapter on this show in *"We'll Have Manhattan,"* Symonds is the first to give the historically important and invariably overlooked *Chee-Chee* its due.

I don't think it is an exaggeration to assert that Rodgers and Hart were the most significant composer and lyricist musical theater team from the 1920s to the early 1940s. Although their songs have eclipsed their shows, the boys from Columbia arguably created the most impressive body of musical theater teamwork between Gilbert and Sullivan in the late nineteenth century and Rodgers (with Hammerstein) in the 1940s and 1950s. In this volume (and its projected sequel in Broadway Legacies) Dominic Symonds gives the boys the royal treatment they so richly deserve.

Geoffrey Block
Series Editor, Broadway Legacies

ACKNOWLEDGMENTS

• • •

Writing a book on a subject about which you are passionate is a labor of love. It has been a joy to immerse myself in this material, written almost a hundred years ago, yet still bursting with life: images, rhythms, witticisms, and personalities spring out of the pages of dusty manuscripts and forgotten shows. Unexpectedly, so much of this has been accessible—it's not always been organized or ordered, and it has sometimes required piecing together, but at least most of it has been there to be explored, carefully warded by some wonderful guardians.

In limiting the scope of this book to the first twelve years of Rodgers and Hart's collaboration, I am able to give significant attention to most of the major shows of this period: nineteen in all. Even so, the book cannot be exhaustive. The pair were so prolific and their work so widely adapted in different contexts that it has not been possible to cover everything. In particular, the work of their varsity days is given a general overview, but I dwell on only some of the more important output from this six-year period. That this leaves out a wealth of their early work is regrettable but is one of the necessary exigencies of compiling a manageable book. Also regrettable is that different versions, rewrites, and touring adaptations of their work have had to be sidelined in favor of giving sufficient coverage to what might be seen as the "main" productions (see figure T.1 for a snapshot of these). Of course, such editorial decisions are part of an inevitable canonizing process, raising the profile of certain shows that may not warrant such attention, while labeling others the "also-rans." The later part of the collaboration, with a similar level of creative output, a flirtation with Hollywood, and a series of classic successes on Broadway, is also left out—the rich seam of a future project, *The Boys from Columbia: Rodgers and Hart, 1932–1943.*

It is a fascinating area of exploration. For much of this period, recording technology was in its infancy, and a general attitude toward musical theater was that it was ephemeral, its shows of passing value, and its materials only working documents. One of the reasons these shows have remained in the shadow for so long is that they have no current record that is accessible or available. Original cast recordings—at least in the manner we know them today—do not exist, though a variety of period recordings, revivals, and "revisiteds" offer us a tantalizing aural glimpse into the sound of the 1920s. Likewise, scripts and scores of material have not been published and were never publicly available, though theater programs are a valuable source of structural knowledge about a show and how it may have changed throughout the production process. That key practitioners—not least Rodgers himself—retained documents, working notes, and memorabilia from the shows has been fortuitous rather than by design, but has enabled an archive of the original creative work to be gathered together in diverse institutions across the globe. My research has been facilitated by archives in the United States and the United Kingdom, and by the support of archivists and curators who have been generous and knowledgeable in their assistance. In particular, the Library of Congress, the New York Library of the Performing Arts, the British Library, the Victoria and Albert Museum, the Rodgers and Hammerstein Organization, and archives at Columbia University and Yale University have been of invaluable help in sourcing and allowing access to materials, and I am also grateful for the generous grants awarded by the University of Portsmouth and the University of Lincoln to enable me to visit these archives and reproduce some of the materials within these pages. Such materials provide wonderful insight into the working practices of Rodgers, Hart, and their collaborators, though by no means do they provide an exhaustive archive of their shows.

I have also benefited from the prior work of other scholars, not least Geoffrey Block, whose careful research into Richard Rodgers provides a real backbone for this book. Likewise, I am indebted to the carefully researched theses of a number of other projects. The work of Graham Wood, which in part focuses on *Dearest Enemy* and *A Connecticut Yankee*, offers a key methodological tool for further research into this area; dissertations by several scholars, notably Jason Rubin, have proved equally invaluable. Finally, there are models for this sort of in-depth study of a practitioner's output: Charles Hamm's work on Irving Berlin's early years (1997), Stephen Banfield's study of *Sondheim's Broadway Musicals* (1994), and Jeffrey Magee's recent focus on *Irving Berlin's American Musical Theater* (2012) are exemplars of the type of book *We'll Have Manhattan* aims to be.

There are times in the writing process when the road seems endless and the journey solitary. At those times the company of folk I have met along the road has sustained my resolve: Dick, Larry, and Herb have been great companions along the way, of course, and others we have encountered en route have offered energy, dynamism, and brilliance: Oscar Hammerstein, Lew Fields, Helen Ford, Cicely Courtneidge, Jack Hulbert, C. B. Cochran . . . These are figures I will not forget, and I hope that in these pages they come to life as vividly as they have done for me as I have leafed through the ephemera they left behind.

But writing a book is not always a solitary pursuit; part of the delight has been to share this journey with others who have offered help, expertise, and advice along the way. Many of these have been the archivists and curators of collections I have explored: Mark Eden Horowitz, Walter Zvonchenko, Alice Birney, and Dan Walshaw at the Library of Congress, Jeremy Megraw at the New York Public Library for the Performing Arts, Jocelyn Wilk at the Columbia University Library. Not only have they shared with me the documents in their collections but also the stories that come with those documents—the anecdotes and oddities that have been passed down orally, the creative links between documents I would not have connected, and the tantalizing new directions their embodied knowledge of the archives gives them. To all of these custodians—and others who remain unnamed—I am immensely grateful.

I am also grateful to everyone who has put up with me fixating on this project: to my kids who have patiently listened to 1920s music on the way to gym every Saturday; to Karen who has held the fort during all my research jollies to the States; to my colleagues at the Universities of Portsmouth and Lincoln, who have been tirelessly supportive. In particular, Colin and Maricar Jagger, George Burrows, and Karen Savage have listened patiently to my late night ramblings, always with enthusiasm, expertise, and gently barbed putdowns.

There are plenty of others who have assisted through conversation: though they may not be aware, little things that have been said or intimated have unlocked thoughts or details and led to important insights. Thanks to Stuart Olesker, Laurie Ede, Sue Harper, Justin Smith, and Searle Kochberg; to Bill Everett, David Savran, Stacy Wolf, Jeffrey Magee, Jim Lovensheimer, Laura MacDonald, and Ben Macpherson; to Larry Starr, to Mark Wilde, and by email Scott Willis.

Thanks too to delegates at the "Song, Stage and Screen / Music in Gotham" conference at City University of New York in 2008 where I first presented research on *Chee-Chee*; and to delegates at the same conference at the University of Missouri, Kansas City, in 2011 where I presented on *Lido Lady*; to audiences at the Chichester Festival Theatre and the University of Bristol, with whom I shared further thoughts during this journey. Testing the water like this is an invaluable opportunity, and I am indebted to John Graziano, Bill Everett, Stephen Banfield, and the staff at Chichester for making that possible.

Finally, a few special thanks to those people without whom . . .

First to Geoffrey Block. I suppose it shows some front to propose a book on Rodgers and Hart to a series editor who is an international expert; but Geoffrey has been gracious in his support, and of course his own publications have been instrumental in showing me where to begin.

Next, Norm Hirschy and his colleagues at Oxford University Press. Many will know Norm and recognize his dedication, encouragement, and enthusiasm for scholarship in this area. It has been my privilege to work with Norm and to benefit from his guidance, support, and constant goodwill.

Closer to home, I have also been privileged to work with Rosalyn Casbard as my research assistant. Ros's help in negotiating the minefield of copyright and permissions has been immeasurable. She's also had to read more of the draft material than I would care to land on anyone.

I would also like to thank Millie Taylor, who has found time in between many projects of her own (and several on which we have been working together) to read some of these chapters and give her feedback, always assiduous, focused, and to the point.

Likewise, special gratitude goes to Bruce Pomahac at the Rodgers and Hammerstein Organization. I cannot imagine anyone more passionate, generous, or knowledgeable about this material; Bruce has been a constant source of support, and wonderful company to boot. His tremendous insights into all things Rodgers have helped me in redrafting several chapters.

But I suppose more than anyone, I should thank two chaps who are no longer around for me to thank in person. Without them this book would be meaningless; but more significantly, without them we wouldn't have all those songs. Here's to Dick and Larry—and also a bit to Herb.

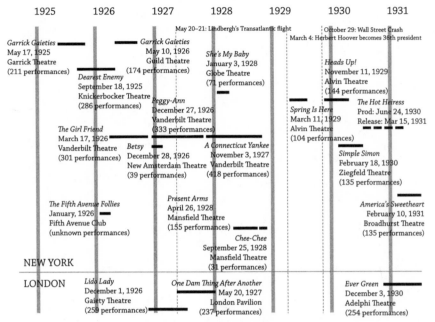

1925   1926   1927   1928   1929   1930   1931

May 20–21: Lindbergh's Transatlantic flight

October 29: Wall Street Crash
March 4: Herbert Hoover becomes 36th president

Garrick Gaieties
May 17, 1925
Garrick Theatre
(211 performances)

Garrick Gaieties
May 10, 1926
Guild Theatre
(174 performances)

She's My Baby
January 3, 1928
Globe Theatre
(71 performances)

Heads Up!
November 11, 1929
Alvin Theatre
(144 performances)

Dearest Enemy
September 18, 1925
Knickerbocker Theatre
(286 performances)

Peggy-Ann
December 27, 1926
Vanderbilt Theatre
(333 performances)

The Hot Heiress
Prod: June 24, 1930
Release: Mar 15, 1931

The Girl Friend
March 17, 1926
Vanderbilt Theatre
(301 performances)

Betsy
December 28, 1926
New Amsterdam Theatre
(39 performances)

A Connecticut Yankee
November 3, 1927
Vanderbilt Theatre
(418 performances)

Spring Is Here
March 11, 1929
Alvin Theatre
(104 performances)

Simple Simon
February 18, 1930
Ziegfeld Theatre
(135 performances)

The Fifth Avenue Follies
January, 1926
Fifth Avenue Club
(unknown performances)

Present Arms
April 26, 1928
Mansfield Theatre
(155 performances)

America's Sweetheart
February 10, 1931
Broadhurst Theatre
(135 performances)

Chee-Chee
September 25, 1928
Mansfield Theatre
(31 performances)

NEW YORK

LONDON

Lido Lady
December 1, 1926
Gaiety Theatre
(259 performances)

One Dam Thing After Another
May 20, 1927
London Pavilion
(237 performances)

Ever Green
December 3, 1930
Adelphi Theatre
(254 performances)

Figure T.1: Timeline of new Rodgers and Hart shows opening
in New York and London, 1925–1931.

WE'LL HAVE
MANHATTAN

INTRODUCTION

• • •

"WE'LL HAVE MANHATTAN"

We'll Have Manhattan
The Bronx and Staten Island too.

It's an iconic couplet, a classic sound bite of the great American song book
from the first resounding hit song of Richard Rodgers and Lorenz Hart:
"Manhattan." Such was the confidence of its writers, flying high with an initial flush of success on the college circuit, that they assert in this hook line a
sort of ownership: over Manhattan, over New York, and in time, over musical
theater. This was 1922. Hit after hit followed, and over the next two decades
the pair created some of the most abiding songs, each encapsulating the spirit
of American popular songwriting at its height: "Manhattan," "Mountain
Greenery," "You Took Advantage of Me," "Thou Swell," "With a Song in My
Heart," "Blue Moon," "The Lady Is a Tramp," "Bewitched" . . . the list goes on.
Each has stayed the test of time in its own right, though each originated in
one of the many musical comedies the pair penned throughout the 1920s and
1930s—close to fifty before their partnership was cut short by Larry Hart's
untimely death in 1943.

Rodgers and Hart were the precursors to Rodgers and Hammerstein, their
output—like the work of other contemporaries—eclipsed by the later team's
gargantuan profile. Although recent scholarship has begun to revisit the lives
and work of the less celebrated figures, dusty archives remain unexplored.
This book is an attempt to dust off some of those archives, adding to work
already published by Geoffrey Block, Frederick Nolan, Gary Marmorstein,
and others. It looks at the first decade or so of Rodgers and Hart's collaboration, from the point when they met in 1919 to when they briefly left Broadway to test their luck in Hollywood in 1931. They were to return—to even
greater success in the 1930s—though that is a different story. This one is

about that first prolific period, exploring some of their most forgotten work, and some of the fondly remembered material from their early years.

There are a number of reasons why a consideration of this period is important. Rodgers and Hart were by no means the figures they are remembered as today, and not yet established on Broadway. These were jobbing writers, competing with the older voices of Jerome Kern and Irving Berlin, and new, more visible kids on the block like George and Ira Gershwin, or Vincent Youmans. And there was other competition to contend with: a vogue for lush European classicism in the manner of Victor Herbert was enabling the romantic sounds of Rudolf Friml, Gustave Kerker, and Franz Lehár to sing out; at other venues, it was the romp of revues and the song hits of Berlin and Gershwin that were more popular, with Florenz Ziegfeld, George White, and Earl Carroll making it clear that girls were a safer bet, clothing merely optional. Against this background, Rodgers and Hart at times seem slightly out of their depth—babes in arms, pretenders to the throne. Yet in their collected work more than that of any other writing team, one can see most clearly the development of the Broadway musical between the wars.

"Early achievement creates a thirst hard to satisfy," wrote Rodgers. And before he was even twenty, he had enjoyed his fair share: "That thirst began with my early experience of writing theater scores and then conducting them before large and enthusiastic audiences," he observed.[1] These were amateur affairs in the late teens and early twenties: summer stock, charity benefits, college revues, but they offered an apprenticeship, and seemingly limitless opportunities. Dick Rodgers and his writing pals threw themselves into projects with relish. There was Ockie—Oscar Hammerstein II (1895–1960)—the mild-mannered head of operations whom Dick looked up to and adored; then there was Herb—Herbert Fields (1897–1958)—the mischievous dance director who dabbled in some of the scripts himself; and then Larry—or Lorry—a funny little chap who tossed off rhyming couplets with glee. After the success of one of their outings, the Columbia University Varsity Show *Fly with Me* (1920), they were spurred to spread their wings. Armed with script and score they marched into the offices of music publisher Max Dreyfus and presented to him a new musical comedy, *Winkle Town*, which they felt sure was the next great hit.

WINKLE TOWN (1922)

The narrative of *Winkle Town* begins at Edith Van Winkle's eighteenth birthday celebrations. Her entrepreneur father is proposing to power the town and then the nation with his wireless invention, the Winkle Radio Light. Edith is in love with Van Winkle's assistant, Tom Kingsly, though a better match for her has been arranged in Harry Perry, the son of Van Winkle's old friend turned adversary, who is funding the invention. Edith and Harry get engaged, though secretly he is already married. When this is discovered, funding is pulled, and the future of the business falters until a mysterious Italian count intercedes and a bidding war ensues to protect American honor. Suddenly the Winkle Light equipment fails and plunges the town into darkness. Tom is sent to the roof of the factory to restore power and Edith follows. They declare their love as power returns and Winkle Town's lights flicker back into life.

This convoluted storyline, modeled around the inevitable romantic pairings of its principal characters, is typical of the period and reminiscent of countless shows from the 1920s or 1930s. Still, Fields and Hammerstein's 1922 script taps into some very contemporary and very American concerns: wireless technology, urban living, Hollywood stars, intrigue, and romance. Stealing the show at its climax is the song "Manhattan," given the most wonderful dramatic setting and therefore demonstrating in the work of its writers an impressive instinct for spectacle, dramaturgy, and poignancy. As the romantic leads climb to the roof of the darkened factory, the spectacle of the night sky takes center stage. First, the ensemble serenades the beauty of the stars; then Tom and Edith declare their love in what the collaborators surely rated as the show's hit. As they sing "Manhattan," the lights of Winkle Town flicker on to illuminate the city, and the show ends with the exhilarating spectacle of a cityscape bathed in the glow of electric light.

In this scenario, Fields and Hammerstein threw down the gauntlet to the lighting designers of 1922, people like Joseph Urban, designer for the Ziegfeld Follies, whose spectacular work at the Winter Garden "laid the groundwork for Broadway musicals for the rest of the century."[2] Here, they offered not only the challenge of portraying a constellation-lit panorama, but also the follow-up of a cityscape lighting up; a city metaphorically born through the wonders of technology. It may be the fictitious Winkle Town, Connecticut, but the suggestion is undoubtedly to create an impression of the Manhattan skyline at night, punctuated with its thousands of windows of electric light and seen from a vantage point that captures its iconicity.[3] In this, the writing team not only announce their fascination with Manhattan but also their fascination with modern technology: the Winkle Light Company does not provide *just* electric light, but *wireless* technology, a fantastical extrapolation riding on the recent invention of radio. As Tom and Edith gaze over the cityscape, they command the city, riding the crest of technology's revolutionary wave. Not only is Manhattan in their sights, but also the Bronx, and Staten Island too. And for Tom Kingsly and Edith Van Winkle, read Rodgers, Hart, Hammerstein, and Fields.

It's significant that this song is called "Manhattan"; it's not, for example, called "New York," though there are many such songs—brash, posturing anthems to "the city that never sleeps," slogans for branding the Big Apple as the megalopolis, capital of the world. But to these boys New York was not a brand, seen and coveted from a distance of geography or time; New York—Manhattan—was the everyday backdrop to their lives; authentic, a constant companion. Thus it is the comfortable detail that emerges in the song, sketched in the laconic, dreamy images of its lyrics and music. Manhattan is the insiders' New York, neither the city that trumpets its pretensions in big band stabs or dizzying skyscrapers, nor the "helluva town" that is seen to the tourist. This is the other New York, the one that New Yorkers know; and in subtle images and quirky miniatures of the every day, Lorenz Hart paints a different iconicity that other writers have followed: the trash collections in Little Italy; eating baloney on a roll in Coney Island; settling down in Flatbush; strolling through Central Park. Years later, Frank Loesser would capture a similar perception of the humble, quiet city in the words of his character Sky Masterson: "when the smell of the rain washed pavements comes up clean and fresh and bold" ("My Time of Day," from *Guys and Dolls*, 1950), while Stephen Sondheim would locate the essence of his character Tony's New York not in its bright lights or hyperbole, but "down a block, on a beach, under a tree" ("Something's Coming," from *West Side Story*, 1957). Although life for all of these characters is vital, and they all bristle—like New York—with the sense that "Something's Coming," the city is home and homely. "Manhattan" captures the quintessence of this paradoxical modern life in the adolescence of twentieth-century New York: with everything to play for, with the world's opportunities right on their doorstep, these boys are perfectly at home, and driven with excitement by the possibilities of modernism.

Rodgers's music, for example, demonstrates key features of an emerging American sound recognizable in his writing throughout his career. First, the chromatic turn on the opening line ("We'll have Man-") shows informality; it sounds slightly lazy, both in the way its melody dips almost imperceptibly, and in the way that the musical phrase misses the beat of the bar. Second, the way the verse material rattles through its introduction is casual, matching the mood of the lyrics and psychologically magnifying the impact of the chorus. In this verse, the melody fashions a simple repeat of two full rising scales, barely acceptable as a conventional melody and giving everything over to information setting up the song's theme. Such scalar motifs would become pervasive Rodgers features; meanwhile, the turn away from a formal verse of aesthetic appeal was a useful facilitator in emphasizing song as an expression of *character* rather than a rendition of *song*. Finally, the way in which Rodgers teases the listener by avoiding tonic resolution in the melody presents a relaxed, conversational impression. At times the melody casually dwells on the leading note without ever reaching the tonic ("(We'll have Man) –hat– (tan)"); at other times it overreaches it to hang precariously on the supertonic ("island too"). Only right at the end of the thirty-two-measure phrase does Rodgers finally commit to the much-anticipated tonic. Thus the chorus also confirms a structure of thirty-two measures as the tight unit of the Broadway song form.

So we meet "Manhattan"—and an unlikely couple from its heart. But who were these boys, who evoked in words and music the thrill of the adolescent city? Pictures of one show a dashing young man, athletic, handsome, precociously talented and a hit with the ladies; with hair swept back stylishly to form a widow's peak, and often grinning infectiously, Rodgers was the epitome of charm. Pictures of the other show quite the opposite: an awkward and funny-looking chap, Hart looked both older and younger than his years—thoughtful and intelligent, but with the confused social graces of a child. This distinction is also reported in their personalities. Rodgers was "quiet, self-contained, and a complete conformist: punctual, organized, sober, precise, diligent and ambitious—just about everything Lorry Hart was not."[4] Hart "drank too much, smoked too much, forgot to eat, spent money he didn't have, stayed up till dawn, [and] slept till noon."[5] In short, they were poles apart, and the impression that comes across from biographies confirms that perspective: Rodgers takes his work seriously, presents himself as the businessman, and wins admirers with his charm; Hart lives a frantic life in the moment, constantly in disarray, and needing to be cajoled into doing any writing. As those who knew them suggest, "Richard Rodgers acted like a stockbroker who happened to be a composer and Lorenz Hart acted like a poet who happened to be a lyricist."[6] Yet between the lines—both those written about them and those they penned themselves—a fuller picture emerges; a picture of two romantics, at times sentimental, at times cynical; two hot-headed youngsters, desperately ambitious yet in the shadow of their peers; and a picture that one (Rodgers) gets to airbrush after the other is long gone (Figure I.1).

It is undoubtedly the airbrushed Rodgers that emerges more favorably in history's recollection of this duo: the "golden boy"[7] of Broadway who became "the darling of the Mayfair set."[8] Hart, by contrast, is invariably if fondly maligned as a "manic-depressive gay tobacco-beclouded lush";[9] or (in Oscar Hammerstein II's words) "an electrified gnome."[10] The fact that he died young (actually from pneumonia) creates the impression that he drank or abused himself to death. Yet to those who knew the boys, suggest Samuel Marx and Jan Clayton, Hart "emerges the more likable, and, in comparison to Dick, who

Figure I.1: Larry Sobel's likeness of Rodgers and Hart in the Morning Telegraph, *June 12, 1927. (Clare Ogden, "The Mad Hatters of Manhattan,"* Morning Telegraph, *June 12, 1927. See NYPL—RRS JPH 85–5, Book 3.)*

comported himself with reliability, sobriety, and dignity, the more lovable of the two."[11] Hart seems more straightforward, more sincere; laden with troubles, perhaps, but carrying his emotional generosity and warmth on his sleeve. Rodgers, on the other hand, seems to have been enigmatically distant. "I don't think anyone really knew who he was," suggested his daughter Mary; "I don't think *he* knew. He was just all locked up in there."[12] His long-term secretary Lillian Leff confided the same: "I've seen him cry, I've seen him happy, worried, angry, thrilled, even. But never once did I know what was going on inside."[13] In fact, Rodgers's life was also beset with issues and anxieties, as becomes clear in the afterword to *Musical Stages,* written by John Lahr with a candor that subverts what the reader has just read in Rodgers's own writing:

> In his alcoholism, Hart seemed to seek death; in his hypochondria, Rodgers seemed in flight from it. Everything spilled out of Hart; Rodgers contained his feelings. In the partnership, the depressed Hart wore the clown's frantic face, which allowed the depressed Rodgers—who feared germs,

flying, tall buildings, elevators, tunnels, bridges—to wear the impassive one. At once cordial and saturnine, Rodgers was finally unknowable.[14]

As time has gone on, the troubles of the real Rodgers have been revealed, most tellingly in a *New York Times* article profiling his grandson Adam Guettel. Though sensationalist and dramatic, Jesse Green's picture of Rodgers as the tormented artist creates a vivid impression of a man whose suffering was carefully hidden beneath a façade of efficiency, correctional spin, and beautiful, melodious music:

> If the anguish and ameliorations of art are an old story, there's a reason we're still interested in why creative types suffer. Some try to eat their piano-playing fingers, some cut off their ears, some stash liquor in the toilet tank to ensure access to oblivion. That last was Rodgers: arguably the greatest American composer, and inarguably an alcoholic, a womanizer, an all-around tyrant. The wayward Hart did everything possible to get away from him when he couldn't face the music.[15]

Despite their troubles, both boys had hearts filled with empathy, emotion, and humor—places in which lovers could sing and youngsters could laugh. As Robert Russell Bennett put it, "Rodgers took great satisfaction in hiding all the warmth and tenderness he ever had in order to come out with it in song and surprise us all."[16] Perhaps it is also in his work—those swell and witty lyrics penned with a cheeky wink and a mischievous twinkle—that the real beauty of Larry Hart emerges.

The Boys from Manhattan

Lorenz Hart was born on the Upper East Side on May 2, 1895, the eldest surviving son of the German immigrant couple Max and Frieda Hart. By the time he was of school age they had relocated to West 119th Street by Morningside Heights, just one street away from the home of William and Mamie Rodgers, who had two sons of their own. Younger son Richard was born on June 28, 1902. The two families grew up so close to one another in a reasonably affluent Jewish neighborhood that it seems extraordinary their paths didn't cross. Nevertheless, despite their proximity the boys themselves—seven years different in age, after all—didn't meet until the Rodgers family had moved away.

In his memoirs, Rodgers writes fondly of his family. For financial reasons, they lived with his maternal grandparents until Dick was in his twenties, an inevitable source of frustration for his proud father, though the youngster felt the warmth of an extended household and doted on his irascible grandfather

Jacob. Despite financial strain, theirs was a middle-class lifestyle, and notably for Dick, a life full of music. Meanwhile, the Hart household was dominated by the larger-than-life character of Max. Ever the bon vivant, Larry's father would entertain until the small hours, planning all sorts of harebrained entrepreneurial schemes with various dubious contacts to put food on the table.

As the older Rodgers recalls, childhood was filled with his love of music and the usual pursuits of an energetic boy: stickball in the street and sledding down Mt. Morris Park hill. He recalls a couple of traumatic moments—not least some surgery on his index finger that might have cost him his musical career—but in general, his seems to have been a relaxed childhood consumed by twin passions for sport and music. Larry's was far more bookish, perhaps a result of the dual-language life to which he was exposed, perhaps a result of his inherited squat physique. At home—as a Jewish immigrant family—they spoke German. Yet although fortunes were up and down thanks to Max's erratic business deals, Larry and his brother Teddy enjoyed a lifestyle that wanted for nothing.

The two Hart boys were educated at Columbia Grammar and DeWitt Clinton High School in Hell's Kitchen. This was a school that would also welcome young Rodgers some years later. While Larry lapped up his academic education, particularly in literature, Dick's preference for extra-curricular activities (the athletics club, his music) meant that he found school work "duller than ever."[17] By that time his sights were set on greater things, and for him, the future was in musical theater.

Theater had a big impact on both boys. Hart was regularly taken to the German-language theater on Irving Place, later to the Star Theatre on 107th Street, and thanks to his father's short partnership with William Hammerstein (Oscar II's uncle), to Hammerstein's Victoria Theatre. Indeed, the Hart boys seem to have been immersed in a theatrical upbringing if the report of Teddy's wife Dorothy is anything to go by: "There wasn't a Broadway show they missed,"[18] she reports. Larry was writing rhyme at the age of six; by 1910, he'd been christened "Shakespeare" by friends. His first lyric was for Max and Frieda's silver wedding anniversary in 1911—a pastiche of "Alexander's Ragtime Band" with both an English and a German verse. Before long— by 1916—he was asked to write his first show by the producer of Irving Place, Gustave Amberg. *Die Tolle Dolly* (*Crazy Dolly*) was a show that "consisted of the usual knockabout German-language nonsense,"[19] presumably something very similar to the Weber and Fields type of Dutch act that had been popular for a generation. It made a play of linguistic malapropisms and physical slapstick, but it impressed Amberg. The following year, when he was just twenty-two, Amberg put him on contract to translate German-language plays indirectly for the Shuberts. In his own small way, Lorenz Hart had arrived.

Meanwhile, Rodgers's influence, which also came from his parents' love of the arts, and in particular their singing around the piano, was more centered on the music: "Songs from the current musical shows on Broadway."[20] He mentions *Mme. Modiste* (*Mlle. Modiste*, a Victor Herbert operetta from 1905), *The Merry Widow* (Franz Lehár, produced on Broadway in 1907), *The Chocolate Soldier* (Oscar Straus, 1909), and *The Spring Maid* (Heinrich Reinhardt, 1910). He was particularly taken by the music to *Little Nemo* (Herbert, 1908) and first recalls attending a show when he was only seven, when DeWolf Hopper starred in *The Pied Piper* (Manuel Klein, 1909). Trips to *The Quaker Girl* (Lionel Monckton, 1911), *Snow White and the Seven Dwarfs* at the Little Theatre (1912), *Carmen* at the Metropolitan Opera House, and Pavlova and Nijinsky at the ballet struck a chord, as did Josef Hofmann playing Tschaikovsky at Carnegie Hall.[21] Barely into his teens, Rodgers's exposure to live music in performance was extensive and varied, and it clearly implanted in the young man a creative desire to emulate what he heard with his own compositions. There's little surprise, then, that Rodgers's first attempts at writing songs came as early as Hart's first stabs at lyric-writing. The first to which he admits is the jaunty but simplistic "Camp Fire Days," written for a summer camp, Camp Wigwam, in 1916. Perhaps more significant is his first published song, "Auto Show Girl," written barely a year later yet with considerably more sophistication and craft: this is also a jaunty number but one showing a knack for form, an instinct for harmony, and—all right—a few wild leaps in the melody line, but plenty of promise.

Where their interests overlapped, the boys would discover, was in a series of little shows that were to leave a big mark in Broadway history. This was 1915. After a dubious project fell through to mount small-scale one-act plays, children's theater, or even Grand Guignol at a newly built boutique theater called the Princess, the inexperienced producer Ray Comstock teamed up with seasoned theatrical agent Elisabeth Marbury and decided to commission a series of small-scale musicals. Their inspiration, according to some, was the Joe Weber hit *The Only Girl* (1914), with its "small cast, simple sets, the absence of extraneous chorus personnel, and specialty acts."[22] That this was a risk is an understatement: Broadway audiences were becoming used to large-scale spectacle from revues like the Ziegfeld Follies and grand extravaganzas like the Shubert shows at the Hippodrome. To mount a musical in a 299-seat theater not only squeezed the possible revenue—and therefore the budget—but also called for a shift in the scope, scale, and size of the production. Yet the risk paid off, and with *Nobody Home* (1915), written by the relatively unknown

Guy Bolton and Jerome Kern and based on Paul Rubens's English musical comedy *Mr. Popple of Ippleton* (1905), Comstock and Marbury launched their acclaimed series: The Princess Shows, named for the theater.

Richard Rodgers's first exposure to the Princess Shows was through the next one, *Very Good Eddie* (1915),[23] which he saw when it toured to the Standard Theatre, a venue on the "Subway Circuit" at 90th Street and Broadway. "What I'd seen earlier was not an American kind of music. Even the Victor Herbert scores were Germanic, and what we got was European operettas—*Spring Maid, Chocolate Soldier*—all wonderful, very good scores, but the Kern scores had the freshness. And I think even as a child I knew that and it did something for me and to me."[24] He saw *Very Good Eddie* several times, then went to all the subsequent Princess Shows. Lorenz Hart was likewise smitten, Philip Leavitt recalls: "Lorry had a habit of sitting in front of an old Victor phonograph and listening to the Kern, Wodehouse, and Bolton operettas, and he loved the lyricisms that were in there, and he developed a style all of his own."[25] Hart would "rub his hands together and beam in satisfaction at Wodehouse's lyrics," report Armond and L. Marc Fields:[26] witty, urbane, intelligent, and sophisticated; eminently suited to the aspirational and intelligent youngster with a mischievous fascination for all things new.

The success of the Princess Shows owes itself not only to a timely combination of talented writers in Kern, Bolton, and lyricist P. G. Wodehouse but also to a sea change in both material and attitude caused by shifts in technology, behavior, and international relations. It's difficult to quantify precisely what changes were happening, though it's clear that a discernible difference came in response to the Great War and with the aid of burgeoning new technologies in transportation and communication. "The war was to bring an excited restlessness," suggests Joseph Kaye, "a reaction against old forms which was to affect the stage greatly."[27]

Until the mid-teens Broadway had been dominated by the sounds of middle Europe and imported successes from London. Among the old guard, Victor Herbert featured prominently with his popular European-style operettas in which swashbuckling vagabonds sparred with the nobility (*Naughty Marietta, Eileen*). In these, European influence is ever-present, thanks to the storylines, the swirling orchestral music, and Herbert's clear pretensions toward the operatic, which in this context represented classical respectability. "At his best," wrote critic H. T. Parker, "we Americans may justly match him against the more vaunted composers of Vienna."[28] This comment—typical of responses to Herbert and representative of attitudes at the time—reflects two of the most abiding concerns of American culture following the Great War: first, to establish a national artistic form that broke free of European influence to represent America; and second, to find a popular expression that could compete with the highbrow respectability of opera.[29] Other European composers—Jean Schwartz, Ludwig Engländer, Paul Rubens, Karl Hoschna—peddled similar fare to Herbert that would dominate Broadway throughout the Edwardian period and into the teens. Later, a younger wave of composers—Emmerich Kálmán, Rudolf Friml, and Sigmund Romberg—would continue this tradition, so it is not surprising that typical narratives of American musical theater point to the prevalence of European operetta, "with its reliance on romantic story, choral singing, ballads and substantial orchestral accompaniment."[30] However, the pendulum was swinging and an even younger wave was itching to find an American voice, a new musical language to match the heady rush of life in modern Manhattan.

An American form

Perhaps more than any other cultural idiom, the Broadway musical strained the fault lines between European and American culture, and between highbrow art and popular entertainment. After all, even before the war, musical theater had boasted numerous examples of work—not always easily distinguishable—that had reflected each of these qualities: voices with the tessitura of opera but legs that prompted letters to the press; characters from Ruritanian principalities with idiolects from the common city streets. Just as familiar as the operettas during this period were the shows of Ivan Caryll and Lionel Monckton, whose work—both collaboratively and individually—was imported to New York from London's Gaiety Theatre. Direct descendants of the Gilbert and Sullivan comic operas with their topsy-turvy tales, these shows profited from Caryll's orchestral scores and operatic finales, Monckton's song-hits that rocketed the partnership to success, a lineup of delectable Gaiety Girls for which impresario George Edwardes was famous, and comic storylines built on anachronistic situations. In *The Arcadians* (1909), a state-of-the-art airship lands in a quaint forgotten land; in *The Quaker Girl* (1910), an austere English Quaker is whisked to the lavish heart of Paris; in *Our Miss Gibbs* (1909), a British aristocrat falls for a Yorkshire shop girl. It is not hard to see how this sort of storyline would resonate some years later in the unlikely setups of *Dearest Enemy*, *The Girl Friend*, or *A Connecticut Yankee*.

Elsewhere, and trading less on storylines or scores than on Tin Pan Alley hits, star turns, and beautiful showgirls, were the lavish and spectacular revues epitomized by the Ziegfeld Follies (from 1907) and mimicked by the Shuberts' Passing Shows (from 1912). These were to be a training ground for many of the Broadway crowd, including Rodgers and Hart, and though their episodic nature and shameless reliance on entertainment bucked the developing trend toward integration as musical theater "matured," the revue must be credited as a fundamental component of Broadway theater at least until World War II.

Exceeding all of the revues for profile if nothing else were the annual long-running spectacles at the 5,300-seat Hippodrome Theatre, such as *Around the World* (1911), *Under Many Flags* (1912), and *America* (1913). These, conceived by Carroll Fleming and Arthur Voegtlin, with music composed by Manuel Klein, would run all season from September to May, reflecting the sort of lavish excess to which New York's musical theater aspired. And if culture reflects its society, as so many commentators have suggested, we can see in the titles of these shows alone the sort of dynamics with which the Manhattan of the developing twentieth century was obsessed: its place in the world, its role as a world city, its plurality, its multiculturalism, and its own identity as American.

As ties with Europe and what seemed like a hangover from the nineteenth century began to unravel, America sought its own voice and its own identity. This began in earnest, J. Ellen Gainor suggests, with former president Theodore Roosevelt's "desire to codify American identity," expressed in his 1911 call to the people to create a "distinctively American" culture that was "no longer imitative of European models."[31] In the same year, composer and conductor Walter Damrosch made his feelings on this very clear:

> The music of many other nations has exerted...influences on us, and we have gained by them, but we have not fashioned out of all of them, as yet, a music which can properly be called American. The Indian does not represent us, the negro does not represent us, and the early European settlers here had no music—they suppressed all music. The real American music, when it comes—and probably it is building now—may be a composite of many national musical expressions, but it must represent an American philosophy of life, and that can only be crystallized in time.[32]

However discomfiting these sentiments are to contemporary sensibilities, it is clear that Damrosch recognizes progress in music with the maturing of an American identity: "Whatever our people may develop into, that their music will eventually express.... Thus America will build her music—carefree, aspiring and inspiring, because of its abounding health. America's musical taste is building—a fine, strong, normal taste."[33]

In fact, America already had a distinctive voice of its own, which Charles Hamm traces back to the mid-nineteenth century, spearheaded by the Czech composer Antonín Dvořák.[34] Other writers point to examples of "Americanness" invoked in the mythic weight of anthems like "The Star-Spangled Banner"

(1814), "My Country! 'Tis of Thee" (1832) and "America the Beautiful" (1895); in a different field, Walt Whitman's whole oeuvre speaks to and of America ("I hear America singing," he writes in *Leaves of Grass*, 1855); George M. Cohan did likewise with his patriotic pronouncements in "The Yankee Doodle Boy" (1904), "You're a Grand Old Flag" (1906), and "Give My Regards to Broadway" (1907), and shows like *45 Minutes from Broadway* (1906), *George Washington, Jr.* (1906), *The Talk of New York* (1907), and *The Man Who Owns Broadway* (1909). Thus, Roosevelt's 1911 call tapped into something already concerning the nation, and the formation in 1913 of ASCAP (the American Society of Composers, Authors and Publishers) consolidated the identity of the American creative writer. Whether any of these events prompted new works or whether they simply acknowledged the increasing artistic articulations of America, a wealth of songs and shows that self-consciously announced themselves as expressions of America appeared: *Seeing New York* (1906), *The Girl from Broadway* (1907), *Up and Down Broadway* (1910), *A Glimpse of the Great White Way* (1913), *America* (1913), *Maid in America* (1915), and *But See America First* (1916), for example. As Raymond Knapp suggests, "American musicals became, in part and in some form, an enacted demonstration of Americanism, and often take on a formative, defining role in the construction of a collective sense of 'America.'"[35]

This "performed trope," as Gainor calls it ("our culture is always constructing and representing itself to itself as well as to others")[36] requires in the collective consciousness not just American *content*, in songs or narratives *about* America or set in America, but also an American *idiom*. As Knapp observes,[37] the form of musical theater (as well as the medium of film and the genre of jazz) offered this in a (more or less) self-contained twentieth-century expression whose center of production and principal practitioners were firmly based in the United States. In the Princess shows, that American voice really seemed to resonate.

Rodgers's observation cited previously—"What I'd seen earlier was not an American kind of music"[38]—and its corollary—"the real birth of the American musical comedy [was in the Princess Shows]"[39]—echoed what countless other commentators were saying. Alec Wilder sums this up: "All the prominent American composers of modern theater music, living and dead, have acknowledged Kern to have been the first great native master of this genre...and his music to have been the first that was truly American in the theater."[40] This should be seen in perspective: there are other contenders to this crown, not least Irving Berlin and George Gershwin. But what was it that made their music so American?

Stephen Banfield observes the very obvious move away from waltz-time to 4/4 in Kern's first hit "They Didn't Believe Me";[41] Gerald Bordman notices the first use of saxophones in a Broadway pit in his 1913 show *Oh, I Say!*;[42] elsewhere, Bordman makes a more detailed attempt to define the difference between European operetta and American "jazz": "The curvilinear lines of operetta... gave way to far more angular melodic lines. The classical harmonies were interspersed with fresh, narrow, 'bluesy' modulations, while the more gently flowing tempos of the older schools were replaced by more staccato, excited tempos, as well as by the distinctive languor of pure blues. The resulting sound was steely, often sardonic, and always thoroughly contemporary."[43] David Savran identifies some of the typical features of this American jazz: "performed in duple or quadruple time and at a faster tempo than waltz songs or ragtime"; "not strings... but brass and woodwind..., sometimes a vocalist, [and] a vigorous rhythm section"; a "playfulness" coming from "syncopated rhythms in both melody and harmonic accompaniment"; and "harmonic complexities" including "blue notes..., lively counterpoints, and unexpected modulations."[44] Meanwhile, Raymond Knapp attempts to identify precisely what the "performed trope" of American-ness is in the American musical, identifying a "basis in African American styles," a "sharply defined rhythmic dimension," "constructed melodic symmetries," and a "focused use of melodies using a 'gapped' scale."[45] In particular, he identifies the "simple dotted figure" as a key element that gives "an even more distinctive rhythmic profile to both American song and its performance on the musical stage."[46]

These, clearly, are qualities found a great deal in Golden Age music, and a gradual move in that direction can be seen in those transitional songs from the mid-teens. Raymond Hubbell's "Ladder of Roses," for example, from *Hip Hip Hooray* (1915) features lots of syncopation, though its repetition becomes a little excessive, as does Sigmund Romberg's "I'm Looking for Someone's Heart" from *Maid in America* (1915). Here the excessive characteristic is the rhythmic ragtime motif of a quarter note, half note, and quarter note in each of the first six measures of every eight-measure phrase. The last note always drops to form an anacrusis. It's like an early draft for Rodgers and Hart's "Blue Room" (1926), which would make a feature of this rhythmic motif, though unlike that later hit, "I'm Looking for Someone's Heart" feels somewhat strained.

Perhaps a more substantial distinction between the older and newer songs can be seen in the song structures in which they were put together. A number of studies have shown marked differences in structural form between songs of an earlier period and those of a few years later, although the diversity of song styles is of course far more complex than a dualist separation suggests. Raymond Knapp and Mitchell Morris, for example, point out that "the vast majority of Tin Pan Alley songs use a verse-chorus structure, in which the 'verse' either narrates a story or establishes a dramatic situation, and the 'chorus' either acts as a punctuating refrain or represents the song promised by the dramatic setup."[47] Knapp and Morris cite Charles Harris's "After the Ball" as an example of the earlier type but suggest that "the 'dramatic situation' song-type came to dominate in the 1920s";[48] this distinction is what makes "Manhattan" stand out as the first song of real caliber in the Rodgers and Hart oeuvre. Up to that point, their work clung to the earlier tendency, even in the rest of the score to *Winkle Town*, in which songs like "Comfort Me," "One a Day," "You're Too Wonderful for Me," and "Since I Remember You" all present a narrative verse followed by a simple musical refrain.

The second structural tendency has been noted by Graham Wood.[49] He observes three distinct structures of song form that became prominent in the transition to the Golden Age: the thirty-two-measure "Parallel Period Chorus," equating to ABAB or ABAC form, an established and at that time, he suggests, slightly conservative structure; the "Lyric Binary Chorus" equating to AABA, which was a relatively recent development in song form, also in thirty-two-measures; and the "Hybrid Form," an altogether different structure equating to ABA but with non-specific length. Wood demonstrates how the different song forms effect a fundamentally different dramatic dynamic and he notices how Richard Rodgers in particular exploits this increasingly through his 1920s shows to connote distinct dramatic situations. In *Winkle Town* this understanding is still nascent—there is no evidence, for example, of a Lyric Binary Chorus at all; however, there is some experimentation away from the Parallel Period Chorus: "One a Day" and "Comfort Me" are both ABAC; "You're Too Wonderful for Me" is ABA'C; "Since I Remember You" is AA'BC; "Manhattan" is difficult to quantify, though its first four-measure motif recurs in each of the eight-measure phrases, making it hauntingly memorable; Alec Wilder labels it in four-measure terms: ABACABCA': it is clearly more innovative.

Whatever qualities do influence the "American-ness" of the great American song book—the rhythms of African American music, the cadences of Jewish liturgy, various dance crazes, the slapstick of vaudeville routines, the melodies of European operetta, the wit of English cross-talk, vernacular language, popular characterization, clearly structured song form, hummable melodies, syncopation, jazz, blues, and ragtime—it's important to recognize that the narratives that support the story of the creation of a distinctly American sound are themselves tied up in particular ideologies necessary for asserting identity statements about America and its people. The dominant story that identifies the mid-teens as being the decisive moment at which America released itself from the shackles of a European legacy to create its own "native" or "indigenous" sounding music is in no small way influenced by the fact that America's relationship with foreign powers was hugely affected by the 1914–1918 Great War, that mass immigration from Europe was reaching its breaking point and would be curtailed by the early 1920s, and that the 1920s themselves are both defined by a booming hedonism and bookended by prohibition and the crash. America was in a state of flux, and one way of stabilizing the wobble of the period was to turn it into a defining moment in which America—and American culture—could come of age. When it did come of age, America's identity was iconicized in far more than just its music. The "rhythms and impulses" are qualities that are paralleled in other defining expressive forms: buildings and institutions, dynamics and trajectories, mythologies and narratives whose very prominence stamps the iconicity on the American urban landscape.

For the younger generation growing up alongside the twentieth century, these changes must have been extremely exciting. Emerging from a childhood and adolescence in which they had absorbed the sounds and spectacles of an older generation, these boys were strutting into the cocky confidence of adulthood, in which they could create their own sounds, in voices that expressed a particular cultural context and a particular common identity. "I was watching and listening to the beginning of a new form of musical theatre in this country," wrote Rodgers; "somehow I knew it and wanted desperately to be a part of it."[50]

Highbrow and Lowbrow

As the characters, language, and musical styles of Broadway turned from the classical European toward the American vernacular, distinctions between cultural values became increasingly contested. To some, the debasing of highbrow culture with the sounds of non-European and (worse) ethnic music was a travesty; to others, the developing idiosyncrasy of an American voice was a liberation. This shift, felt undoubtedly among audiences and practitioners as an exciting or threatening force of change, was underlined by an ongoing debate among a group of critics who contested their opinions not in first night reviews but in cultural critiques published in essay form. Throughout this study of Rodgers and Hart we will more regularly hear from that other set of critics—the newspaper reviewers from the New York and provincial dailies; however, their comments—on the whole about individual productions—were all played out in the wake of a far more significant discussion initiated by Van Wyck Brooks and continued by Carl Van Vechten, Paul Rosenfeld, Edmund Wilson, Gilbert Seldes, and others.

Although the terms had been in currency for several decades, Van Wyck Brooks's 1915 analysis of "Highbrow" and "Lowbrow" as descriptors gained attention. The terms indicated not only assumed degrees of value in different examples of literature but also the different cultural attitudes of authors and perceived statuses of consumers who engaged with them, "differences between a Europeanized, morally and spiritually uplifting art and a vulgar, primitive, commercialized, sensual art; the culture of the intellectual and economic elites . . . as opposed to that of the working classes."[51] On the one hand, Brooks observed a "fastidious refinement and aloofness" in the high-minded, and on the other a "current of catchpenny opportunism" in the low.[52] Significantly, he identified this antithesis as "quite American, authentically our very own," and interestingly, he also considered both terms "derogatory" and the attendant attitudes "equally undesirable": "The 'Highbrow' is the superior person whose virtue is admitted but felt to be an inept unpalatable virtue; while the 'Lowbrow' is a good fellow one readily takes to, but with a certain scorn for him and all his works," he wrote.[53]

While Brooks's remarks focused on literature and the novel, it was the rapid emergence of jazz in the postwar years that really crystallized the distinction between high and low, and the difference of opinions between one set of critics and another, each seeking to define American music and its provenance. To the dismissive Paul Rosenfeld, "American music is not jazz. Jazz is not music."[54] Instead, true musical value was found in the work of emerging figures like Aaron Copland, Edgar Varèse, and Carl Ruggles, all highbrow composers writing in the European tradition. "We have an American music" asserted Rosenfeld, "to be grouped without impertinence with classic European works;" he qualified that this was very definitely "not jazz."[55] Incredulously, enthusiast Carl Van Vechten spluttered disdain for this sort of remark: "When some curious critic, a hundred years hence, searches through the available archives in an attempt to discover what was the state of American music at the beginning of the Twentieth Century do you think he will take the trouble to exhume . . . the recognizedly 'important' composers of the present day?"[56] Instead, he argued, it would be Irving Berlin and the writers of the popular American songbook who would be remembered. He was writing in 1917; soon those other voices would emerge and the songbook would be established as the output of—among others—Berlin, Kern, Gershwin, and Rodgers and Hart.

Irving Berlin and George Gershwin
We have seen already how Kern's music, in the Princess shows, offered a twentieth-century updating of operetta, with a style that was still elegant and fluid. Berlin and Gershwin, in very different ways, epitomized something different: not an Americanized version of the existing European idiom but a

paradigm that sprang from the melting pot voice of America itself. Berlin—lacking in musical education, reportedly only able to play the piano in one key—seems to have almost stumbled into his career, peddling songsheets while still in his junior years, yet gradually building a reputation as the foremost purveyor of Tin Pan Alley tunes. Gershwin sought classical training and was to write music for the classical repertoire, opera house, and concert hall—"Rhapsody in Blue" (1924); the Piano Concerto in F (1925); *Porgy and Bess* (1935)—yet his work is distinctly, unequivocally, and characteristically American: urban, sophisticated, and modern.

Berlin, writes Jeffrey Magee, was "among the first songwriters to embrace the jazz fad, with his summer 1917 publication of 'Mr. Jazz Himself.'" [57] In fact, his interest in creating a "distinctively American musical theater"[58] had underscored all of his songwriting, perhaps due to his status as an immigrant and his desire to understand what being American meant. His first major success had come in 1911 with "Alexander's Ragtime Band," and from that point he became something of a national figure, known as the "Ragtime King"; "Ragtime, in Berlin's words and music, becomes a means by which a pluralistic population can be united, Americanized, and modernized," writes Magee.[59] During the teens, his version of ragtime (modified from earlier instrumental incarnations by the likes of Scott Joplin) became an expression of an exciting and youthful American spirit. His revue *Watch Your Step* (1914), featuring the dancers Vernon and Irene Castle, exploited the popularity of ragtime and dance, and the song "Play a Simple Melody," still widely heard, captures exactly the sort of breezy syncopation that typified this style. By the late teens, thanks to his involvement in writing on the one hand the music for Ziegfeld's *Follies*—including "A Pretty Girl Is Like a Melody" (1919)—and on the other hand the patriotic show *Yip Yip Yaphank* (1917) for his fellow servicemen as they marched off to war, he was seen as the cultural spokesperson of the nation. By 1925, Jerome Kern was able to make his now-famous statement: "Irving Berlin has no *place* in American music—he *is* American music."[60]

Gershwin agreed, and said as much in print: "Irving Berlin is the greatest songwriter that has ever lived," he wrote in 1929; "the first to free the American song from the nauseating sentimentality which had previously characterized it, and by introducing and perfecting ragtime he had actually given us the first germ of an American musical idiom; he had sowed the first seeds of an American music."[61] If this was how Gershwin felt, his work responded to and built on the stylistic idiom of ragtime as an American vernacular—that much is evident in one of his first published songs, "The Real American Folk Song (Is a Rag)" (1918). Like Berlin, his early work was written with revue in mind—he was house composer for *George White's Scandals* from 1920 to 1924, which included "I'll Build a Stairway to Paradise" in its 1922 incarnation—though during this period he also developed an understanding of writing book shows: *La La Lucille* (1919), *A Dangerous Maid* (1921), *Our Nell* (1922), and *By and By* (1922), for example. He would consolidate his growing success with a triple whammy in 1924, when he became the toast of London with *Primrose*, the toast of Broadway with *Lady, Be Good*, and the toast of the concert halls with "Rhapsody in Blue." The following year he tried the same model: *Lady, Be Good!* in London, *Tip-Toes* on Broadway, and the Piano Concerto in F at Carnegie Hall.

Gershwin—more than Berlin—recognized in his early years the legacy of a European sound. Shows like *Primrose* pick up from Kern, and large parts of his Broadway work such as *Strike Up the Band* (1927), *Of Thee I Sing* (1930), and *Let 'Em Eat Cake* (1931) hark back in compositional style to Gilbert and Sullivan. However, Gershwin is more celebrated for the way in which he assertively introduced the vernacular of jazz as the voice of American music. In Savran's words, "Gershwin constructed jazz as the most distinctive and important ingredient in musical modernism and the unique voice of a progressive, democratic, melting-pot America."[62] There are of course many different kinds of music that we nowadays refer to as "jazz," and the term has become a complex fulcrum balancing significant dynamics of race, economics, and social value, as Savran observes.[63] The term also defined something very different in the 1920s than it did in the 1950s when an equally diverse array of popular music and interests contested its cultural space. During the earlier period, the use of the word was both expansive and reductive, slipping between various meanings as musical idioms emerged, yet serving as a catchall for anything popular and un-European. Writing in 1925, Gilbert Seldes refers to "the present elaboration of ragtime we call jazz,"[64] which one takes to mean popular song descending from the Tin Pan Alley sound of Irving Berlin and finding expression on the musical stage in the work of George Gershwin. As Savran puts it, jazz emerged as "a distinctively American—and distinctively modernist—art"; "the key to forging a uniquely American theatre vernacular that could respond to and express the new rhythms and economies of the Machine Age."[65]

America's self-conscious quest for identity is also seen metonymically in the drive to create in New York the dynamic modernist urban metropolis. Part of this was led by the practical exigencies of squeezing a rapidly growing population onto a limited plot of land, and part led by the social phenomenon of diverse ethnic and cultural peoples gathering from all directions. It is an abiding irony that the main exponents of this "all-American" music were themselves of European extraction. But this is a circle that can never be squared: to its credit, it is the multicultural gathering of diasporas that defines America; to its shame it is also the effacing of any indigenous identity that characterizes what America constructed. In part, the American-ness of the new songs was a representation of that diversity and of that city, and if its melting pot sounds didn't exactly mimic the industrial and technological masonry blows of that development (though many would suggest they did), they at least reflected somehow the energies and excitement of that exponential growth.

A More Personal Influence

If Rodgers and Hart's formative years familiarized them with the lush sounds of operetta, the anachronisms of musical comedy, the spectacle of revue and the burgeoning voice of jazz, there was one more type of New York entertainment to which they would have been exposed: the brash humor and vernacular idiom of burlesque, a form straight out of vaudeville. This was best represented by the personality of Lew Fields. As it happened, he was the father of their great friend Herbert.

Lew Fields had been a titanic star of vaudeville throughout the 1880s and 1890s, thanks to his double act with fellow comedian Joe Weber. Weber and Fields, as their characters Mike and Meyer, would perform a typical knockabout "Dutch act"[66] which traded on slapstick camaraderie and linguistic clumsiness. Appealing—perhaps because of a grotesque magnification of their own image—to working-class immigrant audiences on the Bowery, Weber and Fields shot to fame as performers and then bought a number of venues as they moved into producing. By 1904 though, the team had split—not exactly acrimoniously but without much likelihood of a reunion. Both continued to produce and perform, though of the two, Lew Fields probably enjoyed most sustained success.

As family members Armond and L. Marc Fields suggest in their biography, Fields is something of a lynch-pin in the development of the Broadway musical: "the evolutionary link between the popular stage entertainments of the nineteenth and twentieth centuries."[67] Coming out of Bowery vaudeville—which may seem the basest form of entertainment—it is perhaps surprising to note that Fields aspired to both "rigid standards of propriety"[68] and "a script in which the basic elements of the musical . . . could be combined as an integrated whole within a more or less consistent narrative framework."[69] If this attitude—dating from 1904—predates by some margin any of the usually cited calls for integration—Hammerstein with *Rose Marie* (1924), Kern with *Show Boat* (1927), Rodgers and Hart with *Chee Chee* (1928), or Rodgers and Hammerstein with *Oklahoma!* (1943)—it also shows that an aspiration toward credible dramatic works for the musical stage was an important element of the Broadway landscape even before the First World War.

Fields became something of a father figure in his enterprises, not just in the way he nurtured the work of his biological children Herbert, Joseph, and Dorothy, all three of whom followed him into the profession, but also in the way he fostered new talent and remained dedicated to a close community that he considered a "family."[70] This (which Rodgers was to recognize, particularly in regard to *Peggy-Ann*)[71] can be traced right back to his 1890s work with the All-Star Stock Company at Weber and Fields's Music Hall, which they opened in 1895. Here, in addition to a number of regular performers, the team was joined by house composer John Stromberg, librettist Edgar Smith, and—once regular director Joseph Herbert moved elsewhere—dance director Julian Mitchell (who happened to be practically deaf, but who in Fields and Fields's words "redefined the role of the stage director" to become "the creative equal of the librettist and composer").[72] Fields was seeking "consistency" in his shows, and it made sense to have a consistent team putting them together, even if, at this stage at least, burlesques like *Helter Skelter* (1899), *Fiddle-dee-dee* (1900), and *Hoity-Toity* (1901) were more in the knockabout Dutch act vein than they were musical plays. It was really only after the Weber and Fields partnership dissolved—around the same time that Stromberg died—that Fields's ambitions began to bear fruit. He put together a new team, working with Julian Mitchell and Fred Hamlin as producers but now joined by composer Victor Herbert and librettist Glen MacDonough. Their first outing "was an attempt to reconcile the era's two most popular forms of stage entertainment, vaudeville and operetta,"[73] write his biographers. *It Happened in Nordland* (1904) proved a success.

Although Fields's "family" members would eventually move on, he maintained the idea of a stock company. He reunited with Victor Herbert for *The Rose of Algeria* (1909) and *Old Dutch* (1909), while librettist Glen MacDonough became a regular collaborator, complemented by Edgar Smith and lyricist E. Ray Goetz. Two new composers, Raymond Hubbell and Alfred Baldwin Sloane, were brought into the fold, and—though little known today and often described by Fields as "mediocre"[74]— provided scores for several of his musical comedies: Hubbell's *About Town* (1906), *The Midnight Sons* (1909), and *The Jolly Bachelors* (1910); Sloane's *The Summer Widowers* (1910), *The Hen-Pecks* (1910), and *The Never-Homes* (1911), all except the first to libretti by MacDonough.[75] Unlike many of the operettas of the period, these musical comedies were based squarely in America, and typically in New York. "During an era in which English musicals and Viennese operettas overwhelmed the Broadway stage," write his family, Lew Fields "continued to expand the possibilities of indigenous stage forms."[76]

Rodgers and Hart

Such was the musical theater world in which Dick and Larry came of age: the careful, punctilious romantic and the carefree bacchanalian poet. When they tore themselves away from watching the shows they adored, they threw themselves into attempts to reproduce them, pouring out writing, gushing about their plans, and above all dreaming about the prospect of one day having their own work produced. "I knew what I wanted to do and I knew where I was heading," wrote Rodgers.[77] As we explore their early work, we see traces of how they picked up on the influences around them and how they then contributed to the growing confidence of a classic American form. They were younger than Kern (1885–1945) and Berlin (1888–1989), but direct contemporaries of Gershwin (1898–1937), even if their real success was to emerge in his wake, and even if they felt somewhat in his shadow. However, the influences that suffuse their work build on both what their immediate colleagues developed in the teens and what the previous generation had consolidated before that. In Rodgers's music one can hear elements of Kern's romantic grace, Berlin's cheeky vernacular, and Gershwin's jazzy swagger; and in Hart's lyrics, Berlin's language-play and Ira's rhythm. In common with their contemporaries, the spirit of Gilbert and Sullivan looms large in their work, and thanks to librettists from that Gilbertian tradition—Guy Bolton, P. G. Wodehouse, Glen Macdonough, and Herbert Fields—the musical comedies of the 1920s in general become classy comedies of manners with witty language and sympathetic characters. Finally, these shows—collectively—were enthusiastic champions of the desire to dance, recognizing the infectious rhythms of the music and introducing some great dancers (Vernon and Irene Castle, Fred and Adele Astaire) and choreographers (Sammy Lee, Seymour Felix, Busby Berkeley).

Happily for Rodgers and Hart, their youthful jazz sound and contemporary take on tradition struck exactly the right note. Their shows reflected neither the swashbuckling unreality of the fading operetta scene nor the over-provocative kick of hot jazz. They had appeal with theatergoing audiences and they didn't court controversy. The occasional glitch in their consistent output was balanced by an evident integrity in approaching their craft. Most of all, they just kept going, writing lyrics, melodies, songs, and shows incessantly and maintaining an almost continuous presence on the theater scene, consolidating what it meant to be American.

But above all, the identity of "American" is not homogenous, and for all the desire to encompass a monolithic definition, "American-ness" is marked by the dialogue it sustains with inherent others. If American-ness is reflected in anything it is in displacement: the displacement of people, ethnicities, and cultures, and of syncopated rhythms and discordant harmonies. Rodgers's own articulation of displacement is modest (softer than Gershwin's, let's say), but his hyperextensions and pervasive chromaticisms nonetheless point to a psychology in the music that encapsulates what it feels like to be both in and out of your skin, as it were. And Hart's lyrics are nothing if not endemic of this psychology, tossing their anachronisms gamely to the listener: capturing not the balmy breezes of a tropical isle but those of the subway; not a Venetian gondola gliding by, but a Mott Street pushcart.

More than a biography or historiography, this book seeks to explore the shows of Rodgers and Hart. It charts a more or less chronological course through the work of this early phase, though each chapter addresses a particular aspect of that work. For this reason, I deal with some shows slightly out of sequence but where it seems appropriate to consider them. Inevitably, they are products of their time and of the social, cultural, and personal influences informing them. The people themselves will figure, then—both individually and as a partnership; and at times, the wider influences of cultural milieu, historical events, and the social and political landscape undoubtedly impact the products that this team created. In identifying a focus for this book, however, my research centers on the *shows* created by Rodgers and Hart, and how these reveal a developing confidence in writing for the musical stage—one that would influence the Broadway musical of the 1930s and beyond. Specifically, I look at the shows through the prism of three main influences which weave through each of the chapters.

The first considers Rodgers and Hart's continued exploration of how song works dramatically within a narrative. This project was steered partly by Rodgers's musical developments of song form and partly by Hart's exploration of character in the vernacular idiom of popular song. This discussion has as its perceptual bookends the stand-alone Tin Pan Alley song of the teens and the much-vaunted inception of the integrated musical in 1943, staging-posts that demarcate a sense of developing form, that sit respectively at the beginning and end of the Rodgers and Hart collaboration. This discussion emphasizes the fact that their shows—and their breakthroughs—were collaborations: Hart's lyrics work in part through their musicality, exploiting the rhythm and melody of the vernacular idiom, while Rodgers's musical language offers wit that both characterizes and dramatizes through song. This is necessarily a discussion that considers Rodgers and Hart's other collaborators, particularly Herbert Fields, whose influence on the libretti and characters fashioned the particular style of Hart's lyrics and the way in which Rodgers used music. In enabling his collaborators to write for character and situation rather than just for the faceless songster of Tin Pan Alley, Fields helped the boys develop the sort of nuance, detail, and subtlety that would become central to integration.

The second theme focuses on how the business of theater, guided by influences from the media, audiences, economics, and technologies, affected their aesthetic and creative output. This in part considers the role various producers had in enabling and sometimes restricting their development. Rodgers and Hart worked with a dizzying number of top producers during this period, both in New York and London, and at this stage in their career they were playing the producers' tunes. Getting their work performed meant pleasing the money guys, and it was very often a producer's whim that made key decisions, making the producer in effect a collaborative partner. That decisions were guided by economies of the Broadway system meant that shows would lose significant elements or have others brought to prominence as a result of financial imperatives. In particular, the focus on marketing the hit songs of each production would cause interesting and sometimes problematic choices to be made. Some of these, in turn, responded to developing technologies in the recording industry, the music publishing industry, and the film industry, so any discussion of production exigencies necessarily deals with both people and technologies.

The third theme focuses on the significance of identity in the work of Rodgers and Hart, and fits in with other interesting studies, particularly by Raymond Knapp, on how musical theater serves as an expressive voice for both personal and national identity. The work of Rodgers and Hart is certainly affected by the relationships they had with their family histories, with their second-generation immigrant roots, and with their identity as New Yorkers in a booming period of growth. Their work also mounts a discourse between the various cultural influences within song: the traditions of Europe, of a classical training, and of a centuries-old legacy; and the input of African American rhythm, Jewish culture, and Bowery entertainment—in short, between the old world and the new, the classical and the popular, tradition and innovation.

The early period of Rodgers and Hart's collaboration is a period that comes to an end with the double whammy of the stock market crash and the sound film. Both audiences and writers left the theater in droves—Rodgers and Hart among them—to cash in on the new opportunities offered in Hollywood. By the time they returned in the mid-thirties, the theater landscape was very different, and both Rodgers and Hart and the musical comedy they had helped foster were by then mature, polished, big business. This is the other end of that story, though, and we should begin at the beginning, with Act One: *We'll Have Manhattan*.

Who knows what the boys felt as they paraded into Max Dreyfus's office at T. B. Harms? Nervous energy, certainly; excitement and anticipation without doubt. A glittering future lay ahead of them, and like the twinkling cityscape that the denouement of *Winkle Town* so evocatively promised, it needed just a single trigger to have everything brought to life. "We'll turn Manhattan into an isle of joy,"[78] they sang. "There is nothing of value here," was his response.[79] The rest is history.

1

THE SUMMER CAMPS AND VARSITY SHOWS

• • •

The historic meeting between Richard Rodgers and Lorenz Hart happened in the spring of 1919 at the Hart family home on West 119th Street. It was a friend of Dick's brother, Phil Leavitt, who was responsible. "Dick's songs were tuneful, but the lyrics were weak," he writes;[1] "Hart knew something about lyric writing but had no composer," adds Rodgers.[2] The pair talked musicals: Hart impressed Rodgers, and Rodgers impressed Hart. "It was love at first hearing," reports Leavitt.[3]

Rodgers's recollection of the meeting is recorded in his memoirs. Here he gives his first impression of the man he was destined to write with for the next quarter century:

> The total man was hardly more than five feet tall. He wore frayed carpet slippers, a pair of tuxedo trousers, an undershirt and a nondescript jacket. His hair was unbrushed, and he obviously hadn't had a shave for a couple of days.... But that first look was misleading, for it missed the soft brown eyes, the straight nose, the good mouth, the even teeth and the strong chin. Feature for feature he had a handsome face, but it was set in a head that was a bit too large for his body and gave him a slightly gnomelike appearance.[4]

This is a fond memory of Lorenz Hart: Rodgers first evokes his artistic disarray, then admires his classical looks, before slipping in a jibe to diminish the older man's stature. Yet we sense his admiration. As "Larry did most of the talking," Rodgers writes, "I listened with all the reverence due a man of twenty-three from a boy of sixteen."[5] Rodgers was wide-eyed and keen to learn; and Hart had a willing protégé.

Hart's passion was for the Princess Shows, and though he was only twenty-three, he had clear ideas of how emulating these shows but developing their technique could lead to a new kind of musical theater: "He was violent on the subject of rhyming in his songs, feeling that the public was capable of understanding better things than the current monosyllabic juxtaposition of 'slush' and 'mush,'"[6] wrote Rodgers. He "had more ideas than you could shake a chorus girl at," reported the youngster.[7] "It made great good sense and I was enchanted by this little man and his ideas.[8]

The pair began collaborating—Hart with his lofty ideas, and Rodgers with his naïve enthusiasm. There was surely no chance of this going anywhere; but before long, Phil Leavitt used another of his contacts, Dorothy Fields, to gain access to the veteran star and producer Lew Fields.

Fields was at the time appearing as Augustus Tripp in *A Lonely Romeo*, which was playing at the Casino Theatre.[9] His son Herbert—already a friend of Hart and Leavitt—was playing Tripp's son. The story was about a middle-aged milliner who works hard by day and then adopts his son's identity to play hard by night. With this storyline, Fields was showing a keen awareness of the generational changes happening culturally; his family biographers suggest that he "was looking to the younger generation for lessons," turning to Herbert and Dorothy to become "their father's eyes and ears on the changing popular tastes."[10] When their friend Leavitt recommended that Lew hear the new songs of Rodgers and Hart, he was open to the suggestion.[11]

For Rodgers this was a nervous first encounter, made more daunting by the fact that "the entire Fields clan" had gathered to hear his "maiden efforts."[12] Hart—though he had known Herb for almost ten years—excused himself from the audition, leaving Rodgers to play and sing alone.[13] Although they had high hopes for one song, "Venus (There's Nothing between Us)," it was the charm duet "Any Old Place with You" that Fields most enjoyed. He bought the song outright (rather than offering a royalty agreement) and interpolated it into *A Lonely Romeo*, giving the boys their first taste of Broadway.[14]

"ANY OLD PLACE WITH YOU"

"Any Old Place with You" is a delightful song, which—as Rodgers and Hart's first Broadway song—has been widely celebrated. It presents a young couple promising to go to the ends of the earth for one another, and Hart finds playful rhyming opportunities in the various destinations this implies. Commentators regularly cite the final payoff, "I'd go to Hell for ya/Or Philadelphia," but equally witty are other lines, like "Clothes won't encumber ya/ Down in Colombia." There is impudence in these lyrics, but Hart revels in deliberate clumsiness, drawing attention to the fun of lyric-writing, and thereby making the characters endearing. It is interesting to see a transition between the naïve style of "Any Old Place" (1919) and the far more sophisticated

"Manhattan" (1922), particularly since in many ways the songs bear strong similarities.

Another geographical duet, the locations in "Manhattan" are not the fanciful exotic climes of "Any Old Place"; these are regular haunts known by experience, and the fun Hart therefore has in the later song is not so much a game of rhyming but a game of recognition. This has made his lyrics particularly enduring, and here—despite being at the beginning of his career—he is comfortable with playfulness, avoiding the self-indulgence or sentimentality of a more naïve lyricist. At the same time, there is a naivety to the lyrics. This is a couple in love, in a relationship free from the jaded quality that appears in later Hart lyrics (consider "Your brain is dumber / Than that of a plumber" from "I Feel at Home with You" (*A Connecticut Yankee*, 1927), for example).

Musically, a transition is also evident. The verses to both are rhythmically straight and built around scalar passages. "Any Old Place with You" works within the reach of a fifth, while "Manhattan" climbs a complete octave in its first phrase. But the earlier song has a far quicker tempo than its later cousin, accompanied by an insistent syncopated motif that suggests the railroad of the lyrics. By contrast, "Manhattan" is steadier and straighter, though its melody also gestures to an identical syncopation ("-vate all our"/"We'll save our"). Dotted noodles at the ends of the line suggest a more laidback mood than the syncopation of "Any Old Place," as does the descending chromatic harmonization that moderates the assertive scale at the beginning of the verse. The verse of "Manhattan" really is simplistic (AA'), preparing the way to the chorus with a dominant lead-in at the end of the second phrase. "Any Old Place with You" continues, though, modulating surprisingly to the major second for its B material, then enharmonically shifting this key's root note to a dominant lead-in note for the chorus. Here, any differences in the verse material of the songs resolve to offer strikingly similar opening motifs in the refrains.

The refrain of "Any Old Place with You" (Figure 1.1) opens with a rhythmic and melodic call-and-response: a quarter note followed by a dotted eighth pairing is followed by a dotted eighth pairing then a quarter note; a downward semitone turn from the dominant opening note is matched by a downward semitone turn from the higher tonic. This is simple but handsome in its structure, and without being challenging, it is rhythmically and harmonically interesting in its gestures toward syncopation and chromaticism. The motif is then mimicked at a lower pitch before a straight series of quarter notes climbs chromatically up to an unresolved cadence emphasized by a cheeky rhythmic and melodic flick on the word "Timbuktu": this is like a musical wink as suggestive lyrics propose an improper night in an exotic destination. The carefully

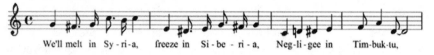

Figure 1.1: Similarities between the opening lines of "Any Old Place With You" (1919) and "Manhattan" (1923). Reprinted by Permission of Hal Leonard Corporation

constructed phrase serves as material for the rest of the refrain, which repeats it in slight variations emulating but inverting the opening melodic turn: the A section establishes a key, the B line pushes its variation of A up a tone, the second A section reverts to the original but leaps on its final note to the seventh to conclude with a C section that steps back down before a final flourish to the tonic. The setup of the unexpected seventh in the music paves the way for a gag line in the lyrics ("Hell for ya/or Philadelphia"), before the song's title line musically and thematically provides the kicker.

Even this early in their collaboration, it shows sophistication. With its gag structure, one can also see why the song appealed to Lew Fields, since the characters' fond remarks and language games resemble the cross-talk for which he and Weber were renowned. Whether through craft or instinct, Rodgers and Hart construct a perfectly delivered joke that works in terms of timing, character, and situation because of the way the lyrics meet the music. The wit is suggestive enough without being vulgar; the music is rhythmically and melodically interesting enough to seem fresh, but it is safe and straight enough to seem harmless. The overall effect is a song that seems to hang between two worlds, evoking the light vaudeville of an earlier generation but ready to fall into the serious fun of the jazz age.

Three years later, "Manhattan" shows that "Any Old Place" has grown up. It starts with exactly the same motivic idea (figure 1.1), though now, rhythmically, melodically, and harmonically, the motif has matured. The rhythmic pattern from "Any Old Place with You" is still evident: an opening note followed by a dotted pairing, answered by a gesture that is formally straight (in the music), though informally often dotted (in performance). It is as if "Any Old Place" wears casual clothes, sauntering in with a snatched delay at the beginning of the bar. The melodic pattern is also practically the same: a downward semitone turn from the dominant followed by a downward gesture from the higher tonic. It doesn't quite reach the tonic, allowing a lazy approximation of the motif to jazz the melody down without returning, exploiting the prominent use of the seventh from the earlier song but now bringing it in much sooner (in the first measure!) and as a weighted note rather than a passing note. As in "Any Old Place," this motif is developed, repeated in a lower variation, then followed by an unresolved cadence in straight quarter notes. Here, though, the resolution is delayed, first by lingering on the major second ("Island too"), then by extending the phrase to indulge the anticipation of its resolution. Finally, the flick of "Timbuktu" ("Any Old Place") is magnified into a half note gesture for "through the zoo" ("Manhattan"). So the first line provides material for the whole chorus, and in three variations of the material (broadly ABA, like "Any Old Place"), it teases our expectations, and delights in its casual disregard for meter and tonality. The last phrase ends by leaping up, this time just to the sixth, before offering the payoff not as an explicit gag—it's matured out of stating the obvious—but as a charmingly wry assertion: "We'll turn Manhattan into an Isle of Joy."

"Any Old Place with You" and "Manhattan" are not so different, then, but what differences they do have define the transition that both these writers and popular music went through in just a few short years. Where "Any Old Place with You" harked back to the teens, "Manhattan" faced the future, with a carefree mood that characterized the mid-1920s. And where the earlier song showed a composer with promise, the confidence of "Manhattan" introduced a composer with style.

Surprisingly, given his upbringing and passion for music, Rodgers at seventeen could barely read music. As he admitted himself, although his mother was "the best sight reader I ever knew,"[15] he resisted both theory classes and piano lessons. This is not to say that he was not musical—indeed, it was perhaps that innate talent that stood in his way: "being able to play by ear made me lazy and I never bothered to practice. Why spend time reading notes when I could play just about anything I heard simply by listening?"[16] And play he could; he was appointed school pianist by his music teacher Elsa Katz, "to play the entrance and exit marches . . . , the traditional hymns and 'The Star-Spangled Banner,'" he explains.[17] Much of this he improvised, displaying a gift honed by ear. But this was to his mother's chagrin: "Richard played only in the key of 'C' til he was 13," she told one reporter—a key which on the piano requires only the white notes.

I never can forget how surprised I was when I went to his public school graduation to find, as the eleventh number on the programme, my son's name with "operatic selections" next to it. My heart stood still. I knew he only played little snatches of everything in the key of "C." He couldn't read a note, and I couldn't imagine him mustering up courage to play for anyone. Judging by the applause, his performance satisfied, but unfortunately there was no encore. The single number had exhausted his repertoire.[18]

Nevertheless, Rodgers demonstrated an extraordinary aptitude for music, and even if he had no formal musical training, he devised "a musical shorthand"[19] with which he could recall what he heard. When he saw a show, Samuel Marx recalls,

[he would] jot onto the margin of his program the songs that were sung and the tunes the orchestra played. He used the alphabet and added a dot or two to indicate tempo. With this method he copied them all down, then went home and played the music from overture to final chorus on the piano, simply reading off the scratches he had scribbled that afternoon.... I never knew anyone else able to do that. I am still amazed by it.[20]

This talent betrays both Rodgers's instinctive musical flair and his lack of any formal training even while he was beginning to compose. Such a peculiarity in Rodgers's musical background may explain the rapid development "from apprentice to musical dramatist"—as Geoffrey Block puts it[21]—that can be seen in his work between 1919 and 1925, evidence of which we can discern in the transition from "Any Old Place with You" to "Manhattan." Gradually Rodgers would acknowledge his technical shortcomings, seeking informal tutelage from Roy Webb in 1920 before enrolling on a more formal program of study at the Institute of Musical Art, now known as the Juilliard School. Even so, it was not until 1925 that Rodgers' writing really gained recognition.

Although the majority of their work in this interim was produced on an amateur basis for school, college, or summer camp shows, the considerable output of Rodgers and Hart in the early 1920s is worthy of a careful study. Over several years we see the growing confidence of jazz emerging (*Fly with Me*, 1920), attempts to integrate songs into their dramatic scenes (*Poor Little Ritz Girl*, 1920), early treatments of themes to which they would return (*A Danish Yankee in the Court of King Tut*, 1923), and sophisticated attempts to create a new type of musical soundscape for the dramatic stage (*The Jazz King*, 1924). Throughout all of this, the boys continued to churn out songs, captivated by a bug they had caught at summer camp when they were still both in their teens.

CAMP FIRE DAYS (1908–1921)

By the 1910s, the tradition of sending city boys off to summer camp was well established. This was partly to relieve them from the intolerable city heat of the summer months but it was also a mission to save adolescents from moral decline. "The summer time is a period of moral deterioration with most boys," wrote Henry Gibson; "boys wander during the vacation time into paths of wrongdoing," he claimed. "The vacation problem therefore becomes a serious one for both the boy and his parent. Camping offers a solution."[22]

Activities at camp included outdoor pursuits like baseball, tennis, swimming, and trekking, overseen by young "counselors" who had graduated from the camps in previous years. Camping upheld the same values as the Scouting movement and was often affiliated to a religious purpose that included some element of Bible study. Camaraderie was encouraged, and campers would champion the identity of their own camp while jibing other camps in the area. As with the Scouting movement, much of this camaraderie was generated in camp singsongs around the fire, and a tradition of revue-type performance developed, featuring songs and skits, and burlesquing the events of the week. Such shows—often modeled around the popular minstrel show and featuring boys and counselors in drag or blackface—gave plenty of opportunities for creative sparks to fly. For young campers like Lorenz Hart, Richard Rodgers, and Herbert Fields, the shows were the sine qua non of camp life.

The boys' camping experiences throughout the 1910s trace remarkably similar paths—attending the same camps, meeting the same people, and eventually finding themselves working together. Indeed, the similarity of their experiences during these early years—although Rodgers and Hart appear not to have met until 1919—points to an extended community in Jewish Manhattan whose families moved in the same circles. Both boys were to start out their summer camp activities at the Weingart Institute—Larry from 1908 and Dick from 1914; then Larry graduated to Camp Paradox from 1910 to 1913 before becoming a counselor at Brant Lake Camp from 1916; Dick attended Camp Wigwam from 1916 before becoming a counselor himself at Camp Paradox in 1920. Meanwhile, Herbert Fields was to match them step for step, working on the summer shows at Paradox with Larry in 1910 and Dick in 1920. The fact that their constellations eventually fell into alignment was surely always inevitable.

In fact, the Weingart Institute was not so much a camp as an elegant school building, Pine Hill, set in grounds near Highmount in the Catskills. This was a retreat favored for their sons by Jewish professionals, and the

roster of summer visitors reads like a who's who of Jewish cultural life—
"a prep school for a Musical Hall of Fame," as Sig Herzig puts it:[23] Larry and
his brother Teddy, David and Myron Selznick, Herbert Sondheim, Oscar
Hammerstein II, and some years later, Richard Rodgers.[24] This was no coincidence: over several years, the Catskills had developed as the resort area of
choice for Jewish New Yorkers, since as Phil Brown suggests, "in the mountains, Jews of Eastern European descent could become Americanized while
preserving much of their Jewishness."[25] This presents an interesting motiva-
tion for parents like Max and Frieda or William and Mamie to send their boys
to a place like Pine Hill. Being packed off to summer camp was a routine adventure for teenage boys, on whom a set of values could be instilled that
broadly reflected all-American ideology; identifying a resort in the Catskills
would ensure close links with others from a similar background, preserving
cultural heritage and consolidating Jewish identity. As Frommer and Frommer
report, "the evolution of the region...mirrored—even crystallized—a two-
fold process: the Americanization of the Jewish population on the one hand,
and the impact of Jewish culture on America on the other."[26]

While at the Weingart Institute, Larry enjoyed his first taste of the theatrical, performing in shows and writing some of his earliest ditties. Sig Herzig
remembers the thirteen-year-old (though "he looked five years younger")
making a splash as End Man in the minstrel show, as "Jim Jimalong, the third
broom" in a farce called *New Brooms*, and as treasurer of one of the ball teams,
a ploy to get out of sporting activity. "His brain [was] so heavy it prevent[ed]
him from growing in a vertical direction," he recalled, though he was obviously popular. In his second season he was, "by unanimous consent, jumped
over the head of a dozen eligible older boys" to become editor-in-chief of *The
Weingart Review*.[27] In these writings he began to develop an acerbic and often
self-deprecatory style, laced with traits that would characterize his later
work: a passion for Shakespeare, a delight in wordplay, and a fondness for
anachronistic juxtaposition. In his biography *A Ship without a Sail*, Gary Marmorstein considers some early Hart material—a short story called "Elliot's
Plagiarism" for the DeWitt Clinton newspaper *The Magpie*, a self-penned interview in *The Weingart Review*, and a stage skit anticipating *The Boys from
Syracuse* (1938, based on Shakespeare's *The Comedy of Errors*) in which "Teddy
and Larry developed a twin-brother routine that both flummoxed and
amused the campers." As Marmorstein suggests, this early work "has Larry's
stamp on every line," exploring ideas he "would be working through in one
form or another, for the next several years."[28]

Following two years in the "sheltered atmosphere" of the Institute,[29] the
boys moved on, Hart to the newly founded Camp Paradox in 1910 and Rodgers

in 1916 to Camp Wigwam in Maine. These camps were far more camp-like, with tents for accommodation and a separate mess hall and club house. At Paradox, sharing his tent with Adolph Zukor's son Eugene and lifelong friend Mel Schauer, Larry met Herbert Fields, and together the two became enthusiastic performers in the weekly shows. At Wigwam, Rodgers penned his first song, "Camp Fire Days," which like much of their early writing, and much of the material performed in summer camps, was both solipsistic and unsophisticated. This early in his development he "had not yet mastered several basic elements of musical notation, including the proper placement of note stems,"[30] observes Geoffrey Block.

The boys' experience over the next few years would develop, with school years spent in the classroom and summers spent at camp. A few years older, Hart would become a counselor in 1917 when three of his acquaintances from Paradox founded Brant Lake Camp. Rodgers too would soon become a counselor, accepting a summer stint along with brother Morty in Camp Paradox in 1920. By this time, the boys had met and enjoyed their first glimpse of success with "Any Old Place with You." At Paradox—along with fellow counselor Herb Fields and the often drafted-in Larry, Dick was both the celebrity and the big brother figure to the campers. Here, closeted away from the hubbub of the city and delighted to practice their craft in the weekly camp shows, the boys could indulge, experiment, and try out ideas away from the judgmental gaze of the industry.

The Paradoxian (the Camp Paradox newsletter) of August 1920 reports on their first amateur night from July 11, when "the yells of the campers caused the entire faculty to mount the stage and sing the new Faculty Song written by that child of genius, Dick Varsity Rodgers and his partner, Herb Lyric Fields."[31] "The Faculty Song"—like most they wrote at camp—was about Camp Paradox and identified faculty members including "Uncle Dick, whose music is sure to knock us flat" and "Uncle Herbie, who promotes the camper's artistry."[32] Such self-references feature regularly in the camp songs, showing how inward-looking the world of the camp could be but painting some interesting character portraits:

Uncle Dicky writes his music nice and neat
Until he finds out that he has missed a beat,
From tent 21 you will hear him yell;
"You can't write music when you feel like hell."

Uncle Herbie has a very easy job,
All he has to do is educate the mob,
And from the clubhouse you will hear him say
"You can't get talent from a bale of hay."[33]

Such material—albeit simplistic—was enormously popular with the boys, as a retrospective in *The Paradoxian* from 1925 suggests: "no startling events revert to memory until 1920, when the advent of Herbert L. Fields—a camper of 1910—and his Pythias, Richard C. Rodgers, wrought a tremendous change in the dramatic policies of Paradox. Gone forever the last moment 'sketches', the slapstick comedy, the humor of class or creed! In their place arose drama, comedy, music. Camp became the proud possessor of its own songs—worthwhile music, with worth-while lyrics. And with the songs, a new spirit."[34] Sometimes, the song material was quite literally about the activities at Camp Paradox, as in "A Paradox Day" from the boys' first summer. At other times, the writing would become more satirical, staging thinly disguised portraits of Camp Paradox in fictitious camps like "Bloody Gulch Camp" and "Lillycup Camp."[35] One song, "The Mayor of Paradoxo," written for a 1921 camp show based on *If I Were King*, lampooned Gilbert and Sullivan's "The Duke of Plazo-Toro" but was set, predictably, in the environs of Camp Paradox. At still other times, Fields and Rodgers would exercise their writing in *The Paradoxian* itself, starting a trend for self-reflective journalism that would continue throughout their early twenties. "Music and the Camper" (1920) by Rodgers (calling himself Victor Herbert Rodgers), is a satirical swipe at how even the most musical of campers will lose any musical ability by the end of the summer because they are otherwise engaged with outdoor activities.[36] These writings exude the infectious energy of both the boys and their campmates; for all of them their campfire days offered space and opportunity to indulge their writing, exercise their creativity, and develop the charismatic confidence that would help guide their later success.

Occasionally, material penned by Lorenz Hart would be smuggled into these shows, and it is fair to say that while Herbert Fields's work as director and librettist might have been applauded, the sophisticated quality of Hart's lyrics far outshone his. One song showcased was "The Geography Song," the same song that under a different guise—"Any Old Place with You"—had marked the start of Rodgers's and Hart's professional career.

THE AKRON CLUB SHOWS (1920–1921)

Away from camp, though Rodgers was still in college, the siren call of the theater beckoned. The boys took every opportunity to throw themselves into projects, and as Geoffrey Block notes, "no theatrical venue was too lowly."[37] Rodgers and his writing partners found themselves in great demand, creating revue material and shows for groups and fundraising clubs all over the New York Jewish scene.

The Akron Club, a "local social-athletic group,"[38] was set up in 1912 and started raising money for charity with entertainment nights—at that time minstrel shows—in 1914. Rodgers, through his elder brother Mortimer, had already been involved with the Akron Club before he and Hart met: he wrote music for their one-night-only vampires-in-Hollywood show, *One Minute Please* (1917), a benefit for the Sun Tobacco Fund's campaign to provide cigarettes to American soldiers fighting in France. Now two years older (though still only seventeen), he had his own lyricist and a Broadway profile, even if that amounted to just one song. With the continued support of Lew Fields, who provided "professional assistance," the boys began *You'd Be Surprised* (1920), "an atrocious musical comedy."[39] The show was genuinely a team effort, so although Rodgers provided all the music, at least five individuals contributed lyrics: Lorenz Hart, Milton G. Bender ("When We Are Married," "Princess of the Willow Tree"), Oscar Hammerstein II ("That Boy of Mine"), Robert Simon ("College Baby") and Herbert Fields ("Mary, Queen of Scots"). Although the show was a spoof loosely based on *Carmen*, with Lew's fifteen-year-old daughter Dorothy playing the lead, the title *You'd Be Surprised* perhaps deliberately echoed that of an Irving Berlin hit from the previous year. Berlin tells the story of shy young Johnny and his sweetheart Mary. Though her friends can't understand his appeal, Mary explains: "He isn't much in the light but when he gets in the dark/You'd be surprised." Inadvertently, her candor backfires: Johnny becomes a casanova and she loses her man. So goes the Irving Berlin song. In Milton Bender's script for this musical with the same name, the first act opens with "Don't Love Me like Othello," in which Carol hints that her boyfriend Ralph might be a similarly dark horse: "Girlies never clamor to make love to me," he sings; however, all that is set to change as the characters are whisked to China and the beguiling Toy Ming—played by Dorothy Fields in a parallel role to Carmen—falls for Ralph.

"Don't Love Me Like Othello" was one of two songs that stood out. This is a pleasant foxtrot that was later recycled in several shows. Hart's lyrics display erudition and wit as the characters relate a series of tragic love affairs, warning each other how not to behave: "Don't love me like Othello," pleads Carol, "I'm much too young to die"; Ralph responds, "Don't love me like Salome,/I'd hate to lose my head." Although unmentioned, the affair of Carmen and Don José in Bizet's opera is similarly doomed, as he stabs her to death outside the bullring. This morbid fascination is a consistent theme in *You'd Be Surprised*. Later, another deathly relationship is recounted in the dark humor of the dance-craze song "The Boomerang," in which "a dusky beauty" discovers her lover's infidelity and tries to kill him: "Poor dusky wife/ Let fly a knife;/As she stood on the strand,/It came back to her hand."[40]

Finally, to round off the quota of tragic murderous relationships, Herbert Fields recalls the story of "Mary, Queen of Scots," presaging Hart's ideas for "To Keep My Love Alive" in the *Connecticut Yankee* rewrite of 1943:

> Ain't it awful what they done to Mary, Queen of Scots,
> She was as full of husbands as a leopard is of spots.
> She kept them in a haunted flat,
> Killed each one off just like a rat.[41]

The following year's Akron show *Say Mama* (1921)—or *First Love*—provided the second half of an evening's fundraising for the Oppenheim Collins Mutual Aid Association (a cooperative supporting employees of the women's clothing store on 34th Street). It was held at the Brooklyn Academy of Music on February 10, and directed by Herb. The show featured Carol King as Ellen, an artist's model who sits for a portrait titled "First Love." Again Dorothy appeared. Here was a show that really allowed Larry's wry humor to come out: in the song "Watch Yourself," for example, he warns singletons to avoid getting married—"When the she-male wants the he-male / You're no free male!" cries the refrain. The first verse ends with a "poor simpleton" being pushed up to the altar; in the second verse—using a device that was to become characteristic—he cranks up the acerbic comedy:

> It's until death do us part!
> Oh! How those words do burn![42]

Later in the show Dorothy Fields introduced the "Chorus Girl Blues," which would subsequently be used in *Say It with Jazz*. This is another example of Hart's wit, sung by a chorus girl fed up with the perception that her life is "all fun and revel" when in fact it is tedious. Instead of traveling in limousines and dining at expensive restaurants, she takes the late night Metro home and eats soup "à la can." As she sings,

> I've Johnnies by the score
> With flowers at the door they're waiting.
> The flowers don't look big—
> A steak is more invigorating.[43]

Dorothy clearly appreciated the work that her brother and his friends were producing. Following their shows for the Akron Club, she recommended them for three more commissions from the Benjamin School for Girls: *The Chinese Lantern* (1922), *If I Were King* (1923), and *The Prisoner of Zenda* (1924). For all three, Herb directed, Rodgers wrote the music, and Dorothy starred (often in a beard). Hart was less involved, though he did contribute lyrics to the historical drama *If I Were King*, in "The Band of the Ne'er-Do-Wells," and the title song, recycled from *Winkle Town*.

THE VARSITY SHOWS (1920–1921)

Far more significant, however, were the productions the boys threw themselves into at Columbia University: the popular Varsity Shows, renowned for their energy and wit. Hart, being a few years older, had been involved with these since 1915, writing a sketch for *On Your Way* and playing a lead role based on Mary Pickford. As it happens, he had also rubbed shoulders—literally—with Oscar Hammerstein II, a Columbia student who was also forging a career in musical theater. Hart and Hammerstein performed in the Varsity Show of 1916, *The Peace Pirates*, mounted at the Hotel Astor's Grand Ballroom from April 12 to 15. This was scripted by Herman J. Manciewicz (later to write *Citizen Kane*), with music by Ray Perkins, who over the following few years would be instrumental in tutoring Rodgers in notation and conducting. It was directed by the veteran Varsity Show director Kenneth S. Webb. The plot lampooned Henry Ford's attempt to mount a peace mission to Europe the previous year. Hart—in drag—played the protagonist's wife, Mrs. Rockyford, while Hammerstein—in blackface—played Washington Snow, "a dark secret." One photograph from the Columbia University archives shows the two together in this show, a bizarre snapshot of two men (one in drag, one blacked up) who were to write some of the most celebrated contributions to the great American songbook (Figure 1.2).

The Varsity Shows had begun as fundraisers for Columbia University's sports teams. Initially known as "The Strollers," the Columbia College Dramatic Club was founded in 1886. By 1904 its shows were popular enough to be staged for their own merit and as Columbia University Players, the well-managed student organization became independent of the athletics club. By the time Rodgers, Hart, and Hammerstein were on the scene, the Varsity Show had become a perennial favorite.

The next year's offering, *Home James*, played at the Astor Ballroom from March 28 to 31. This time, Hammerstein had a hand writing the show, also appearing as head waiter Armand Dubonnett. In the audience was fifteen-year-old Richard Rodgers, whose older brother Morty was a classmate of Ockie's. "That afternoon I went home with one irrevocable decision," he admitted later; "I would also go to Columbia and I would also write the Varsity Show."[44]

It was in 1920's show that Rodgers and Hart hit success. As always, suggestions for material were competitive, and among the year's bumper batch of five submissions had been their proposal. The selection panel—which included

Figure 1.2: The cast of The Peace Pirates *(1916), showing Oscar Hammerstein II in blackface (far left), and next to him, Lorenz Hart in drag.*
Courtesy of the Columbia University archives.

Hammerstein—had liked the songs but had rejected the script. They were teamed with fellow students Milton Kroopf and Phil Leavitt (who had first introduced them), whose script for *Fly with Me* told a fantastical story set fifty years in the future (in 1970). Picking up on the government's fear of communism, the script established Manhattan as an island ruled by the Bolsheviks and carefully controlled by draconian laws. One prevented anyone from remarrying if they had children, so a complex plot involved lovers Mrs. Houghton and Mr. Larrimore trying to conceal the identity of their offspring, students Emmy and Jimmy, while also trying to prevent them from falling in love. This does not prove to be easy, not least because the first act is set in the Love Laboratory of Bolsheviki University, where Mrs. Houghton is teaching the Fine Art of Soviet Lovemaking, a technique called the "Fly with Me" embrace.[45] In an extended metaphor with lots of double entendres ("When we take off in my aeroplane, we'll wake up all the neighbours"; "My aeroplane doesn't have any landing gear"),[46] the students are taught the art, only to find in Act Two that acts of intimacy have been banned (undoubtedly a reference to the previous year's prohibition of alcohol). Trying to trap any flouters, Chinese characters Ming Ying and Tien Tong rig the garden kissing bench with an alarm. Before long, the dean of the college, Professor Theophilus Lamb (professor of safe-cracking and dirty tricks), who has been chief whip for the Soviet laws, nestles down on the bench with two college lovelies and sets off the alarm. Everyone revolts, and the play ends with plenty of smooching.

Although amateur, the Varsity Shows were widely reviewed by the New York papers. In general, the script was panned: "It isn't bad. It isn't good. It just isn't," wrote the *Globe*.[47] The *Evening World* thought likewise, reporting that "there is not the semblance of a plot to the play, as the authors admit,"[48] while the *Spectator* thought that the book was "almost completely devoid of humour."[49] On the other hand, the scenario very much revealed the things that were "on the minds of Columbia's typically intelligent witty, frightened, jaded, hormone-driven 17-to-21 year-olds"[50]—Prohibition, the Red Scare, the Golden Age of aviation, university life, and sex.[51]

With their topical references and college-based antics, the Varsity Shows were contemporary, if self-obsessed, burlesques. Added comedy would have come from the casting, made up exclusively from the ranks of the male students. In particular, audiences had come to delight in each production's celebrated Pony Ballet, "a bunch of skirt-wearing, sweaty, muscle-bound behemoths, rouged and wigged to the hilt, clunking round in high heels with the barest sense of grace or rhythm."[52] This was dyed-in-the-wool frat humor: as Phil Leavitt, in a program note to the 1980 revival of this show at Columbia comments, "Chest hair peeked through their costumes. Even if one were fooled by the padded-out shapes and makeup, it all fell apart when they joined in the singing. You expected a high treble chorus, and instead, booming bass voices came forth."[53] One can imagine the incongruity of romantic lead Jimmy Danford taking up with a bevy of these girls to spite his sweetheart Emmy Childs:

> JIMMY: You're sweet little things.
> GIRLS: Oh, thank you, sir.
> JIMMY: Petite little things.
> GIRLS: Oh, thank you, sir.[54]

As Leavitt remarks, "a lot of people fell right out of their seats."[55]

However early this may be in their development as songwriters, *Fly with Me*'s lyrics and music—both praised by critics—show elements that would become characteristic in Rodgers and Hart's later work. Rodgers makes liberal use of chromaticism in "Inspiration" (Figure 1.3), for example, moving through four then six steps of the chromatic scale in the first line of the refrain; Hart concocts some virtuoso triple and quadruple rhymes ("When springtime is alluring us/Assuring us/Of curing us/Of winter's melancholy"; "Down with all Ecclesiastics,/Moral teachings by bombastics,/We're our own

Figure 1.3: Rodgers' chromaticism in "Inspiration," from Fly With Me *(1920).*
Reprinted by Permission of Hal Leonard Corporation

iconoclastics,/Teaching plastics by gymnastics"),[56] though interestingly he also mocks this penchant in the lyric for "Kid, I Love You":[57] "Never try to waste your time/Looking for a triple rhyme."[58] It's true that in other places he uses some rather saccharine lyrics, such as those in "Dreaming True" or "Moonlight and You" ("In my dreams I'll kiss you,/And I'll never miss you"; "Sweetheart mine, the moon and you are melted in a dream");[59] however, there are other rather better lyrics—such as in "The Third Degree of Love"—that show not yet the jaded Hart of later years but still a young man with a suspicion of romanticism: "You think you're wise,/You're other-wise."[60]

In many ways, the score of *Fly with Me* reflects its era, with music closer in style to the sounds of the teens than the twenties (and to contemporary ears, closer even to the nineteenth century than the twentieth). The *Evening Telegram* compares Rodgers's music (favorably) to that of Victor Herbert, Alfred Robyn, and Raymond Hubbell, prominent composers of the old school, and the positive reviews the music received ("Music that sparkled from the rise of the curtain to its last descent"; "the real strength of the production")[61] probably reflect the fact that it did not challenge too much the traditionalist sensibilities of the critics. Jimmy's first song, "A Penny for Your Thoughts," for example, is straight out of the Gilbert and Sullivan textbook, with little swing or syncopation to mark it as a song of the early jazz age; instead, it has a very straight, regular, eighth-note melody which provides clarity for some very wordy lyrics. Rhythmic patterns elsewhere ("Inspiration," "Dreaming True," "Always Room for One More") likewise avoid syncopation or even dotted rhythms, giving the songs a period feel. Indeed, in some ways, Rodgers's music bears its influences on its sleeve: "Another Melody in F" adopts the theme to Anton Rubinstein's "Melody in F" (1858) for the girls' vocal line (in C and greatly sped up). After the boys sing a variation of this material, Rodgers combines the theme and its variation in counterpoint, in a style of "double song" that Irving Berlin had introduced to popular effect in "Play a Simple Melody" (1914).[62] "Another Melody in F" concludes with a very classical coda in the style of Rossini or Sullivan. Later, an extended musical sequence typical of pre-war operettas reprises earlier themes to draw the act to a conclusion.

Despite these period features in the score, a number of moments stand out for their light, jazzy feel. Both "Peek in Pekin'" and "A College on Broadway" were noted by critics as highlights, and these use more syncopation than elsewhere: in the opening phrase of "Peek in Pekin'," for example, Rodgers dots the rhythm to give it a swing feel, and then preempts the barline of the second phrase to create syncopation ("Summer breezes blowing,/Soon we will be going/China").[63] These "ragged" rhythms give it a light and casual feel, which is both very youthful and very up-to-date for 1920. It is rather ironic that this song—perhaps the most obviously American song in the score—is sung by the two Chinese characters. It could be seen as the halfway point between "Any Old Place with You" and "Manhattan." The refrain of "A College on Broadway," too, features dotted sequences that make it extremely catchy, while the second act song "Gunga Din"—placed in what would become recognized as the "Eleven O'Clock" spot—is the one that most obviously embraces jazz in its up-tempo foxtrot style. This song celebrates a new novelty dance, the "Gunga Din," in the explicit vocabulary of jazz ("It is not a jag step;/Just a lot of rag step") and with a particularly syncopated beat ("Do the syncopation that appeals").[64] This is an instructional number ("There: you've done it!"), similar to *Lido Lady*'s "Try again tomorrow," and in both its mood and music it captures the spirit of the dance crazes that would sweep America and Europe throughout the twenties.

While this show allowed the first full-length collaboration between Rodgers and Hart, it also brought together a team of other contributors who would form a wider collaborative network: Oscar Hammerstein wrote lyrics for two of Rodgers's songs;[65] Herbert Fields was the choreographer; Roy Webb was to orchestrate the show, as he later would the *Garrick Gaieties* and *A Connecticut Yankee*.

Above all, though, the reviews comment on the fact that Rodgers was so young: "the first Freshman ever to compose a complete score for a Varsity show";[66] "the youngest orchestra conductor in the city at the present time";[67] "the youngest composer in the country."[68] Although not yet full-blown Broadway professionals, these boys were making inroads into the business and were certainly getting themselves noticed.

Fly with Me undoubtedly exceeded the expectations of the Varsity Show, and it was favorably compared to Broadway productions by at least one reviewer, for whom it was "Full of echoes of the Charles Dillingham manner, the Flo Ziegfeld insouciance, the Shubert nonchalance";[69] the next year's production—created by much of the same team, including Rodgers and Hart—was not in the same league. Press reviews of *You'll Never Know* focused on twelve-year-old prodigy Edward Roche Hardy, who had been admitted to study at Columbia and who had a bit part showing off his skills in Chinese, French, Spanish, and Gaelic. Aside from this, neither the show nor the contributions of its writing team get much of a mention.

POOR LITTLE RITZ GIRL (1920)

Lew Fields was impressed that the moderate success of *You'd Be Surprised* had so swiftly been followed by the great success of *Fly with Me*. Rodgers and Hart seemed to be a team who worked quickly and productively. That their material bubbled with youthful energy and infectious rhythms appealed to him, and as the writers of Fields's own generation seemed to be increasingly distant from the contemporary mood of this new decade, he was prepared to take a gamble on their "juvenile joie de vivre."[70] *Poor Little Ritz Girl*, due to open in out-of-town tryouts by the end of May, was in any case saddled with a current writing team that was causing him doubts.

Fields had initially approached songwriters Al Bryan and George Meyer to write the score to a script by the unknown Adeline Leitzback. Bryan's "Peg O'My Heart" (1913) and Meyer's "For Me and My Gal" (1917) were their most well-known hits, though each had been jobbing songsmiths for Tin Pan Alley and Broadway revues throughout the teens, most recently working for the Shuberts at the Winter Garden. Their score for this show, however, fell short of Fields's expectations, and with little time or money, he went in desperation to Rodgers and Hart. Since the script was also a cause for concern, he brought in Henry B. Stillman and the new collaborators set to work.

Poor Little Ritz Girl is a backstage comedy about a group of chorus girls appearing in a Broadway revue (called *Poor Little Ritz Girl*). New recruit Barbara Arden has rented an upmarket apartment on the cheap, not realizing that it is already let. When she takes her chorus buddies back after rehearsal, they are astonished at her digs and suspect her to be a Gold Digger, no matter how much she protests. After they leave, wealthy bachelor William Pembroke returns home and is at once smitten when he finds a beautiful chorine in his apartment. He agrees to let her stay and calls his psychiatrist friend Dr. Stevens to act as chaperone. At the beginning of Act Two, Stevens hypnotizes Barbara so that Pembroke can find out her feelings. But her sister Dorothy arrives and a second love match develops between her and the psychiatrist. Stevens takes Dorothy to the theater for opening night and afterward, after some soul-searching of their own, Pembroke and Barbara admit their feelings—this time out of hypnosis—and marry as the show concludes.

Perhaps because of a shortage of time, Rodgers and Hart borrowed heavily from their existing repertoire. They incorporated "The Boomerang" and "Mary, Queen of Scots" (lyrics by Herbert Fields) directly into the show, and redrafted lyrics to five songs from *Fly with Me* and *You'd Be Surprised*, creating "You Can't Fool Your Dreams," "Love Will Call," "All You Need to Be a Star," "Will You Forgive Me?" and "Love's Intense in Tents."[71] Thus six of the twelve Act Two numbers and one number from Act One used recycled material. The rest of the material, including the whole of Act One up until its last song, was new.

Throughout the show, the big ensemble numbers take place in the show-within-a-show, in rehearsals or performances of *Poor Little Ritz Girl*. The opening number ("Poor Little Ritz Girl") is interrupted when several chorus girls mess up the rehearsal to the director's frustration. "The Gown Is Mightier than the Sword" and "Drink in to Your Eyes" also occur as part of the rehearsals, giving an opportunity for Hart to practice satirical lyrics without requiring a link to the narrative: "The Gown" comments on the influence of the fashion industry, while "Drink" tackles prohibition. In the second act, there is less *Ritz Girl* material as the contrivances of the plot are resolved, but "The Boomerang" offers that all-important dance craze number, and a new song, "The Daisy and the Lark" provides a glimpse of opening night.

In terms of the development of Rodgers and Hart as writers, however, these stand-alone numbers are not as interesting as the book numbers that drive the plot forward.[72] Act One's three book numbers in particular work lines of dialogue into the lyrics, thereby integrating the songs into the scenes. "The Midnight Supper," sung by the four chorus girls after their late-night rehearsal, preempts the lament of the "Chorus Girl Blues" from *Say Mama* (1921). However, rather than having each chorus girl sing a stanza, as might ordinarily have happened, Hart pitches the girls' comments within a conversation, each jostling to contribute in the manner of dialogue:

LILY: Ain't it awful to be moral?
MADGE: Lily, hang the crepe, I'm dead!
ROYAL: If you've passed away, don't quarrel,
         But butter the bread.
         In the Ritz I dreamed we dined
         Dressed in plumes and silk;
MADGE: Gawd, you're getting unrefined!
         Lil, don't spill the milk![73]

Along with "Will You Forgive Me?" this song stood out most for reviewer Philip Hale of the *Boston Morning Herald*. Like other critics, he found the chorus girls' banter to be "realistically frank, funny [and] illuminative."[74] In their biography of Lew Fields, his family biographers credit this "youthful" and "up-to-date" dialogue to Herbert. Though he is not explicitly named as a writer, his work as choreographer gave him "daily observation of the behaviour and speech patterns of chorus girls," and Fields and Fields suggest that he may have influenced the writing: "Here was dialogue with the nervous, hyped-up rhythms of jazz, and the verve and jaundiced wit that would characterize Herbert Fields's librettos for Rodgers and Hart in the mid-1920s."[75]

Such dialogic construction in the lyrics is also seen in the next number, "Lady Raffles Behave." Again, this presents a scripted conversation, in which Pembroke discovers Barbara in his apartment (see Figure 1.4). Here, Rodgers's music also contributes to the effect of the number: the same musical motif begins both chorus and verse, using straight half notes in the chorus though displacing these to an eighth-note pickup and dotted quarter note in the verse, which gives the dialogue a nervy quality. Since Pembroke has pulled a gun on Barbara, the effect is appropriate.

Although Rodgers and Hart had employed this style of dialogic writing in *Fly with Me*, particularly in Act One's ensemble finale "Call Me André," the extent to which they do this in the score of *Poor Little Ritz Girl* is significant. In *Fly with Me*, for example (with the exception of "Call Me André"), "dialogue" is constructed within the lyrics either as comment-and-riposte character play ("A Penny for Your Thoughts"), or by allocating whole musical phrases (i.e., eight measures at a time) to each character in turn ("Working for the Government"). By contrast, a number of the songs for *Poor Little Ritz*

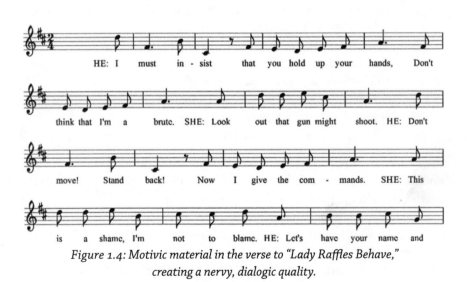

Figure 1.4: Motivic material in the verse to "Lady Raffles Behave,"
creating a nervy, dialogic quality.
Reprinted by Permission of Hal Leonard Corporation

Girl establish dialogic musical "scenes," as described: in addition to "The Midnight Supper" and "Lady Raffles Behave," "You Can't Fool Your Dreams" and "All You Need to Be a Star" resemble far more closely a scripted conversation.

"You Can't Fool Your Dreams," which recycles the music of "Don't Love Me like Othello" from *You'd Be Surprised*, stages the hypnosis scene with a very conversational verse, distributing dialogue between the characters to continue the scene:

DOC: Look into my eyes again.
PEMBROKE: Take her pain away.
DOC: Read my eyes and see your pain is better.
BARBARA: Yes, there isn't any pain.
DOC: Do just what I say,
            One deep breath now[76]

This differs markedly from the way the same song is used in *You'd Be Surprised*, in which the first verse and chorus are sung by one character and the second verse and chorus by another, thereby halting the action of the scene to indulge in the moment of song.

Another example is seen in "All You Need to Be a Star," which in *Fly with Me* had appeared as "Inspiration," a group number sung by the whole of Mrs. Houghton's lovemaking class as a block verse and refrain. In *Poor Little Ritz Girl* (as "All You Need to Be a Star"), the lyric is distributed among the four characters on stage:

DOT: Waves of art are roaring, roaring in my brain!
BAB: It's her inspiration soaring up again.
DOT: I hear voices calling, they kindle the spark!
DOC: Like Joan of Arc!
DOT: I will enter in the center, passion pent!
TAN: Heaven help the cast, for she has temperament.
ALL: Give her (me) publicity, gowns and a car,
      That is all you need to be a star.[77]

In this sense, although material is recycled for *Poor Little Ritz Girl*, its integration into the plot of the show is carefully considered and displays a marked development in Hart's songwriting expertise.

Despite favorable reviews, Lew Fields chose to redraft the show significantly before its New York premiere on July 28. To some degree this was reasonable: Stillman's script left "a great deal to be desired," according to one reviewer,[78] and though the banter of the chorus girls had been praised, scenes between Pembroke and Stevens were "weary work" and "might well be rewritten."[79]

Wilbur Theatre, Boston, May 24, 1920.   Central Theatre, New York, July 28, 1920.

1. The Poor Little Ritz Girl
2. The Midnight Supper
3. Lady Raffles—Behave
4. The Gown is Mightier than the Sword
5. Drink In To Your Eyes
6. Will You Forgive Me?

1. Call The Doc
2. You Can't Fool Your Dreams
3. The Lord Only Knows
4. The Boomerang
5. Love Will Call
6. All You Need to Be A Star
7. Love's Intense in Tents
8. The Daisy and the Lark
9. Souvenirs
10. Mary, Queen of Scots
11. I Surrender
12. Finale

1. Poor Little Ritz Girl (Romberg / Gerber)
2. Mary, Queen of Scots
3. Love Will Call
4. Pretty Ming Toy (Romberg / Gerber)
5. I Love to Say Hello (Romberg / Gerber)
6. When I Found You (Romberg / Gerber)

1. You Can't Fool Your Dreams
2. What Happened Nobody Knows
3. My Violin (Romberg / Gerber)
4. All You Need to Be A Star
5. Love's Intense in Tents
6. The Daisy and the Lark
7. In the Land of Yesterday (Romberg / Gerber)
8. The Phantom Waltz (Romberg / Gerber)
9. The Bombay Bambeshay (Romberg / Gerber)
10. Finale

Figure 1.5: Running order of songs in Poor Little Ritz Girl *before (left) and after the Rodgers and Hart material was culled. Reprinted by Permission of Hal Leonard Corporation*

Drafting in George Campbell as a new bookwriter was one thing, but it is less understandable that Fields cut eleven of the Rodgers and Hart numbers—including the entirety of Act One—and recruited another pair of songwriters, Sigmund Romberg and Alex Gerber. In redrafting, the storyline was kept more or less the same, though eight new numbers by Romberg and Gerber now reshaped the score (Figure 1.5).

It's tempting to speculate why Fields may have done this. Some commentators, picking up on a remark in *Variety*, wonder whether it was to avoid charges of nepotism for employing his son's friends Dick and Larry;[80] Fields could certainly be sensitive to this sort of charge, as he was sensitive to accusations of plagiarism.[81] It's possible also that the oldtimer became nervous about relying on the talents of such youngsters—as many reviews mention, Rodgers was still in his teens, and there was no way that the names of Rodgers and Hart could yet command audiences. Either way, replacing the youngsters with Romberg and Gerber was, if nothing else, safe—Romberg was by far the most prolific Broadway composer at that time, having notched up twenty-three Broadway productions and 3,800 performances of his shows since 1913. His style, though, was also "safe," and his contributions to this show, as William Everett puts it, "are much less daring [than Rodgers'] and consist largely of sentimental and nostalgic numbers that recall the sound world of the operetta."[82] "When I Found You" in particular is a typically European waltz with a very straight rhythmic feel, a heavy tonic-dominant bass on the first beat of the bars, and a lilting melody stretching the high tenor range. "Pretty Ming Toy" is a jaunty number and "In the Land of Yesterday" a pleasant refrain, though both are dated by their prominent oompah bass lines. "I Love to Say Hello to the Girls but I Hate to Say Goodbye" has a ragtime syncopation giving it a jaunty air appropriate for a charm song, and "The Bombay Bombeshay" (or "Bambeshay"), replacing "The Boomerang" in suggesting another dance craze, introduces the most dotted rhythms in Romberg's contribution to the show. But the different musical styles were mismatched, and Romberg's "serious and sentimental" songs, though "pleasing," were "hardly as striking as the lighter numbers" by Rodgers and Hart.[83] In the end, one reviewer summed up the New York production of *Poor Little Ritz Girl* as "a sort of cross between a revue and a polite American musical comedy with a plot. The plot is rather short and not too husky, and there aren't a great many revue scenes; but the two together make an odd and rather satisfactory entertainment."[84]

Cobbled together though it may appear, and the result of dubious ethical production practices though it undoubtedly was, the combination of revue and musical comedy was Fields's vision for a new type of musical theater:

> I decided that the new type of musical show ought to be a blend of the Princess Theatre intimate style of show and the revue type of production. The story of "The Poor Little Ritz Girl," which switches back and forth from the apartment of the chorus girl to the stage of a theatre, was ideal for this purpose. In the girl's apartment, we had the "intimate" touch. On the theatre stage we had the revue effect—result: something absolutely novel and a success.[85]

Still, in the transition from Boston to New York, the sense of integration seemed to fade, as the old vaudevillian shoehorned the big comedy number "Mary, Queen of Scots" into the first scene in the apartment, and heavy-handedly inserted a number of specialty acts elsewhere: a violin routine by Ardelle Cleaves, dances by Dolly Clements and Michael Cunningham ("The Phantom Waltz") and Donald Kerr (in "The Bombay Bombeshay"), and the song hit "Dear Heart My Sweetheart" by Bide Dudley and Ted Barron. All were to be viewed favorably by the press, vindicating Fields's interpolations and supporting his belief that "revue has come to stay";[86] but what had taken two steps forward in terms of integration was now taking one step back.

Rodgers and Hart were disappointed that so much of their material had been cut from *Poor Little Ritz Girl* and that "their" show—their first Broadway show!—was now half-written by a team they had never even met. "Even now," Rodgers would later write, "I can still feel the grinding pain of bitter disappointment and depression."[87] If this was galling, the fact that Lew Fields had not even told them that their songs had been replaced smarted considerably. It wasn't until they arrived at the Century Theatre for the opening night performance that they discovered what Fields had done.

THE INSTITUTE OF MUSICAL ART (1920–1923)

Around that time, although Rodgers was enrolled as a freshman at Columbia, he decided to relocate, and for the first time he acquiesced to some formal musical education at the Institute of Musical Art (IMA). It was his opportunity to train with some of the highest caliber music teachers in the world,[88] though Rodgers's attraction to the Institute was not purely academic; each year the IMA put on a show, and it was just as much this that interested him. Indeed, so keen was he to make his mark that he shipped in both Larry and Herb, neither of whom were remotely connected to the school. At the end of Rodgers's first year, the students offered a "travesty" of Rimsky-Korsakov's *Le Coq d'Or* (1907), entitled *Say It with Jazz*. This was set in the Classic Realm of Music, "declared to be threatened by enemy modernists and jazz demons,"[89] and then Jazzland. In the loose storyline, the "Three Bees" of the Classic Realm (Bach, Beethoven, and Brahms) are confronted by modernists Deboozy, Ravelled, and Dandy, who encourage Queen Jazz to entice King Classic with her ragtime "Hymn to the Moon." In the end, the Cock (Coq d'Or), representing the Rising Generation, pecks King Classic to death and runs off with the sexy Jazz Queen amid much dancing and delight.[90]

The *New York Times* confessed its surprise that such cavalier material could be condoned "in a sanctum of classic art that looks askance at any music later than Brahms."[91] Indeed, this sentiment was one also expressed (though mockingly) by Dick and Herb in a short stanza published in the newly founded college newsletter the *Baton*. Here, the mischievous confidence of their summer camp articles easily transferred to the Institute's publication: "An institute where music's taught/Is one place that you hadn't ought/To poke a single joke at!"[92] Nonetheless, the IMA's response to these burlesques was tolerant, if not encouraging, and for the first time in his life, Rodgers claimed, "I realized that my fellow students didn't look down their noses at someone whose aim was the tinselled world of Broadway."[93] If this shows a self-consciousness about his love of the popular—and perhaps about his lack of musical education—it was reassuring to find that "faculty and fellow students alike displayed support and respect for the kind of music Rodgers wanted to compose."[94]

Still, the main musical diet at the school was resolutely the classics, so in the end-of-year productions it tended to be these—alongside faculty staff—that were burlesqued. While the 1921 show had the semblance of a coherent plot, 1922's *Jazz à la Carte* didn't claim to be anything more than a series of sketches based around the experiences of IMA students. It opened in the newsroom of the *Baton* (edited by virtually the same team responsible for the end-of-year shows, so nothing if not an incestuous clique) and went on to present a skit on "The Joys of Enrollment" [*sic*] at the school. The influences on Rodgers, Hart, and Fields are evident throughout this program; between sketches, student Cyril Towbin gave his impersonation of the violin master, Franz Kneisel, in a Dutch Act that could have been by Lew Fields himself.[95] The second act departed from the school to present a short sketch set in the Nut Islands of the South Sea, before burlesquing the classics in "Geraldine à la Mode" and "Liliom at the Bat." The first ribbed the Met's prima donna Geraldine Farrar, with skits on her most celebrated characters; the second took Ferenc Molnár's 1909 play *Liliom* as its influence, which had been staged to great acclaim on Broadway in 1921. *Liliom* would later be even more significant to Rodgers, since it was the source material for *Carousel* (1945); at this stage the link was to Hart, since this was one of the playtexts that he had translated for Amberg.[96] Like the previous year's show, *Jazz à la Carte* ends with a jazzed rewrite of Tschaikovsky by Sigmund Krumgold, this time of his "Pathétique Symphony." Rodgers's own music included a few new songs with lyrics by Herb Fields and Frank Hunter, and "for insurance, a few of the better applause getters which I had written for previous amateur efforts".[97] "Another Melody in F" and "Moonlight and You" were drafted in from *Fly with Me*; "Breath of Springtime" and "Mary, Queen of Scots" (lyrics by Herb, and again the hit of the evening) from *You'd Be Surprised*.

Perhaps the most interesting of the three shows staged by the IMA during Rodgers's studies was *A Danish Yankee in King Tut's Court*, performed on May 31 and June 1, 1923. Based on the Twain novel *A Connecticut Yankee in King Arthur's Court* (1889), it drew topical references from the recent discovery of King Tutankhamen's tomb.[98] As the *New York Times* review reported, this was "What might have happened in Tut-ankh-Amen's tomb, had he been found 'more alive than dead.'"[99] The Danish Yankee of the title was George Nielsen, the Institute's janitor, who was soon to retire. "At the opening," reports the reviewer for the *Baton*, the celebration of his majesty's three thousandth birthday is rudely interrupted by the capture of Nielsen, the Danish Yankee, who has been, digging down to find King Tut, who he hoped would replace him officially in the I.M.A.[100]

King Tut is alive and well and celebrating his birthday, though his daughter Sulphite cannot be roused. The Danish Yankee offers to revive her and is duly rewarded by becoming director of the new "Insti-Tute-ankh-Amen." A comedy scene had Nielsen interviewing new teachers (which allowed for current faculty members to be satirized) and then mounting an operatic production, in which several of the classic operas (performed straight at the IMA the previous week) were burlesqued.

A Danish Yankee was an overwhelming hit, and excited by its success, the boys approached Charles Tressler Lark, who controlled the rights to *A Connecticut Yankee* through the Twain estate. They were delighted to secure the stage rights without a fee: Rodgers and Hart had a valuable option on the material; now all they needed was a producer prepared to support it.

The juxtaposition of a contemporary vernacular with a historical milieu was clearly something that fascinated the boys, and something they explored on numerous occasions. The song "Mary Queen of Scots" reveled in this conceit, and Herb would continue in the same vein reinterpreting classic operas in contemporary parlance for the *Baton*. "A Spanish Omelette" revisioned *Carmen* framed as a wedding announcement ("Mr and Mrs Timothy Tobasco announce the betrothal of their little daughter, Carmen, to Don José, a grenadine in the Spanish Boy Scouts of America");[101] while his spoof of *Lucia di Lammermoor* ran

> From sorrow and debility
> Her brain snaps with agility
> And dexterous Lucia throws a mad scene that's a beaut!
> She sings a shrill cadenza
> With a final C that ends her
> And she dies while Donizetti does contortions with the flute.[102]

Meanwhile, Hart is delighting in the same sort of impish tricks, as *Shakespeares of 1922* shows. This is a short review sketch he wrote with Morrie Ryskind for vaudevillian George Price to perform. "I'll make Shakespeare seem the cat's pajamas," quips the opening verse, revealing the intentions of the sketch: a very staple burlesque device that had been popular in both London and New York for decades.[103] Hackneyed though the idea was, 1922's colloquial idioms give it a fresh edge, and Hart and Ryskind have fun translating the best-known soliloquies into 1920s Manhattanese. Price plays, in turn, Shylock, Hamlet, King Lear, Julius Caesar, and Romeo; each character is introduced in a short refrain leading into a ribbed version of a famous soliloquy and a burlesque of a popular Al Jolson song. Shylock (from *The Merchant of Venice*) becomes a Jewish garment trader, and the soliloquy morphs from the original "hath not a Jew hands, organs, dimensions, senses, affections, passions" to continue the list with "broadcloth, velveteen, sateen, tricolette and different quality serges?" "If you gyp us," he continues (using slang meaning "cheat" rather than "prick"), "do we not bleed? If you do not pay us, do we not sue?" Shylock goes on to sing a version of the Al Jolson hit "The Spaniard that Blighted My Life" (1911), substituting Jolson's trademark vocalese with exaggerated Jewish davening sounds ("tiddly-i-ti-ti-ti-ti-ti-ti-" becomes "diddy diddy ei, die, die, die"). Next comes Hamlet, whose "To be or not to be" soliloquy poses the dilemma "whether 'tis nobler to buy your Gordon's gin, and pay the prices of outrageous bootleggers, or to take arms against this sea of highwaymen, and make your own home brew!" For audiences recently plunged into prohibition, this is a very topical handling of the "Danish pastry Prince." Hamlet goes on to sing "Mammy" ("The sun will shine, and the sun will drop,/ But the sun won't shine where you sent my pop!"). Next, King Lear becomes a tenant evicted by his cruel landlord, and the famous storm scene puts him out on the street in the rain. The pastiche of another Jolson hit, "April Showers," which he was at that time performing in the Broadway show *Bombo*, is perhaps the highlight of the whole sequence, partly because it is so appropriate for the scene and partly because of Hart's masterful tweaking of the lyrics: "It isn't raining rain at all,/It's just a stage effect." The fourth episode turns Mark Antony's "Friends, Romans, Countrymen" speech into a commentary on the baseball player Babe Ruth, who that season had been suspended for six weeks following disciplinary action after he embarked on a prohibited "barnstorming" tour of the baseball circuit. At the same time, to capitalize on his popularity following a record season in 1921, he launched a vaudeville career. Following the soliloquy, Price sang a short stanza of the 1891 perennial "After the Ball." The Hart/Ryskind commentary on these events is certainly topical, though it is perhaps the weakest of the five episodes in this Shakespeare sketch. Finally, Price became Romeo, in a balcony scene updated to the Manhattan streets some thirty-five years before *West Side Story*: "Ah, there she sits, my Juliet, on the fire escape!" he exclaims, continuing with gag after gag in the "What's in a name" soliloquy. "Nellie Melba, she's a peach…Napoleon is a cream cake!" The final song is Jolson's "Yoo-hoo," which he had also interpolated into *Bombo*. Here Hart's ribaldry sneaks in as Romeo describes his ascent up the fire escape: "While I'm climbing up the ladder/And I get a worm's eye view"—one can imagine the audience's roar as Price finishes the final lines of the refrain.

Price—who was some years younger than Hart—was keen to try the sketch in his act, though he urged them to stay away in case the material fell flat. Doing this, Price could claim that the sketch was mediocre and that audiences hadn't really responded; he paid Hart and his colleague just $100, which for politic reasons Hart accepted. But the boys had seen everything and had noted the success of their work. Not for the last time, Hart had been duped.

THE JAZZ KING (1924)

If the early 1920s were frustrating, it was Dick more than Larry who felt the rub, sensing parental pressure to embark on a "proper" career. Although there is no report of William and Mamie actively rebuking their son, Rodgers senior was a well-respected doctor, and a similar profession would have been expected for his offspring—music was a worthy pastime, but the stage was no place to build a respectable livelihood. Larry's background was different in this sense: his father took whatever work he could and got by on his pluck and charisma. The odd payments that came in for skits like *Shakespeares of 1922* complemented Larry's earnings from Amberg and generous handouts from his old man (the "O.M."). Easy come, easy go, any money Larry made funded his social life: "Larry would gather a group around him and take them out on the town, paying for everything with crumpled bills from his pocket—never a wallet—saying, 'Here, I've got it! I've got it!' "[104] Free and easy, then; though not free of cares. "Larry's war with himself was intense," suggest Marx and Clayton, picking up on some amateur psychology from author Jerome Lawrence: "Unless you were an Arrow Collar ad guy or a Gibson Girl, unless you had that Princeton look," he opined, "it was 'beat me.' It was 'I'm no good.' It was 'Nobody's heart belongs to me.' " Due to his stature and his looks (and perhaps his sexuality), the common assumption goes, Larry saw himself as worthless; and to Lawrence this sense of self-loathing pervades his songs: "*Every* lyric has some masochism, every single one."[105]

By 1924 the boys were becoming disconsolate about their prospects of ever hitting the big time. This was not for want of trying: they had courted high profile producers and music publishers; they had been feted in the press; they had scored significant successes on both amateur and professional circuits (*Fly with Me*; *Poor Little Ritz Girl*). But the rejection of *Winkle Town* was hard to take.

Perhaps it wasn't them so much; perhaps it was musical theater that was the problem. Musical shows were expensive properties: not only did they require greater numbers onstage, but they also demanded significant numbers in the pit. Moreover, there was the expectation of spectacle, and if this demanded complex stage machinery, as *Poor Little Ritz Girl* had, the wage bill for stagehands increased too. In this climate, and with names yet to draw box office, Rodgers, Hart, and Fields Jr. wondered if breaking into musical theater was just too much of a mountain to climb.

> Larry and I reasoned that we should next try something more modest, a comedy perhaps, which might have an easier time getting on the boards. At the very least it would get our names known in the profession, and we could always sneak in a song or two just to let everyone know the direction in which we were still heading.[106]

If getting their names known was the intention, it was an odd idea to disguise their identity: although they filed their script at the Library of Congress using their full names (ordered Rodgers, Hart, Fields), they promoted *The Jazz King* under the pseudonym Herbert Richard Lorenz (Figure 1.6).

Loosely based on Charles Klein and David Belasco's 1904 David Warfield vehicle *The Music Master*, which Fields had already burlesqued in 1905, *The Jazz King* was described as a "combination comedy, musical comedy and melodrama";[107] but if this composite approach—both in terms of authorship and form—was intended to manufacture a coherent piece, not every critic approved.

> It exhibits a farcical flair at the start....As it progresses to the second act it becomes legitimate comedy, and before the third has gone very far one realises that here is something else again.[108]

Some called this innovative, others confused. "Every act is a different play," wrote the *Chicago Herald and Examiner* reviewer.[109] Only a handful realized that Herbert Richard Lorenz was a pen name for three writers,[110] though several believed Lew Fields to have written the play himself, using "a trick combination of the names of his family" as a pseudonym.[111]

The elderly Franz Henkel is a classical composer, who in his native Austria studied under Liszt and wrote the acclaimed "Dresden Sonata." Now, having emigrated to New York, he is working as an arranger for the Al Tyler Music Publishing Company, where his classical training is at odds with the jazz sounds the public craves. "I'm willing to write your 'breaks' and to make it 'nasty'...but this da-da-da-daaaa! I won't do it!" he protests,[112] though the hoofers who are buying this hack material find Henkel's arrangements completely outdated. Tyler's hit songs are all steals from the European classics, and when Henkel discovers that his own "Dresden Sonata" has been ragged

*Figure 1.6: "Herbert Richard Lorenz": Herbert Fields, Richard Rodgers, and
Lorenz Hart (1927). Photo by Vandamm Studio © Billy Rose Theatre Collection,
The New York Public Library for the Performing Arts.*

to create "Moonlight," he is furious, storming out of the office and threatening to sue the publisher.

Act Two takes place in Henkel's apartment, which he shares with his
daughter Elsa. During this act, it is revealed that Henkel fled from Austria
after finding out that his success there had been sponsored by an admirer of
his wife, with whom she later eloped. When Henkel discovered this deceit he
flew into a rage and killed the man; for eighteen years he has been wanted for
murder. Now Tyler has found out about his past and threatens blackmail. But
the publisher is also in love with Elsa, and before blackmailing Henkel, he
offers to split the royalties for "Moonlight" with the expectation of getting
her hand. Henkel is again furious and vows to proceed with the case.

But a year later, Act Three has Elsa and Tyler returning from their European honeymoon. The case went to court and Henkel lost, though to his
surprise, Tyler didn't reveal his secret. Indeed, the publisher has secured an
official pardon for Henkel from the authorities. Henkel realizes that the old

world is where he belongs, and decides to leave the happy couple to return to his old life and music.

The Jazz King started tryouts in Bethlehem, Pennsylvania, on March 24, 1924, before having its name changed to *Henky* (to avoid sounding like it was a musical),[113] and finally *The Melody Man* (which sounds *more* like a musical) as it moved onto Broadway on May 13. The change in name is of course interesting: as *The Jazz King*, the show emphasized the contemporary and suggested Tyler as the "lead" role; as *The Melody Man*, the new name was more ambiguous, though if the name refers to Henkel it certainly diminishes the stature of classical composition (and with that, seniority). With Fields in the role of Henkel, and husband-and-wife team Eva Puck and Sammy White playing Stella Mallory the office girl and Bert Hackett the vaudevillian, the cast was strong—as critics agreed. Indeed, out-of-town critics generally raved, calling the production "striking,"[114] commending its "real substance,"[115] and citing its "distinct departure from the conventional ending"[116] as a major virtue. But with only lukewarm reviews in pre-Broadway tryouts ("plenty of minor faults and absurdities";[117] "creaks badly at the beginning but warms up as the first act progresses";[118] "the performance as a whole dragged"),[119] its momentum faltered, and it closed after seven weeks. According to the *New York Times*, *The Melody Man* was "about as far as possible from being a good play";[120] the *New York Herald and Tribune* called it "pretty poor stuff..., it belongs among the trundle bedtime stories, feeble, immature and meandering."[121] The failure was blamed on various things: the summer heat, the fact that it had opened late in the season, and an ending that seemed to contradict its opening:

> Here something happened to Mr. Lorenz' plot. He may have been called out of town or something. At any rate the third act contradicts the other two. The sudden turn of events is at least surprising. Perhaps the actors forgot, in the hurry of a first night, to play the act in between which would have explained what was happening and then again it may all be a part and parcel of the jazz age in which we live.[122]

Flop though it was, *The Jazz King* is still interesting for a number of reasons: as the last major project before Rodgers, Hart, and Fields hit the big time, it shows the boys in their amateur endgame; as a play rather than a musical it reveals an unusual detour away from musical comedy; as a piece that explicitly pits old against new it reflects the significant cultural change taking place; and with a storyline emphatically written by the integrated character "Herbert Richard Lorenz" it embodies their understanding and practice of collaboration.

The Jazz King is a rehearsal of the voguish classical versus jazz refrain that would appear on stage and film in any number of other shows during this period and which Rodgers and Hart were perennially exploring, not least in *Say It with Jazz* (1921) and *Jazz à la Carte* (1922); the tensions brought out in this theme—in particular the tensions between European sophistication and an American vernacular—are endemic to the period, and these and their meta-phorical associations were recurring obsessions of Rodgers, Hart, and Fields as they tried to gain status in the complex strata of New York culture. The old/new dichotomy was also reflected in the script's generation gap between father and daughter, and it is not hard to see this struggle at the core of this young writing team's psyche. The figure of Lew Fields, after all, towered over them not only as their sole professional producer to date but also as a reminder of old-school vaudeville trying to rebrand itself for the jazz age. In this show, one might have thought (particularly at this stage in their career) that Herbert, Richard, and Lorenz would have sided with the young generation, presenting a tale that showed the energy, verve, and pizazz of American jazz trumping the staid clas-sicism of a former generation. That they resist this autobiographical indulgence reflects developing sophistication in their writing, but perhaps it also mani-fests a complexity regarding their own relationships with the classics and with the varying statuses of cultural forms. Notwithstanding the fact that they were actively promoting everything new and modern and doing their bit to engineer an all-American twentieth-century sound, their work in this period reveals tre-mendous respect and allegiance to the classics of the past. Not for nothing was Hart known as "Shakespeare"; and burlesques though they may have been, the virtuoso updating of soliloquies in *Shakespeares of 1922* shows his admiration for the language, the characters, and the form.

Most of all, it is interesting to consider why Rodgers, Hart, and Fields—so committed to musical theater—would mount a piece that seemed to cry out for songs yet only half-heartedly include them. In the second and third acts *The Jazz King* has the pace and feel of a play; Rodgers at least intended to write it as such. However, the fact that its subject is music and its characters musicians gives ample opportunity for music and song to feature. In fact, the first act suggests that it was far closer to musical theater than Rodgers admits.

This act, set in the reception area of the music publisher's, features music throughout and moves with the pace and tone of a musical comedy. At cur-tain rise, two separate songs—a vaudeville ballad and a jazz number—are being rehearsed simultaneously in two anterooms, establishing song as part of the sound palette of the show. A few pages later, the vaudevillians Hackett and La Marr rehearse one of their routines, a run-of-the-mill gag with a kick-line that serves as the cue for a song ("The Sheik of Battle Creek"):

HACKETT: Play it for me, will you, and I'll give you an idea of how we're gonna do it. *(Stella goes to piano and starts to play. Hackett stops her).* Let's take it from the cue. The cue is "Oh Daddy!"

LA MARR: *(Leading in).* Who was that lady I saw you with?

HACKETT: That was no lady, that was a female impersonator. *(He kicks her).*

LA MARR: Oh Daddy!

   (Stella starts. They begin verse).[123]

This is typical musical comedy fare. What makes it different, however, is when the song is interrupted and, according to the stage directions, the sound palette of the scene is made more prominent:

They are interrupted by the entrance of Al Tyler. As he comes in the noise in the office is increased. Ruth Davis is singing loudly in [Room] A. Miss Sands is typewriting and Sidney is stamping copies. Hackett and La Marr are trying to top the noise by their singing.

This suggests a fascinating complexity to an otherwise standard routine. The convention of the musical number being introduced and then situated in relief from the diegesis serves as a way in for the song, but then the stand-alone number becomes naturalized back into the scene and the scene itself becomes stylistically exaggerated. In one sense we are made aware of the chaotic noise of the office; but in another, the writers build a musical soundscape from the diegetic sounds of Sands typing, Sidney stamping, and Davis singing in the background.

Following this episode, the next song is "Moonlight," the musical focus of the narrative, which Tyler has adapted from Henkel's "Dresden Sonata." At the end of the act, it is hearing this that tips Henkel over the edge; shortly beforehand we hear the composition in its "original" form as the "Dresden Sonata," played by Stella on the piano. The use of the song at this point— much earlier—is partly to introduce it so that we recognize it at the end of the act, and partly to underscore dramatically the romantic tension between Elsa, Don, and Tyler. This happens over three short scenes during which the song is rehearsed in Room A. In the first, we see Tyler and Elsa together in an unrequited love scenario; in the second, we see a bonding scene between the girls (Elsa, Stella, and Sands); and in the third, we see the true lovers Elsa and Don recalling the glory of the "Dresden Sonata" and sharing their own romantic hopes over the imagery from a dream Don has had. Underscored by an enchanting ballad, one imagines, these three scenes would work extremely effectively and would consolidate that ballad as a significant musical feature in the show. Quite what that ballad was is unclear—the song that eventually featured, "Moonlight Mama" (which does not seem to suggest this pathos), was published a whole year after this script was copyrighted, by which time many changes may have been made.

The next musicalized sequence shows Henkel arguing with Hackett. They bicker about a particular refrain in the most recent song Henkel has arranged, and the two trade what are scripted almost as scat passages in their argument:

> HACKETT: At the end of the dance we do a break. See? *(Does step and sings)* Dum-de-de-dum-dum-DUM DUM- That's got to be good and loud.
>
> HENKEL: But the way I got it, it's so *cute: (Sings it with a little flourish at the end).* Isn't that darling?[124]

This, then, is a different way of naturalizing song as part of the diegesis of the scene.

Two pages later, the next number is used, again to magnify the emotional pathos:

> *Henkel is over-wrought and despondently sinks in a chair. As he sits there, Miss Davis in Room B starts a loud jazzy chorus. Henkel writhes. As the music becomes softer Sidney enters.*[125]

Although there is no indication of how long this moment is sustained, what the song is, or how much is used, the music is clearly intended to contribute to the dramaturgy. In common with the music, Henkel's mood softens. Later, as he argues with his daughter, *"Miss Davis in Room B starts singing loudly to the crash of the piano"* (presumably the same song).[126] Thus the song articulates the emotional trajectory of the character through the scene.

With such a musical palette energizing this act, it seems likely that the writers saw *The Jazz King* originally as a musical, and Rodgers's subsequent claim that a play had always been their intention seems more correctional spin than authorial ambition. After Hart's experimentation working the structural expectations of song form into the give-and-take of dialogic interaction in *Poor Little Ritz Girl*, was this a further experiment, in which the scenes and songs are even more closely integrated? And was the adoption of the pseudonym Herbert Richard Lorenz an attempt to fuse the writing team's identity into one, as a sort of performative metaphor for the close integration they sought; or was it rather, as Fields and Fields suggest, a "sheepish attitude towards the enterprise,"[127] an attempt to hide their real identities to avoid recognition in the press?

The truth about the development of *The Jazz King* and its eventual appearance as *The Melody Man* on Broadway is likely to remain shrouded in mystery, though some of the evidence challenges the story we have been told. For a start, a draft script was filed for copyright as early as April 1923 (though the piece was not staged until March 1924). It was credited to Rodgers, Hart, and Fields Jr. (as individuals), and it clearly contained a significant musical element and a number of songs in Act One. By the time it appeared on Broadway (in July 1924), *The Melody Man* had just two identified numbers, "Moonlight Mama" and "I'd Like to Poison Ivy."[128] Whether or when other songs had been written and removed is unclear.

Still, the two published songs themselves are interesting in the way they position notions of the contemporary stylistically within this narrative of the old and new; for neither *sounds* particularly new—at least not new like George Gershwin's "Fascinating Rhythm" from that year's *Lady, Be Good* (1924). These both evoke the end of an era rather than the beginning of something new. "I'd Like to Poison Ivy" is a straight-out vaudeville number, pitting him against her with witty banter ("I'd like to poison Ivy because she clings to me!"). Meanwhile, "Moonlight Mama" is a plaintive refrain in ABAC form. With a generous use of internal chromatic movement it is by no means old, though it is reminiscent of a pre-1920 wind sound, and its gauche title phrase, with both racially and sexually dubious overtones, shows a clumsy appropriation of voguish mores. The slightly dusty sound may be dramaturgically appropriate, in the sense that "Moonlight Mama" derives from the music of the European old guard. Even in classical circles, though, the tide had turned, with composers like Berg and Stravinsky reinventing that classical sound, and with American classical composers appropriating jazz (not least George Gershwin with "Rhapsody in Blue"). As Rodgers would articulate years later through the script of his subsequent collaborator, Oscar Hammerstein II, "Country a-changin', gotta change with it!" Perhaps toying with this story of old and new sounds just at the moment the musical idiom of American music was a-changin' was so timely it tripped itself up.

The first few years of Rodgers and Hart's collaboration (1919–1925) (Figure 1.7) have always been seen as a frustrating amateur period, at the end of which a combination of pluck, luck, and talent led them to score their first Broadway success. This telling of the tale—corroborated by Rodgers's own autobiographical account—consolidates a rhetoric of perseverance and the idea that hard work will eventually be rewarded. It also sustains the sort of rags-to-riches mythology of Broadway that still beguiles young hopefuls today. Yet it also obscures some of the facts about the Rodgers and Hart partnership, whose actual story is not so clear-cut; they experimented considerably, for example,

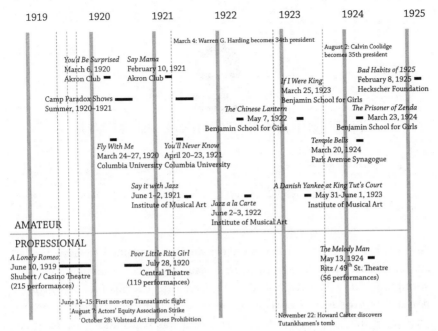

The timeline figure contains the following:

Years across top: 1919　1920　1921　1922　1923　1924　1925

March 4: Warren G. Harding becomes 34th president

August 2: Calvin Coolidge becomes 35th president

You'd Be Surprised
March 6, 1920
Akron Club

Say Mama
February 10, 1921
Akron Club

Bad Habits of 1925
February 8, 1925
Heckscher Foundation

If I Were King
March 25, 1923
Benjamin School for Girls

Camp Paradox Shows
Summer, 1920–1921

The Chinese Lantern
May 7, 1922
Benjamin School for Girls

The Prisoner of Zenda
March 23, 1924
Benjamin School for Girls

Fly With Me
March 24–27, 1920
Columbia University

You'll Never Know
April 20–23, 1921
Columbia University

Temple Bells
March 20, 1924
Park Avenue Synagogue

Say it with Jazz
June 1–2, 1921
Institute of Musical Art

Jazz a la Carte
June 2–3, 1922
Institute of Musical Art

A Danish Yankee at King Tut's Court
May 31–June 1, 1923
Institute of Musical Art

AMATEUR

PROFESSIONAL

A Lonely Romeo
June 10, 1919
Shubert / Casino Theatre
(215 performances)

Poor Little Ritz Girl
July 28, 1920
Central Theatre
(119 performances)

The Melody Man
May 13, 1924
Ritz / 49th St. Theatre
(56 performances)

June 14–15: First non-stop Transatlantic flight
August 7: Actors' Equity Association Strike
October 28: Volstead Act imposes Prohibition

November 22: Howard Carter discovers Tutankhamen's tomb

Figure 1.7: Timeline of Rodgers and Hart's amateur and professional engagements, 1919–1925.

reconceptualizing a new, sophisticated musical theater; thanks to Lew Fields—at least by proxy—they also had two Broadway successes in *Poor Little Ritz Girl* (1920) and *The Melody Man* (1924), even if these were bastardized or doctored, and even if they don't "fit" the standard telling of the tale. In developing their craft, perhaps the most significant lesson was to recognize the balance between creative license and commercial exigency. Pleasing the press, public, and producers would inform their work from now on. Learning to juggle those requirements while maintaining creative integrity was a trick they seemed to grasp at this point, and as they moved into 1925, it would be their ticket to success.

2

THE BREAKTHROUGH IN REVUE
• • •
THE *GARRICK GAIETIES* (1925, 1926) AND *FIFTH AVENUE FOLLIES* (1926)

As 1925 began, prospects for Rodgers and Hart seemed to have stalled. Although Larry remained upbeat, Dick was despondent. "I hated myself for sponging off my parents, and I hated myself for the lies I would rattle off about this producer or that publisher being so impressed with my work that it wouldn't be long before everything was just dandy," he recalled.[1] Rodgers's ego was bruised, his self-confidence deflated—though as it happened, this time it really wouldn't be long before everything was dandy. Increasingly frustrated and sensitive to the successes of peers like George Gershwin with *Lady, be Good!* (1924) and Vincent Youmans with *No, No, Nanette* (1925), he made a decision. "I felt that the time had come for me to restore some measure of self-respect by going out and getting a job."[2] Through a friend to whom he owed money, Rodgers got in touch with a Mr. Marvin and interviewed for a job selling babies' underwear "('And, failing that, my own,' he adds)."[3] This was a big decision, turning his back on everything he had dreamed of and going to work in a business for which he had no passion and in which he had no experience. When Marvin offered him $50 a week as a starting salary, Rodgers asked for twenty-four hours to think things over.

Then, according to the tale, fate shone on Richard Rodgers over dinner that very night with his parents at West 86th Street. The telephone rang and a voice on the other end—the voice of theatrical lawyer Benjamin Kaye—offered a lifeline: "Dick, some of the kids from the Theatre Guild are putting on a show. I told them you'd be just the right fellow to write the songs."[4] It's a tale well told. On this cliffhanger, Rodgers finishes chapter five of his autobiography, having rehearsed the same story in a variety of earlier interviews. Chapter six begins from the same point, and with mounting excitement, Rodgers realizes this is the phone call for which he has been waiting. His narrative gains momentum, a first success leads to another, and before the end of the book, Rodgers has reached the summit of theatrical achievement. It's a classic rags-to-riches story and grist to the mill of the Broadway musical. Modified only slightly, Rodgers's narrative could become his own *America's Sweetheart* (1931) or *Babes in Arms* (1937).

The impression from those memoirs is that the Theatre Guild itself commissioned *Garrick Gaieties* from the boys, though this polishes the events somewhat: Rodgers's invitation from Benjamin Kaye was his attempt as chairman of the fundraising committee to assist the Guild's Junior Players, who were enthusiastically developing material. The Guild producers Theresa Helburn and Lawrence Langner were happy to accommodate the Junior Players and even financed their production, but they did not exactly commission Rodgers. In fact, once Kaye had introduced him to the Juniors and he had brought in Larry, the next step was for them to audition. After their experience with Max Dreyfus this may well have been an ordeal.

> They had been writing some songs and sketches which they hoped might be put on in a special performance at the Garrick some Sunday night. Sitting on the empty stage of the Garrick, Dick Rodgers played the songs and Larry Hart...sang them for us. When they came to the song "Manhattan" I sat up in delight. These lads had ability, wit, and a flair for a light sophisticated kind of song.[5]

According to Edith Meiser, the activities of the Junior Players took off thanks to Sterling Holloway, who had gained recognition as the constantly reappearing servant Henry in the Guild's *Fata Morgana* the previous year. "He *would* imitate Emily Stevens on parties during the hottest part of last summer," she writes. "Not to be outdone—you know how actors are—several of the other young Guild aspirants developed parlor stunts."[6] Over time, the junior members, usually playing walk-on or chorus roles in the main shows, developed enough material to consider a showcase, and then convinced Theresa Helburn to give them a Sunday slot when the main stage was not being used. It was a fundraising venture to buy tapestries for the new Guild theater on 52nd Street. As the young company's excitement grew, Helburn recalls Rodgers pitching to oust *The Guardsman* and its stars Alfred Lunt and Lynn Fontanne: "Please pack up the Lunts and let the *Gaieties* open," he begged.[7]

The accounts of Helburn and Rodgers clearly differ, though the enthusiasm to succeed is evident. What is unequivocal is that the show, when it appeared, was an enormous success, hailed by critics and therefore extended by Langner and Helburn to run for 211 performances. For most observers, it was the youthful attitude of the show that charmed them: "Everything about *Garrick Gaieties* was young, hopeful and spontaneous. It gave the impression of having been whipped up casually in a two-room apartment by a few kids having a party," wrote Margery Darrell in her commentary to *The Rodgers and Hart Songbook* (1951).[8] Other reports concur:

> It is absolutely fresh in word, song, dance, skit and bit of skittishness. The juniors have taken full advantage of their juniority, have thrown to the winds all respect for the works of their seniors and for pretty much everything else in the season's theatrical line, and have just galloped and galumphed home with the bacon.[9]

As usual, Rodgers and Hart brought in Herb to oversee the staging and choreography, and if there was an influence, it was recognized as the "peppy" style of Lew Fields.[10] This was a funny show, not far removed from the college antics of the Varsity Shows and with a cast just as young. But it brought to Broadway a fresh evening's entertainment, a world away from both the intensely serious plays of modernist drama and the lavish spectaculars of the Winter Garden. Although it was only officially announced for two performances, "it is pretty well acknowledged that the directors have more ambitious plans if it proves successful. If it attracts the attention they hope it will, the plan is reported to be to put it on as a regular summer attraction, the first of a series and somewhat similar in idea to the Grand Street Follies."[11]

The Grand Street Follies was a benchmark for the company. This was another revue, conceived by Albert Carroll in 1922 and responding to a sea change as small-scale revues rich in singing and dancing but lacking any pretence of a plot or theme began to emerge, contrasting with the grandiose perennials mounted by the big impresarios. Revue was at this time the most prominent type of entertainment on Broadway, with no fewer than seven kicking off the start of the summer season in 1925.[12] Most offered lavish excess, with sumptuous sets and costumes and a plethora of girls. *The Grand Street Follies*, staged in the Neighborhood Playhouse, was different, following a number of smaller-scale European revues. The Russian impresario Nikita Ballieff had brought *Chauve-Souris of Moscow* to Broadway in 1922; the French producer André Charlot had triumphed with *Charlot's Revue of 1924*; *The Grand Street Follies* had matched their intimacy and plotlessness, and was by 1925 a hot property. Almost all the *Garrick Gaieties*'s critics compared them: "'The Grand Street Follies,'" they wrote, had "active rivals."[13] "Here is something even grander."[14]

With a cast of virtual unknowns, the success of the *Garrick Gaieties* propelled its performers into the spotlight. Sterling Holloway would become a celebrated comedian and the voice of Disney's Winnie the Pooh; Edith Meiser had a distinguished career as a performer, writer, and director; Romney Brent wrote the libretto for Cole Porter's *Nymph Errant* (1933); House Jameson went on to a successful TV career; and Lee Strasberg founded the celebrated Actors' Studio. Meanwhile, June Cochrane went on to work further with Rodgers, Hart, and Fields, playing Irene in *The Girl Friend* and Evelyn in *A Connecticut Yankee*; Betty Starbuck likewise played Alice in *Peggy-Ann*, Li Li Wee in *Chee-Chee*, and Betty Boyd in *Heads Up!* Though Rodgers and Hart would become the most auspicious alumni of the *Garrick Gaieties*, this was a show that serviced many of its graduates extremely well.

In the *Garrick Gaieties* these young hopefuls of the chorus lambasted the theatrical establishment in a series of burlesques: two travesties of *The Guardsman* ("The Guardsman" by Benjamin Kaye and "The Theatre Guild Enters Heaven" by Edith Meiser), a pastiche of *They Knew What They Wanted* (1924) (entitled "They Didn't Know What They Were Getting" by Benjamin Kaye), and "a third brickbat hurled back at the Guild's seniors"[15] in a ribbing of *Fata Morgana* (1924) ("Fate in the Morning").[16] This sort of travesty had been popular for decades and was a Fields influence from his days with Joe Weber. The success of these sketches naturally relied on the audience having seen the material that was being pastiched, though since the Guild operated on a subscription basis, the team could probably assume that their references were familiar. Holloway's performance in drag for "Fate in the Morning" (based on his party piece) was particularly acclaimed, as were Peggy Conway's "remarkable impersonation"[17] of Pauline Lord in *They Knew What They Wanted*, and Edith Meiser's impression of Lynn Fontanne in *The Guardsman*.

Further topical sketches—both by Morrie Ryskind—poked fun at events of the day. "Mr. and Mrs." ribbed Calvin Coolidge, to the applause of many and the disgust of others.[18] "And Thereby Hangs a Tail" mugged a high profile creationist trial known as the "Scopes Monkey Trial," in which a Tennessee teacher had been hauled in front of the courts for teaching evolutionary theory. This sketch had the jurors dressed as monkeys and ripped into the prosecuting attorney, William Jennings Bryan, a former presidential candidate. Hart contributed to the sketch with a lyric that shows him being uncharacteristically political:

> BRYAN: I started Prohibition on its way,
> And all of us are lawbreakers today;
> And every speech I make for home and mammy
> Goes to build another cabin in Miami.
> I am very glad to hand out good advice
> To any group of folks who pay my price.[19]

Meanwhile, the second act opener "Rancho Mexicano" offered "authentic" spectacle, choreographed by Rose Rolanda to music by Tatanacho. Her traditional folk dance, "El Jarabe-Mexicano," finished with "the lady dancing around the brim of the gentleman's hat which she afterwards claps on her head."[20]

Rodgers and Hart joined the theatrical mockery gleefully in a number of songs, including "Soliciting Subscriptions" and "Ladies of the Box Office," written to the same music and revealing "secrets of the American theater,"[21] and the "Stage Managers' Chorus," a mediocre song whose gimmick was to reveal the tricks behind theatrical sound effects. Hart's attitude toward contemporary theater is particularly significant in regard to this show, which adroitly placed itself in a position of commentary. "Soliciting Subscriptions," which opened the show, set his stall. As translator of the great European dramas for United Plays, he found "both American contemporary drama and American musical theater emotionally flat and theatrically timid."[22] "All commercial art is hollow," the opening number cried, proceeding to mock the theatrical fare of competitors at the Neighborhood Playhouse, the Provincetown Playhouse, and the Actor's Theatre.

"Soliciting Subscriptions" is a typical, self-conscious opening number, reminiscent of their summer camp shows, and the sort of routine that Cole Porter would pastiche in "We Open in Venice" from *Kiss Me, Kate* (1948): "We bring drama to your great metropolis, / We are the little theatre group," sing the players. References to theatrical and popular culture (Gene O'Neill, Oscar Wilde-ish, Yeats and Synge and Shaw) are complicated by the use of puns, such as a reference to the "Macy-Gimbel line."[23] This is clever, though it shows inexperience, since the lyrics, written as "patter," are fiendishly difficult to sing and challenging to hear. The way that some of the denser phrases mismatch the meter of the music means that the stress falls on unexpected syllables ("The PROVince TOWN playHOUSE still OWNS"), so there is no surprise that some critics called the lyrics "clever but unsingable."[24] At one point, to condense the three-syllable word "museum" into two syllables, the writers force its rhyming pair "see 'em" into one syllable, creating a very clumsy phrasing for the line: "Grand STREET folk WE neVER see 'em / THEY think THE place IS a MUseum." It's witty, but this is lyrical pyrotechnics at the expense of intelligibility.

In "Ladies of the Box Office" Hart introduces the audience to three girls, one dressed as Mary Pickford, one as a Ziegfeld chorus girl, and one as Sadie Thompson in the long-running success *Rain* (1922), then still playing on Broadway. Here he exercises his contempt for what he saw as "writers who mistrusted the audience because their own level of intelligence wasn't very high to begin with":[25] "Using up your brains with great frugality / Is the Broadway Theatre hunch."[26] Mary Pickford goes on to sing about Hollywood stars who "act half well" and the "half-wits" who lap up their films; the Ziegfeld girl criticizes other revues for their mediocre music and comedy and their reliance on titillation ("Even Mother Eve's old fig leaf / In my show would seem a big leaf"); and Sadie Thompson reveals that any scandalous pornographic storyline will do for 1920s Broadway. Each girl finishes the verse with disdain for her audience: "we seldom let them think," sings Pickford; "I never let them think," responds the Ziegfeld girl; "I let them think they think," concludes Thompson.[27] Interestingly, Hart's wordplay and rhyming in these lyrics is far more accomplished than in "Soliciting Subscriptions."

Generally, the lyrics were recognized as "literate and witty,"[28] "suave,"[29] and "intelligent";[30] indeed, one letter to the *Herald* claimed Hart to be "the only inspired writer of lyrics within a radius of a few thousand miles,"[31] even if Alexander Woollcott was critical of their "distinct Varsity Show character."[32] In this respect, the young lyricist was to counter in practice what he criticized in conversation: the fact that "rhyming in general was elementary and often illiterate."[33] He felt that "the public was capable of understanding better things than the current monosyllabic juxtaposition of 'slush' and 'mush'"; something better was what he attempted, though he was not averse to recycling material. The "hell for ya / Philadelphia" couplet from "Any Old Place with You" reappears in "Ladies of the Box Office"—this was a rhyme Hart was to use on a number of occasions.

With success—at last—came attention. Having worked for six years to get themselves noticed, the boys now could not escape the press. From this point forth, news of their activities on stage and off would become staple reading matter for the New York public. Typically, interviewers would ask the boys about their writing process, and in particular whether music or lyrics were written first. Recent commentators usually suggest that Hart wrote lyrics to Rodgers's music (in a reversal of Rodgers's later collaboration with Hammerstein),[34] though their writing arrangements seem to have been less clearly defined, and as far as they maintained, "there is no answer."[35] On the other hand, as Block notes, the pair would often establish a song title first, to which Rodgers could assign a melody. "In one important sense," he therefore concludes, "the lyrics do in fact come first."[36] Since it is unusual for Larry to offer much in the way of interviews, it is particularly interesting to hear his thoughts:

If I am trying to write a melodic song hit I let my composer . . . get his tune first. Then I take the most distinctive melodic phrase in his tune and work on that. What I choose is not necessarily the theme or first line, but the phrase which stands out. Next I try to find the meaning of that phrase and to develop a euphonic set of words to fit it.... Of course, in a song of this sort the melody and the euphonics of the words themselves are really more important than the sense.[37]

Hart's concern with euphonics shows musicality and a sense of the performative in the sounds of the songs, and it is easy to see in his lyrics how he picks up on musical sequences provided by Rodgers. "Gilding the Guild" is one example, repeating the title verbatim in its first two phrases of repeated music and then echoing the musical sequence of the next two phrases in the lyric arrangement of the lines. In particular, when the second musical phrase is shortened, the second lyric phrase follows suit (Figure 2.1).

Further into the song, the triple sequence of the music offers Hart a triple rhyme opportunity: "But we've built this cozy little shack, / Tho we lack Shubert's Jack!" This rhyming response to Rodgers's musical sequences would become a characteristic feature of their work: "And if there's a moon above you, / I'll carve 'I love you,' upon the bark" ("A Tree in the Park," from *Peggy-Ann*, 1926); "We'll have a blue room, / A new room, / For two room" ("Blue Room," from *The Girl Friend*, 1926); and still in the same manner many years later, "I'm wild again, / Beguiled again, / A simpering, whimpering child again" ("Bewitched, Bothered and Bewildered" from *Pal Joey*, 1940). All are examples of songwriting that seem driven by the music, in which "the patterns and schemes of... [melody]... dictate rhyme."[38]

Hart reveals in an interview an experienced understanding of lyric writing, going on to consider the surprising success of "Manhattan" despite its complex lyrics: "Strangely enough, the song hit of the show is the number with very intricate and elaborate rhymes, though the song hit of a show is usually a very simple one with monosyllabic words."[39] He also worries about the impact of jazz and particularly syncopation on his writing.

Figure 2.1: Words following music in "Gilding the Guild" from the Garrick Gaieties *(1925).*
Reprinted by Permission of Hal Leonard Corporation

I find that the prominence of jazz makes things very difficult for the lyric writer because of the offbeat in the music. The natural accents of ordinary words have a tendency to fall in with the accent of regular rhythms, but syncopation throws the rhythm out of gear, as it were, and compels, simultaneously, an adjustment of word-accents.[40]

This comment certainly suggests a keen awareness of the relationship between words and music, a fact that impressed Rodgers at their first meeting. If at times the arrangement of his lyrics with the music was slightly awkward, as in "Soliciting Subscriptions," it points to the complexity of what the team were trying to accomplish: songs that were not only melodically memorable and lyrically intelligent but that also developed the craft of songwriting and raised the standard of musical theater.

The team were delighted that a number of "hits" from *Garrick Gaieties* were picked up by publisher Edward B. Marks: "Manhattan," "Sentimental Me," "April Fool," "Do You Love Me (I Wonder)," "On with the Dance," "The Three Musketeers" and "Old Fashioned Girl," with a lyric by Edith Meiser.

"Sentimental Me (and Romantic You)" is, in its published version, a fairly standard charm duet structured ABAC and built around a descending pentatonic motif. Musically, it shows characteristic Rodgers features, such as ascending scalar passages. Lyrically, it "departed successfully from the stereotyped 'Moon-June' doggerel of most of the current love ditties," as the *Morning Telegraph* reviewer put it, printing the first page of the music and going on to commend one line in particular for showing "originality, verve and alliterative rhythm almost unrivalled in any song revue of the last decade."[41] It's not quite clear what "alliterative rhythm" is, exactly, though the line he commends ("I sit and sigh, you sigh and sit upon my knee") is certainly alliterative, even though this reviewer misquotes it in his review. Nevertheless, this high praise must have gone some way to help promote the show through the sale of its songsheets. Though the song is not classic Rodgers and Hart, one suspects what made it stand out in the show was a final comedy verse and refrain sung by a different, elderly couple, which completely deflates any sense of schmaltz and shows typical Hart humor. In this verse, not published in the songsheet, "sentimental me and poor romantic you" becomes "poor asthmatic me and poor rheumatic you"; now, "I sneeze and sit, you sit and sneeze upon my knee."[42]

A similar self-deprecatory trick brings humor to "April Fool," another song that risked sentimentality but was described by one reviewer as "a rhapsody in undergraduate joy."[43] Its first verse and refrain are sung straight by Romney Brent, but when Betty Starbuck takes over for a second verse the sincerity is undercut: where he sings "I simply must be admirin' / Some pretty siren," her line becomes "And my affection I pour on / Some pretty moron."[44]

Aside from "Manhattan"—the outstanding number not just of this show but of their partnership thus far—the other published songs are less notable. "Do You Love Me" has a Viennese feel and was clearly a dance feature of the show; "On with the Dance" was the compulsory dance-craze number (though unlike "The Boomerang" or the "Crime Wave," this goes without a name). Here, Rodgers pulls out all the syncopated stops, basing the whole AABA refrain around two-measure phrases whose classic ragtime rhythm extends over the barline, giving a sequence of three motifs, each one stressed differently. This was very contemporary, though really just a rhythmical device; five years later, they would be building a dramaturgical dynamic into the same rhythmic pattern to comic effect in *Ever Green*'s "The Color of Her Eyes." Nevertheless, even at this stage Hart uses his lyrics to support the stress of the syncopation, particularly in the verse, where he sets a strong internal rhyme on and then off the beat: "There's a revolution / CUT-ting LOOSE like THE deuce; / It's a thunderbolt."[45] "The Three Musketeers," another trunk song from *Winkle Town*, exploits a juxtaposition of vernacular language and classical characters, as we have seen elsewhere. Here, the musketeers are three lads about town, offering some opportunity for double entendre, but mainly trading on linguistic anomalies: "Athos, Porthos and Aramis, / We are the kitten's pajamas."[46]

The most innovative contribution of Rodgers and Hart in terms of developing the musical theater idiom was their attempt to write "An American Jazz Opera," in "The Joy Spreader." This was an extended musical sequence based in a department store. When staff leave for the night, colleagues Tom and Mary—who have been honored with employee awards for their virtue—are locked in the store. Two versions of the script exist, and according to Hart and Kimball, it is unclear which was performed.[47] In both, the couple declare their love and embrace as church bells ring and night falls; in the longer version, scene two reveals Tom and Mary sleeping on the counter as the employees return the next morning. They are confronted by the store manager Mr. Price and fired, but their fellow employees rally round and to the infectious sounds of jazz back the boss into a corner and overthrow his tyranny. The metaphor is not hard to pick out here, with the strains of youth winning out over a prevailing old-school figure. However, the attempt to blend jazz with opera (rather than simply usurp its dominance) shows a complexity, even a confusion, in Rodgers and Hart's approach.

"The Joy Spreader" was dedicated to Gilbert Seldes, whose book *The Seven Lively Arts* (1924) and essays such as "Jazz and Ballad" (1925) had been manifestos championing popular American culture. Seldes disliked the terms "highbrow" and "lowbrow" and their implications, viewing popular culture as "lively," and this spin on the rhetoric surrounding their milieu appealed to Rodgers and Hart. Bernard Simon in the *Morning Telegraph* wrote that "One of the more important numbers was a worth-while attempt at the jazz-opera idea that has received so much publicity this Winter." The reviewer commented on the lyrics, which were "always in American idiom," and the music, which was "always jazz, but none the less enough in the operatic style, in the use of themes stated and repeated, to be more than ordinary jazz."[48] Nevertheless, this foray into a new kind of writing was less than successful: "the lyrics weren't so good, but one strain plugged constantly and the general bumness as a musical proposition made it a howl," wrote Sisk in *Variety*.[49] The *Zits* reviewer likewise called it "a tedious bit of American jazz opera,"[50] while Alexander Woollcott, who was not enamored of the *Garrick Gaieties* at all, wrote "There are some wearisome stretches at intervals, notably one long, lifeless jazz opera, which cluttered up the stage interminably at the end of the first act."[51]

Perhaps in response, the Theatre Guild reverted to a shortened version as the show progressed. However, as Hart and Kimball suggest, "the simpler and shorter second version lacks the fantasy and romantic spirit of the first." Still, it "probably satisfied those who might have objected to a story in which the juvenile and the ingenue spent the night together in the department store."[52]

In the end, "The Joy Spreader" was dropped, much to Rodgers's disappointment. Its place was taken at the end of the first act by "Rancho Mexicana," and the team wrote more material to cover the gap, turning once again to self-reflexive theatrical fodder for a new finale to the show. "It's Quite Enough to Make Me Weep" presented George Bernard Shaw as a patriarch of high art theater whose popularity was being usurped by a bunch of cocky Theatre Guild juveniles. As several of his characters warn about the modern threat of light entertainment, Shaw exclaims:

Peace, my children, whatever they do
Your Bernard Shaw can do it too
And I will be a play physician
Writing these brats a new edition.[53]

He goes on to pen new verses to "Manhattan" and "Sentimental Me," in which Caesar and Cleopatra "turn the desert into an isle of joy," and in which Blunchi and Raina (from *Arms and the Man*) "make sad efforts to be funny/ While Shaw gets all the money." The sequence ends with the whole cast dancing across the stage in a reprise of "Gilding the Guild."

All in all, the *Garrick Gaieties* was a great success and was recognized by the powerful newspaper critics whose voices were so significant to a show's longevity. Still, one senses that as in previous less successful ventures, Rodgers and Hart's luck could easily have gone the other way. In typical tones of the day, *Variety* critic Sisk makes the most extraordinary comments, revealing what mindless opinion the reviewers could peddle:

> Worked over a bit and some of the junk eliminated, an unnecessary cuss word or so cut, the chorus work speeded and some of the clowning stopped, "Garrick Gaieties" on the strength of its excellent cast and material may easily draw Sunday audiences to the Garrick for several weeks and radically restaged, figures to hold its own on a regular basis.[54]

Even if this sort of review seems baffling, and even if the praise of the revues in general was often couched in rather patronizing terms (viewing the enterprise as a commendable attempt by "the young Guilders"), Rodgers and Hart, singled out as "Two Broadwayites," were finally given the recognition they had long desired as pros in the field.[55]

THE FIFTH AVENUE FOLLIES (1926)

Much happened to the boys' fortunes in the wake of the *Garrick Gaieties*, but their next foray into revue was to strike a different tone. Where the *Gaieties* had sparkled with the charm of youth, the *Fifth Avenue Follies* presented charms that were far more adult.

The boys were of course adults by now—in fact, Larry had just celebrated his thirtieth birthday—and their pursuits were exactly what you might expect from eligible young bachelors in the mid-1920s. Dick was a good deal more restrained; he'd catch a movie or take girls dancing rather than frequent the illicit speakeasies that flourished despite prohibition. But Larry and his willing accomplice Herb were game for anything, and as Nolan suggests, "If you wanted to be self-destructive there were plenty of people around to help you do it":[56]

> at the Dizzy Club or the Aquarium, the Hotsy-Totsy, Texas Guinan's, Tony's East 53rd or Tony's West 49th, the Clamhouse, the West 44th Street Club or the Richmond, Frank and Jack's, Felix's, Louis's 21 West 43rd Street, Jack Delaney's, Billy Duffy's McDermott's, Sam Schwartz's, the Type and Print Club, the Bandbox, and half a hundred more speakeasies, blind pigs, gin joints, and beer flats scattered all over the great big city.[57]

In short, for Larry, "liquor became an added compulsion, mixed with drunken companions."[58] And along with the alcohol came a relaxed attitude to behavior; behind their enforced closed doors, the party palaces were places where "Anything Goes," as Cole Porter would later put it.

The original title of their next show, *Billy Rose's Sins of 1926*, gives some indication of its content. It ended up as the *Fifth Avenue Follies* and played only briefly at Billy Rose's nightclub, on the corner of 5th Avenue and 54th Street, in January 1926. Program covers to the *Gaieties* and the *Follies* reveal the difference in tone between the shows—one clearly presenting entertainment in the Parisian style for an elegant top-hatted audience, the other promising nudity in abundance but masquerading as something more demure (Figures 2.2 and 2.3).

Rose—born William Rosenberg—had known the boys for years. He was a successful Tin Pan Alley lyricist whose hits would include "Me and My Shadow," "Does Your Chewing Gum Lose Its Flavor on the Bedpost Overnight?" and "It's Only a Paper Moon." He first got to know Larry back in the late teens when he would visit Brant Lake Camp and the two would go furtively off in a boat for the day. There, for three weeks, according to Arthur Schwartz, they "would go over the melodies that Billy was working on, and at the end of the day Larry would show me a hundred dollar bill."[59] That was big money in 1919, so whatever Larry traded with Rose must have been valuable. Many people—including Rodgers—speculate that Rose's song successes were actually written by Hart.[60] Still, Rose had also invested in the Rodgers and Hart franchise, stumping up $1,000 dollars to get *The Melody Man* into New York in 1924. He would also be a driving force behind the extraordinary show *Jumbo* a decade later (1935), Rodgers and Hart's bold return to Broadway. Now he came to the boys for song material for his new enterprise, originally intended to feature sketches by Noël Coward and Avery Hopwood, though in the end using some by Harold Atteridge, a Shubert librettist from the Winter Garden, and Ballard MacDonald. Rose's out-and-out commission of Rodgers and Hart was surprising given that he generally took songwriting credit; however, his sights were set in a different direction and he had already branched into the nightclub trade, opening a speakeasy on West 56th Street the previous year. The "Backstage Club" had been closed down "because of violent gangland interference in the liquor trade,"[61] so to avoid the same problems with his upmarket venture, the Fifth Avenue Club was dry. It was probably this that accounted for its failure; later, Rose would celebrate the end of prohibition by opening a third club, the Casino de Paree on 54th Street (now Studio 54), which boasted an extensive wine list and presented its own series of revues.

Figure 2.2: Program cover to the Garrick Gaieties *(1925). Billy Rose Theatre Collection, The New York Public Library for the Performing Arts, Astor, Lenox and Tilden Foundations.*

The Fifth Avenue club had cost Rose an investment of $50,000, and its appearance in this class-conscious neighborhood concerned many of New York's elite. Not only did this bring to the avenue a worrying Broadway presence (theatricals were vulgar and their entertainments suspect), but it also placed in their midst a venue provocatively peddling exoticism and eroticism. Rose had the walls painted with the salacious murals of erotic artist Clara

Figure 2.3: Program cover to Fifth Avenue Follies *(1926). Music Division, The New York Public Library for the Performing Arts, Astor, Lenox and Tilden Foundations.*

Tice, and in an outer room he offered a "Perfumed Garden with three Assyrians playing weird Oriental tunes for the atmosphere."[62] Fountains graced the reception, and red tables and chairs against black paneled walls gave a modernist elegance to the club. The surroundings were intimate, with just the eight-piece Harry Archer band accompanying the singers.

The show opened with a female chorus of six girls singing "Do You Notice Anything." The implication was that the chorus, usually overshadowed by the principals, were going to be noticed in this show. Each time the song was reprised—six times in all—the girls reappeared with a little less clothing, promising by the finale "the unbaring of the plot."[63] This served a double meaning: modern revue had notoriously shed its pretensions to plot, and a common gimmick introduced by George M. Cohan in *Hello, Broadway* (1914) was to labor the point, as "at intervals throughout the evening one character or another carried a hat box on stage [which] supposedly contained the plot of the revue"[64] but which would be opened to reveal nothing. In the context of chorus girls gradually stripping, this plot's "unbaring" would clearly offer something of a titillation.

But the show featured more than just striptease, and with a cast of sixty there was plenty on offer. Cecil Cunningham, Bert Hanlon, and Doris Canfield were the individual stars, countering the parade of girls with their number "In the Name of Art" and then seguing into Harold Atteridge's sketch "Fatigue." Throughout the show the principals took comedy solo numbers—Cunningham sang "Mike," Hanlon sang his own song "An Olive" and Jack Donohue's "My Mammy's Knee," and Canlon sang "Susie," similar in tone to "The Midnight Supper" from *Poor Little Ritz Girl* and "Chorus Girl Blues" from *Say Mama*. Hanlon and Canfield also sang "A City Flat." The sketch "Literally Speaking" took figurative colloquialisms ("you kill me," "I'm falling for you") at face value; and in the second act, the trio's opening number "Lillie, Lawrence and Jack" burlesqued Beatrice Lillie, Gertrude Lawrence, and Jack Buchanan, then appearing at the Selwyn in *Charlot's Revue of 1926*. "Maybe It's Me," sung by Johnne Clare and Albert Burke and danced by Elizabeth Brown and Dan McCarthy, scored well with critics, though the preceding sketch "The Morning After" was considered a "naughty skit."[65] Specialty acts were featured in Mignon Laird's acrobatic harp dance and in contributions from the singing trio Adler, Weil, and Herman, who performed "High Hats" and "Where's that Little Girl."

To round off the plot, the principals finally concede that the Fifth Avenue girls have been the delight of the show. With that announcement, however, a group of "Third Avenue Girls" enters. This "misfit chorus girl brigade"[66] from Billy Watson's famous vaudeville troupe the Beef Trust each weighed over 190 pounds and critics agreed that their appearance was by far the funniest moment.

The *Fifth Avenue Follies* did make some concessions to the fact that it was staged in a nightclub: it lasted just over an hour, and the writers avoided sentimental songs. Nevertheless, this was no cabaret, and Rose made a point of presenting it as a theatrical show: dinner service was suspended while it was performed, and the writers (Rodgers, Hart, and Atteridge) received a royalty based on ticket sales, which was Broadway procedure though not standard practice for cabaret or vaudeville.

Variety considered the show "Quite an ambitious entertainment"[67] but questioned whether—in a period of prohibition—it was the right sort of entertainment for a New York supper club: "The consensus is that the material is too smart for supper club appreciation, with its audiences in varying stages of attention, and that it would click on Broadway with greater effect."[68] Rose's plan was to showcase the material at the club as a pre-Broadway tryout. In the end, although critics were positive, the revue didn't transfer.

THE *GARRICK GAIETIES* (1926)

Following such success in 1925, and given the Broadway appetite for revue perennials, a second installment of the *Garrick Gaieties* was inevitable. This time, the Guild Juniors' intentions were loftier and the weight of expectation heavier.

One of their earliest decisions was to formalize the Junior Group and reconsider their name. Feeling that "Juniors" was a bit juvenile, they seized upon the loaded term "The Theatre Guild Studio," redolent with hints of pretension and knowingly aware of Nemirovich-Danchenko's Moscow Arts Theatre Studio. What the underlying politics of this decision was is unclear: they were by no means forced into using this name, though Romney Brent at least, writing albeit flippantly in the program for *Garrick Gaieties of 1926*, is acutely aware of comparison:

> "Why not call yourselves 'The Studio'?." Silence. A look of awe came over the faces of the heated members. As one man we all salaamed in the direction of the city of the Czars. Some of the more sensitive artists to this day swear that at that moment they heard the Kremlin bells.[69]

Whatever politics was at stake—and it's worth remembering that these Juniors were also apprentices to the worthy aspirations of the Theatre Guild—there is certainly an escalation of expectations and a marked self-consciousness about the *Gaieties'* value. Reviewers were quick to notice: "Last year it seemed to be saying, 'Ain't I cute, I'm only six', which it was. But this time it is a wise and flippant ingénue, well versed in the ways of the world, though a bit awkward in pursuing them," wrote the *Herald Tribune*.[70] The *Sun* also registered the self-consciousness of this installment, inevitably compared to the previous year's: "The opening chorus and the closing chorus are both defence mechanisms, arguing the matter out for you."[71] The opening chorus made bold the statement "We can't be as good as last year," while the closing chorus staged a mock trial in which the jury voted on the quality of the piece. This was self-consciousness writ large, Guild Juniors still very much displaying the inexperience of youth.

Concerns about living up to public expectation almost dissuaded Rodgers and Hart from getting involved: "The first *Gaieties* had sneaked into town. . . . What we'd lacked in polish we'd made up for in fledgling enthusiasm, and audiences and critics appreciated the show for what it was."[72] Now, the charm of the show's naivety was no longer going to carry any inadequacies. Indeed, in contrast to the previous year, newspapers turned this feature into a subtle put-down: the *Morning Telegraph* titled its review "Children's Hour at the Garrick,"[73] while the *Evening Post* jibed that the Theatre Guild "parked its perambulators" out front.[74]

Of course, there were mixed views from the critics. The *Brooklyn Standard Union* led the cheers: "A bit more sophisticated, a bit more naughty, a bit more self-conscious than at its first appearance last year, 'The Gaieties' is just as original and just as youthful and vivacious, and just as chuck [*sic*] full of tuneful songs and peppy dances."[75] On the other hand, Brooks Atkinson was critical of Rodgers and Hart, considering their work "inferior in quality" to the previous year.[76] Discerning views suggested that the first act was a success but that the show "slump[ed] badly in the second half."[77] The creative team would respond to the critics' calls for "surgery...on the overlong and dull second half,"[78] and after a number of problematic elements were axed,[79] the second *Garrick Gaieties* managed to run for 174 performances, "only about a month less than the first."[80] John Anderson summed up the critical consensus: "It is not as witty a time as last year's. There, that's said. But...it is far and away the best of the tribe of young revues in the town."[81]

One of the most heavily criticized elements was the performance of Sterling Holloway, who had received warm accolades the year before. Holloway, perhaps unfortunately, took the lead in two of the most maligned items, "a dreary travesty of 'Lulu Belle' (with Mr. Holloway as Lulu) and a somewhat afflicting song entitled 'Sleepyhead,' sung by Mr. Holloway for several hours."[82] The gimmick of "Sleepyhead" was that it was sung to a dog, "an inexplicably resentful terrier who writhed and fretted last evening as though labouring under the apprehension that the song was titled 'Insomnia.' "[83] When the dog yawned it stole the show; on the other hand, the dog yawned. Holloway's number was dropped without further ado.

However, there were also high points, particularly in the first act. "Six Little Plays" and "The De Bock Song" lambasted the Guild's main season of shows, which in 1925–26 had not been particularly successful. As the curtain rose, an undertaker greeted the audience with a lament for the failures, *Arms and the Man*, *The Glass Slipper*, *Merchants of Glory*, *The Chief Thing*, *Androcles and the Lion*, and *The Goat Song*, each personified by one of the cast. This requiem ("Requiescat in Pace") preceded the familiar fanfare kicking off the *Gaieties* proper ("The *Garrick Gaieties* is coming down the street"), and the cast launched into the opening chorus, "We Can't Be as Good as Last Year." A spirited march wove in motifs from 1925's "Gilding the Guild" and pointed forward to a similar clarion call from the youngsters in *Babes in Arms* (1937). Next, "The De Bock Song" ribbed not only the Guild's unsuccessful shows but also the pedagogical lectures the theater had established to explain "the symbolical, metaphysical or allegorical meaning of the most pretentious drama of the moment."[84]

Lightening the tone came Sterling Holloway and new girl Bobbie Perkins singing "Mountain Greenery," a deliberate riposte to "Manhattan": "Here, instead of the boy and girl finding the city 'a wondrous toy,' they decide to leave the city to discover a more romantic setting in the country. The whole attitude was one of urban sophistication amid a rustic atmosphere," writes Rodgers.[85] This was touted as the hit song of the show, and the later number "Four Little Song Pluggers" made fun of the fact that, as such, it needed a reprise:

> The publisher who prints the stuff
> Has told us ever since the stuff
> Was printed—he'd be cheated
> If it were not repeated.
> So while they change the scenery
> We'll do the "Mountain Greenery."[86]

Other moments scoring highly—alongside sketches "Burglary à la Mode" and "Addled"—were the obligatory dance routine "Keys to Heaven," the cross-dressing "Tennis Champs," and the catchy "What's the Use of Talking," which along with "Mountain Greenery" Rodgers was to record onto a piano roll.[87] "Keys to Heaven" was intended to be performed around a pianist who had impressed the team during auditions. "'Can't you write a number,' I said to Dick and Larry, 'about a piano, and she can sit at a piano in the middle of the stage playing while the chorus dances'?"[88] When she dropped out of the show before opening night, the gimmick was lost, though the song and its dance remained. This was to be an idea that would stay with the boys, though, providing a high point in their London revue *One Dam Thing after Another* the following year. Likewise, both "Gigolo" and "Idles of the King" reappeared in *One Dam Thing*; little mention is made of them in newspaper reviews, though "Idles of the King" is worth exploring.

In dramatizing the characters from Camelot, "Idles of the King" marks Rodgers and Hart's second excursion into *Connecticut Yankee* territory (after *A Danish Yankee in King Tut's Court*). Rather than pasticching Twain directly, this song is a nod to the Alfred Lord Tennyson poem "Idylls of the King." Its humor—presaging a Pythonesque ribaldry by almost half a century— is characteristic Hart, with homoerotic suggestions playing up to both his mischievous personality and to his rumored sexuality. In the second verse, for example, Sir Lancelot seems to be enjoying bisexual relations with both Arthur and Guinevere:

> SIR LANCELOT: Just one damsel I never can stick to,
> I invented the triangle scene.
> I've been caught in flagrante delicto
> And I bat for the King with the Queen!
> My song of love to both I sing,

To both of them I'm dearer than a brother.
God Save the Queen! God Save the King!
It's six of one and half a dozen of the other!

Later on, Sir Galahad is portrayed even more provocatively with the suggestion—"Who put the gal in Galahad?"—that he is transsexual:

SIR GALAHAD: I've just been psychoanalyzed;
I'm neither a sister nor a brother.
It's the odd way I am devised:
It's six of one and half a dozen of the other![89]

If this reading of "Idles of the King" layers a twenty-first-century queering
onto Hart's lyrics, it is worth considering how, in his writing, Hart could
release some of the insecurities he seems to have felt about his sexuality.
"While he professed to like girls, there was no question he liked boys, too,"
writes Frederick Nolan;[90] yet he remained guarded about what was at the time
taboo. Larry frequented the bathhouses of New York and—in the company
of his unsavory friend "Doc" Bender—is assumed to have actively sought
male prostitutes. Still, at least one observer—Edith Meiser, from the *Garrick
Gaieties*—sees Larry's sexuality as "his biggest unhappiness."[91] How much of
that perception is the rhetoric of a conservative voice speaking in a closeted
world is unclear (though one other report emphasizes the extreme homo-
phobia of later reportage: "Now and then you hear . . . a baseless and offensive
innuendo about Larry and homosexuality. No, Larry was not queer!")[92]; in
cheeky lyrics at least, any and every kind of lifestyle could be imagined.

If "Idles of the King" was one euphemistic swipe at the British monarchy,
"Queen Elizabeth" was another. Here, Rodgers and Hart took on (and took
off) Noël Coward, whose revue material from *London Calling* (1923) and *On
with the Dance* (1925) had been brought to Broadway by André Charlot in his
revues of 1924 and 1925. Coward offered demure English propriety thinly dis-
guising improper suggestions in songs like "Roses Have Made Me Remember
What Any Nice Girl Would Forget" (1925). "Queen Elizabeth"—sung by Edith
Meiser as the virgin Queen herself ("don't laugh!")—traded exactly the same
conceit: "When my army / Failed to charm me / I would call out the reserves,"
she sings; after all, "Even a Queen has her moments . . . and one must have
a moment or two."[93] As the *Evening World* commented, this song "carries in
its frankly naughty lines the program's sole suggestion that the 'Gaieties'
youngsters are by way of growing up."[94]

The most celebrated element of these *Garrick Gaieties* was the "magnifi-
cent"[95] spoof operetta "The Rose of Arizona," which concluded the first act.

This was "really delightful,"[96] according to Alexander Woollcott, and far more successful than its equivalent "The Joy Spreader" the previous year. Herb's libretto took "a melodrama, a comedy and a revue and rolled it into one, and burlesqued the whole affair."[97] The story is set on the border between Mexico and Arizona, at the Rosa Raisa Hotel. Gloria van Dyke is in love with the chief of police, Captain Sterling. When the Mexican bandido Casaba Caramba kidnaps her, Sterling musters the men of the force and springs into action to save her. He does, and they marry.

The show-within-a-show was packed with topical references. Most obviously, it spoofed the Rudolf Friml operettas *Rose-Marie* (1924) and *The Vagabond King* (1925), which had opened at the Casino Theatre in the same week as Rodgers and Hart's *Dearest Enemy* opened next door at the Knickerbocker. Although *Dearest Enemy* had been successful, it was due to close while *The Vagabond King* would continue to play to packed audiences until the end of 1926.[98] Friml's operetta was fair game not just because it was a rival show but also because its source, Justin Huntly McCarthy's *If I Were King* (1901), was a story with which Rodgers and Hart were familiar. *If I Were King* had been the inspiration for a Camp Paradox show in 1921 in which Rodgers and Fields both performed, and also the Benjamin School for Girls' show in 1923, with Rodgers's music and Herb's direction.

"Rose of Arizona" kicked off with the opening chorus "Back to Nature," extolling the virtues of the great outdoors. Where *Rose-Marie* (1924) had opened in a hotel setting on the Canadian border, "Rose of Arizona" established a location on the Mexican border. The outpost they chose, Rosa Raisa, was named for the Italian soprano who had played Turandot in Puccini's world premiere just two weeks earlier, bringing a topical and highbrow reference to the pastiche.

Then came "It May Rain," a parody of the trite moon-June song Rodgers and Hart so vehemently disliked: "It may rain when the sun stops shining. / It may rain when the sky is gray."[99] Its lyrics were deliberately banal and its music captured "a little bit of almost every sentimental song ever written,"[100] according to Rodgers. He cheekily invited the audience to spot various melodies (see Figure 2.4): "Till the Clouds Roll By" from *Oh, Boy!* (1917), "April Showers" (1921) by Buddy de Sylva and Louis Silvers; even "The Love Nest" from *Mary* (1920), sung as the song concludes to the line "Til the clouds go rolling by."[101] More than this, there was one further satirical stab in ribbing one of their own songs from *Dearest Enemy*. That show's principals, Helen Ford and Charles Purcell, were rumored to have taken a dislike to each other; under Herbert Fields's direction, Blanche Fleming and Jack Edwards performed "It May Rain" with "a palpable and growing distaste for each other,"[102] emulating the Ford-Purcell

Figure 2.4: Intertextual references in the pastiche "It May Rain," from the "Rose of Arizona" section of the Garrick Gaieties (1926). In this section, spot Jerome Kern's "Till the Clouds Roll By" and Louis Silvers's "April Showers" ("It May Rain" from the Garrick Gaieties (1926); music from sketches in LC—RRC, Box 6, Folder 22; lyrics from Hart and Kimball, Complete Lyrics, 72).

animosity in a gentle bit of self-deprecation that would have endeared audiences to Rodgers, Hart, and Fields. The boys had the grace, charm, and confidence to send themselves up as much as anyone else.

Next appeared a comedy song, "Davy Crockett," whose alternative title "Who Kept the Wolves Away from the Door (When Davy Crockett Went to War)?" recalled the popular Jolson number "Where Did Robinson Crusoe Go with Friday on Saturday Night?" (1916).[103] This was fairly meaningless vaudeville, with no context in "The Rose of Arizona," but in speculating about Mrs. Crockett's sexual shenanigans in Davy's absence, it generated laughs through a series of double entendres and the unlikely humor of the setup.

Following this, "American Beauty Rose" pastiched the glamorous Ziegfeld Follies shows at the Winter Garden. As these spectacular revues had become ever grander, costumes had become increasingly absurd: 1919's show, for example, featured an opening number called "The Follies Salad," in which girls dressed as different salad ingredients, were tossed into a bowl by the chef Eddie Dowling. "American Beauty Rose," by these standards, was rather restrained, with the girls dressed as flowers. In a stab at the quality of the songwriting in these songs, Hart paired a series of clumsily rhyming words: "France" with "immense," "no land" with "Holland," "drizzle" with "Brazil" and "replenish" with "Spanish."

It is in the final song, "Mexico," that the most obvious ribbing of *The Vagabond King* appears. Both lyrics and music are recognizable references to the Friml/Harbach "Song of the Vagabond," in which the hero Villon stirs up the people to march against Burgundy: "Come all you beggars of Paris town / You lousy rabble of low degree," sings Villon. Rodgers and Hart extend this as Captain Sterling leads his men against the Mexicans. They jibe the fraternal orders that were popular in the 1920s ("All you Shriners and Elks and Pythian Knights") and add to this list "Babbitts of low degree,"[104] a reference to Sinclair Lewis's 1922 novel *Babbitt*, which became used pejoratively to criticize unthinking conformists. In his music Rodgers exploits Friml's motifs in the pastiche: a dotted and triplet feature from the verse, and a stirring theme of repeated notes and dotted turns from the refrain; in the B section, both composers offer a phrase starting on the higher tonic which is then repeated a fourth lower. Finally, where the original's last line exclaims "To Hell with Burgundy," the spoof yells "To Hell with Mexico." It's clearly a direct crib.

The lampoonery of "The Rose of Arizona" was sustained, and it registered with audiences familiar to Broadway. Still, while the satirical swipes were "intended as deadly weapons of jeering intensity,"[105] reviewer John Anderson observes the irony that "as the audiences depart...the hummers in the crowd may be heard humming, after every performance, the music for 'It May Rain.'"[106] The song was so accurate a pastiche of a catchy show hit that it became one itself, to Rodgers and Hart's astonishment. They acknowledged that, had it been published, they might have made a fortune.

The show concluded by returning to the idea from its opening number that the *Gaieties* of 1926 was not as good as its predecessor. A judge summons Sterling Holloway, representing the *Gaieties*, and a jury comprising Johann Strauss, Gilbert and Sullivan, and Irving Berlin offer their thoughts on the revue. Hart mimics the lyrical style of these composers in successive verses, offering Strauss's in German, Gilbert and Sullivan's as patter, and Irving Berlin's in a perceptive bit of ghosting: "You can't be as good, remember? / Just remember last year."[107] This exercises the sort of characteristically Berlin-like repetition that Jeffrey Magee discusses, and it shows Hart to be well attuned to the nuances of his contemporaries' craft. Magee's analysis of Berlin's songwriting is astute, and one comment in particular could be equally applied to Hart's own craft, "writing with an ear tuned to performance—to *oral* delivery and *aural* reception."[108] This recalls Hart's commitment to the euphonics as much as the meaning of the words and reminds us how his rhyming patterns are often dictated by the musical phrases. Just as Magee recognizes Berlin's "distinction between songwriting and composition," Hart's skill as a song lyricist rather than a poet can be seen: his lyrics, "rhythmic roguery" that he "appears to find as easy as breathing," are viewed (with considerable admiration) as "more sound than substance,"[109] and as Lincoln Barnett suggests, his "primary concern was with...*how* he said something rather than with what he actually said."[110] These were songs for singing rather than texts to admire. When his lyrics adopt more of a poetic slant, as they do in "A Little Souvenir," conceived for this show but dropped before the opening, they become dull and heavy:

> Love will always cry to love,
> You can't lie to love,
> There is no goodbye to love
> For us two.[111]

On the other hand, "Mountain Greenery" gives Hart ample opportunity to compile a list of unlikely but playful rhymes, some of which sacrifice any sense whatsoever to become, literally, meaningless sound bites. "Beans could get no keener re- / Ception in a beanery" is Hart at his most errant: if the rhyme works, any sense will do.

The matter of songwriting technique was one explored by both Rodgers and Hart in the program notes to the *Garrick Gaieties of 1926*. Reading their accounts, one gets the impression that they are already rather fed up of answering questions about technique, and particularly questions about whether the music or the lyrics come first. Hart invokes Shakespeare and Poe and offers a couple of tips, but he is generally vague. He signs off his account claiming "I wish I knew how. Had I that knowledge, gentle reader, I should never have instructed you in its methods. But it is always safe to be a philosopher when you don't know what you are talking about."[112] Rodgers is just as evasive: "Writing songs isn't the sort of thing you have habits about....I haven't any idea how any other composer goes about his work but the chances are there are as many methods as composers."[113] These remarks seem disingenuous, though; seven years into their collaboration, and a good many more into their individual practice as songwriters, these are writers who have carefully developed their technique and studied the craft of their colleagues. In their series of revues in the mid-*1920s* that technique is evidenced; elsewhere, they were exercising other elements of technique in their construction of full-scale musical comedies.

3

THE RODGERS AND HART REVOLUTION
• • •
DEAREST ENEMY (1925)

The success of the *Garrick Gaieties* was a significant step for Rodgers, Hart, and Fields, though revue did not offer the form they so keenly desired to make their own. The first opportunity audiences had to see the team working at musical comedy was *Dearest Enemy*, a complete book show without interpolations, and with a coherent storyline from start to finish. If these boys really did have a new approach to writing for the musical stage, this was their chance to show it.

The show and its script went through several drafts before it was presented on Broadway. Initially *Sweet Rebel*, it was known as *Dear Enemy* during out-of-town tryouts, *Betsy* in pre-Broadway rehearsals,[1] and finally *Dearest Enemy* by the time it reached New York.[2]

The story is set during the American Revolutionary War and involves the invasion of New York by the British. Led by General Howe, the invaders landed at Kip's Bay, separating American forces camped at the Battery from the main army on Harlem Heights. When the British stopped to rest at the house of a wealthy merchant, his wife, Mary Lindner Murray, waylaid them, enabling the American forces to regroup. The event was "a turning point in the American revolution,"[3] and a commemorative plaque at Lexington Avenue and 37th Street was erected to honor the act. To this historical narrative, Herb Fields added three romantic liaisons: one between Mrs. Murray's niece and Captain John Copeland of the British army, one between her daughter Jane and Copeland's comrade Harry Tryon, and a third between Mrs. Murray herself and General Tryon. Although the initial flirtations with the British soldiers are a part of their daring plan, the ladies soon succumb to British charm. At the climax of the play, Mrs. Murray's niece sends a signal to the rebel forces. The British discover her subterfuge and leave to attack but not before the American rebels have retrenched and met with General Washington on Harlem Heights.

The story of the Murray deception had long been a project the boys wanted to stage, so they were thrilled to interest rising Broadway star Helen Ford in the show. Ford had been hitting headlines since her debut in Oscar Hammerstein II's first Broadway show, *Always You* (1920), playing the French ingénue Toinette Fontaine. She joined Fred and Adele Astaire in a supporting part in *For Goodness Sake* (1922), then took lead roles in two successes, *The Gingham Girl* (1922) and *Helen of Troy, New York* (1923). By the time the boys approached her, Ford was a box office draw; getting her support was significant—and it would prove to be more significant than they realized.

Courting Broadway's rising star was not just a production decision; Dick was smitten. Where Larry sought clandestine encounters after dark and wrestled with his sexuality, Dick was unequivocally straight—in John Lahr's words, "a romantic and a womanizer."[4] In fact, as Michael Feinstein has suggested (in what may be a rather animated impression), "he was known as a notorious womanizer who freely grabbed the derriere of any beautiful chorus girl close at hand."[5] In Helen Ford he found a beautiful young lady who was just as passionate about (his) music as he was. Writing *Musical Stages* over fifty years later, he is discreet about their relationship—for she was married, and he was later to meet the love of his life—but in Meryle Secrest's opinion "he was more than a little in love with her and she with him";[6] he nostalgically recalls walking in Central Park with her, discussing "our two favourite topics, ourselves and music," and concedes, "she was many things to me—teacher, mother, confidante and companion."[7]

Ford became *Sweet Rebel*'s biggest promoter, carrying the script round with her "every day for about a year."[8] She showed it to the producers of her most recent hit, *No Other Girl* (1924), and although A. L. Jones and Morris Green were not interested, they arranged a meeting with John Murray Anderson, one of their directors whose revue work (*Greenwich Village Follies*, *Music Box Revue*) was very successful. Then, Ford found a backer: New Hampshire lawyer Robert Jackson who happened to have gone to school with her husband. With Jackson on board, she next involved her husband, who had dabbled in theater production and for a while had run a stock company upstate . George Ford was recruited as producer, and he arranged for a tryout at the Colonial Theatre in Akron, Ohio, with Helen playing the lead and the rest of the cast drafted in from local talent. The tryout production—by now *Dear Enemy*—was rehearsed for just a week, so opening night at the Colonial on July 20 was shaky. Nevertheless, Ford and the local cast were commended by the press for their work, and buoyed by the reasonable reception, the team decided to proceed to New York. John

Murray Anderson (who a decade later would direct *Jumbo*) replaced George Ford's brother as director, a Broadway cast was selected, and after an out-of-town week in Baltimore, *Dearest Enemy* opened at the Knickerbocker Theatre on September 18, 1925.

It was an unusual path to Broadway, but despite the short out-of-town period, the show was significantly developed on its journey into town. Two extant scripts—of *Sweet Rebel* and *Dearest Enemy*—show how it emerged and give a fascinating insight into the way a piece changes between conception and production.

SWEET REBEL

The country is at war with the British. The girls of the Murray household have been without male company for so long they have forgotten what men are like. As they sew, the girls sing the opening number, "Heigh Ho": "Our hearts are smitten so, / All day we sit and sew / Heigh-ho!" they sing; "Our lads are in the war, / But till they win the war, / Heigh-ho!" General Putnam, we learn, is at the Battery with 3,000 men; he expects to march on the Heights the next day. Margot Burke, the niece of the Murrays, is fishing in Kip's Bay. The British have already seized Long Island and are rapidly advancing. Mrs. Murray, singing "War is War!" warns the girls what might befall them if the enemy attacks: "Ev'ry soldier is a frightful brute who / Snatches ladies for his loot..." To our surprise, this thrills the girls: "Hooray, we're going to be compromised!"[9]

News comes that the English have landed at Kip's Bay (where Margot is fishing). Mrs. Murray sends the stable boy Tony to establish a plan of action from General Washington. Her daughter Jane climbs a tree to see what is happening, and when the British captain Harry Tryon enters, seeking quarters for the troops, she is smitten. Harry points out that it is not becoming of an officer of the British Army to trouble young ladies and that they are under strict instructions not to touch anything that doesn't belong to them. Jane and Harry sing "Here in My Arms," proving that despite orders, love will out. Generals Howe and Tryon (Harry's father) arrive and arrange to headquarter at the Murray house overnight. When a dog enters with Margot's clothes, the girls panic, thinking she may have been killed. Tryon sends the soldiers off to search, while following a tip, he makes his way to Kip's Bay.

The scene cuts to reveal Margot entering in a barrel, accompanied by Captain Sir John Copeland. She is angry because he is more interested in interrogating her about the whereabouts of the rebel leader General Putnam than helping her find her clothes. As they arrive at the Murray residence, Mrs. Murray comes out, relieved to see her niece is safe, and while still in the barrel, Margot and John sing an unnamed duet. Mrs. Murray scolds John, then sends him off after the other soldiers to confirm that Margot is safe.

Meanwhile, Tony returns from his errand and reports that Washington has asked Murray to house the soldiers overnight so that while the British are distracted, Putnam and the troops can sneak up the island to join the main army. Murray convinces the soldiers to stay, enticing them with a fine meal and high-quality wine. Margot, meanwhile, plots her own strategy to get the men to stay: she confesses her love for Copeland and urges him to leave, singing with him the duet "Here's a Kiss." However, he is suspicious, assuming that Margot's volte-face is because she is trying to conceal a rebel meeting. As she expected, he determines to stay and catch the rebels. An ensemble finale concludes the act.

Act Two begins after dinner, with Mrs. Murray concocting more ruses to keep the British from leaving. She sends Tony off again to get orders from General Washington, but he can't get past the guards on the door. Margot hatches a plan, inviting the soldiers to watch a pantomime and suggesting that Tony take part so they can smuggle him out as part of the action.

The oriental pantomime begins, with Tony playing a Genie. During the course of the play, he is hidden in a laundry basket and thrown from the balcony. Thus he escapes to get word to Washington. After the pantomime, Mrs. Murray plies the soldiers with more alcohol and then helps discuss their strategy, inviting them to map out their plan on her bare back. Her intention is to reveal the plans to General Washington in the morning. As everyone beds down, the guards drag in the captured Tony. They are suspicious that he is a spy and imprison him upstairs. As he goes, he points at a lamp behind Margot, and she interprets this as a message: the household should send a signal when all the troops are asleep; Putnam will slip by with his men and re-group with the army on Harlem Heights. Margot and John reprise their love duet before going to sleep. Once he is asleep, she slips downstairs to give the signal. But he awakes and she is caught in the act of lighting the lamp. John shoots it out, thinking that will disrupt the signal. However, this inadvert-ently sends it (Light on, Light off). Putnam's men start to march. The house-hold is wakened and Margot arrested.

Act Three begins the following morning with Margot's trial. General Howe tries to ascertain if Margot knowingly gave a signal. If she did, she will be sen-tenced to death for spying. But John springs to her defense, admitting that it was him. He claims he is therefore a traitor and that he should be put to death to let her go free. He even suggests he lit the signal as a rebel spy in the service of Washington. Margot is freed and his trial for treason is scheduled. Finally, Tony reveals that he didn't pass on a message about a signal; indeed, there was no signal. When he pointed (at the lamp) he was just trying to get everybody to turn around so he could run away. There was no signal, and the fact that the troops marched at exactly that time was just a coincidence—or at least that is the story they are going to tell.

I have spent time detailing the events of *Sweet Rebel* because the show was to change substantially in its development into *Dearest Enemy*. At this stage, as can be seen, *Sweet Rebel* offers a complicated but workable plot, with opportunity for both stirring romantic ardor and coarse, knockabout comedy. At the same time, one can understand why its complex plot may have seemed rather convoluted: the device of the show-within-a-show could be confusing, while extensive comedy material, particularly in Act Three, was long-winded. It is not clear exactly how much of this treatment remained when *Dear Enemy* opened in Akron, Ohio, though critics did report leaving the theater before the third act had started in order to hit their copy deadlines—the show, it appears, was well over three hours in length. Still, a two-month hiatus between the Akron tryout and the subsequent pre-Broadway stint in Baltimore gave plenty of time for Herb to refashion the script into the *Dearest Enemy* audiences saw on Broadway.

DEAREST ENEMY

One significant change that happened in this period is that the name of the heroine was changed from Margot to Betsy, prompting the *Long Beach Life* to report in August that the show was in fact called *Betsy*. By the time it opened in Baltimore on September 7, the title was confirmed as *Dearest Enemy*.

Much of Act One remained the same. It still begins at Murray Hill with "Heigh-ho, Lackaday!" and "War Is War," though when Jane meets Harry, their coy flirting takes place in a new song. "I Beg Your Pardon" pushed "Here in My Arms" further into the act, where it became the love song for Betsy and John and therefore the hit of the show. The messenger role of Tony the stable boy is now taken by Betsy's brother Jimmie, and there is no panicky search for Betsy. Instead, though still introduced wearing nothing but a barrel, the story has Betsy swimming rather than fishing when the British arrive.

As in the previous version, Betsy is at first antagonistic toward the British, though when Jane reveals General Washington's plot, she assumes control. She dispatches Jimmie to communicate with General Putnam. However, in this script, the dramatic tension is increased in two significant ways. First, Generals Howe and Clinton are far more assertive about returning to their stations, meaning that the job of the Murray household to distract them becomes more difficult. Second, Betsy's role is more pronounced, and the juxtaposition of her role as rebel leader with the love scenes in which she forgets her animosity toward John is very marked. "Here in My Arms" is now given far more prominent dramatic weight; Betsy is torn between her love and her rebel sentiments, and she warns John to leave for his safety. This makes him suspicious, and for the wrong reasons, he assumes Betsy has been misleading him. A reprise of "Here in My Arms" in a minor key reveals his disappointment and shows Betsy's dilemma. Just as the troops prepare to march, John snaps into military mode and warns of "some sort of rebel intrigue."[10] The act finishes with their dramatic decision to remain at Murray Hill.

More significant changes appear in an almost totally rewritten Act Two. This now begins, after dinner, with a stately gavotte, offering a strong ensemble opening. General Howe begins to express suspicions, especially when Jimmie is dragged in from the woods by soldiers. Having caught Jimmie and suspecting Betsy to be loyal to the rebel cause, Howe and Clinton decide to return to their troops. It is clear that Jimmie failed to make contact with Putnam, so Betsy resolves to take the message herself.

As everyone becomes careless, plied with alcohol and forgetting their duties, we see a cut-away of Betsy reaching Putnam's camp, where he gives her instructions to send a signal when the household is asleep.

Betsy returns to find everyone retiring for the night. John has been stationed downstairs to keep watch. They have a final romantic scene, singing "Here's a Kiss," before she heads upstairs. As he falls asleep, however, Betsy steals down and hangs a lantern in the window as the signal. Suddenly John awakes. He rushes forward to extinguish the light; there is a scuffle, and she gets shot. John thinks he has put out the signal, though as Betsy reveals, he has actually confirmed it (Light on, light off). As the household awakes, we hear General Putnam's troops marching up the island. It is too late: the rebels have achieved their goal, but the injured Betsy collapses in John's arms. He becomes a suspect and is arrested by his own men.

Act Three in this version is reduced to an Epilogue and extends to just six pages of script. The war has ended and the troops are coming home. Among them is Jimmie, who is now a lieutenant. Harry and Jane are married and are heading up to Niagara for their honeymoon. This reminds Betsy of John, and she sings a reprise of "Bye and Bye." Suddenly a fanfare sounds, heralding the arrival of General Washington. He honors the rebels, and offers particular thanks to Betsy, promising her a gift. The strains of "Here in My Arms" are heard, and John and Betsy are reunited.

Though these versions clearly differ, and though *Dearest Enemy* was an improvement over *Sweet Rebel*, there are qualities in the first script that are worth exploring. The libretto shows Herb juggling comedy inherited from his father with pathos inherited from serious drama, a curious clash of writing styles that seem barely compatible. Act Three of the first draft, for example, includes an extended section in which Tony is hidden underneath Mrs. Murray's skirt for a considerable period of slapstick; meanwhile, General Tryon is an out-and-out buffoon, a lecherous, drunken Falstaff with laugh-lines aplenty. At other points, the serious characters Margot and Copeland revert to melodrama: "I love you, as the woman in me loves the man in you.... But what does the woman in me matter, when my heart cries out against your tyrant King? When all my soul cries out for freedom for the nation? It is a nation you are fighting, not a colony!"[11]

Despite this heavy-handed script, there are other moments when dialogue is used rather well to give the characters dramatic depth, adding strength to the protagonists and political clout to the events:

MARGOT: (*softening*) It's not your fault. It isn't you. Not you alone . . . it's your people . . . You British . . . I'm not thinking of myself, it's these noble hearts over here, fighting with their backs against the wall. Facing impossible odds . . . , facing poverty, privation, death! Only for an ideal, for liberty. You come here to beat them down, and then ask me to love you.

JOHN: War is man's business, Margot.

MARGOT: No. THIS war is woman's business. Because it's at the home you're striking. We want our sons to be free men, not slaves. This wilderness was made livable by the women. The men came over here as colonists, but the women made a country of these colonies. That country has to live, and we'll fight for it. Every one of us. (*They sing Duet.*)[12]

Here, the strength of the female protagonist is nurtured through her words. As the script changes she maintains that strength, though by the time the show became *Dearest Enemy* and Margot changed to Betsy, her strength was as an action hero, her dialogue diluted.

Despite this change, the strong female character remains a feature of Herb Fields's shows, as we shall see. For him, men are lovers or comedy foils; and in this script, which could so easily have ennobled Washington, Putnam, or even Mr. Murray, it is unquestionably the women who command events.

When George Washington does appear at the end of the play (as a figurehead rather than a real person), his speech of recognition honors women for their role in the Revolutionary victory: "It is to the nobility of our women, their strength and confidence, that we owe our victory. America is proud of you, and as her servant I come to thank you, and to kiss your hand."[13]

DEAREST ENEMY ON TELEVISION (1955)

Dearest Enemy had one more articulation of note, in a 1955 TV film, part of a series by Max Liebman (which also included *A Connecticut Yankee*). In common with many filmed adaptations of stage musicals, Liebman makes considerable adjustments to the script and structure of the show. In particular, he bookends the narrative with two scenes set in England, in which the British officers reminisce about their exploits in the Revolutionary War. The song "Cheerio" is used as a transitional sequence, its first verse sung by the officers in London, its second flashing back to New York in 1776.

The action switches to Mrs. Murray's house, with a period map as illustration, and for a time follows the plot of both *Sweet Rebel* and *Dearest Enemy*. The girls sing "Heigh-Ho Lackaday," Jane brings news that the British have arrived, and we learn that Betsy is stranded swimming in the cove. Then the action departs from the stage script to show the riverbank scene in which Betsy is discovered by John. Rather than the celebrated barrel, he offers her his coat. Though in black and white and mediatized through the technologies of camera and screen, the proxemics and dramaturgy of this encounter are powerful. It is interesting in this scene to see Betsy—the American rebel— dressed in British colors, for example; in the following scene where they arrive back at the Murray house, Mrs. Murray and the girls stand on their porch with shotguns trained on the couple. This is palpably tense. Then a message from General Washington arrives to urge the ladies to keep the British at the Murray House at all costs.

Act Two begins with the gavotte scene. Then a courier arrives from the British army and is misled by Mrs. Murray so that he cannot get his message to General Howe. The girls torture him with delicacies from the larder; he eventually relents, and hands over the message. The girls spin a ruse, telling the soldiers variously that General Washington, Thomas Jefferson, Benjamin Franklin, John Adams, and Patrick Henry are due to meet at the house that night. Each soldier sees a potential honor if they remain to capture one of the Americans. Howe announces the decision to stay, the courier escapes, and Howe realizes that Murray has stalled him.

At the opening of Act Three, Betsy admits she has feelings for John in "I'd Like to Hide It." Troops interrupt the scene as John is dragged in, under arrest, and locked in the cellar. Betsy takes John his meal, and he convinces her to release him. He escapes, and she sings a reprise of "Here in My Arms."

A final scene returns to the British Officer's Club in 1778, where General Howe and John conclude their story. They learn from the newspapers that Mrs. Murray and Betsy are visiting Britain, so rush to meet them at the dock. A finale medley of "Here in My Arms," "Old Enough to Love," "Bye and Bye," and "The Hermits" concludes the telecast.

A REVOLUTIONARY SHOW?

To understand *Dearest Enemy*, it is worth recollecting the context in which it hit Broadway, especially if it seems odd that the first hit book show by young Rodgers, Hart, and Fields was a period piece. More than that—and contrasting starkly with the *Fifth Avenue Follies*—this was a show with fully clothed girls and very little syncopation: "It did seem funny to see no flesh. You simply have to imagine legs. You couldn't see any," one reviewer lamented.[14] Still, they had tried sex and jazz in varying degrees over the past few years and though popular, these elements had not yet provided the hit the boys wanted. Despite a popular turn in productions toward newer and younger forms, Broadway's influential reviewers and producers, usually older and always opinionated, were wedded to formulae that were tried and shows whose standards of decency were intact. In *Dearest Enemy*, there are enough of these elements to appease traditionalists.

Not surprisingly, the writing team gets linked to Gilbert and Sullivan in many reviews and the show to operettas like *Blossom Time* (1921),[15] *The Student Prince* (1924), *Rose-Marie* (1924), and *The Love Song* (1925).[16] "It's different, very different, from most of the musical plays of the season," commented the *Evening Post*, "for it isn't syncopated at all and there isn't the slightest suspicion of jazz";[17] "not even a furtive breath of jazz," agrees the *Evening Telegram*.[18] The critic for *Women's Wear* was even more blunt: "In these days of jazz music and semi-nude women on our stages, 'Dearest Enemy,' although a little old fashioned, is as welcome as a cool breeze on a hot night."[19]

On the other hand, the script flaunts its 1920s values, even if the narrative is set in the eighteenth century. The *Baltimore News* noted "many heavy-handed attempts to project risqué dialogue,"[20] and the *Times* complained that "the humor is rather banal, and when it leans toward the vulgar it offends the general scheme of gracefulness."[21] Betsy's initial appearance, naked in a

Figure 3.1: Promotional flyer for Dearest Enemy, *showing Helen Ford in her risqué opening costume: nothing but a barrel. Billy Rose Theatre Collection, The New York Public Library for the Performing Arts, Astor, Lenox and Tilden Foundations.*

barrel with a little red parasol (see Figure 3.1) is one that undeniably sexualizes Helen Ford, though critics were generally enticed: "When a man fishes a fair and bare girl out of the river and then takes her home in a barrel, he is very apt to fall in love with her," opined the *Baltimore News*;[22] several of the other (male) reviewers wrote similar things.

In fact it was partly this gimmick that attracted Ford to the show in the first place:

> I knew this would make a star of me. I knew this instinctively.... You know what sold it to me? The entrance.... It was a wonderful entrance, and it was cute and it was funny with this English redcoat soldier chasing me with one of my slippers in his hand, and obviously I have no clothes.[23]

Effective though it might be, and although like many of Rodgers and Hart's later shows it is the women who stand out as the stronger characters, one can't help feeling that this costume decision is a way of injecting titillation into the opening scenes, and the humor of the script hardly contradicts this impression. In the first scene, Jane's comments set the tone when she returns after taking provisions to the troops: "how grateful the soldiers were for their provisions," she remarks, in an apparently innocuous comment that soon becomes suggestive in the light of other lines in the script. Betsy, we learn, has "already had experience with the British army...she dropped her petticoat right in front of the State House."[24] Later, Harry defends the honor of the British soldier: "We try to behave. It's our military training," he says. Jane's response is tart: "Then you've been overtrained,"[25] she retorts. The double-play is the same in some of the songs: the conceit of "War Is War," for example, is to build a picture of the archetypal domestic scene and then undercut it. Here is a crowd of virginal girls sewing and skipping, and an older matriarch warning of the dangers of men. The girls' riposte of "Hooray, we're going to be compromised!" turns completely on its head the expected etiquette of 1776, thrusting *Dearest Enemy* squarely into the roaring twenties. Still, in contrast to the sexual suggestions of other shows on Broadway in this period, *Dearest Enemy* clearly appeared charmingly inoffensive: a safe, clean show upholding standards of decency.

As the reviewers' comments make plain, though, a considerable threat to this decency was jazz, the all-pervasive new music that appropriated black rhythms, encouraged sexualized dancing, and referred symbolically to the sexual act itself. Rodgers and Hart were no strangers to jazz, as we have seen (*The Jazz King*, *Jazz à la Carte*, *Say It with Jazz*), and they were undoubtedly part of a generation infected by the licentious opportunities it promised. Yet critics' positive comments about the music in *Dearest Enemy* reveal that although there *were* elements of contemporary styling, jazz was distant from its main musical mood. Instead, Rodgers colored his score stylistically with the impression of operetta, even layering deliberate musical references into the score. One critic found "Cheerio" reminiscent of Sigmund Romberg's "Homeland" from *Louie the 14th* (1925),[26] though it was clearly a pastiche of the First World War song "Goodbye-ee" by R. P. Weston and Bert Lee (1915); another was reminded by "Here in My Arms" of the spiritual "Nobody Knows de Trouble I've Seen," recently recorded by Marian Anderson;[27] the song "Ale, Ale, Ale," which disappeared from the show before it opened, was presumably a pastiche of "The Drinking Song" ("Drink, Drink, Drink") from Romberg's *The Student Prince* (1924); another critic recalled in Rodgers's music the strains of French composers Émile Waldteufel and Charles-François Gounod.[28] While these were one-off observations, the most consistent stylistic reference that many critics noted was "more than a chance flavor of Gilbert and Sullivan."[29] Given Hart's admiration for the Savoy Operas, this is not surprising. "Old Man Gilbert was the greatest lyricist who ever turned a rhyme," he stated,[30] and as Earl Bargainnier notes, "Rodgers and Hart were soon called 'the Gilbert and Sullivan of America.'"[31] Marmorstein rather romantically pictures Hart studying the Gilbert and Sullivan material: "atop the upright piano the Harts kept in the sitting room there were all those Gilbert and Sullivan operettas to pore over, the librettos studied time and again."[32] In this show, Rodgers also shows his close familiarity with Sullivan's style, and a sense of Gilbert and Sullivan pervades the whole score.

The opening chorus, "Heigh-Ho Lackaday" is one such reminder, surely a pastiche of any one of Gilbert and Sullivan's girls' choruses: "Twenty Lovesick Maidens We" from *Patience*, "Tripping hither, tripping thither" from *Iolanthe*, "Climbing over rocky mountains" from *Pirates of Penzance*, or "Braid the raven hair" from *The Mikado*. Elsewhere, though not a girls' chorus, *Yeoman of the Guard*'s opening number ("When maiden loves, she sits and sighs") is itself a song ruminating on the remark "Heigh-Ho" and other colloquialisms. Establishing the musical atmosphere of the show in this way would undoubtedly have reminded audiences of the Gilbert and Sullivan style. Later in the same song, Rodgers and Hart make use of another classic Gilbert and Sullivan technique as they introduce the first of several patter verses. Rich in triple-rhymes and inverting in these verses the syntax of sentences, it is not surprising that Hart became recognized as "a deep student of Gilbert":[33]

> MRS. MURRAY: I behold in consternation
> You have taken a vacation
> Fingers in your occupation please employ.[34]

Further into the act, Mrs. Murray and General Tryon sing "The Hermits," whose patter shows similar features:

> TRYON: In the spring when we make merry
> Hermits feel unnecessary.
> Springtime is the best narcotic
> To induce the sense erotic.[35]

Finally, the Act One finale incorporates a third patter verse, this time between General Howe and Mrs. Murray:

> HOWE: Tho' we've no authentic reason
> To suspect the maid of treason
> From her actions I begin to
> See some things we must look into.[36]

Significantly, these songs are always associated with Mrs. Murray, played in the original Broadway production by Flavia Arcaro, who had just portrayed

Lady Jane in *Patience* at the Provincetown Playhouse. Rodgers and Hart have fun with this biographical detail in the song "Full Blown Roses," which was written late in the process and introduced in pre-New York tryouts by Arcaro herself. This is the most self-conscious reference to Gilbert and Sullivan in the show. In the same way they pieced together refrains reminiscent of other popular songs in "It May Rain" from the *Garrick Gaieties*, Rodgers and Hart ransack the Gilbert and Sullivan repertoire to structure this song. In *Patience*, Arcaro performed the patter duet "So go to him and say to him." For "Full Blown Roses," Rodgers and Hart take one of the main themes of this song and adapt it to their purpose: "Sing 'Hey to you –/ Good day to you' / And that's what I shall say"[37] becomes "A curt'sy, Sirs, we'll pay to you / And say to you / Good day to you."[38] Rodgers's music closely follows Sullivan's, forming the basis of the pastiche: a dotted rhythm followed by straight beats gives a distinctive rhythmic pattern in each measure; meanwhile the melody of each measure steps down and back up (see Figure 3.2).

Other lines also come from intertextual origins: the officers' "Such faces hardly bear inspection. / Their beauty is their own protection" seems to stem from *The Mikado*'s "The sun whose rays are all ablaze"; "Let us have a little chat" resembles the same show's "Taken from the county jail."

Of course, the music is not entirely derivative, and a number of musical motifs recur throughout the score, giving it consistency. Some become characteristic Rodgers traits as his style develops: scalar passages, for example, are fundamental in "Cheerio," "Full Blown Roses," and "Sweet Peter" (see Figure 3.3); the latter two both begin on the third of the scale, offering the same tonal ascent, "Full Blown Roses" to the upper tonic, and "Sweet Peter" one step higher. "Sweet Peter" subsequently descends back to the lower tonic in another scalar phrase interrupted by passing and pickup notes.

Figure 3.2: References to Gilbert and Sullivan's Patience *in "Full Blown Roses."*
Reprinted by Permission of Hal Leonard Corporation
(Richard Rodgers, Dearest Enemy *(1925), reconstructed piano-conductor score,*
edited by Larry Moore, RHO, 65–66.)

"Cheerio"

Cheer-i-o, lit-tle moth-er of mine! Don't be wear-y o - ver the sea and the home-land.

"Full Blown Roses"

Full blown ros - es are sweet - er.

"Sweet Peter"

Sweet Pe - ter, sweet Pe - ter had a wife and could - n't cheat her,

Figure 3.3: Rodgers' characteristic scalar motifs in Dearest Enemy.
Reprinted by Permission of Hal Leonard Corporation

The score also makes bold use of arpeggios, which gives a martial stamp to some of the music. The refrain of "What Do all the Hermits Do in Springtime," for example, is built entirely on arpeggio patterns, while elsewhere they are prominent in "Sweet Peter" ("Homeward he'd stumble"). The combination of scalar motifs and arpeggios in "Bye and Bye," John and Betsy's Act Two duet, is worth considering. The verse to this is structured in five phrases of four measures, the first and second of which establish the use of arpeggio. A descending root arpeggio in measure two is mimicked in measure six by its descending first inversion. In phrases three and four a rising scalar sequence ascends over a seventh before leaping down the first inversion of the arpeggio again. In the re-frain, the title phrase ("Bye and bye") is not only repeated on the tonic, mediant, and dominant of the scale in the first eight-measure phrase but is also aided in its step up through this arpeggio sequence by a short ar-peggio turn between sub-phrases (see Figure 3.4). The B phrase emulates this same patterning up a tone, before the A is repeated. In the final eight-measure C phrase, the melody descends over an octave, interrupted only marginally by alternate pickup notes.

"Bye and Bye" is another classic Rodgers and Hart song, whose triple-rhyme motifs work dramaturgically to consolidate the rhetoric of the music and lyrics: "Our happy days will come / Though slight delays will come / The bright sun's rays will come"[39] is a prime example. Toward the end of the refrain, Hart takes the musical lead from Rodgers in a sequence that marginally extends

Figure 3.4: Arpeggios and scalar passages in "Bye and Bye," measures 25–32 and 49–56.

Reprinted by Permission of Hal Leonard Corporation

the expected rhyme to great effect: "Ev'ry cloud just flies on ,/ Love is on the far horizon."[40] Again, the impetus has come from the music but resounds because of the consonance of the lyrical match.

Perhaps the most defining motif in the score, though—and one that helps put these stylistic features into context—is a cascading phrase central to the main love song "Here in My Arms" (see Figure 3.5). This—again built around an arpeggiated structure—appears in both the verse ("a merry place") and the chorus ("-able, it's de-"), moving from the sixth of the scale to the fifth before dropping down the root arpeggio to the tonic. The subliminal impact of this motif is magnified by a persistent reminder of its prominent tonal drop ("can while" and "you smile" in the verse, and all the "ab-le"s in the chorus) and an echoing semitonal drop ("a-way"). It is also consolidated by a reverse sequence that sweeps up to the cascading motif ("in my arms"). The main cascading motif is found elsewhere throughout the score, perhaps most significantly in the girls' line "Hooray! We're gonna be compromised!" from "War Is War," but also in different modulations in "Where the Hudson River Flows" and twice in the first phrase of "Sweet Peter" (see Figure 3.6).

Significantly, this is an example of what Raymond Knapp calls a "gapped scale," a pentatonic feature that to his mind "can be taken as particularly

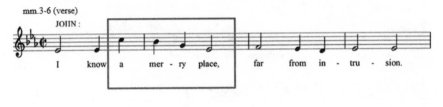

mm.3-6 (verse)

mm.19-22 (refrain)

Figure 3.5: *The cascading "Here in My Arms" motif, demonstrating the quintessentially American "gapped scale."*
Reprinted by Permission of Hal Leonard Corporation

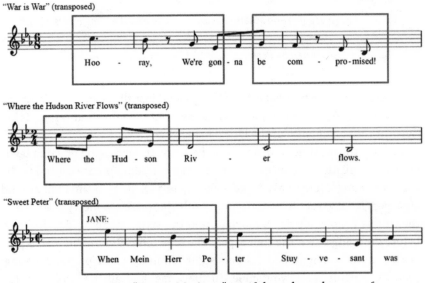

"War is War" (transposed)

"Where the Hudson River Flows" (transposed)

"Sweet Peter" (transposed)

Figure 3.6: *The "Here in My Arms" motif throughout the score of* Dearest Enemy.
Reprinted by Permission of Hal Leonard Corporation

American,"[41] raising the possibility that Rodgers may have been deliberately writing material that nationalistically contrasted with the Britishness of the Gilbert and Sullivan pastiches. Knapp discusses the Americanism of the gapped scale in regard to Gershwin's "I Got Rhythm," which is built of "many constructed melodic symmetries" and which uses a very similar motif to the "Here in My Arms" cascade: "In the four note opening figure and its manipulation, Gershwin produced an emblem of elemental American energy powerful enough to serve as a generative motive within the classical tradition."[42] This fits his thesis that "American musicals become, in part and in some form, an enacted demonstration of Americanism, and often take on a formative, defining role in the construction of a collective sense of 'America.' "[43] Clearly, the narrative of *Dearest Enemy* is trading on a significant moment in national history, and not surprisingly, it is celebrated in the press on this account, representing "that longed for quantity, the 100 per cent American operetta, as to which many of us have sighed because so generally we have found it not."[44] Indeed, it pulls no punches in consolidating this impression in the narrative, not only showing the Americans triumphing over the British but also welcoming the messianic figure of George Washington to the stage. The appearance of Washington in the epilogue is noted by several reviewers:

> Of all the stage Washingtons we have seen in play and tableau he came nearest to reproducing the ideal of the great American. Tall in stature, dignified and courtly in bearing, yet intensely simple and human, the actor conveyed an understanding of the reason for the devotion of Washington's contemporaries and his place in their admiration as well as in that of the generations since. That brief scene gave a real value to a stage production designed only to amuse.[45]

So *Dearest Enemy* is clearly "an enacted demonstration of Americanism" in its presentation of a significant historical moment, its characterization of key American figures (Mrs. Murray, General Putnam, George Washington), and its referencing of other notable American icons (Peter Stuyvesant); if there was ever a show that offered a chance for the cultural separation of American music from European to be symbolically staged, *Dearest Enemy* was it. However, a glance at the real history of the events reveals that, in fact, this show presents an extremely sensationalist account.

On September 15, 1776, General Howe, commander-in-chief of the British forces, sailed into New York harbor and up the East River, landing his troops at Kip's Bay (where 34th Street now crosses FDR Drive). The American forces were camped in various positions around Manhattan: Washington was stationed at Fort Washington, north of the city on Harlem Heights; General Henry Knox was stationed at Bayard's Hill Redoubt (Bunker Hill), at the intersection of Grand and Mulberry Streets. Anticipating a landing attempt by the British, American militia had been lined up strategically along the East River shoreline. Around dawn, Howe's flotilla of five frigates sailed into the East River, docking by the Long Island shore within easy sight of the continental army. Throughout the morning, the British offloaded some eighty-four smaller boats into which they squeezed an estimated 6,000 troops. At ten o'clock, the five frigates began their bombardment, shelling the Manhattan shoreline so heavily for three full hours that "the militiamen could do nothing but keep well under cover."[46] Shielded by this bombardment and protected from counter-fire by the dense smoke, Lieutenant-General Clinton and Earl Cornwallis led their infantry in the small boats to land at Kip's Bay.

Faced with this onslaught and the arrival of 6,000 well-organized troops, the defending militia panicked and scattered westward in confusion. Washington responded to the guns by riding down from his Harlem position to gauge the situation:

> As soon as I heard the firing, I rode with all possible despatch towards the place of landing, where to my great surprise and mortification I found the troops...flying in every direction....I used every means in my power to rally and to get them into some order; but my attempts were fruitless and ineffectual; and on the appearance of a small party of the enemy, not more than sixty or seventy, their disorder increased, and they ran away in the greatest confusion, without firing a single shot.[47]

He quickly comprehended the enormity of the invasion and issued commands to retrench on Harlem Heights, sending General Putnam to withdraw Knox's troops from the Bayard's Hill Redoubt. Thus the American troops were split, with a formidable British army encamped in the middle of the island. Putnam's rescue of the stranded troops was only possible thanks to two things. First, his aide Aaron Burr had an intimate knowledge of the Manhattan topography: skirting the western-most edge of the island, they were able to creep through the wooded area north of Greenwich, evading detection thanks to a raised spine of land running northward up the center of the island, which hid them from view. Second, rather than consolidate his successful invasion of Manhattan with a full-scale rout of the enemy, Howe chose to wait to allow his troops to gather, and requisitioned the house of the wealthy merchant Robert Murray to set up temporary headquarters: "By this happy incident," reports Johnston, "General Putnam...escaped a rencounter with a greatly superior force, which must have proved fatal to his whole party. Ten minutes, it is said, would have been sufficient for the enemy to have secured the road at the turn and entirely cut off General Putnam's retreat."[48]

As it was, Putnam escaped and regrouped with Washington on Harlem Heights. "Washington," suggests Alan Axelrod, "who had left his army vulnerable through poor tactics, was reprieved by the lethargic conservatism of the British commander."[49] Although skirmishes ensued over the coming days, the British proceeded to occupy the whole of Manhattan island, though it took them a month to do so. In time, Washington was chased across New Jersey, Howe successfully occupied Fort Washington, and by the end of the year the British had full control of New York and its environs. It was to be several years before the tables would turn and Washington would be able to claim victory for the continental army over the forces of the King.

If this is closer to the truth of what happened in the events of Kip's Bay, it is clear that historical accuracy has been subject to a revisionist reading in the script of *Dearest Enemy*. Where Washington appears as the victor in the glorifying epilogue, it would be more appropriate to see him as the vanquished leader who presided over "an ungovernable panic" that "served to increase existing jealousies between the troops from the different States, and so far impair the morale of the army."[50] Moreover, the suggestion that Betsy Burke may have gone out swimming in Kip's Bay on the morning of the invasion beggars credibility: it would be a fool indeed who took a dip with a flotilla of gunboats preparing a three-hour bombardment on the other side of the river. Equally, for Mrs. Murray to suggest meeting Tryon "in the forests of Manhattan...where the Hudson River flows" would have been revolutionary suicide: this was precisely the area through which Putnam was leading his troops, so Mrs. Murray would hardly have guided the British in that direction.

Of course, dramatic license is perfectly acceptable on the stage, and the writing team made no claims that this was a factually accurate account. Nor are Rodgers, Hart, and Fields solely responsible for turning this national travesty into a story of heroic glory. Their account was part of a sustained revisionist historicizing as America became increasingly self-conscious about its independent identity. The writing of American history to suit America— which began in earnest toward the end of the nineteenth century—led to the formation of celebratory organizations such as the Daughters of the American Revolution, and their erection of a plaque to commemorate this event was just as much an exercise in educating Americans about the sanctioned story as it was about honoring heroes of the Revolutionary War. Thus although "Dearest Enemy may do violence to the facts of history and cause an historian to shed bitter tears of anguish,"[51] it played its own role in reconstituting American history as part of the mythology of manifest destiny.

One significant tool in revising American history has been America's appropriation of cultural statements to suit its own ends, and in both obvious and subtle ways *Dearest Enemy* does this with its music. In another direct musical quotation—this time explicit—Rodgers makes liberal use of the Revolutionary anthem "Yankee Doodle," signifying to twentieth-century audiences the triumph of the Continental forces. Used as it is in the second act—sung by the

British at the Murray house while the cut-away scene depicts Betsy delivering rebel messages to General Putnam—the song's dramaturgical role is complex: it is well known that "Yankee Doodle" was a song first used by the king's troops but then appropriated by rebel forces as they gained power over the invaders. Here, it is seen in both of these guises, working on different levels to create irony, pathos, and drama. On a more subtle level, *Dearest Enemy* is a part of the constitution of the musical as an American art form (despite Gilbert and Sullivan's obvious influence). In *Dearest Enemy*, Rodgers and Hart had the perfect opportunity to exploit the difference between "old world" and "new world" music, thereby demarcating the boundary between one paradigm and another. With warring factions established as culturally distinct—English and American—a clear, self-conscious use of musical motifs can be seen as stylistically distinct—English (Gilbert and Sullivan) and American (the gapped scale).

In turning away from a European sound to establish one of American identity, the popular music industry in general—and exponents such as Rodgers and Hart—developed over time a new paradigm that became accepted as American. One of the few close analyses of the music of *Dearest Enemy* explores this in detail. Graham Wood discusses not the surface qualities of the music but the structural patterns. Through these, he suggests, Rodgers used song form to consolidate character and to strengthen the dramatic dynamic, and he insists that "to ignore the relationship of these formal patterns to their surrounding musical-dramatic framework is to miss a crucial layer of the show's dramatic meaning"[52] (and, we might add, its complicity in consolidating the Americanism of the Broadway musical). Wood demonstrates how different song forms are used by different characters to connote distinct dramatic situations: in *Dearest Enemy*, the Lyric Binary Chorus (AABA) is "associated with the younger couples and their direct expressions of love," while the Parallel Period form (ABAB or ABAC) is "associated with the older couple, with formal romantic expressions, or with future sentiments of love, both romantic and patriotic."[53] It is not hard to map these functions metaphorically onto the identities of the "younger," "direct expressions" of American culture and the "formal romantic" expressions of European. However, far from simply structurally distinct patterns, Wood sees distinguishing these two forms a fundamentally different dramatic dynamic—a performativity—wherein the Lyric Binary Chorus (AABA) pattern generates more "Romantic excitement," heightening the sense of drama and performing modernity.

The three statements of A material in the lyric binary model—which might be characterized as recognition, repetition and resolution—produce a more intensified final statement than the parallel period's second statement of A material. The elegant classical proportions of the parallel period are contrasted here with a more Romantic dramatic intensity. In this way the final A section of a lyric binary chorus is able to pack more musical and emotional punch than a parallel period chorus.[54]

On the face of it, the four songs structured with Lyric Binary Choruses—"Here in My Arms" (Betsy and John), "I'd Like to Hide It" (Betsy and Jane), "Sweet Peter" (Jane and Harry), and "Old Enough to Love" (General Tryon)—share little in terms of dramatic situation, though Wood presents plausible explanations as to why these songs and not others are structured with Lyric Binary Choruses. "Here in My Arms," he suggests, is "direct, unmediated and spontaneous" and "is associated with young lovers who have set aside both convention and cultural difference";[55] "I'd Like to Hide It" is "another unambiguously direct expression of youthful love";[56] in "Old Enough to Love," Wood argues, General Tryon "adopts a strategy of youth" to imply that older couples "are indeed capable of just as much passion as younger couples";[57] finally, in the least convincing argument, he suggests that "Sweet Peter" has a Lyric Binary Chorus because, in contrast to the "genteel restraint" of their previous song "I Beg Your Pardon," Jane and Harry "are more able and more willing to express their love directly."[58] Despite this, Wood's is a compelling thesis, and he grants to Rodgers and Hart considerable expertise in fashioning the short-form, thirty-two-measure song as a building block not just of the American musical but of American identity.

Although Rodgers and Hart were just one pair of prominent contributors to a gradually evolving shift, the techniques the pair were developing are very evident with the benefit of hindsight: "I Beg Your Pardon" may still be in the "old-fashioned" Parallel Period Chorus form, but it is the first song that sounds both contemporary and American, with its blues notes and its informal manner. Triple rhymes like "It seems so sweet / I beat / A maidenly retreat"[59] show typical Hart traits, pitting a vernacular tone against a more formal articulation, thereby both popularizing and elevating the idiom of popular song. Meanwhile, the laconic seventh at the end of the first phrase of the chorus ("I should not hold your hand") stamps an undeniably jazzy mark and harks back to the flippant modality characterizing Rodgers and Hart's writing in "Manhattan." At the same time—and just like "Manhattan"— this song is evidence that the thirty-two-measure AABA form had not yet become fully established as that quintessential American expression: this has a twenty-six-measure verse and a twenty-measure chorus.

Elsewhere, Rodgers and Hart's technique is seen in the way they were developing the use of the sound palette of a stage production to dramaturgical effect. They had already shown this in *The Melody Man*. In *Dearest Enemy*, in equally integrated ways, the use of both music and sound effects creates an aural diegesis beyond the stage space. At key moments, tension is provided by both offstage songs ("Cheerio" as Howe readies his forces to depart) and sounds (the calls of the nightwatchmen as the household beds down); elsewhere, the dramatic arc is resolved when we hear offstage singing (the final rendition of "Here in My Arms" before John enters at the end) and effects (the marching feet of Putnam's forces, indicating that the rebels have won). This use of an offstage aural diegesis magnifies the impact of the play, emboldening it with an epic quality and affirming the iconicity of real and life-changing events. A similar strategy is used iconographically in that other musical on a revolutionary theme, *1776* (1969), in which the final (rather undramatic) roll call of names is set against the iconic tolling of the Liberty Bell. Reaching beyond the immediacy of the play's material (script, stage, diegesis), both in the use of external expressive effects and in the referencing of historical significances, was key to the efficacy of *Dearest Enemy* and Rodgers and Hart's wider work.

Dearest Enemy was a revolutionary show for Rodgers and Hart in more ways than one; still, critics at the first night performance agreed that it lacked pace in the second act and for that reason had reservations about its quality. Some even suggested that Act Two slipped back into a revue-like reliance on "speciality numbers and patriotic tableaux"[60] like the toe dance by Jane Overton tacked onto "Where the Hudson River Flows" and the comedy kick line of one-legged Peter Stuyvesants during the showstopping "Sweet Peter." However, many of the reviewers remarked that *Dearest Enemy* was driven by its plot and its characters, and one even reports that he sought out the commemorative plaque on his way home and "tipped [his] hat to the lamplit bas-relief" in an act of homage; as he explains, "plots are too rare in musical comedy not to deserve extreme deference."[61]

4

PLEASING THE PRODUCERS

• • •

HERBERT FIELDS, LEW FIELDS, AND *THE GIRL FRIEND* (1926)

One reporter's performative salutation to the plot may seem idiosyncratic but it reflects the overwhelming hangup of the day, a lament rehearsed incessantly in both revues and reviews. Where comedians would bring onstage empty boxes in which to safe-keep the elusive plot, commentators would point out time and again, incredulously, that a show had a plot, didn't have a plot, or had sacrificed its plot to performative antics best kept elsewhere. The requirement of a plot seems to have been of tantamount significance, regardless of form.

Despite the fact that we might assume plot to be the quality that distinguishes vaudeville (plotless) from revue (thematic) and musical comedy (narrative), there was significant slippage between forms and practices, and in a Broadway melting pot whose creative artists worked variously in and with all three theatrical forms (and any other that periodically claimed the stage), boundaries were not blurred so much as whimsical. Critics got equally incensed lamenting the lack of plot in revue as they did in musical comedy.

That plot emerges in the 1920s as such an important expectation emphasizes the hybridity of the musical stage during this period, brought about by the increasing commercialization and organization of the industry. With its heavy demand on resources, theater has always been a high-cost business, and musical theater especially so, thanks to large casts, full orchestras, grand spectacle, and lavish production design. Of course, it stands to make money too—it would not be a viable business model if there were not profit-making potential, and the possibilities for generating high-dollar profits from a long-running hit were in the 1920s just as enticing to speculators as today. But by the 1920s, Broadway had seen significant changes in the ways productions were financed and business arrangements handled. These occurred throughout the second half of the nineteenth century when what was formerly a "push-cart-type enterprise" catering to individual actor-managers shifted to a "big business" model.[1] In the new setup, it was increasingly the businessmen—the producers—who wielded the power, and though we may refer today to shows of that period as "Rodgers and Hart," "Gershwin," or "Kern" shows (though not "Herbert Fields," "Bolton," or "MacDonough" shows), their very existence was due to the fact that they were supported, commissioned, or bankrolled by a producer. Pleasing the producer was everything.

During their career, Rodgers and Hart worked with nearly all the big producers on Broadway; eventually Rodgers would seize control himself and set up with his subsequent collaborator Oscar Hammerstein II one of the most powerful producing teams in Broadway history. However, at this stage he and Hart were still dependent on the support of a top dog; and courting the producer's whims, egos, and vicissitudes was a skill in itself.

By the 1920s, Broadway was dominated by a small coterie of extremely powerful producers, all of whom in one way or another impacted the early careers of Rodgers, Hart, and Herbert Fields. The big boys were those who owned or controlled the theater circuits, and that landscape had been a contested ground since the turn of the century. Lee and J. J. Shubert, who by 1924 had eighty-six theaters nationwide, had successfully managed to break up the powerful Theatrical Syndicate in the 1910s. There had been trouble throughout the teens, culminating in the Actors' Equity strike of 1919. But although that had been resolved in favor of the actors, theater artistes were still reliant on those who coordinated the complex business arrangements of a production and those who were willing to invest; it was still the producers, managers, and theater owners who wielded power. The problem for new writers trying to break into the business was that—like today—neither investors nor producers were keen to take risks. "Whenever there was uncertainty about the prospects of a show—and uncertainty was chronic—Broadway's aging musical producers would fall back on the same old writers and composers: Harry B. Smith, A. Baldwin Sloane, Raymond Hubbell, E. Ray Goetz, Victor Herbert."[2] Still, as one generation passed away (Manuel Klein in 1919; Ivan Caryll in 1921; Victor Herbert, Louis Hirsch, and Lionel Monckton in 1924; Baldwin Sloane in 1925; and Silvio Hein in 1928), a door was opened for a new wave of writers to come to the fore.

A show's potential was calculated by how long it might need to break even and start turning a profit. Producers calculated how much a show would "take" according to the ticket price, audience numbers, and capacity of the venue, against how much its running costs would eat away at that yield. A straight play with a small cast and modest design would cost little to run but would generate only modest box office takings thanks to the size of the venue and low ticket prices. A musical, on the other hand, could be a lavish affair with exorbitant running costs that would need a theater of enormous capacity to stand a chance of breaking even. The bottom line was very much the bottom line—producers could not afford the risk of keeping a show running if weekly receipts dipped and they didn't meet their running costs. Not surprisingly, commercial exigencies encouraged producers to work with tried-and-tested formulae, to meet audience expectations, and to handle their spending cautiously.

There is little surprise, then, that producers would turn to anything that would offer a box office draw, be it girls, gags, or stars. By the mid-teens, the cross-fertilization of forms had already begun as impresario Charles Dillingham established an efficient approach of recruiting vaudeville stars into musical comedy, making his shows hot properties while keeping costs as low as possible. In quick succession, he produced *Chin Chin* (1914) and *Watch Your Step* (1914), both capitalizing on popular vaudeville talent and both scoring huge successes. This initiative guaranteed revenue, though it led to a very particular type of star-driven entertainment. Attracted to the "legitimate" stage as they were, Dillingham found he could sign big acts up for less than their usual fee while creating a vehicle for their performance. Vaudeville sensations Vernon and Irene Castle, for example, were recruited to *Watch Your Step* (1914) for $1,000 per week—"a generous sum certainly, yet a steep drop from the $1,600 per week they had made in big-time vaudeville."[3] *Watch Your Step* hung a loose storyline around the Castles' act in a curious hybrid of vaudeville and musical comedy. "What may surprise us," writes Margaret Knapp, "is that given the nature of the performers he had hired, Dillingham bothered to have any libretto at all." Knapp reveals that incorporating book material identified a show as "legitimate," thereby allowing producers to charge legit prices: "Dillingham had to justify charging his audiences two dollars a ticket—around $50 in today's prices—to see the same performers who regularly appeared in vaudeville houses where the top seats cost from fifty cents to a dollar,"[4] she writes. The ruse was entirely economic, and Dillingham stood to generate a huge commercial reward.

With a smorgasbord of entertainers in the shows, Dillingham's librettist Harry B. Smith—who would become prolific on Broadway over the next few years—had a challenge: "faced with the preponderance of vaudevillians in the cast," writes Knapp, "Smith was forced to allow a great deal of latitude in his script so that the specialities of the performers could be introduced."[5] Thus a type of show emerged that would rely on its headline act. This was "less a plot and characters than a flexible scaffold on which to present his vaudevillian headliners."[6] Even by the time Rodgers and Hart worked with Dillingham on his vehicle for popular Canadian performer Beatrice Lillie, *She's My Baby* (1927), he was still exercising the same formula: lavish production values and a token book framing the existing act of a vaudeville headliner.[7] "Dillingham must have invested a young fortune," wrote one reviewer of *She's My Baby*; "it reeks of riches—elegance, exquisiteness."[8] At the same time critics noted "the slashed wreckage of a book"[9] by Guy Bolton, Bert Kalmar, and Harry Ruby; "a wonderwork of inanity," as the *Herald Tribune* put it.[10] The *Washington Daily News* pinpointed a problem: "Its immediate fault lies in its tendency to go revue at any or no provocation," commented the reviewer.[11] But when Beatrice Lillie "managed to sweep [the plot] to one side with all [her] 'I-can-explain-that-to-you-in-the-morning's [sic]' and 'Say-Gene-I-want-you-to-throw-a-white-spot,'" wrote the *Times*, "everyone sat down eagerly to bask in the radiance of her clowning."[12] As Jeffrey Magee notes, "early twentieth-century musical theater was a form of entertainment dominated by two forces: producers and star performers. The writers—composers, lyricists and librettists—existed to supply raw material with which these agents added luster to their celebrity and prestige, but their significance ended there."[13]

Nevertheless, the obsession with plot also implies that the role of librettist was key, so it is somewhat surprising that the writers who are remembered from this period are generally the composers and lyricists, rarely the librettists. Though the significance of some librettists has been recorded in the history books—notably P. G. Wodehouse—many libretti have been lost, neither published at the time like the songsheets nor collected in retrospective anthologies like the lyrics. Writers like Glen MacDonough, Harry Smith, Guy Bolton, and Herbert Fields were all prodigious exponents of their craft, though they are barely remembered today.

It is a testament to the overshadowing of Broadway librettists that Herbert Fields is not better known and is rarely recognized as part of the Rodgers and Hart team. Their shows at least in these first few years were the shared collaborations of a triumvirate, a fact acknowledged in the press, and—as we have seen—even on one occasion in a nom de plume. The three worked exclusively together on at least seven shows in their professional period—*Dearest Enemy*, *The Girl Friend*, *Peggy-Ann*, *A Connecticut Yankee*, *Present Arms*, *Chee-Chee*, and *America's Sweetheart*—not to mention the early works *Winkle Town* and *The Melody Man* and the screenplay for *The Hot Heiress*.

HERBERT FIELDS

Herb (Figure 4.1) seems to have been a speedy writer, and he could certainly keep up with the prodigious output of his writing colleagues while taking

Figure 4.1: Herbert Fields, cartoon by Joseph Margulies in the Jewish Tribune, *October 28, 1927.*

on further commissions such as *Hit the Deck* (1927, with Vincent Youmans) and *Fifty Million Frenchmen* (1929, with Cole Porter). Although various shows demonstrate marked differences in approach, engaging with historical themes (*Dearest Enemy*) and parody (*A Connecticut Yankee*), his typical script is characterized by a contemporary American setting and a plot revolving around new technologies, trends, or topical themes: Connecticut and the wireless (*Winkle Town*), Connecticut and the navy (*Hit the Deck*), Hawaii and the marines (*Present Arms*), Hollywood and the talkies (*America's Sweetheart*). *The Girl Friend* is no different, with its setting in Long Island, its focus on the fashionable sport of cycle racing, and its plot propelled by the relationship between the young couple Mollie and Lenny.

The Girl Friend tells the story of good-natured and clean-living Leonard Silver and his sweetheart, Mollie Farrell. He is a passionate bicycle racer, and when sports promoter Arthur Spencer visits to consider him for his squad, he is naturally delighted. Although unimpressed by Lenny's setup, with a girlfriend as his casual trainer, a bike hooked up to a butter churn, and a personal best gauged by how fast he can churn ten quarts into butter, Spencer is persuaded to try Lenny out. Once at the velodrome, Lenny makes enemies, both with rival teamsters because of his talent and with the jealous fiancé of Spencer's sister Wynn because she won't stop flirting with him. The fiancé plots to discredit Lenny by claiming he forged his references, and two shady trainers are enlisted to cause an accident. Lenny is brought in with his leg in plaster, and everyone assumes he is out of the running. But the ever-faithful Mollie is suspicious. She arranges for the cast to be removed and proves that Lenny can still walk. Lenny wins the race, with a prize fund big enough to allow him to propose to Mollie. But at the celebration party, the seductress Wynn plies Mollie with alcohol, knowing she will embarrass herself and hoping the clean-living Lenny will disapprove. When Spencer finds out he is appalled at his sister's actions. Secretly he arranges to get Lenny drunk too, and once the pair are both in the same condition, they drunkenly dance the night away as the jazz band plays and the curtain falls.

The Girl Friend relies on its two central characters to function successfully only when they have each other. Lenny is brilliant on a bike but hopeless at self-promotion and stilted socially; Mollie balances his weaknesses and complements them with her strengths, so we see in their trajectory an inevitable union, destined for success. This model would serve as a template for musical comedy pairings throughout the Golden Age (Curly and Laurey, Frank and Annie, Fred and Lilli, Sky and Sarah), and although it may be excessive to claim it as a Fields innovation, it is certainly one of the step-changes brought about by this new generation of writers. Fields creates couples whose togetherness is at the heart of the show. Even in the historical milieu of *Dearest Enemy* this is true, to the extent that the plot-turning signal sent to the rebels is an (unwitting) collaboration between the central couple Betsy and John.

As can be seen from even the brief synopsis above (which necessarily omits some of the nuances), there is a very definite plot to *The Girl Friend*, and the characters are clearly drawn. Even if some of these may be stock roles, and even if the show concludes rather weakly, it can hardly be described as plotless. Nevertheless, the main criticism of the show was that "the book, like most of them, plays but little part in the evening's doings."[14] Its "anemic plot"[15] was "the weakest part of the show," according to reviewers who judged that "Herbert Fields must do better work if he is to be mentioned with the other Fields who have helped to make American theatrical history."[16] In short, this show's "mediocrity could not very well be placed on the shoulders of Hart or Rodgers . . . , but on the book builder's, one Herbert Fields."[17]

Of course, the script handed down to us and carefully archived in the Library of Congress is the one filed originally for copyright purposes. It is this that Herbert Fields wrote and intended for production, and something close to this, it would seem, that appeared in tryouts. But with the out-of-town run reportedly lasting until one o'clock in the morning, something had to give. Between that Saturday and the Broadway opening on Wednesday, it was rewritten extensively. The first act (of three) was reduced—according to an interview in the *Sun*—from forty minutes to eight, and merged with the second.[18] This streamlined the show, but it came at a cost. "There may once have been a bigger and better book attached to 'The Girl Friend,'" wrote Gilbert Gabriel. "You can imagine it as starting off with three full sized acts and a plot which was a plot and you can also imagine what happened to act III and that much of the plot while en route from Atlntic [*sic*] City."[19] That an overlong show should be severely cut down is entirely appropriate, though the manner in which this happened reveals a great deal about the working practices of the 1920s, and particularly the status of the writers and their producer.

LEW FIELDS

Over twenty-five years on the stage with partner Joe Weber, Lew Fields (Figure 4.2) had become used to the traditions of nineteenth-century self-promotion in which acts defined their own terms. Weber and Fields's separation as a performing team in 1904 more or less coincided with the change in the industry landscape, and since Fields was used to managing his own business affairs (alongside the far more shrewd Weber), it would have seemed only natural for him to continue to play a part in the production of his theater ventures. After a brief partnership with stage director Julian Mitchell and producer Fred Hamlin, Fields signed an agreement with the Shubert brothers in 1906, staking equal claim to a business capitalized at $20,000. Fields had creative responsibility for the shows and worked to a set of parameters with which he was familiar, faring reasonably well for a number of seasons. He was almost always the star performer, and his shows were structured around his own brand of "hokum" and his familiar routines. He was flanked by a large and well-costumed supporting cast, offering audiences what they wanted: quality entertainment at an affordable price. The problem was that this sort of quality came at an increasing cost, and Fields's weakness in managing his accounts would lead to problems: an excessive costume budget of $7,000 for *About Town* (1906)[20] raised eyebrows; an excessive supporting cast for *The Summer Widowers* (1910)[21] accounted for the show's short run, claimed the press. That show came off the road, the Shuberts removed its high-salaried performers, and a leaner company was put back into action. Fields was relegated to a low-level directing position in the Shubert enterprise, respected for his artistic know-how but seen as a liability with the money. "Where the

Figure 4.2: Lew Fields as Henkel, with Sammy White in The Melody Man *(1924). Photo by White Studio © Billy Rose Theatre Collection, The New York Public Library for the Performing Arts.*

Shuberts were experts in cutting and trimming, Fields was a big spender who paid high salaries to his employees and spared no expense in giving each of his shows the best possible production value," writes Hirsch.[22] This was to be his downfall: by 1921 Fields declared himself bankrupt, and withdrew from Broadway for the best part of three years.

Always more of an artist than a producer, Fields nevertheless had high aspirations to develop musical comedy, pushing for greater integration years before that became a sort of holy grail. "'This is my principle theory of what the public wants...,' declaimed Fields in 1904, 'coherency'.... Fields wanted 'to unfold a story in a natural way... to play a character role in a bright musical play without feeling every time I walk on stage like an intruder.'"[23] This was a progressive ambition coming from a slapstick vaudevillian known for his hokum; yet torn between an artistic desire to create quality musical comedies with coherent books and the commercial necessity of hitting budget and bringing in audiences, Fields would invariably revert to type, making crude changes to institute tried and tested formulae, or bringing in crowd-pleasing interpolated song hits. In 1905 he appended a knockabout burlesque of David Belasco's *The Music Master* to the otherwise coherent *It Happened in Nordland*;[24] in 1911 he slashed Glen MacDonough's careful script to *The Hen-Pecks* with the result that "important plot-connecting information was deleted or telescoped into the barest tidbits of connecting tissue";[25] and in 1920 he replaced half the score of Rodgers and Hart's *Poor Little Ritz Girl* with a new score by Sigmund Romberg. Indeed, as daughter Dorothy reported, "he didn't want a coherent libretto or a book show. He wanted music, yes, but the rest should just be gags, blackouts, and belly laughs, whereas Herb, Dick, and Larry were obsessed with the necessity of having a strong story."[26]

That had been Rodgers and Hart's first real encounter with a producer: a frustrating and disillusioning experience but one that signaled very clearly the power balance on Broadway. Producers would veto anything to keep their budget in trim; the integrity of the product was subservient to the power of the bottom line.

THE GIRL FRIEND (1926)

It was of course a great boon to the boys to have a prominent theatrical figure close at hand, however faded he may have become by the early 1920s. What Lew Fields could offer the Rodgers, Hart, and Fields team was a Broadway "in"; what they could offer him was the energy, vigor, and contemporary insight of a younger generation. In many ways, suggest commentators, it was the work of these youngsters that gave old Lew a new lease of professional life: "In no small measure," write Fields and Fields, "Lew Fields owed his renaissance to the emergence of his son Herbert as a first-class librettist."[27]

Lew had already shown considerable interest in the young writing team, using their material in *Poor Little Ritz Girl* and more prominently *The Melody Man*. But these had been *his* vehicles, into which he had co-opted the boys as scribes. When it came to supporting work initiated by the writers, Lew was hesitant and even standoffish. He had clearly followed the antics of his own children as they toyed with theater through college: Herb had been involved with the Columbia Varsity shows; Dorothy had headlined the all-girl casts at the Benjamin School for Girls. However, he was resistant to their pursuing the theater as a profession (even though they all did): "as soon as matters with Dorothy threatened to turn even semiprofessional," writes Charlotte

Greenspan, "Lew stepped in."[28] The same was true with Herb—and it might be because he only saw Herb's involvement with the theater as amateur or casual that Lew seemed to ignore his son's early scripts. Perhaps more to the point, the material developed by Herb and his friends did not offer any roles for Lew: for all his identity as a producer, he was at heart only interested in producing work that showcased his own performance; and for all his suggestions of cohesion, Lew still saw musical comedies as vehicles for the star.

Eventually, Fields was to relax the prohibition against his children working on the stage, and as history has revealed, this was to the benefit of the Great American Songbook and the great American stage: Dorothy's prowess as a lyricist won her lasting acclaim for songs like "I Can't Give You Anything but Love" (1928) and "On the Sunny Side of the Street" (1930), and an Oscar for "The Way You Look Tonight," written with Jerome Kern for *Swing Time* (1936); Joseph went on to write the libretti for *Gentlemen Prefer Blondes* (1949) and *Flower Drum Song* (1958), among others, and won a Tony award for *Wonderful Town* (1953); and Herb would be respected right across the industry for his libretti not just with Rodgers and Hart but also Vincent Youmans (*Hit the Deck*, 1927), Cole Porter (*Fifty Million Frenchmen*, 1929), Sigmund Romberg (*Up in Central Park*, 1945) and Irving Berlin (*Annie Get Your Gun*, 1946, co-written with his sister Dorothy). In the end, Lew, Herb, Dick and Larry would become a team to be reckoned with, and by 1928 the *Morning Telegraph* even depicted them as Broadway muses, as if they were the dream team of American musical theater (see Figure 4.3). But that was yet to come.

For all that their connection with Lew Fields was a great advantage, Herb, Dick and Larry could not have picked a worse time in his career to exploit that contact. Just as they needed his help, Fields was bankrupt (1920–1923), and following this he emerged cautiously—no doubt a protective instinct brought about by a fear of taking risks. He knew his star vehicles packed with vaudeville hokum worked; coherent books (despite his confident assertions) were an unknown quantity. *Dearest Enemy*, with its historical storyline, he felt, was a dangerous risk, though he must have kicked himself when it proved tremendously successful. Similarly, he would take years to agree to producing *A Connecticut Yankee*, though in that instance he was relieved that he eventually did. But in 1926, following the success of *Dearest Enemy* and the profile of *The Garrick Gaieties*, Lew Fields decided to gamble on *The Girl Friend*; this gave him a piece he felt was youthful, exuberant, and American (Figure 4.4).

Indeed, Fields said as much in interviews, announcing that he had surrounded himself with the new generation and that this would render the new show slick and up-to-the-minute. "To prove that we are up to the minute, 'The Girl Friend' will contain both jazz and the Charleston, a jazz band and

Figure 4.3: Rodgers, Hart, Lew Fields, and Herb as the muses, cartoon in the
Morning Telegraph, *April 22, 1928.*

a satire on the popular dance," he enthused.[29] It was indeed remarkably up
to date, showing the younger generation's influence and capitalizing on new
fads that were thrilling America. The opening chorus, set on a dairy farm, has
the farmworkers listening to the latest jazz while they work:

> Out in the fields we let the radio stand.
> Plowing is grand, in time to a band.
> Now that the radio is ruling the land
> We hear the froans [*sic*] of saxophones.
> It isn't toil to till the soil.[30]

The farmworkers hardly resemble laborers, it is true, though they sometimes sing of hard work and the rural life. Instead, these kids come across as
sophomores, and much of the music during the first act resembles more the
marches of Rodgers's Columbia days than the sophisticated score of *Dearest
Enemy*. Indeed, "Goodbye, Lenny," sung as Lenny leaves for the velodrome,

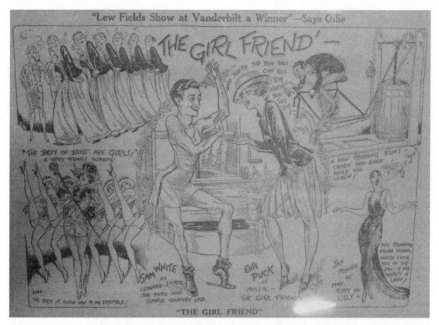

Figure 4.4: Humorous Zits *cartoon of events in* The Girl Friend *("'Lew Fields Show at Vanderbilt a Winner'—Says Ollie,"* Zits, *March 27, 1926.)*

appears little more than a cheerleading call, with confusing references to his skill at the Charleston and to Broadway:

> Oh, he's gonna win the race with the Charleston!
> He will lead the pace with the Charleston!
> And he'll get first place with the Charleston!
> And it's Hay, Hay, Hay on Broadway![31]

Still, in this show it was the song hits that counted, and most reviewers predicted these accurately to be "The Blue Room" and "The Girl Friend," the latter of which became the best-selling song in the country.[32] It "can be whistled by people who don't know even how to whistle!" wrote the *Evening Journal.* "That's what you call popular music."[33]

If this populist approach to the songs reflected Lew Fields's guidance, so too did the casting, though it had been the younger collaborators who had conceived the show as a vehicle for vaudevillian husband and wife team Sammy White and Eva Puck. They had encountered this pair working on *The Melody Man* two years earlier and had promised to write them a show. Perhaps this demonstrates just how ingrained the tendency had become to crowbar vaudeville acts into musical comedy; perhaps it just shows how much the forms had cross-fertilized. In any case, Herbert obligingly "bunched as many ancient puns and situations as his memory permitted, and mixed them with a slapstick brand of comedy that the two leads fetched with them from the two-a-day."[34] Reversing the characters of their act, White played the country hick to Puck's shrewd go-getter. In the longer (original) version of the show at least, that switch made their performance less of a "turn" than a genuine musical comedy partnership. On the other hand, with knockabout comics Jack Kogan and Water Bigelow—"laugh-getters of no mean stripe"[35]—cast as shady trainers Mike and Duffy, and contortionist Dorothy Barber as a specialty dance act, the show seemed to get its lifeblood from the two-a-day rather than the pen of the playwright.

With its Atlantic City tryouts running way over time, Lew Fields claimed a sort of droit du seigneur, dispensing with the services of director John Harwood and wading in as "Dr. Fix-It"[36] with the show remedies he knew best. As Fields and Fields report, "though John Harwood was credited with staging the book and Jack Haskell with the musical numbers, Lew Fields was *The Girl Friend*'s hands-on producer throughout the rehearsals and tryouts."[37] Reporters with access to rehearsals painted a picture of the energy and excitement of the Lew Fields rehearsal room,[38] and if nothing else, these reveal a man with unbounded energy and utter commitment. Some reports suggest the company was forced to work through the whole night that Tuesday to ready the transfer for its Vanderbilt opening, though this was not unusual for Broadway productions of the period; a similar thing would happen for the next show, *Peggy-Ann*, when the stage crew were called on to work thirty hours straight.[39] But Fields's commitment was not to the show that had been written; it was to the show that would be staged. Once the written material became embodied in performance, it effectively became the producer's to do with what he chose. What happened to the plot, as Fields and Fields suggest, is that "the burlesque tendencies of the elder Fields overran the dramatic logic preferred by Herbert, Rodgers, and Hart."[40] Although a vestige of the storyline and the integrity of the main numbers for the dramatic leads was maintained, material elsewhere seemed "shoe-horned into the text, recalling the flimsiness with which Fields and his collaborators had introduced numbers into their musical shows."[41] As the script was whittled away, what remained must have seemed a ragtag concoction of slapstick, stunts, and song hits: "a curious spectacle of two schools of musical comedy at war in a single production."[42]

With all the compromises of this collaboration, it is difficult to inspect Rodgers and Hart's material in the same way as *Dearest Enemy*. In that show, the writing was coherent, with a score that showed consistency and character-based logic. That model would be the direction in which Rodgers, Hart, and Fields would travel as their work became better respected and their methods more independent. However, *Dearest Enemy* was effectively a vanity project, funded by personal contacts and "produced" by Helen Ford's husband George; to get a step up, Rodgers, Hart, and Fields needed to court a real producer. Today we might talk in terms of "selling out"—sacrificing artistic integrity to benefit from greater profile or success. Even if they didn't exactly do that, Fields and Fields at least suggest that with *The Girl Friend*, the writing team "retreated from the aesthetic ambitions of *Dearest Enemy*" in order "to meet Pop Fields halfway."[43]

Hence the largely uninspiring score that veers erratically between musical styles. It is brought together in a kind of coherence, it is fair to say, but this is simply by repeating material from "The Blue Room" and "The Girl Friend" which therefore inevitably become its "take home tunes." These, to be sure, are wonderfully written songs and have stood the test of time. Moreover, they do represent a musical palette of a sort for Mollie and Lenny's relationship: both songs use similar repeated and extended motifs in a syncopated style, and it is not unreasonable to suggest that they are in a sense variations on a theme. In this emphatically jazzy material, Mollie and Lenny are distinct from the crowd, who tend to sing in Sousa-like marches ("Town Hall Tonight") or sophomoric chants ("Goodbye, Lenny"). To an extent, then, we can see the dramaturgically integrated skills of the writing team at play. However, the incongruities in the rest of the score are legion. The "Creole Crooning Song," Rubin suggests, capitalizes on a resurgence of the "coon" songs being made popular at the time through the hits of Al Jolson;[44] "I'd Like to Take You Home" revives material from a round-the-world style revue number from the previous year that they contributed to *Bad Habits of 1925*; and the "show-stopper"[45] "What Is It?" had all the men cavorting in a drag routine reminiscent of the Columbia Pony Ballet. Rodgers's music is generally undistinguished (with a "made to order ring to it," according to the *Evening Post*),[46] though it went down reasonably well with reviewers. All in all, though, reviews were lukewarm: "I've known Dick Rodgers and Larry Hart for quite some time now and they've never let me down yet," wrote one report, hedging its bets, "so why should you think they start doing it with 'The Girl Friend'?"

Variety at least was quite surprised the show survived the summer,[47] reporting average weekly grosses of around $11,000—"Okay for house but not profitable for show."[48] By May 26, the cast's salaries had been cut and "summer arrangements" put into action to keep the show afloat.[49] Nevertheless, it did cling on for an impressive 301 performances; what's more, it also transferred to London for an astonishing 421 performances: not bad for a mediocre hotch-potch, though—significantly—the London show was substantially changed. When it opened at the Lyceum Theatre on September 8, 1927, *The Girl Friend* had a script by Philip Bartholomae and Otto Harbach, and music and lyrics by Con Conrad and Gus Kahn. This was not *The Girl Friend*, though it bore the name; this was *Kitty's Kisses*—a modest hit from lesser-known writers riding on the success of the popular Rodgers and Hart song. That and just three other songs was the extent of their input; Herbert Fields' input was nowhere to be seen.

5

A LONDON ODYSSEY

• • •

LIDO LADY (1926), *ONE DAM THING AFTER ANOTHER* (1927), *EVER GREEN* (1930)

The 1926–27 season was a hectic time for the "busy little bees of Broadway."[1] They had undoubtedly made their mark, but securing the commitment of the money men for a new venture was a different matter. Even Lew Fields wouldn't take a gamble with the idea of revisiting *A Danish Yankee*, which they were keen to revive. The main prospect for Rodgers and Hart presented itself in a trip across the Atlantic. They were intrigued, excited—and international.

The opportunity came as a commission. Following their own success on the British stage, husband and wife team Jack Hulbert and Cicely Courtneidge had brought their successful revue *By the Way* to New York. While there, they had been struck by the energy and vigor of American shows, so different from the typical fare of the respected but staid West End. Hulbert was a dancer, and for him the infectious excitement of jazz dance was "quite staggering." In a breathless autobiography, he recalls his excitement:

> There was so much I had to learn to catch up. Several shows I saw over and over again, trying to absorb some of the more effective steps. I began to form new routines for future chorus work and got steps together for a routine of my own. Tap Charleston was the vogue. I had to keep practising what I had collected.[2]

Hulbert determined to take back to London this exciting American energy; but more than simply learning and performing American dances, he was keen to recruit genuine American talent, and he consulted Louis Dreyfus about suitable collaborators. Louis and his brother Max were the titans of Tin Pan Alley music publishing company T. B. Harms, and Rodgers had already had material rejected by each of them: Louis had heard his songs in 1920 and had told the precocious boy, "keep going to High School and come back some other time";[3] two years later, it was Max who heard the score of *Winkle Town* before announcing "there's nothing of value here."[4] Though they had "discovered" Jerome Kern, and though they had Victor Herbert, George Gershwin, and Vincent Youmans on their books, the Dreyfus brothers were lukewarm about Rodgers and Hart, at least until the successful run of *Dearest Enemy* made them difficult to ignore. Now, they were keen, and they recommended the boys to Hulbert. Even so, the British producer considered the team with care: their American Revolutionary War storyline in *Dearest Enemy* might be too American for an English audience, and bicycle races were surely a bit of a fad. Still, Hulbert fell for "Here in My Arms," so Dick and Larry were invited to contribute a score to his new project, *Dancing Time*. The book was to be written by Guy Bolton, and the show was due to open in London's Gaiety Theatre by the end of the year. Rodgers and Hart were thrilled. Immediately after Dick served as best man for his brother's wedding on June 8, he and Larry took a break to Europe to research the Lido in Venice, to connect with Morty and his new wife, Ethel, on honeymoon, and to visit Paris, which had always been an aspiration.

At this time, it was certainly the sensational American productions that were making their mark in London: Fred and Adele Astaire, "London favourites,"[5] were performing in the Gershwins' *Lady Be Good* at the Empire; it played for 326 performances and a first night audience of more than 4,000 people had had to be turned away.[6] The Gershwins' next show, *Tip-Toes*, opened on August 31, and that too played until the end of the year. Kern and Hammerstein's *Sunny* opened on October 7 at the Hippodrome where it stayed for over a year; other shows by Romberg (*The Student Prince*), Youmans (*Wildflower*), and De Sylva (*Queen High*) had enjoyed modest recent runs. So to bring American writers in to invest British shows with that energy and vigor seems a shrewd move on the part of Hulbert.

It didn't sit well with the British press though: "I suppose [the producers] couldn't find any English lyrists and composers! Well, well!," crowed the *Referee*;[7] "Many will regret that two of the authors and the writers of the songs came from America, but you must be in the fashion, I suppose," moaned the *Daily Express*;[8] the *Illustrated Sporting and Dramatic News* found the show "not *too* awful ... despite the fact that three American gentlemen wrote the original book."[9] Referring to the new Tin Pan Alley songs as "ridiculously incongruous Trans-Atlantic jingles"—incongruous because the show is set in Venice and cast with quintessentially English characters—the critic continued:

[*Lido Lady*] has had its not specially interesting book revised by Ronald Jeans from that of a presumably American triumvirate. Almost as banal and commonplace are the lyrics (very poor stuff some of them), by Lorenz Hart, and there is a good deal of familiarly sounding, if tuneful, engaging and not aggressively ragtimish music by Richard Rodgers and others.[10]

The experience was not a happy one, according to Rodgers's testimony in *Musical Stages*. He bristles at the indifferent reception they received from their hosts, though it is perhaps the creative process that most bruised their first London encounter. By the time the boys arrived in London for rehearsals in late summer, they found an already finished book which Bolton had put together over the summer while also working on *The Ramblers* and *Oh, Kay!* "Making songs fit into an already written script…was certainly less stimulating than the give-and-take sessions we were accustomed to with our old librettist buddy Herb Fields,"[11] Rodgers writes. Though the boys had jumped at the chance to work in England, they were really no more than hired guns.

In fact, Hulbert's enthusiasm to secure top American writers proved something of a gimmick: far from collaborating with Rodgers and Hart to make *Lido Lady* coherent, their librettist didn't even meet them during the project. Bolton's commitments meant he did not arrive in England until *Dancing Time* had changed its name to *Lido Lady*, been on a pre–West End tour of the provinces for several weeks, and had its first act extensively rewritten by English playwright Ronald Jeans.

LIDO LADY (1926)

The story is set in Venice, at a party thrown by rich businessman Rufus Blake. Blake's daughter Fay (Phyllis Dare) is in love with "good-for-nothing scatter-brained idiot, Harry Bassett"[12] (Jack Hulbert), and Blake is keen to prevent their impending engagement. Meanwhile, Blake's new sporting product, a synthetic tennis ball, is keenly sought by criminals masquerading as South American Tennis Champion Luis Valeze and his sister Rita. As the criminals plot to steal the formula for the miracle tennis ball, Blake forbids his daughter's engagement until Harry can prove his sporting excellence in competition. Harry arranges a rigged fight with middleweight boxing champ Spencer Weldon in exchange for tips on how to woo Harry's cousin Peggy, a ludicrously exaggerated film star played by Cicely Courtneidge. The plan goes wrong and Harry gets knocked out by Weldon. Undeterred and desperate to win Fay's hand, Harry arranges another sporting contest, this time a tennis match against Valeze. But Valeze and Rita—really conman Steve and his girlfriend Letty—steal the tennis ball formula and elope, causing the whole gathering to decamp to the cruise liner *Futuria* on which they are making their getaway. The stage of the *Futuria* provides a perfect location for a finale of song and dance, and in an eleventh-hour mixup, somehow the formula is planted on the innocent, blundering American Bill Harker and he gets locked in the brig. As dusk falls and everyone gets ready for the final concert, a gust of wind miraculously blows a copy of the paper with the formula into Harry's hand from out of Valeze's cabin window. The imposter Valeze is arrested, and Harry and Fay united. The final scene plays out as a stylized dance by Harry, and in the re-written version he pledges to win that sporting competition after all (and the love of his sweetheart) in an on-deck tap-dancing contest.

It's a convoluted scenario, particularly complex in the original draft libretto. In its redraft (introduced in Liverpool during the first week of November), the first act is tightened up considerably, and a more conventional exposition established in which the smitten Harry chases the disinterested Fay, eventually winning her affection. This makes the storyline easier to follow and creates three pairs of lovers: Harry and Fay (the ingénues), Spencer and Peggy (the slapstick comedians), and Bill and Peaches (the foils). The heist of the miracle tennis ball formula by the fourth couple (Valeze and Rita aka Steve and Letty) is really only a narrative driver against which the trajectories of the three relationships can be spun out.

Still, reviews generally dismiss the plot, which according to the *Telegraph*, was "so negligible that one almost marvelled at the discovery that no fewer than three authors were concerned in the writing of the book."[13] Rodgers was also dismissive about the libretto, which he later saw as "some fluff about a flapper tennis champ on the Lido."[14] On the other hand, despite their apparently hostile remarks, and revealing generally superficial expectations of musical comedy, most reviewers were in the end positive about the "compact, crisp, and well finished"[15] show,[16] and applauded in particular the performances of Hulbert (Harry), Dare (Fay), and Courtneidge (Peggy). Courtneidge's character was clearly written with her in mind, and in this respect the show was a star vehicle for her "characteristic manner."[17] Her character pastiches the shameless self-promotion of film stars (at that stage, of course, still silent icons); Peggy Bassett is desperate to be recognized as a Hollywood star, though "she foozles one publicity stunt after another,"[18] and each increasingly ludicrous promotional ruse goes wrong. Courtneidge is supported by comedy sidekicks Billy Arlington (Bill Harker) and Harold French (Spencer Weldon); the humor is both slapstick and verbal, offering a perfect stage for her knockabout antics and giving Lorenz Hart a wonderful palette for his characteristically sharp lyrics.

In the song "Camera Shoot," for example (which was cut from the show and later recycled in *She's My Baby*), Peggy is acerbic about typical celluloid heroines.

PEGGY: She's chaste
  And she's strait-laced [*sic*], –
  I mean her waist.
  No man could kiss her in
  Her tears of glycerine,
  When she gets saccharine
  You'd like to smack her in
  The bean;
  But she's a queen
  Upon the screen.[19]

This is a gratuitous sequence, no more than an excuse for a comedy routine. But its lyrics are vintage Hart: triple rhymes ("chaste-laced-waist"; "bean-queen-screen") are characteristic of his "pyrotechnics in the 1920s,"[20] and quick-fire, short rhyming phrases amplify the comedy of a number that is entirely a divertissement from the action.

Elsewhere, in "I Want a Man" (a number also cut before the opening, later to appear in *America's Sweetheart*), the spiky tone of Hart's lyrics inflects the badinage between fat businessman Bill Harker and dizzy blonde Peaches. This show appeared just a year after Anita Loos's *Gentlemen Prefer Blondes* was first published (1925), and this relationship shows Hart characterizing contemporary social stereotypes.

PEACHES: Your features make the weather
  Get cloudy, dark and rainy;
  In sex-appeal you're lower than Lon Chaney.
  And your table manners are hardly polite,
  You prove by each bite
  That Darwin was right.[21]

The contemporary references in these lyrics—Darwinism surely beyond the intellectual understanding of a character such as Peaches—allow Hart to make topical jokes that still remain amusing. Perhaps in empathy with the butt of this hostile wisecrack, Hart allows Bill to retaliate with an equally acerbic jibe:

BILL: Life on a desert island with you would be quaint.
  You'd have no complaint –
  I'd act like a saint.[22]

While in London, the boys were put up at the Savoy Hotel, which would have satisfied their aspirations to feel a part of the musical stage. This was the hotel built by Sir Richard D'Oyly Carte alongside the Savoy Theatre, home of the Gilbert and Sullivan operettas. On the other hand, if they expected superior treatment, Rodgers and Hart would have been disappointed. "Instead of the large rooms with a sweeping view of the Thames that we had been promised, we had to be content with two small dark rooms with no view at all."[23] Still, the lifestyle at the hotel might have made up for that: the new Pinafore Room had just opened with its impressively designed wooden paneling by Basil Ionides; the resident Savoy Orpheans were considered the best dance band in Europe (very soon they would be recording hits from *Lido Lady*); only a few months beforehand it had hosted the London premiere of Gershwin's "Rhapsody in Blue"; and every afternoon tea was offered in a ritual that has now become celebrated around the world. The opportunity for Rodgers and Hart to step outside their habitual milieu to experience a strikingly different culture in London served as a magnifying prism for their thoughts.

> "It occurred to us," Larry wrote, "that we might not be able to reach the British audience with no more than rudimentary knowledge of what that audience cared to see."[24]

With this cultural naivety troubling them, the writers made sure that they immersed themselves in English culture, the better to represent people and places referred to in the script. And for the thoughtful and self-critical Hart in particular, this was important research. He didn't want to fall into the same trap that English writers fell into when trying to emulate American idioms:

> Their music is too feathery. The English composer strives to imitate American jazz, and because his feet do not touch American soil, he falls just short. Whether we live in the North or the South, [African American] music has influenced us. Lacking that influence, the English musical writer can only echo an echo.[25]

So a whistle-stop schooling in English idiolect, geographical resonances, and cultural pastimes is evidenced in *Lido Lady*. For example, the opening number extols the British passion for tea, leaning on Gilbert and Sullivan in suggesting that such a predilection might have supported the naval might of the Empire:

> Tea has made them hear us,
> Cheer us, fear us on the sea.
> Tea has always paid us,
> Made us brawny, brave and free.[26]

Similarly, "A Cup of Tea" recalls the Finale to Act One of *The Sorcerer*, "Now to the Banquet We Press." Here, Sullivan's music is a rousing pastiche of Rossini, pitched against the mundane incongruity of Gilbert's lyrics to ridiculous comic effect.

CHORUS: The eggs and the ham
And the strawberry jam,
And the rollicking bun!
The rollicking bun
And the gay Sally Lunn
And the strawberry jam.
WOMEN: Jam!
MEN: Bun!
WOMEN: Jam!
MEN: Bun!
CHORUS: Oh! The strawberry, strawberry jam!
WOMEN: Bun!
MEN: Jam!
WOMEN: Bun!
MEN: Jam!
CHORUS: Oh! The rollicking, rollicking bun![27]

The pastiche in both examples certainly mocks Britishness, though it is fair to say that Gilbert and Sullivan's innate understanding of British cultural codes (in the characters, language, and musical references) allows a more sophisticated effect than Rodgers and Hart's second-hand understanding. Hart has been self-effacing on this point, attempting, as Nolan has observed, to use English phrases such as "What, ho?" and—to his own chagrin—"You can say what / You may, what / Care I? / Eh, what?," which Hart suggests will "probably be intelligible only to someone who lives within ten miles of Soho."[28] Clumsy they may be, though these should be considered alongside the many hundreds of other lyrics which reveal Hart's credibility as a lyric-writer. Besides, the first example criticized belongs to "Morning Is Midnight," another song cut prior to the West End opening, and the second lyric appears in neither draft script so it was either rejected early in the writing process or never seriously considered as a lyric. Moreover, it is also worth considering that stereotypes and language just as caricatured and ridiculous were typical of English-born dramatists such as P. G. Wodehouse, Guy Bolton, or Nöel Coward; indeed, they very much fit into the formal presentational manner and class values of theatrical character tropes on the British stage of the time.

Nevertheless, Hart's foray into English idioms is rather superficial, and reminiscent of Rodgers's later though better documented approach to different cultures in *The King and I* and *Flower Drum Song*, a sort of "if it sounds about right to the untrained ear, it's good enough for me."[29] We can be critical of this approach, accusing it of an ignorant, orientalist cultural appropriation, as does Kenneth Tynan in his "more than a smidgen of pidgin" review of *Flower Drum Song*;[30] on the other hand, we can also interpret this as an impressionist or stylistic technique of musical theater, one of many simplified articulations of artifice in which theater trades in preference to diligent verisimilitude. Perhaps more problematic than this flirtation with British cultural tropes is the more pervasive orientalist fascination with exotic cultures manifested in the lengthy "Queen of Sheba Pageant" during the second act (much of which had also featured just as incongruously in *The Girl Friend*). This spectacular, noted in particular for its costumes, stages a quasi-Egyptian ensemble scene, fronted by Cicely Courtneidge. Its resonances are nothing if not confused, and the repeated lyric reference to "Mammy" in the songs conflates an orientalist fervor for the exotic with the (now dated) Americanized minstrelsy of the New York stage.[31]

> SHEBA: There's a word of just five letters starts with M and ends with Y
> Mammy! Mammy!
> A word of sixteen letters starts with X and ends with I
> Mammy! Mammy!
> . . .
> Take me to your arms I mean
> Mammy, Mammy, here's your queen!
> . . .
> There are red, red roses hanging round the door
> Little Shebaninnies playing on the floor.
> When I get way down South
> I'm gonna kiss the ground
> 'Cause my heart is Sheba-bound![32]

The linguistic reference to "Little Shebaninnies," the call-and-response structure of the chorus, the theme of being called by one's home, and the reference to "way down South" are all idiomatic of the minstrel show. Later on, in the Act Two Finale, such references become even more pronounced, though in pastiching this trope of the American musical in his lyrics, Hart creates more of a hollow simulacrum than anything typical. As well as the Egyptian, Lebanese, African American, and Jewish eccentricities of the song itself, it is sung by a quintessential English character actress playing a Hollywood film star on the Venetian Lido.

> PEGGY: We're going way down South to the land of Sheba.
> Back to Uncle Isaac and our dear Aunt Reba.

Hear that great big choo-choo with the whistle blowing
It knows we're going to-day! (Choo-Choo!)
The Pullman Porters wait and their faces shine up;
We'll be at the station a dusky line-up.
We'll get off at Sheba with some prancing steps.
He'll come back to London with some dancing steps.[33]

Lido Lady is typical of other shows of the period in its use of the primary song forms we have seen Graham Wood analyze in Dearest Enemy. The main comedy number for the stars of the show, Courtneidge and Hulbert, is the song "Try Again To-morrow," whose parallel period (ABAC) chorus is based around a pentatonic motif. The parallel period form is also used for "Atlantic Blues," a wistful lament for home that Phyllis Dare sings as part of the Act Three concert.[34] The A section of this chorus is also restricted to a pentatonic scale and makes use of a repeated rocking melody over both minor third and major second intervals. This song's chorus begins plaintively with a subdominant seventh chord, its melody falling from the mediant to the submediant, which amplifies the idea of pining for home. In these respects, Rodgers uses the music dramatically to reflect the subject of the lyrics and the emotions of the character, and this song fits well within the dramatic mood, in which Fay is deep in thought in the moonlight on deck. Indeed, throughout this third act the different narrative elements are played out in different dramatic settings: couples (Fay and Harry, Peggy and Spencer) come together in the romantic space of the deck, while the chase narrative is played out as a farce using the corridors and many cabin doors of the interior.

On the other hand, the score is not a coherent musical dramatization of characters or their expression, as Dearest Enemy's is. Although Rodgers and Hart reprise the interpolated "Here in My Arms" a number of times and use it as the love theme between Harry and Fay, and although it shares melodic and harmonic features with other songs in the score (such as a melodic arc through doh-lah-soh-doh; see Figure 5.1),[35] it would be stretching credibility to say that this song is fundamental to the dramatic cohesiveness of the show.

Rodgers and Hart elsewhere employ the familiar ensemble structure that Wood recognizes from Gilbert and Sullivan:[36] the finales of both Acts One and Two (the show is in three acts) use this, before incorporating short reprises of some of the featured songs of the act. Several other ensemble numbers throughout the score (including some, like "Chuck It," another song excised but used very shortly afterward in Peggy-Ann) make similar use of the chorus to accentuate the contributions of the soloists.

As is clear, the influence of American jazz is treated with considerable suspicion by the British press. The concern is presumably not only about the

"Here in my Arms"

I know a mer-ry place far from in-tru-sion.

Here in your arms it's a-dor-a-ble, It's de-plor a-ble that you were nev-er there.

"Try Again To-morrow" (transposed)

Try a-gain to-mor-row, Where there's a will, there's a way.

Figure 5.1: Recurring melodic features of the Lido Lady score.
Reprinted by Permission of Hal Leonard Corporation

music but also about the lifestyle it evokes, the tastes that consume it, and, one suspects, a protectivist alarm that traditional English values might be eroded. This is astonishing given the rapid acceptance of American musical idioms in British culture throughout the rest of the century, and the attitude of the press seems somewhat at odds with the tastes of the British public, for whom Hulbert's appropriation of American talent was intended. Rodgers walks a fine line, though, and ultimately his music wins favor because of its discreet use of a jazz inflection. The attitudes of the newspapers toward his music offer a consistent refrain: in 1926, it is considered "not aggressively ragtimish";[37] the following year, One Dam Thing after Another "is not over-burdened by jazz";[38] and in 1930's Ever Green, the music is "mercifully discreet, far from the all-too-violent vagaries of jazz; here and there melodious, always joyous, English music too, with a little air of raciness."[39]

Both audiences and critics, it seems, were astutely sensitive to the different styles, idioms, and performance energies of the different cultures, and there is clearly something about American music that was notably different from English music. Some of the pejorative language in these newspaper comments undoubtedly veils racist dismissals of black influence on American music in general, though black American performers had toured England regularly during the teens to great acclaim; some of the hostility may be more wrapped up in the high versus low discourse that clung to popular music and especially that stemming from America.[40] Indeed, a lively debate in the music press, variously championing or vilifying the "new" American music, accompanied the encounter of the British public with jazz throughout this period. Of course, Rodgers and Hart had been brought over specifically because they were American, so their agenda was to write songs that were American-sounding to the British audience. Whether this made them artificially exaggerate American traits, or conversely, whether it made them dilute American sounds to mollify the English taste, is an interesting question. Against a backdrop of Kern and Gershwin we can reason that London audiences had already been acclimatized to an American sound, and the public was calling for it.

Since Gershwin was at this time dominating Broadway and the West End, there is perhaps no surprise that Rodgers's score for *Lido Lady* borrows from Gershwin's popular hits of the day. George and Ira had traveled to London two years previously to write *Primrose* (1924), a self-consciously English show that would serve as a reference point for Rodgers and Hart in exploring English idioms. *Lido Lady*'s "A Tiny Little Flat in Soho" borrows unashamedly in both lyrical and musical style—not to mention theme—from "I'll Have a House in Berkeley Square" (see Figure 5.2);[41] "Try Again To-morrow" uses a motif in its title melody that is undoubtedly responding to Gershwin's "Fascinating Rhythm"—characteristically softened into a compound feel rather than heavily syncopated as it is in the original (Figure 5.3). By the same token, Gershwin had rewritten his score for *Lady, Be Good!* to include the new song "I'd Rather Charleston" for the London opening, a song that is so similar to the contemporaneous title song of Rodgers and Hart's *The Girl Friend* that they could almost be variations on a theme (Figure 5.4).[42]

"I'll Have a House in Berkeley Square" ("Berkeley Square and Kew") (transposed)

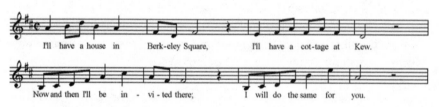

"A Tiny Flat in Soho" ("A Tiny Flat Near Soho Square") (transposed)

Figure 5.2: Motivic connections between Rodgers' "A Tiny Little Flat in Soho"
and Gershwin's "I'll Have a House in Berkeley Square."
Reprinted by Permission of Hal Leonard Corporation

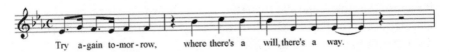

"Try Again To-morrow"

Try a-gain to-mor-row, where there's a will, there's a way.

"Fascinatin' Rhythm"

Fas-cin-a-ting rhy-thm, you got me on the go; fas-cin-

a-ting rhy-thm, I'm all a-qui-ver.

Figure 5.3: Motivic connections between Rodgers' "Try Again To-morrow"
and Gershwin's "Fascinating Rhythm."
Reprinted by Permission of Hal Leonard Corporation

"The Girl Friend" (transposed)

...her beau-ty's il-le-gal, she's the girl friend!

"I'd Rather Charleston"

Take a les-son from me. I'd ra-ther Charles-ton!

Figure 5.4: Motivic connections between Rodgers' "The Girl Friend" and
Gershwin's "I'd Rather Charleston."
Reprinted by Permission of Hal Leonard Corporation

There was clearly a vogue—as Hulbert had anticipated—for the Charleston. The new dance step had been introduced to the United Kingdom in the summer of 1925, and popular press reports made a great deal of its difficult rhythms:

It is not the steps, but the rhythm, that is going to make the new dance difficult. The beat is on the first and third note, and it makes an ordinary fox-trot seem quite dull by comparison, it is so sprightly and vivacious.[43]

Indeed, so difficult was the syncopation of the new dance that for some time it seemed that the Tango and then the Paso Doble would win favor as the popular dances of the day. By October the *Daily Mirror* declared the Charleston dead thanks to the spread of "Charlestonitis" around the dance-floors:

> In time our leg muscles [will] thicken and grow knotted, and our calves bulge and assume the proportions of a Russian dancer's... [D]ancing on one's toes is fatal, and causes that leg thickness.[44]

A good deal of dismissive commentary in the society pages—not least the scornful posturing of the *Daily Mirror*—accused the Charleston of being first improper and then dangerous, and roundly condemned it for its "vulgar nigger movements."[45] Elsewhere this scathing racism is toned down, though still latent in the responses of the establishment to the popular craze that continued to escalate:

> I was amused at the semi-savage contortions of the dancers, only to learn to my dismay that it was the Charleston, which, it seems, we poor creatures dare not ignore if we are to consider ourselves fashionable. My partner observed that some of the nearly-shaved Eton crops looked positively cannibal, and seemed only to need a gold ring through the nose. *What* a criticism of "we Moderns!"[46]

As we shall see, this comment could serve as a blueprint for the sketch "Progress" in *One Dam Thing after Another*.

The jibes at ragtime and jazz in reviews in this sense reveal some hostility—however veiled—toward the inflections of black influence. England had not had the same experiences or cultural tensions as America over the presence or treatment of the black population, though the country was only beginning to emerge from the pall of its Empire-building crusades, and attitudes toward race were undeniably problematic. Almost a century later, the rhythms and cadences of American music have become so ubiquitous that it is difficult to see how basic jazz features of these catchy dance tunes (syncopated rhythms and pentatonic melodies) can have been so startling to British ears. Still, the various comments from reviewers flag up the differing expectations of English and American entertainment around this time, highlighted in a distinction noted by the *Daily Mail*, which saw in the music "a compromise between the jazzing and the old-time flowing melody."[47]

The syncopations and opportunities for dance are clearly a prominent feature of what is seen as American in this "latest American style";[48] equally significant, however, is the more casual vocal style typical in performance. The show's main hit, "Here in My Arms," was recycled from *Dearest Enemy* (and subsequently, no fewer than eleven of the songs from *Lido Lady* would find themselves cropping up in future Rodgers and Hart shows). However, while the song was accepted in that incarnation by American audiences without any real criticism, its reception by English audiences (or at least critics) was more hostile. One reason for this was the way in which the producers exploited new technologies in order to commodify the song as a hit:

> "Here in My Arms" was "song-plugged" as the tune of the show, and even when you leave the auditorium for the foyer, or the bar, it follows you, because microphones carry all over the house the sound of the orchestra still playing. This is a new idea—from America, where they hate quiet.[49]

The *Sunday Pictorial* is even more critical of this practice:

> There is no escaping the Two Big Tunes, even in the intervals, for if you wander out into the foyers and the bars, there, lying in wait, are musical instruments, still yawching into your ears the songs you have heard thirty times already. At the end of the evening you are so accustomed to them that they seem quite old-fashioned.[50]

Several reviewers bemoan the incessant repetition of the main melody:[51] finally, the *Sunday News* quips about music that is elsewhere considered rather "haunting":[52] "'Didn't it haunt you?' somebody asked. 'Hardly that,' I said, 'it *hunted* me.'"[53]

The other reason that "Here in My Arms" receives criticism is because of its lyrics, and particularly the way they prove problematic to sing. The *Sunday Times* voices a sentiment also expressed in the *Sunday Express* and the *Queen* magazine:[54]

> In plain English, Miss Dare is jolly good. But I think she has some right of quarrel with a lyrist who should commit her to such English as "Here in my arms it's adorabull, It's deplorabull that you were never there." ... The melodic accent falling on the last syllable of these dreadful words, the singer has to take the choice of pronouncing them properly and ineffectively or effectively and ridiculously.[55]

This incongruity between the popular vernacular of the (American) song and the formal style of the (English) voice singing it can be heard on the British Columbia recording. The lyric, created by a New Yorker for an American voice to sing and American ears to hear, emphasizes the different pronunciations of New York American and received pronunciation (RP)—particularly in the tessitura of the early twentieth-century English soprano. Short vowels such as the schwa sound in "ble" are placed farther back in the mouth in a New York accent and are often weighted more than in RP, particularly when followed by the heavier "l" of the American idiolect; thus it would make sense for Rodgers and Hart to provide a reasonably weighted note for this syllable, and Phyllis Dare's vocal tuition would have encouraged her to emphasize the syllable in order to allow the resonance of the note to carry. However, this would conflict with her habituated pronunciation of the word (adorable), whose phonetic spelling in RP (/əˈdɔː.rə.bl̩/) indicates no vowel at all in the final syllable's pronunciation (/bl/).[56]

These cultural differences in performance style, audience reception, and popular expectations reveal a fascinating performative dimension to the trade between American and English cultural products, and perhaps explain why contemporary British performers often affect an American accent when they sing "American" (popular) song. If *Lido Lady* is Hulbert and Murray's attempt to offer American culture to London audiences, it is an interesting potpourri of resonances. Perhaps predictably, and despite British success, this show was not taken back across the Atlantic, and thus it is perhaps more typically English than any of the English realized. Certainly, Rodgers and Hart remained unimpressed, and their culturally unfamiliar experiences also extended to the processes of theatermaking. They were struck by the lack of rehearsals, which were "quite the most leisurely things in the world," according to Hart.[57] Indeed, it is unclear when the company actually rehearsed: the stars and producer of the show were taken up with continuing performances of *By the Way* until September 18 (*Lido Lady* opened in Bradford on October 4). It is hardly surprising that the *Daily Mail* reviewer later considered the show "scarcely...rehearsed at all," or that during opening week, according to his account, "Mr. Jack Hulbert was rehearsing some of his dances at five o'clock on Monday morning; and Miss Cicely Courtneidge was found asleep in her dressing-room by the theater fireman about 6 a.m., after the rest of the company had gone!"[58] English attitudes were indeed very different from American ones, and Rodgers and Hart left the country with some disgust on September 6. "I thanked them heartily for their excellent contributions to *Lido Lady*, expressing the genuine pleasure I had had in working with two such amiable chaps and wished them the best of luck when they got back to America," reports the still-breathless Hulbert.[59] "We didn't give a damn whether we ever saw *Lido Lady*," was Rodgers's unhappy retort.[60]

Interestingly, this Anglo-American tension has continued to dog the narrative of Rodgers and Hart in contemporary historiography. Frederick Nolan's account of this show contradicts press reports of the time. Jack Hulbert, he suggests, was "a so-so actor whose dancing would never give Astaire any sleepless nights,"[61] while Phyllis Dare (playing ingénue Fay) was "considerably longer in the tooth than [Rodgers and Hart] had been led to believe."[62] Yet British reviewers explicitly single out both the dancing of Jack Hulbert ("The Astaire…of England," according to the *Evening Standard*)[63] and the juvenile charm of the leading lady (who is "extremely attractive"[64] according to the *Star*, and whose "all-pervasive charm," according to the *Observer*, makes her "still without a rival as a musical comedy heroine")[65] Nolan's observations are an attempt to undermine the value of this show in relation to other Rodgers and Hart shows; this serves his narrative and is something he continues to do in reference to the other English shows, *One Dam Thing after Another* and *Ever Green*. Yet all three of these shows were perfectly successful, with runs of 259, 237, and 254 performances, respectively (compared to *Dearest Enemy*'s 286 and *The Girlfriend*'s 301 New York performances).

Indeed, Hulbert's ability both as a dancer and choreographer were highly commended by the *Daily Mirror* following the Professional Charleston competition at the Charleston Ball in London in December, an event that indicates the continuing vogue for American dancing and that offered a perfect opportunity to promote *Lido Lady* (with a bit of one-upmanship over *Lady, Be Good!* and the celebrated Astaires, one suspects). Hulbert's principal dancers Billy Shaw and Dave Fitzgibbon won first and second prize, while the Lido Lady Eight, a group he trained, won the Stage Troupe Championship. The *Daily Mirror* concludes, "Hulbert is not only a great dancer himself, but possesses the priceless gift of making brilliant dancers of others."[66] In short, there is little evidence to support Nolan's critique of *Lido Lady*, and this throws new light on its merit and its place in the Rodgers and Hart narrative. Its marginalization, one suspects, may well be a symptom of its Englishness, or more likely the fact that, like the other English shows, it never enjoyed a production on American soil.

Rodgers and Hart were less than impressed with their experiences on *Lido Lady*, so it was with some consternation that they returned to England in January following reports of its popularity. Aside from catching up with the run of this show, they were also keen to nurture interest in *Peggy-Ann* from Lee Ephraim and Jack Buchanan, and in *The Girl Friend* from Herbert Clayton and Jack Waller. Both productions would go ahead, though in heavily revised versions. To their surprise, *Lido Lady* was proving to be a bigger success than anyone could have guessed; central to that were the idiosyncratic performances of the charismatic Courtneidge, Hulbert, and Dare. A fluffy tale about Brits on the continent, it turned out, was exactly what audiences wanted.

ONE DAM THING AFTER ANOTHER (1927)

If their London trip the previous year had been something of a disappointment, it is perhaps because it paled in comparison to the rest of their travels.

Dick and Larry were making the most of their glamorous new lifestyle, finding in Europe a playground for the rich and famous. In Venice they hooked up with Dick's brother and his wife, Morty and Ethel, but met by chance their acquaintance Noël Coward and his host, Cole Porter. Rodgers waxes about that encounter, at which the three maestros traded songs long into the night. "Though I was unaccustomed to such glittering grandeur, Noël and the Porters turned the occasion into one of the warmest, most relaxed and happiest evenings of my life."[67] Rodgers clearly thrived on company and attention, without which he quickly reached his boredom threshhold—Paris some days later "was a disappointment." "We had no friends there and had to be content with the usual Eiffel Tower—Arc de Triomphe—Louvre—Sacré Coeur sightseeing round."[68] Likewise in London, "we didn't know a soul there, but apparently [our hosts] couldn't have cared less.... We had little more to do than write our songs and take in the tourist attractions."[69]

Their return in January—though ostensibly to review *Lido Lady*—was an excuse to continue this whirlwind tour of Europe. They sailed on the *Aquitania* on January 14, arriving in London on January 21, where this time they stayed at a privately rented residence. But three weeks later, by February 13, they were in Paris—about ten days later than expected thanks to business discussions. They left for Cannes by car on February 22, arriving a week later and writing March 1 from Le Grand Hotel, then via Vienna en route to Budapest, from where they wrote on March 7. The next day they took a train to Berlin, before returning to London by March 15 for rehearsals. It wasn't long before they were back in Europe again, though: the high time continued in Paris for five days in April, where they discussed orchestrations with Robert Russell Bennett; and they still found time to visit Budapest again in May before the opening of their next show on May 20. On the Continent, they were able to witness the popularity of Rodgers and Hart all over Europe: they had discussions about *Peggy-Ann* being produced in Budapest and *Dearest Enemy* and *Lido Lady* being staged in Berlin. "In Berlin," Rodgers reports, "we went dancing one night, and in the course of the evening I heard Tree in the Park, Girl Friend, Blue Room, Sing, and Here in My Arms! Silly!"[70]

Yet between visiting glamorous destinations and basking in their own success, the boys did find time to continue their work. Something must have appealed about London because they agreed to take on a revue for the producer C. B. Cochran. Cochran was a British impresario whose name is often compared to Ziegfeld's. He started his career as an actor but by the 1920s was producing all manner of entertainments for the British public. He was instrumental in launching the career of Nöel Coward and would consolidate his success in the 1930s with a string of Coward hits including *Bitter Sweet* (1929),

Private Lives (1930), and *Cavalcade* (1931). He also produced the London productions of *Porgy* (1929) and *Anything Goes* (1935), and was manager of the
Royal Albert Hall from 1926 to 1938, presenting not only classical music con-
certs but also rodeos and boxing matches. His aim was to entertain, and he
made every effort to create spectacle. Most of all, Cochran was renowned for
his revues at the London Pavilion: *Dover Street to Dixie* (1923), *On with the
Dance* (1925), and *Blackbirds* (1926).

In fact, it was one of his revues that first introduced a Rodgers and Hart
number to British audiences. "Maybe It's Me," from the *Fifth Avenue Follies*,
had first sparked Cochran's interest and he had interpolated it into *Charles B.
Cochran's Revue of 1926*, changing the title to "I'm Crazy 'Bout the Charleston."
Now Cochran was to reunite Rodgers and Hart with Ronald Jeans for a revue
entitled *One Dam Thing after Another*.

This was a far cry from their experience with *Lido Lady*. They speak in
glowing terms of both their London stay and their host:

> This stay was far more enjoyable than the first. The man most responsible
> for this was unquestionably Cochran, who entertained us frequently in his
> home and who went out of his way to introduce us to many interesting
> people. Cochran himself was an admirable blend of gentleness, intellect
> and courage.[71]

The actual process of putting together the revue is described by Nolan as
rather casual:

> [Cochran] tended to put his shows together by guess and by God, trying
> things out with various artistes until he felt they would work.... No deci-
> sions were made in advance about who would sing which song, who would
> be better or funnier in that sketch or this routine.[72]

Eventually, a framework came together for the diverse collection of material.

Six sandwich girls establish the conceit of the show: the public is too contrary in its tastes, so Mr. Cochran is holding a ballot to decide once and for all
which of the performing arts should hold sway in the theater. The vote will
be cast tonight, and the winner will command the stage. One by one, the contenders enter and perform a song or routine: Mr. Melo Drama is a "typical old
melodramatic actor," Miss Ballet dances, and Miss Shakespeare (as Portia)
recites rhyming couplets. Moss and Stoll, two cross-talk comedians, represent Variety,[73] Miss Musical Comedy enters to a waltz song, and Mr. Broadway Play holds everyone up like a gangster. Miss Modern Comedy enters,
then Signor Opera. There is one more candidate but everyone is surprised
when the character Revue is introduced. Revue, they argue, is dead; but after

a mock-requiem, Revue goes on to win the contest and thus is granted the stage for the rest of the evening.

This is a rather corny framework but it responds to attitudes toward revue on both sides of the Atlantic, particularly about the consumption of theater and class. Mr. Melo Drama makes this clear from the beginning: "If I am to be beaten, I hope it'll be by a candidate of dignity—Shakespeare, sir, or Opera."[74] Miss Ballet and Miss Shakespeare suggest that various areas have preferences for certain forms—the ballet is a favorite in Chelsea, Surrey has a taste for Melodrama and Shakespeare, while Musical Comedy appeals to schoolgirls in Streatham—which defines geographically the patterns of culture (and affluence) in and around London. In between the book-ends of the framing device, the acts reflect the skills of their performers. A number of specialty acts were recruited, including the celebrated pianist Edythe Baker on her white grand piano, the singer Art Fowler on his ukelele performing "Ain't that Baby Neat" to great acclaim, and the thirteen-year-old coloratura soprano Gwen Stella who received rave reviews for her rendition of "Lo, Here the Gentle Lark" by Sir Henry Bishop. Rodgers and Hart also borrowed songs from elsewhere—"Shuffle" from *Betsy* (1926), "Paris Is Really Divine" from the discard pile, and "Gigolo," "Idles of the King," and the premise of "Requiescat in Pace" from the second *Garrick Gaieties* (1926).

There is a suggestion built into the conceit of this show that revue's popularity was waning, and a part of this may have stemmed from Cochran's own announcement the previous year that he was no longer going to produce revues.[75] As this show attests, he did, and it ran for an impressive 237 performances.

The name of the show was taken from a little-known John Masefield novel of the previous year (*One Damn Thing after Another*, initialized to *ODTAA*). Reviews of opening night suggest that it consisted of twenty-three separate acts,[76] though by September 1927, the show boasted a running order of twenty-two "Dam Things."

While simple in its format, *One Dam Thing* did attempt some sophistication in the way that its songs and sketches related to one another. For example, the early song "Paris Is Really Divine" is paired with the "Tourists Sketch," whose comedy arises from misunderstandings when a tour guide tries to show English tourists around Paris. There is a further tenuous link from this sketch to the next song, "Gigolo," "an almost savagely true burlesque on young male (presumably) dancers and their elderly partners,"[77] whose cheeky theme perhaps surprisingly escaped the censor's blue pencil:

If you are fat and forty,
You can be just as sporty,
Go get a young Gigolo.[78]

The following sketch, "The Lady of the Lake," which is again somewhat suggestive ("very saucy," one reviewer called it),[79] has no connection to the previous material and was cut soon after opening night; then come two further unconnected acts that were considered highlights of the show: "My Heart Stood Still," sung by Jessie Matthews and Richard Dolman, and Edythe Baker's "Piano Act," featuring "The Birth of the Blues" (Ray Henderson) and "Play Us a Tune" (Cole Porter). Almost all of the reviews praised Baker in particular, whose "bizarre,"[80] "somewhat 'freakish' "[81] playing was "comparable with Gershwin's."[82] Even if many were bemused by her combination of dancing and playing, they were impressed by the syncopated jazz style she adopted, "treating the piano to a course of manipulative roguery," as the *Manchester Guardian* wrote;[83] she "slaps at a white piano as though she is only imitating a real musician, but all the time is playing like one," claimed the *Queen*.[84] *Sketch* called her "a little virtuoso on the piano, whose right hand is the artist and her left a clown—swooping down on the keys like a bolt from the blue."[85] If Edythe Baker's piano playing mimicked Gershwin's style and layered it with a performative frisson, as seems to be the case, she must have been accomplished indeed; the *Daily Mirror* at least christened her "the Queen of jazz musicians," suggesting that "Miss Baker plays with much more artistry than most performers of this type."[86]

"Lucky Star" and "One Dam Thing after Another" were two other highlights of the show, the first sung by Mimi Crawford and Sonnie Hale and the second by Jessie Matthews. These are introduced by preliminary scenes that establish their theme and contextualize their comedy: "Lucky Star" laments the lot of two chorus members forever consigned to the ensemble; the show's title song, "One Dam Thing after Another" dresses the ingénue Matthews up as a startlingly coy baby (see Figure 5.5) who not only talks eloquently but also offers a precocious critique of her entire family; "Community Singing," a hit with some reviewers, is a sketch in which all the characters communicate in traditional English song, ordering breakfast in their rooming house from their landlady, played by Douglas Byng in drag.

Perhaps the most interesting sequence in the show, for a number of reasons, is the sketch "Progress," closing Act One and incorporating the song "Make Hey! Hey! while the Moon Shines" (a direct reference to the Gershwins' *Primrose*). It was by no means the most popular of the sketches, though it does serve as an interesting example of Rodgers and Hart's thinking in 1927.

The scene satirizes contemporary society through its pastiche of song and dance styles from various eras, enacting a commentary on the discussion about the Charleston in the British press. This sketch is just one of several in *One Dam Thing* that thrusts jazz—particularly Charleston—at its audience.

Figure 5.5: Jessie Matthews in a publicity still for the title song of One Dam Thing after Another. *(From* Sketch, *June 8, 1927, 503.) Mary Evans Picture Library. Used with permission.*

Earlier in the show "Gigolo" poked "shafts of irony at the modern grandmother with her mania for the Charleston";[87] later, when the trial scene from Shakespeare's *The Merchant of Venice* gets "jazzed," remarks are lofty in their disdain:

> Upon the incitement of some hitherto unsuspected lilt in the words, the *cacoethes Charlestoni* seized not only upon plaintiff and defendant, but also upon the Doge of Venice, who, mounting upon the senate-house table, delivered himself—if I mistake not the gender—to the worship of St. Vitus.[88]

In the same vein, reviews of "Progress" draw predictable jibes: "I gathered that our modern jazz does not register any very striking advance upon the methods of prehistoric amusement,"[89] sniffed one reviewer.

Interestingly, this satire shows the boys flirting once again with an Arthurian setting; and the fact that they also shipped in "The Idles of the King" wholesale from the second *Garrick Gaieties* shows how compelling their long-term fascination with Twain's *Connecticut Yankee* was proving to be.

"Progress" begins in a modern dance club, where the flighty Billie (Jessie Matthews) is playing unattractive Monty and sparky Jack off against one another. First she pretends to Jack that she and Monty are engaged. Jack is upset, but Billie and Monty go off to dance to the first verse of "Make Hey!," a typical jazz tune of the 1920s:[90]

> You gotta make Hey! Hey! Hey! Hey!
> While the moon shines!
> Wake up! Shake up! And you're a wow!

Jack leaves, but bumps into Lady Betty Carstairs (Mimi Crawford), costumed in the style of the "Beaucaire" period. She is astonished that Jack hasn't challenged Monty to a duel, and illustrating how to defend one's honor in the eighteenth century, Sir Benjamin Rip and his adversary Charles Ruffle challenge one another over the hand of Lady Betty. The second verse of the song is played as a minuet:

> Heigh-ho, milady! Heigh-ho, milady-o!
> Moonlight is glancing—as we a'dancing go!
> Hands all a'tremble
> Pray don't dissemble, lady!

As the fops leave to duel, a medieval fool enters. "It takes a fool to understand lovers, Mistress,"[91] he says, and shows her how his master, the Baron, deals with the scheming Marmaduke when he tries to woo the Lady Anne (Matthews after a quick change). Both are thrown in the dungeon and the Fool is told to entertain the Baron. The third verse is a medieval pastiche:

> Good Master Owl doth hate the sun
> With a Heigh-o-heigh,
> For the night's the time for mating.
> At morn the owls sleep deep each one
> With a heigh-o-heigh and a nonny-nonny-o.

The Fool takes his turn to reflect on the past and offers to sing the Baron a song about how savages conduct their love trysts. The scene changes to reveal savages grouped exactly the same as the dancers in the modern scene. They dance to the fourth verse, sung in an assumed primitive dialect:

> Hotdoggyboy. Hey! Hey! Hey! Hey!
> Bubbly! Binjoz
> Umpho! Gumpho! Issippi! Wow!
> Oo-googli! Dozat! Shiveree!
> Whozat! Quiveree jumpo!

Glook and Bunk argue over Zab-Zab. Bunk gets drunk and collapses, and Zab-Zab goes off to dance with Glook. Finally, the lights change and the scene returns to the present. Billie is plying Monty with alcohol. He falls asleep and Jack comes over. Billie and Jack dance.

It's a fun scene, though one that did not receive particular praise from the press, many of whom—like this reviewer from the *Telegraph*—found it to labor the point and drag on too long:

> ...a fanciful conceit...which, satirical in conception, seems to aim at pointing a contrast between eighteenth-century formal manners and the present-day lack of them. But, somehow, the scene loses its point by over-elaboration, and becomes involved and meaningless.[92]

It certainly bears similarities to the idea behind *A Connecticut Yankee*, however, with a time-slip narrative, a juxtaposition of contemporary and historical idioms, and a conflict between rival partners of a love triangle. The inevitability of the boys staging that Twain novel was looking increasingly likely.

Meanwhile, "The Idles of the King"—still presenting the Arthurian figures with ambiguous sexualities—did not fare well in London. The *Times* suggested that it was "occasionally in rather bad taste";[93] others gave it unequivocably negative criticism. Due to this feedback the sketch was soon cut: "The humor did not quite come off," reported the *Telegraph*,[94] while the *Evening News* considered it "a weak idea weakly carried out."[95]

The main hit of the show, though, aided in its popularity by a well-chosen anecdote, was "My Heart Stood Still." The anecdote relates to an incident in Paris, during the runup to work on *One Dam Thing after Another*, when Larry and Dick were sharing a taxi with acquaintances Rita Kempner (or Heiden or Hayden; there is some confusion) and Ruth Warner.

> While we were escorting the girls back to their hotel one night in a taxi, another cab darted out of a side street and missed hitting us by a matter of inches. As our cab came to a halt, one of the girls cried, "Oh, my heart stood still!" No sooner were the words out than Larry casually said, "Say, that would make a great title for a song."[96]

Rodgers explains how he wrote down the possible song title in his address book, then forgot about it until flicking through the book and being reminded of the incident. Inspired, he wrote a refrain for a song, and offered it to Larry, who couldn't even remember the near miss.

This makes for a great bit of marketing for what became the show's hit; and it may be a true story—it is certainly told in almost every biography of Rodgers and Hart, by different witnesses of the event and with sufficient detail to make it sound credible. On the other hand, an early version of "My Heart Stood Still" among the *Lido Lady* material in Rodgers's scrapbooks shows that

Figure 5.6: An early draft of "My Heart Stood Still," calling into question the authenticity of popular promotional anecdotes about this song. Reprinted by Permission of Hal Leonard Corporation

the germ of the melody at least comes from mid-1926 (see Figure 5.6). What is significant in terms of this anecdote is that the words "My Heart Stood Still" don't scan; the music at least predates those lyrics. Once given that title, though, Rodgers was able to rewrite it to accommodate the exclamation from the tall Parisian tale.

Still, the veracity of this anecdote is not really the point. What is interesting is the fact that neither Rodgers's music for "My Heart Stood Still" nor Hart's lyrics are in any way suggestive of this heart-stopping moment of terror. On the contrary, the melody line of the song is lyrical and flowing, comprised of scalar passages, as Block and several other writers discuss.[97] Furthermore, in performance, singers extend phrases and sustain some of the long notes within the melody, even where there might be an opportunity to exploit syncopation and—literally—stop the melody. Likewise, Hart's lyrics are romantic (one might say even bland) for such a mischievous cynic: "Though not a single word was spoken, / I could tell you knew; / That unfelt clasp of hands / Told me so well you knew."[98] Are these *really* lyrics by Hart?

ODTAA was a great success, profiting from the ease with which it could be refreshed, with sketches and songs that were less popular removed and others interpolated as appropriate. Following its West End season, it was taken into the provinces where it toured for several months.

Once the show had opened (May 20, 1927), Rodgers and Hart barely paused for breath before sailing back to the United States (arriving June 3), where their next project beckoned: the *Connecticut Yankee* idea, which would prove their biggest hit of the twenties. Although several of their other shows were mounted in London in the coming years, only one was to be an original. It is a testament to their mutual admiration and the enjoyable experience of *One Dam Thing after Another* that when Cochran asked them to write another show for him, they jumped at the opportunity.

EVER GREEN (1930)

It was 1929, and Cochran was in New York launching Coward's *Bitter Sweet*. This was a significant show in the trade between the UK and United States, since it was the only British book musical (as opposed to revue) to make it to Broadway during the 1920s—a sure sign of changing trends and of a vogue for "American" music on both sides of the Atlantic. Cochran was scouting for a star vehicle for Jessie Matthews (whom they knew from *One Dam Thing after Another*). Several successful Broadway productions had already transferred that season, including the Henderson, De Sylva, and Brown hits *Hold Everything* and *Follow Thru*, and *A Connecticut Yankee* (whose London title was changed to *A Yankee at the Court of King Arthur*). That left a number of shows to choose from, though

> [Cochran] told Larry and me that he had seen nothing on Broadway that he wanted to produce in London. What he did want was an original show with a score by Rodgers and Hart, but this time he thought it should be a book musical instead of a revue.[99]

Taking their lead from *Bitter Sweet*, in which an elderly woman recalls her youth, and in which both parts are taken by the same actress, Rodgers and Hart sketched out the bare bones of a plot. Cochran loved it, and Rodgers and Hart were sent to Germany to develop the idea with playwright Benn W. Levy, at that time writing for the film company UFA.

Levy (1900–1973) had established himself as a playwright during the late twenties, with the successful transfer of *This Woman Business* (1925) to New York. This was a drawing-room comedy with the *Love's Labours Lost* idea of five men shutting themselves away from the society of women, only to find their misogyny softened and eventually thwarted when a young woman turns up. The drawing-room comedy style would be a dominant feature of Levy's work, as it was for his contemporaries, Shaw, Coward, Priestley, and Rattigan. However, it was his play *Mrs. Moonlight* (1928) that most closely resembled what *Ever Green* would become, and it was probably recalling this storyline that made Cochran introduce the boys to Levy: Sarah Moonlight, thanks to a turquoise necklace she is given, is granted a wish, and she chooses to remain forever young so that her beloved husband Tom will continue to love her. However, nothing else remains trapped in time, and as the play follows her next fifty years she faces the consequences of this foolish fantasy: she has to feign suicide, flee her home life, then revisit as her own niece to avoid arousing suspicion and being cast as a freak; finally, she visits the senile Tom on his deathbed, wearing the dress he gave her just before she disappeared. A moment of recognition unites them just as her husband dies; she is left behind, forever young.

Ever Green opens with a beauty contest at the Royal Albert Hall, judged by the "Belle de Soixante Ans" Harriet Green, the sensational sixty-year-old beauty (who is in fact a twenty-three-year-old fraudster). The winner is chosen and Harriet leaves to star at the risqué Casino des Folies[100] in Paris, stopping overnight at a guesthouse run by her (middle-aged) "daughter," Mrs. Platter. Harriet arrives with her business manager Mary Tucket and they meet fellow guests, variety performers Tommy Thompson and Eric Merivale. Tommy and Harriet are at once attracted, though she spurns his advances lest he discover her ruse. The boys arrange to accompany the ladies to Paris, and once there, Tommy and Eric both audition for the show. When Tommy lands the part, Harriet is furious and insists the director St. Didier fire him. Tommy is incensed, punches St. Didier, and storms out. Some time later, Harriet tracks him down to Neuilly Fair, where he has been recruited as Gentilli the lion tamer's assistant. The two make up, and she invites him to the opening show at the Casino. On opening night, the show builds to its climax, the revelation of the "Woman of Sixty." Harriet is revealed and Tommy—believing she really is sixty—is horrified as the first act curtain falls.

Act Two begins in Spain a year later. Harriet and Mary are holidaying there with Mrs. Platter. When Eric visits and reveals that Tommy is now working at the Cabaret de l'Abbaye in Paris, Harriet decides to return to Paris where she will tell Tommy everything. Back in Paris she fantasizes about being back with Tommy, and in a spectacular showstopper, "Dancing on the Ceiling," the room is turned (literally) upside down for the lavish routine. After the number, St. Didier enters and asks Harriet if he can marry her daughter (Mrs. Platter), but he is forced to sneak into the bathroom to avoid being discovered in a lady's room. An intruder breaks in claiming to be Harriet's estranged husband and demanding money. She sends him packing but the next night at the Cabaret Tenorio in Paris, we see the stranger sharing his secrets with Tommy. Tommy takes to the stage, and during his number, launches a hostile tirade of abuse at Harriet. Later, back at the Casino des Folies, Tommy admits that he doesn't care if she is sixty—he still loves her. She confesses that she is not sixty but twenty-three, and that Mrs. Platter is her mother not her daughter. She agrees to prove it on stage, and in the finale number—in which Harriet is supposed to be revealed as the girl in the moon—she runs on stage and admits the truth to the audience, then breaks down. The compere and St. Didier try to cover up the gaffe and start the number again. This time, when the moon opens, Mrs. Platter steps out in feathers and sequins. Tommy runs on stage and he and Harriet are united.

Constructing a show around a cast of performers and show folk is an obvious way to allow what might otherwise be incongruous songs to become a part of the narrative. Thus, the diegetic situations of audition, rehearsal, and performance play a significant role in *Ever Green*. Indeed, the original program for the production highlights this by including a second mock program, for the Casino des Folies, inside the first.

The opening is a Gilbert and Sullivan–style ensemble number introducing the chorus girls who in this scenario are beauty contestants. Its lyrics alone signal a direct pastiche of *The Mikado*:

> BEAUTIES: If you want to know who we are:–
> We're not gentlemen of Japan,
> But we've travelled from near and far
> For the Beauty Prize;
> We represent the nation's femininity,
> But pulchritude's our only consanguinity –
> Our homes are stretched from Greenwich to infinity;
> Each one's the local queen of her vicinity.[101]

The second song, "Harlemania," is purely an opportunity to stage an energetic tap Charleston, sung by Madeline Gibson and choreographed by Buddy Bradley as part of the beauty contest entertainment. The song celebrates the "crazy tunes" coming out of Harlem, picking up on the recent notoriety of venues such as the Cotton Club. The lyrics are sassy and suggestive: the Charleston is celebrated as both a degenerate influence and a provocative come-on.

> MISS L. S.: With the best of intentions,
> Folks who used to be nice,
> Shake what nobody mentions,
> Not once, but twice![102]

Musically, this B section emphasizes the humor of the third and fourth lines by dropping a repeated sequence progressively down a tone, a technique that Rodgers would also employ to emphasize the comedy in "The Color of Her Eyes" (see Figure 5.7). "Harlemania" also identifies the black influence of the Charleston in language very much of its time: "Dark eyes blaze with an off-beat gaze; / The world is turning brown." As in other shows, the Charleston is seen as a representative example of this new "American" culture, which is often a euphemism for "black" culture. Buddy Bradley, the choreographer, was himself black and it is likely that the inclusion of this otherwise incongruous song was to exploit his talent for jazz choreography and the British enthusiasm for the Charleston.[103] Indeed, although Bradley had been working on Broadway shows (such as the *Greenwich Village Follies*, 1928) for some years, problematic attitudes about race in New York left him regularly uncredited. His recruitment by Cochran for *Ever Green* offered not only a chance for the

"Harlemania"

Shake what no - bo - dy men - tions, not once, but twice!

"Lovely Woman's Ever Young"

Truth is beau-ty, beau-ty truth, And they have e - ter-nal youth.

Fa - ther Time can-not de - ny, Charm can ne - ver die!

"The Color of Her Eyes"

Al-most ev-ery-bo-dy said who'd seen us She was like a sta-tue in her charms,

Af-ter one small ar-gu-ment be tween us She looked like Ve- nus; I broke her arms!

Figure 5.7: Recurring use of dropped phrasing to emphasize comedy in Rodgers'
score to Ever Green.
Reprinted by Permission of Hal Leonard Corporation

show to include authentic black American jazz dance but also an opportunity for Bradley's work to be recognized. Bradley stayed in London for several years, working alongside choreographers such as George Balanchine and Frederick Ashton, and choreographing a number of stage shows and films.

The third song, "Doing a Little Waltz Clog," is a rehearsal for two variety performers. They later audition for the Paris Casino des Folies with "Nobody Looks at the Man," and "Waiting for the Leaves." When the action cuts to the Neuilly Fair, the lion taming act is introduced with a song called "The Lion King," a later addition to the show. The final sequence of the first act is a series of performances from the revue show: "When the Old World Was New," "Lovely Woman's Ever Young," and a pageant of spectacles including Carlos and Chita (an acrobatic act) and culminating in the climax of the act, "La Belle de Soixante Ans."

This use of diegetic song, a trope that would come to feature heavily in the developing musical theater and film of the 1930s, was something that other artists were exploring. We have already seen its use in *Poor Little Ritz Girl* to facilitate what Lew Fields saw as the incorporation of revue or vaudeville material within a musical comedy storyline. In *Ever Green*, there are only two non-diegetic numbers in the first act, "Dear! Dear!" and "No Place but Home," both sung by the principal couple Tommy and Harriet, and both at significant points on the trajectory of their relationship. "Dear! Dear!" is sung during their first encounter; "No Place but Home" is sung as a brief reconciliation between one falling out and the next. This is also the thematically reprised hit song of the show, which recurs several times during Act Two.

Act Two begins with a traditional Catalonian procession, the "Festa Major," whose music was separately composed for authenticity by the Spanish musician Pedro Morales. It also features two more sequences of diegetic song, both of which are ostensibly performances. The first is at the Cabaret de'l'Abbaye club halfway through the act: the "Hot Blues" dance capitalizes on the skills of Dave Fitzgibbon and his partner Jean Barry; the "Impromptu Song" (or "The Talking Song") is Tommy's specialty act at the club, which has dramatic resonances for the plot. The second diegetic sequence is the finale of the Casino des Folies show, which stages the extravagant revue number "The Moon and the Stars" to end both the revue show and the musical. However, in Act Two there are far more non-diegetic songs, particularly as resolution points between the other two couples in the show. "The Color of Her Eyes" is a comedy character number sung by Mrs. Platter and Eric; "In the Cool of the Evening" is a bluesy ballad for another comedy character, Mary. Yet another comedy character, Saint-Didier, provides "Je M'en Fiche Du Sex Appeal!" while Mary and Eric resolve their differences and complete the trajectory of the secondary love match with "If I Give In to You." The only other song in the act is, in fact, one of the highlights of the show, and a dazzling bit of staging enabled by a dream sequence in which Harriet imagines herself reunited with Tommy. "Dancing on the Ceiling" famously revealed an enormous chandelier "hanging" from the stage floor, to give the impression that Jessie Matthews, Sonnie Hale, and the many dancing girls were in fact dancing on the ceiling. This was of course their main opportunity to show their dancing skills and was in a sense the raison d'être for their casting in the show.

Ever Green is an odd show and Levy's only stab at musical theater. In many ways, it reads like either a straight revue or a straight play, or to be more precise, like several straight plays: at times a melodrama, at times a farce, it has a script that is sometimes in English and at other times (and for quite considerable stretches) in French. This uneven writing is characteristic of Levy, whose ability "was blunted by the lack of a consistently strong focus of either style or content" and whose plays "seem divided in their purpose and loose in plot construction."[104] This play lurches from one location to the next, with no real justification. Most of its significant action takes place in Paris, so it would make sense to have made that the primary location: the two performance venues, the hotel room, and the rehearsal hall would offer ample opportunity for scenic spectacle while giving the setting of the play a consistency and a coherency. That it begins in London, moves to the South Coast, drops in to Paris, then a fairground in the French countryside, a Spanish village, a Parisian hotel room, and finally the performance venues of the Casino and the Cabaret makes the play very episodic. Nor are these episodes given equal weight: the Neuilly fairground scene, one of the highlights of the evening according to reports, lasts for just two minutes while the second act hotel room scene takes up an inordinate amount of the act. Clever though it is, with Levy exercising his talent for farce, this scene seems out of place: its purpose is to engineer the forced revelation about Harriet's true identity, but this is interior, domestic British theater, a scene whose walls symbolize the mask of identity, whose foil character from outside threatens exposure, and whose action is set against the farcical machinations of situational comedy. The libretto archived at the British Library bears the marks of the Lord Chamberlain's renowned blue pencil throughout this scene, objecting in particular to a repeated gag in which Saint-Didier loses his trousers in the bathroom. This, apparently, was too risqué for the censors of 1930.[105] Significantly though, the scene isn't even mentioned in the synopsis included in *Ever Green*'s program, despite its length. By contrast, several of the other more striking scenes in the play offer evocative outdoor settings (a Catalonian village; the Neuilly Fair) or exotic performance spaces (the Casino revue bar; the Parisian cabaret), and it is these that receive all the critical reception.

These many and varied settings are there for a reason, however—and so too the ensemble of 150 performers. The reason is spectacle. This is, after all, a Cochran show, and one designed to take the best elements of revue and weave them into a storyline. Here, as Sheridan Morley suggests,

the techniques that had been learnt in his own lavish revues—rapid changes of set and a fast-shifting sequence of sketches and songs—could actually be harnessed to some semblance of plot.[106]

Because of the various performance settings, this show has endless opportunity for song, whether in English or French, and at Cochran's request it also exploited a multi-locational storyline to show off a series of stunningly designed sets. In this it is rather filmic, a quality enabled by the innovative employment of a revolving stage, the first in British theater history. Indeed, several reviewers note its filmic quality and even suggest that Cochran is deliberately throwing down the gauntlet in offering live spectacle that rivals film: "Mr. Cochran has decided to go the whole Hollywood," crowed one reviewer;[107] "it is a Circus, a Revue, a Musical Comedy, a Pageant, a Peep-show, a Kaleidoscope, a Merry-go-round, a Miracle, All Hollywood and Half Heaven," said another;[108] this is "a shrewd blow for the stage against its rival, the cinema," reported the *Play Pictorial*;[109] while the *New York Times* suggested that

> Showmanship of the quality of Mr. Cochran's flourishes gaily upon fierce rivalry; . . . and in "Ever Green" he has taken the opportunity to maintain that the stage can present, in rapid sequence, spectacles as numerous, as varied and as gorgeous as any film has shown.[110]

In particular, Cochran reminisces with delight about the staging of a complete fairground scene with illuminated rides:

> When the stage revolved one had the impression of a jostling crowd moving naturally about the side-shows and the roundabouts. The shouts of the barkers and the shrieks of the calliope, the French hunting horns, played to attract the spectators to particular shows, mingled with the ceaseless chatter of the crowd, the screams of the people on the slippery slides, and the roaring of the wild beasts in the menageries. The applause which invariably greeted this scene never failed to hold up the action of the play.[111]

Cochran's own description of the scene is matched by similar descriptions in newspaper reviews. The fairground scene was clearly the highlight: "that alone would justify the revolving stage," admits the *Play Pictorial*.[112] One wonders whether this atmospheric scene was in Rodgers's mind when he came to create the evocative music for a similar fairground scene at the beginning of *Carousel* sixteen years later.[113]

Despite the inconsistencies of the plot and the whimsy of its conceit—"the most strenuously inane idea which could be conceived as emanating from the human cranium," according to one critic[114]—the show received almost unanimous praise. Reviewers respected Cochran's having found a way to make something more substantial of his usual revue material, and if songs, scenes, and even interpolations have little to do with the plot or characters, this is overlooked because of the spectacle and the Cochran legacy. According to one reviewer, this is "a show that admits of interpolations more easily than the average musical piece." Thus a thrilling gymnastic act by Carlos and Chita is warmly received, while the interpolation of a fakir act into the Catalonian village in Act Two is accepted with "no feeling of irrelevance."[115] Likewise, the interpolation of three songs by the American "diseuse"[116] Marion Harris into the Cabaret scenes is applauded (though for the reviewer to make a point of commenting on these interpolations rather undermines the point she or he is making).

The role of Rodgers and Hart in this spectacle might have been simply to provide stand-alone songs and instrumental color were it not for the fact that there are at least recognizable characters and credible character situations on which to hang the musical numbers. Again there are three couples: the ingénues Harriet and Tommy, the comedy characters Saint-Didier and Mrs. Platter, and the rather unevenly written sidekicks, Eric and Mary. Reviews give an indication of character—Jessie Matthews (Harriet) is warmly regarded for her sensitive acting, while her husband and partner Sonnie Hale (Tommy) plays "in a more serious manner than we have known him for in the past";[117] these are the straight characters, bringing dramatic weight to the production. Jean Cadell (Mrs. Platter) and Leon Morton (Saint-Didier) are both "exquisite"[118] and clearly play their characters for comedy: "somebody had the entirely right notion that to keep this part 'straight' would throw other absurdity into greater relief," observed reviewer James Agate; "between them the pair ran away with the piece."[119] Finally, Albert Burdon (Eric) is noted by several critics for his comic ability: he is "nearly funnier than most of the established zanies, and he brings to his work the peculiar properties of Lancashire gusto and Yorkshire relish," suggests Agate;[120] other reviewers also pick up on this regional humor, calling him "more robust in style than our London comedians."[121] Although his counterpart Joyce Barbour (Mary) is barely mentioned, it is clear that this third couple offers a different type of comedy to the piece, with a recognizable regional (northern) flavor.

This northern identity is revealed in the early numbers sung by Burdon, "Doing a Little Clog Dance" (or "Doing a Little Waltz Clog"), which he sings with Sonnie Hale in the boarding house scene as a rehearsal of their double act, and "Waiting for the Leaves to Fall," which is his (unsuccessful) audition song for Saint-Didier at the Casino des Folies.

"Doing a Little Clog Dance" showcases the Lancashire progenitor of tap dancing, popular since the industrial revolution and exploiting the wooden-soled footwear worn by workers in the industrial cotton mills. Informal competitions would take place in factories to judge competitors' speed and rhythmic innovations. The dance form was introduced into the nineteenth-century music halls (Dan Leno was a clog dancing champion) and influenced the creation of tap dancing following the immigration of working-class migrants to the United States. The "Waltz Clog" specifically was a softer version of clog dancing, more akin to the soft-shoe shuffle. Placing "Doing a Little Clog Dance" early on in *Ever Green* establishes Eric's northern identity and characterizes a particular type of British humor, typical of the sort performed at working-men's clubs in the north of England.

The resonance of a northern working-class character would not have been lost on the audience, acutely aware of the worldwide depression that had struck when the New York stock exchange crashed in October 1929. The situation had already been bleak in Britain since the general strike (May 1926), when a mass national walkout in support of beleaguered miners had brought the country to a standstill. It lasted for just over a week and had a particular impact on the transport infrastructure and industrial productivity. But the situation deteriorated, and by 1929, mass rallies were being called to protest high levels of unemployment. The slump was devastating in the north of England, which since the Industrial Revolution had been reliant on heavy industry. Shipbuilding suffered a 90 percent drop in output over three years; the textile industry around Lancashire was also badly affected. Although unemployment in most areas peaked at around 25 percent, some towns reported unemployment figures of up to 70 percent. An inexperienced Labour government, led by Ramsay MacDonald, was disbanded at the general election in 1931, when a National government was instituted instead, a coalition headed by MacDonald but with an overwhelming conservative majority.

In this climate it is appropriate that reference should be made to political matters, and it is significant that this show chooses to address politics and regionality in a way that neither *Lido Lady* nor *One Dam Thing* did. Eric's Lancashire character comments on the unemployment, and targets the ineffective stewardship of Ramsay MacDonald:

ERIC: The Labour Party rules today,
　　　And many workers get no pay!
　　　The government does not repent,
　　　Hear the good prime minister say:

　　　I'm doing a little waltz clog,
　　　While you are collecting the dole.
　　　One – two – three! One – two – three! Toe, heel and toe!
　　　Doing a little waltz clog! Oh, doing a little waltz clog![122]

In his second song, "Waiting for the Leaves to Fall" (by which time the action has repaired safely to Continental Europe, where it can offer some escapism from the economic realities of life at home), Eric sings of his Lancashire Moll:

ERIC: She was poor but she was pure, poor thing
Dressed in rags but still she kept her wedding ring.
When the birds flew to the south
She lived from hand to mouth
She was bold but she was cold, poor thing
She was turned away from butcher shops and dairies
But was watched over by all good little fairies
But she waited till October for my call
Waiting for the leaves to fall.[123]

This song has the feel of a folk ballad, and its lyrics offer evocative images lamenting poverty but suggesting it to be a natural concern. Although the lyrics appear to be entirely serious, they are reminiscent of Billy Bennett's comic monologue "She was poor but she was honest," also from 1930, which presents similar sentiments (culminating in the suicide of the poor but honest girl):

She was poor, but she was honest
Though she came from 'umble stock
And an honest heart was beating
Underneath her tattered frock

It's the same the whole world over,
It's the poor what gets the blame,
It's the rich what gets the pleasure,
Isn't it a blooming shame?

Both songs have satirical and political bite. It's tantalizing to speculate how a mention of October in these lyrics may have resonated with audiences, October being the month in which the Stock Market had crashed; in that light, it's also easy to see the birds that are mentioned flying to the south representing the disappearing opportunities for employment as factories closed in the north of England leaving poverty and desperation in their wake. This migration of opportunity to the south of England and the impression that the British government only really related to what was going on in the immediate environs around London has been a significant contributor to what is known as the "north-south divide," a feeling of social inequality between the affluent south and the impoverished north that is still sensitive today.

Eric's Lancashire character—played by the apparently very funny comic Albert Burdon—is able in this song to comment on contemporary British politics and social issues in a way that not only resonates with audiences but also deals with the issues with typical English discretion and typical northern "grit."

In *Lido Lady*, Hart's depiction of the English would remain superficial and his exploration of character limited to hackneyed idioms. This time, aided by Benn Levy's political passion and native understanding of regional nuances,[124] Hart is able to offer subtleties in his characterization of Eric that show a real connection with the British type he is portraying.

Our introduction to Tommy and Eric shows them rehearsing for their variety act, a rapid-fire exchange of gags between comic and straight man:

TOMMY: How do you stop a cock from crowing on a Sunday morning?
ERIC: Wring its neck on a Saturday night.
. . .
TOMMY: We all come out of the same mould.
ERIC: Yes, only some are mouldier than others.
. . .
ERIC: We're a musical family. I had a brother who died of music on the brain.
TOMMY: How was that?
ERIC: Someone hit him over the head with a harmonium.[125]

Rather than performing this as a set piece in this rehearsal scene, the pair step back to comment on their performance, sometimes venturing to repeat material ("Give me that again, old boy"), sometimes offering directorial advice to one another:

ERIC: I dried up twice this afternoon.
TOMMY: It's because you don't concentrate. Where do you want to go from? "Is red cabbage greengrocery?"[126]

Each punchline is punctuated by a "Kick behind" or a "Fall behind," slapstick maneuvers that Tommy and Eric do not actually perform in this rehearsed setting but instead indicate. The routine and its self-conscious staging is reminiscent of the self-deprecatory discourse of northern double acts, typified in the later TV comedy routines of Lancashire comedians Eric Morecambe and Ernie Wise. In the dramaturgical conceit of the rehearsal badinage, it is the characters of the performers rather than their slick stage personas that come across. We become fond of them—particularly the comic who is always the butt of the joke—and this helps set up the character as more rounded than, for example, the comparable though two-dimensional character Billy

Arlington in *Lido Lady*. A further nuance is added by a running gag about Eric's lack of height—something that Hart shared and with which he would have empathized.

The ongoing relationship between Eric and Mary trades on the sort of frosty banter we have noticed in *Lido Lady*. However, the double meaning and subtextual affection between these characters becomes more evident as their cross-talk gets more aggressive. By the end of the play. Eric is enchanted by Mary's outpouring of abuse:

> You're stunted, snub-nosed, knock-kneed, pigeon-chested, chicken-livered, short-sighted, quarter-jointed, half-witted, thick-skinned, self-centred and the rottenest comic in Europe. In a word, dearest, you're spiritually nauseating and physically obscene.[127]

Whether Hart felt any connection between Eric's "stunted . . . pigeon-chested . . . physically obscene" body and his own is not documented, though the song that follows this tirade, "If I Give In to You," is sensitive, endearing, and heart-felt:

> ERIC: Please do not be vain;
> That my mind is all askew.
> I'm a little bit insane
> For I love you.[128]

This is a touching moment, and dramaturgically it offers a moment of tenderness and a respite from the dominant narrative of Tommy and Harriet's relationship, and from the farce comedy earlier in the act. Of course, in classic musical comedy style, this scene is concluded with a kick:

> ERIC: Now I needn't ask you to marry me at all. Dear Mary! *(He presses her hand and leaves her)*
>   *(Mary is stupefied)*
> MARY: *(when she recovers)* Damn![129]

Elsewhere, the characterizations are not so much related to character but to type, and to comic stereotypes in particular (after all, Eric is a comic character). As we have seen, it was becoming a feature of Rodgers and Hart shows to offer a rhythm song for the comedy couple whose banter becomes increasingly sarcastic. In this show, "The Color of Her Eyes" provides a variation of this formula, taking comic characters from two different relationships and letting their sarcasm loose on previous partners. The song, whose title is suggestive of a tender relationship between two lovers, actually becomes an outpouring of dating disasters from both Eric and Mrs. Platter (with some suggestion that it may have been one another they were dating). The song works in this context, though it started life in the previous year's show *Spring Is Here* (1929).

"The Color of Her Eyes" starts conventionally enough; the music's pleasant melody and bouncing feel work well with the initial verse and chorus, in which Eric reminisces about his first love.[130]

> ERIC: I remember she was eighteen, maybe nineteen,
> Maybe I'm wrong.

The fusion of music and lyrics is perfect: Eric corrects his memory three times ("she was eighteen / maybe nineteen / maybe I'm wrong"), and these three remarks are matched with a sequence of three motifs in the music. The music constructs a cross-rhythm with its 3/4 phrasing mapped onto a 4/4 beat, which gives the impression that each new thought interrupts the last (see Figure 5.8). The memory, we gather, is slightly hazy, despite his assurances (in the verse) that "I remember her so well I've never missed her"; thanks to this we sense the story is not all it appears, and later in the chorus both music and lyrics unsettle the memory further. The B section establishes another sequence that descends over four phrases, giving the suggestion of increasing disappointment, a motif we have already noted of Rodgers's music in this show (see Figure 5.7, page 151). In this first chorus it is not quite clear what causes the disappointment, though by the end we have reassessed what he means by saying "I remember her so well I've never missed her": the double-edged meaning in this sentiment becomes the motive guiding the song.

Mrs. Platter takes up the song with her own anecdote, and we are now alert to the double-edged meaning. Hers is the voice of experience recalling her youth when she was just an innocent girl (maybe eighteen, maybe nineteen, maybe the girl in Eric's story?). The verse reveals nothing (though it contains a number of incongruous American allusions—her suitor was as "virtuous as Lincoln"); but in the chorus, the wry memories are becoming clear:

> MRS P: I remember he was half shot, maybe all shot!
> Maybe I'm wrong!
> Anyway his beard was all there, it was all *there*
> And it was strong!

I re-mem-ber she was eight-een, may-be nine-teen, may-be I'm wrong.

Figure 5.8: Use of cross-rhythm to dramatic effect in "The Color of Her Eyes."
Reprinted by Permission of Hal Leonard Corporation

This time the sequence of three motifs works to magnify her observation that "he was half shot / maybe all shot! / maybe I'm wrong!"; the second A sequence repeats this effect: not only was he unshaven, but Mrs. Platter experienced the heavy stubble of this boozy suitor more intimately than she would have liked. As the B section initiates the descending sequence, what might otherwise be a romantic scenario becomes soured until the punchline on the final cadence reveals that this fellow stripped off his clothes to reveal a tattooed lady on his chest. The final A section pushes the humor further by mentioning his (oversize) underwear, all too well imprinted on Mrs. Platter's memory, unlike the color of his eyes.

Although the script in the Lord Chamberlain's collection offers no further lyrics, a third chorus exists in which the recollections of this encounter become even more horrific.

> ERIC: I remember she had two legs, maybe one leg,
>   Maybe I'm wrong!
>   Anyway her arms were all there, they were all there
>   And they were strong.
>   Almost every body said who'd seen us,
>   She was like a statue in her charms;
>   After one small argument between us,
>   She looked like Venus:
>   I broke her arms.
>   At twelve o'clock she'd park the torso,
>   She could snore so,
>   To my surprise;
>   I see it all
>   But can't recall
>   The color of her eyes![131]

The double meaning occurs in almost every line, and we can imagine the effect of a clever comedian performing this number: her arms were all over him, so he ends up breaking them; she was as charming as a block of granite, and snored terribly in bed where she lay like a parked car. Though its gender politics may be dated, the song is carefully crafted lyrically and musically to create increasingly funny laugh lines assisted by the music.

The chorus is constructed in AABAC form, with an extended B section that adds to the comedy. The initial A section—with its musical and lyrical "triptych" (discussed above) establishes the tone and immediately undermines the character of the singer by both questioning the veracity of the narrative ("Maybe I'm wrong!") and disrupting the conventional meter of the rhythm.

The effect of repeating the A section exactly is to consolidate this impression. The descending phrase of the B section, which modulates awkwardly down through whole tones, further diminishes the status of the storyteller in an acoustic "lowering" by steps; and because the B section is extended to twice the length of the A sections, this diminishing appears to continue inexorably. This section ends in a musical and lyrical "punchline" (e.g., "I broke her arms"), a short phrase that allows for instrumental "laughter" to accompany the audience response before the final A section provides a further cross-rhythmic joke. The concluding C section, more or less identical in each verse, provides the over-arching punchline of the whole song—the fact that these faded lovers can't recall one of the most defining romantic features of young love ("The Color of Her Eyes"). In some ways—and considering the fact that Eric is a cross-talk comedian—the music provides "banter" with the lyrics, emulating the sort of dialogue we have seen between Tommy and Eric that provides both comedy and character.

In this, Rodgers and Hart show themselves to be at the top of their game and by now extremely experienced in the craft of constructing songs to suit character, type, situation, or effect. They are versatile in the styles of song they have in their repertoire, and they are able to use originality when required or to pastiche a variety of idioms effectively and in the service of the show.

If each show at this stage was exploring a particular dynamic of musical theater, *Ever Green*'s contribution to their growing knowledge may well have been the exploration of how *diegetic* song can be used to *dramatic* effect. This is not necessarily a new direction. Indeed, the denouement of *Lido Lady*, in which Harry's emotional decision is played out through dance, is another example of their exploration of how song and dance can be used dramatically, anticipating the dramaturgy of dance shows like *On Your Toes* or devices like the dream ballet of *Oklahoma!* In the stage directions, this dramatic device is evident, though the actual choreography remains unnotated:

> Harry throws away the rose and gradually becomes engrossed in the dance. As he dances he glances at the rose as if half wanting to pick it up, but curbs his impulse. FAY also dancing returns. Reconciliation in dance form. FINALE.[132]

This serves the purpose well, not only *showing* a decision being made but also articulating this in an appropriate idiomatic language for the character. In *Ever Green* the exploration is slightly different. In this, the dramatic effect is not wholly internal to the scene but makes use of the audience's dual role as spectators of both the musical and the show-within-a-show.

The first example of this is at the end of Act One, when Harriet's secret is revealed to Tommy as a performative act. Here the audience of *Ever Green* is also positioned as the Casino des Folies audience, which creates a dramaturgical distance in which tensions can play out: as the *Ever Green* audience, our hope for Harriet and Tommy's relationship is dashed by her unexpected revelation and his horror; as the Casino audience, our reaction to the spectacle is disrupted by a fellow audience member breaking the illusion of the show. Combining these effects in a single moment enables the performative distancing to magnify the dramatic impact.

The second example allows for a further level of distancing to be added. The synopsis in the program explains the situation toward the end of Act Two:

> Tommy has now become a great success at the Café de L'Abbaye, where each night he makes up witty verses about the guests. Seeing Harriet there with a party, he begins to sing about "La Belle de Soixante Ans," but breaks down after flagrantly insulting her.[133]

Not only do the layers at the end of Act One work in a similar way, but in this example the diegetic performance also breaks down, causing an additional sense of performative distancing: for the Cabaret audience, this is between what was intended (entertainment) and what was achieved (embarrassment), and between who the audience expected to be performing (witty raconteur Tommy) and who was witnessed performing (bitter ex-lover Tommy). For the *Ever Green* audience, the resonance is created in our perception of a gap between comic and pathetic versions of the same thing: this song portrays one character making snide and acerbic comments about another, which we have seen to be a typical device of Rodgers and Hart; in this example the tone and characterization are not comic but personal, and as such its already more potent dramatic force is magnified because we have laughed alongside the petty jibes of the comedy characters in "The Color of Her Eyes."

The song begins with several stanzas that depict other guests, before he turns to Harriet:

> I ask you now to gaze upon
> La Belle Charmante de soixante ans
> All hail—she wears fair Helen's wreath
> Yet her heart is falser than her teeth.
> And though she uses golden dye
> Her hair, her words, her love's a lie
> Oh Grandmother, where's your gray hair?

Your dear old wrinkles, deep with care?
Why are those painted lips so glad?
To make men mad! To make men mad!
Come let your lovely shoulders shake—
They aren't real! It's all a fake!

. . .

Some people say—say she suffers from—from Sex-mania. But I don't
think that's true, do you? After all, what's a husband discarded here or—
or a lover cheated there? The world's full of men—what does one more
or less matter? You've heard of growing old gracefully—well—well, we
know better now. We know that youth, like love, is something anybody
can have for the paying for? Ask Miss Green, ask Miss Green, the celebrated—[134]

In dramatizing Tommy's emotional breakdown, Rodgers and Hart choose to
move away from the metered confines of song form, so the song collapses
into inarticulate speech. This is particularly interesting given the dominant perception that songs in the integrated musical happen at moments of
heightened emotional intensity; here (at such a heightened moment), song
falters—yet this is an excellent example of integration in a musical from well
before the integration period.[135]

The final moment of Rodgers and Hart exploring the drama of the perfo-
mative is in the last sequence of the show. Back at the Casino des Folies, the
grand finale takes place. Again, we are positioned as audience of both *Ever
Green* and the Casino revue. In *Ever Green* our engagement with this scene
is loaded with the anticipation that Harriet will resolve the confusion. However, we also experience a surprise resolution of the Mrs. Platter storyline, in
which her dowdy, comic character is elevated into a position of grace as the
iconic "Belle Charmante de Soixante Ans." As part of the Casino audience, our
engagement is excited first of all by the show's finale going wrong; then by an
offstage scandal interrupting the performance; and finally by the recapitula-
tion of the show's finale resulting in an unexpected ending.

In exploring the dramatic potential of the diegetic performance, Rodgers
and Hart find a number of potent ways for staged events to offer a double (or
sometimes triple) dramatic meaning. The devices they exploit here are almost
identical to those of subsequent shows, most obviously *Gypsy* (1959). Indeed,
Mama Rose's breakdown at the end of "Rose's Turn," expressed in dramatic
and character terms through the celebrated interplay of the musicodramatic
language of that show,[136] leans heavily—although probably unwittingly—on
the prototype developed here.

Ever Green was another hit for Rodgers and Hart and was subsequently turned into a film, *Evergreen* (1934), a starring vehicle for Jessie Matthews and a great success for British Gaumont Pictures. As is common, the film bears little similarity to the stage show, though it does retain the conceit of a young starlet pretending to be older than she is for promotional purposes. Only three Rodgers and Hart songs are kept: "Dancing on the Ceiling," "Dear, Dear," and "If I Give In to You," and a number of other songs by Harry M. Woods are interpolated. "Dancing on the Ceiling" becomes less prominent than in the stage version, though its placement of the song and dance number as an expression of the psychological anticipates Hollywood's subsequent reliance on this device in films such as *An American in Paris* (1951) and *Singin' in the Rain* (1952). Instead, the musical showstoppers become "When You've Got a Little Springtime in Your Heart" and "Over My Shoulder," both choreographed to lavish routines by Buddy Bradley. The film is a well-respected favorite in the UK, though it is not really Rodgers and Hart's work. Indeed, lost as it now is from the public's recollection, and eclipsed by the success of this film, Rodgers and Hart's *Ever Green* remains an intriguing though forgotten piece of theatrical nostalgia, most significant because of its contribution to their repertoire.

Rodgers and Hart's London odyssey—played out against the challenging economic conditions of a general strike, mass unemployment, and a worldwide depression—was a whirlwind experience (Figure 5.9). Starting out little

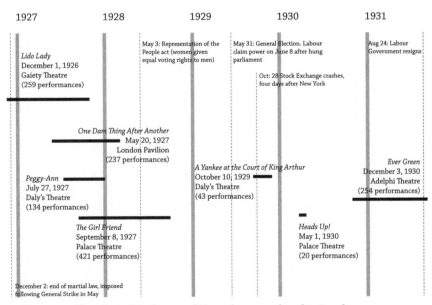

Figure 5.9: Timeline of Rodgers and Hart shows produced in London, 1925–1931.

known and with a disappointing beginning at the tail end of 1926, it's a narrative that can be spun in two ways: possibly it is a great success story—seven West End productions and a total of 1,368 performances in little over three years, including four shows playing simultaneously during 1927, a feat bettered only by Andrew Lloyd Webber's domination of the 1980s. Or possibly it is a story of hits and misses—shows sustained thanks to the popularity of their stars (*Lido Lady*, *One Dam Thing*, *Ever Green*); shows ripped apart and interpolated with other writers' material (*The Girl Friend*); the shortest run of the pair's professional career (*Heads Up*, which closed after twenty performances). Either way, this corpus of work represents a vivid snapshot of Rodgers and Hart, and can even be seen as a microcosm of their whole career: successful at points, and hit and miss at others.

6

BIG FISH

• • •

PEGGY-ANN (1926), ZIEGFELD, AND A FLOP CALLED BETSY (1926)

Dick and Larry's first trip to London had been a mixed experience, and in their own recollections they seem pleased to have left behind the very different theatrical scene. Back home, both *The Girl Friend* and the second *Garrick Gaieties* were still going strong, and they were keen to get properly started on Herb's next idea, which he had put to them before they left for England.

But for Dick at least the voyage back would offer a distraction. Among the passengers was a young lady with whom he was already acquainted, the sister of his friend Ben Feiner. Rodgers recounts having met Dorothy some months earlier at the Feiner house, where he had been captivated. Now the couple had four long days at sea to become properly acquainted. "The two of us spent all our waking hours together, from the morning walks around the promenade deck to the late-at-night sessions on the sun deck. By the time we reached New York we had managed to get to know each other well enough to know that we wanted to know each other better."[1] They were smitten, and it wouldn't be long before, in 1930, Dorothy Feiner became Mrs. Richard Rodgers. As they sailed into New York harbor, she must have been impressed by her new leading man: the cast of the *Garrick Gaieties* was there to greet the ship in a specially chartered tugboat with an enormous banner: "Welcome home, Dick and Larry," it read. Welcome home, indeed.

PEGGY-ANN (1926)

The *New York Times* had already announced that the boys' next show would be *Peggy-Ann*; now they had to start work. Herb's idea had come from scouring his father's back catalogue and pulling out a popular success called *Tillie's*

Nightmare, which Lew had produced with the Shuberts in 1909. That show, written by Edgar Smith with music by A. Baldwin Sloane, had starred the larger-than-life comic actress Marie Dressler, whose character Tillie—already popular from Smith's earlier play *The College Widower*—went on to be featured in three silent movies.[2] *Tillie's Nightmare* is a Cinderella story. Long-suffering Tillie is forced by her mother to stay at home doing the chores while the family and their boardinghouse guests go out on the town. Tillie falls asleep and dreams of her own glamorous adventure. In her dreams, she becomes the toast of New York, boarding her own yacht and then taking to the skies in a startling new invention, the airplane.

Quite why Herb selected *Tillie's Nightmare* so enthusiastically is perplexing. Although the show had been successful in New York, it was very much a vehicle for Dressler. "No one much cared that *Tillie's Nightmare* was nearly plotless and most closely resembled a musical revue. No one much cared that the songs were largely forgettable," writes Matthew Kennedy.[3] "It was her show entirely. The rest of the cast was there to service her comedy."[4] Without Dressler, one suspects, this show would have been an out-and-out turkey. More than this, the pre-Broadway period had been for Lew Fields one of the most excruciating of his career. "Ill will flowed in all directions," reports Kennedy. "Morale was low, notices were bad, expenses were high and Marie was on her worst behaviour."[5] Dressler and her husband were intolerable, the chorus lacked discipline, and tour manager Henry Winchell seemed profligate with company expenses. Lew Fields—having invested heavily—had to plead with the Shuberts not to scrap the production before it reached Broadway, and it was only after Winchell was dismissed and seasoned director Ned Wayburn was instated that it began to show any signs of improvement.

Despite its lack of promise, Herb convinced Dick and Larry that a revision of *Tillie's Nightmare* could work. Retitling it *Peggy*, he proposed splitting the central character's role into two; one character would be the Cinderella character, but more of a romantic lead than Tillie; the other would be the comedy part, and this would provide the slapstick.

The plot hewed close to that of its predecessor. Peggy-Ann is engaged to grocery clerk Guy Pendleton, but losing hope that they will ever marry. When she is left at home to do the chores, Guy announces that he is leaving for New York to open his own store and save for their eventual wedding. Peggy-Ann falls asleep and dreams she is on Fifth Avenue, where Guy's new store has opened. They agree to marry, but plans are scuppered when her spiteful sister Dolores sprays everyone with a sleeping drug. Act Two finds the company sailing to Havana on the steam yacht *Peggy*. When a pirate ship pulls alongside and the yacht is boarded, Peggy-Ann saves the day by tickling the pirates into submission. The couple attempt again to tie the knot, but again Dolores spoils their plans, pulling the emergency propeller lever and sinking the ship. Stranded in a lifeboat taking on water, the company are only saved when a talking fish pops up and tows them into Havana. Here Peggy-Ann and Guy—still not married—win a castle and racetrack in a bet. Once more they try to marry but yet again Dolores thwarts them. Meanwhile, Peggy-Ann's talking horse Peggy wins the big race and is whisked to Paris to become a continental star. And Peggy-Ann wakes up. In the dream, she had everything; now she realizes the only thing she does want is Guy. They go off together to the Halloween Dance as the company sing the finale.

Although with its whirlwind of fantastical non sequiturs *Peggy-Ann* seems a bizarre concoction, it struck a chord with critics and enjoyed glowing plaudits. It was "far more satisfying fare than their late success, *The Girl Friend*," in the opinion of the *Sun* reviewer,[6] while the *Times* called it "Bright and fantastic,"[7] and the *American* "a fast-moving show with not a dull moment."[8] The score was "one of the best of the season"—considerable praise given the number of shows produced in 1926–27—and Rodgers was noted to be "fast becoming a second Gershwin" with "a shining gift as a tunesmith." The same reviewer spoke highly of Larry too: "the lyrics of Lorenz Hart were a joy," he suggested. "They always are."[9]

Naturally, there were detractors: the *Herald Tribune* took a dislike to the show, saying that "the musical score was utterly without flavor, originality or distinction of any sort" and that "many of the jests were not fresh."[10] The reviewer for the *Telegram* sounds bad-tempered, disliking the "silly horse" and griping that "the enthusiasm evoked by what is called a 'musical comedy' may be in inverse ratio to the wit of the book and the importance of the music."[11] In the Philadelphia tryouts, reviewers also criticized hackneyed comedy routines, like the staging of the horse race and a seasick woman routine. "As for the music," continued one, "the worst of it is now that the good numbers are poorly sung and the poor ones sung the best."[12] But these points seem picky, and in general the notices were at least favorable and often effusive. Many critics spotted the musical's link to *Tillie's Nightmare* but enjoyed the one major difference—the new comedy character (Mrs. Frost), played by vaudevillian Lulu McConnell "whanging her comedy business across with broadax";[13] she reminded critics of Marie Dressler[14] and is credited with stealing the show.[15] Exactly two months after opening night, Alexander Woollcott finally gave his judgment, and he loved it: *Peggy-Ann* was "Nutty fudge brought in hot from the kitchen in a pan," he waxed; compared to the lavish Ziegfeld show *Rio Rita* (which had just opened as the first show in the new Ziegfeld Theater), this was a "small, scrubby, tattered rag-doll of dubious ancestry"; but it was this rather than the "great, big, richly-dressed, eye-rolling doll" of the Ziegfeld event that Woollcott preferred.[16]

Although there are familiar musical comedy characters and a dramatic trajectory based on romance and subterfuge, the conceit of the extended dream scene introduces some unlikely characters in a whimsical chain of unexpected events. In this, it borrows heavily from two obsessions of the time: the work of Sigmund Freud and the emergence of American expressionism on the stage.

The public fascination with Freud had led to a populist understanding of both psychoanalysis and his theories relating to dreams. Freud had visited America in 1909 with Carl Jung to give a series of lectures at Clark University in Massachusetts. The translation into English in 1913 of his *Interpretation of Dreams* was eagerly received, and in the mid-twenties, lucrative invitations to write for Hollywood and to act as expert witness for the Leopold and Loeb murder trials (both of which Freud turned down) showed that his work was recognized and admired in America. Varying accounts suggest he was both thrilled that his theories were becoming international and skeptical about what he saw as the popularization of his "scientific" enquiry.

Meanwhile, Broadway's fascination with expressionism had blossomed through the 1920s with successes from playwrights like Eugene O'Neill and Elmer Rice. Their assertive move away from naturalism, which they judged an inadequate reflection of the world, grappled with heightened theatricality to reflect "the essential life of the soul that exists beyond everyday reality."[17] If the tone of American expressionism from these writers was weighty, it was balanced by the more uplifting pastiche of others such as George S. Kaufman with *Beggar on Horseback* (1924), with which *Peggy-Ann* was frequently compared. These took on the aesthetic and form of expressionism—"nightmarish visual images," "exaggerated caricatures or abstract types," "episodic and often disconnected" scenes[18]—to comic effect, relying on the audience's familiarity with tropes of expressionism but spinning them into quirky, dream-like scenarios and introducing characters such as talking fish and horses.

Although *Peggy-Ann* is hardly a Freudian tract, its dream conceit plays mischievously with the popular understanding of how dreams process material from our waking life; and in resolving Peggy-Ann's dilemmas through this device it gestures toward a sort of figurative psychoanalysis. Meanwhile, the show bursts with references to topical issues, public figures, and popular theatrical styles. The staging of the final scene at a Cuban hotel and racetrack, for example, responds to Cuba's becoming an alternative holiday location and enjoying a flood of US tourists following a devastating Florida hurricane earlier in the year. John McEntee Bowman's Sevilla-Biltmore and Oriental Park

Racetrack, "the most glamorous hostelry in Cuba,"[19] became inspirations for the hotel and racetrack that Peggy-Ann and Guy acquire.

Peggy-Ann's first encounter in her dream world is with a policeman on Fifth Avenue, whose instructions on how to follow the traffic light system are ludicrous. The scene takes an obvious satirical swipe at the police force and the city management. Peggy-Ann can't leave until the light changes to green (though there is no green), and when it turns white all traffic is suspended. This is a scene in which, so to speak, Kafka meets Stalin, and the impression of the latter in the policeman's appearance reinforces the reference (see Figure 6.1). More locally, the caricature mocked recently retired New York Police Commissioner Richard Enright, who had campaigned widely about traffic congestion during his controversial term of office. Staged "in one"—on

Figure 6.1: Helen Ford and Patrick Rafferty in the Fifth Avenue scene from Peggy-Ann. *Photo by White Studio © Billy Rose Theatre Collection, The New York Public Library for the Performing Arts.*

the strip of stage in front of the curtain as the main scene is being changed—the street scene is illustrated with a backdrop of wildly bowing skyscrapers, and the dialogue is the show's first real indication of Peggy-Ann's nonsensical journey: she asks directions to 42nd Street, just around the corner, to be told "You gotta go down here to Broadway, up Broadway to 59th Street, through 59th Street to 8th Avenue—down 8th Avenue to 42nd Street, and through 42nd Street to Fifth Avenue—There you are!"[20]

The aspirational destination of Fifth Avenue signals Peggy-Ann's desires and reflects the cultural obsession New Yorkers had with affluence and glamour. Saks Fifth Avenue may have been the model for the upmarket department store, the company having relocated to its flagship premises around 50th Street just two years previously.[21] In any case, the *Peggy-Ann* customers reflect the height of glamour; they are greeted by name and prove to be the millionaire socialites Mrs. Astor, Mrs. Gould, Mrs. Biddle, and Queen Marie of Romania, who at the time was visiting the United States. One unnamed customer spends $600 (around $8,000 in today's money) on hats and gowns. Glamour is key, then—and even if the internal psychoanalytic integrity of Fields's idea is light, we might speculate that this in fact reveals something about the psyche of the authors or even American audiences.

The scene in Guy's department store concludes Act One with a hurried wedding sabotaged by Peggy-Ann's spiteful sister and her fiancé Arnold Small. The chorus begins, reprising the theme of "Where's That Rainbow?," one of the song hits and Peggy-Ann's "I Want" number, heavily plugged already throughout the act. "Here's that wedding you hear about," sing the chorus, with a bright ensemble feeling cut through by classic Hartian wit: "Here's that torture they cheer about / Here's the females that hang around as the bridesmaids," and eventually "Here's the deadly and fearful fate that betides maids."[22] As Arnold enters, substituting himself for the Minister, a sinister undercurrent of Beethoven's Seventh Symphony emerges in the music. Unsure of how to lead the service, he begins reciting the Gettysburg Address as the ensemble sing. When Dolores sprays the congregation with a poppy seed sleeping potion, Peggy-Ann is left the only character still standing, plaintively singing snatches of "A Tree in the Park" (her rueful lament for Guy) and "Where's that Rainbow?" as the act concludes.

The structure of this ensemble finale is right out of the Gilbert and Sullivan textbook, and given the narrative use of a sleeping drug, it is once more reminiscent of the Act One finale to *The Sorceror*. This is not the only reference to Gilbert and Sullivan in the show; it's not hard to spot the homage to the genteel Pirates of Penzance in Act Two, when Peggy-Ann's yacht is attacked by a hapless bunch who are easily overwhelmed by her plucky charm. However, an even more uncanny similarity can be seen in Moss Hart, Kurt Weill, and Ira Gershwin's *Lady in the Dark* from fourteen years later (1941), which virtually recreates this nightmare wedding scene ("The Woman at the Altar") in just one of many Gilbert and Sullivan–infused parallels. Here, the chorus sings a bright ensemble, "What a lovely day for a lovely wedding," overlaid by movie star Randy Curtis crooning the romantic "This Is New," Russell Paxton performing the nonsensical patter song "It's Never too Late to Mendelssohn," and the voice of the Freudian Dr. Brooks, God-like, challenging the integrity of the marriage: "This is no part of heaven's marriage plan; This woman knows she does not love this man!" As Liza protests and then collapses, a chaotic maelstrom of these themes ends the act. With their mix of Gilbertian topsy-turveydom and Freud-inspired expressionism, *Peggy-Ann* and *Lady in the Dark* seem cut from the same distinctive cloth—it's reasonable to assume that both Moss Hart and Ira Gershwin would have seen *Peggy-Ann* (Weill was at that time still based in Berlin), but was it really an influence?

If the production process for *Tillie's Nightmare* had been a challenge, the preparation for *Peggy-Ann* would not exactly be plain sailing. *Tillie's Nightmare* had been a star vehicle and was carried by its star. *Peggy-Ann* relied as much on the vaudeville skill of Lulu McConnell, and the team was fortunate to have such a solid performer on board, a veteran, as it happened, of *Poor Little Ritz Girl*. Elsewhere, the company leaned on other familiar faces, causing Rodgers, Hart, and Fields to talk in terms of a "family," noting "the genuine fondness and admiration we had for each other."[23] The *Garrick Gaieties* ended its run on October 9, meaning that two of its graduates could join—Edith Meiser as Dolores and Betty Starbuck as Alice. Roy Webb, from Rodgers's Columbia days, was the musical director, and Seymour Felix, whose choreography would be so much admired, late of the *Fifth Avenue Follies*, directed the dancing. There was still that lead part to fill, though, and that was proving tricky.

From the start, Herb had Helen Ford penciled in for the role, though since she was still touring the country in *Dearest Enemy*, she was contractually unavailable. In any case, the history between Ford and Rodgers now that he had a permanent girlfriend may have complicated things. This meant that the production team had to sit through a protracted series of auditions, which Rodgers documents in his letters to Dorothy. Helen Ford is passed over; then second choice Ada May jumps ship to another Ziegfeld vehicle; Ona Munson is cast in a different show, *Twinkle Twinkle*;[24] so the team auditions Dorothy Dilley, recent star of *Kitty's Kisses*, and finally Jane Cochrane, "the only possibility left."[25] In his own way Rodgers is charmingly forthright about the attractive candidates, though this may not have sat well with seventeen-year-old

Dorothy, away at college while Dick led the glamorous life of the Broadway composer. Eventually, with the touring production of *Dearest Enemy* coming to an end in Cincinnati, Helen Ford became available and agreed to take the role. "We were all disheartened and unhappy when Herb decided to give Helen Ford one last try," Rodgers reassured Dorothy; "to be forced into such a disagreeable position was rotten."[26] On the other hand, Rodgers was smitten with her performance in rehearsal: "I'm crazy about 'Peggy' and pray for success as there is something we can point to with some reasonable pride. Helen is simply wonderful in the part."[27] Whether their passions continued to burn is left unclear.

It becomes apparent from the reviews that the show was principally a dance show, which chimes with the increasing emphasis given to dance in the Rodgers and Hart canon as their careers developed. *Lido Lady* was already heavily driven by dance; in *Peggy-Ann*, the choreography of Seymour Felix merited attention in a number of the reviews.

Felix was even commissioned to write an article in the *Herald Tribune*,[28] where he offered his thoughts: "Until not so long ago the staging of musical comedy dances entailed not much more effort than the mere teaching of a few dance steps," he began, quickly dismissing the early 1920s crazes such as the Charleston and the "mechanical dolls" of the Tiller lineups; "it was all very lovely, all very interesting until the bag full of tricks was emptied." The thrust of his article argued for dance to service the narrative of a show and for routines to be (in his words) "'book' numbers," something Rodgers and Hart would undoubtedly have embraced, and something that would have delighted former dance director Herb Fields.

Felix cited two of the numbers from the first act of *Peggy-Ann*, "Howd'y to Broadway" and "Charming, Charming." Both are really no more than establishing numbers, the sort of "Here we are in [interchangeable location]" numbers that have graced plenty of musical comedies before and since *Peggy-Ann*. Nevertheless, Felix at least claimed a more dynamic role that he obviously wanted to underline. In "Howd'y to Broadway" "the girls convey the idea of tradition [does he mean 'transition'?] from country to city by pantomime and by a change of costume right before the eyes of the audience." Meanwhile, it was reviewers who recorded their impressions of "Charming, Charming": "the boys and girls danced until every bone and muscle in their body must have ached," wrote one (referring to the composer as "Richard Dodgers");[29] they "danced until the chorus was almost gaspless," joked another.[30] This, according to a third, was "probably the most sustained bit of jiggling now rattling the boards of Broadway. Yet they caper through it with the willingness of daisies dancing in the breeze."[31]

Felix clearly valued his contribution to the show, but as he continues to discuss the second act numbers, he reveals not so much that his choreography was groundbreaking but that the *process* was unexpected and stimulating. He notes that the second act dispensed with a full chorus opening number and marvels at such innovation: "Imagine a dance director who could overlook the opportunity for a 'flash' in the old days. Not he. Here is where he would 'pep up' the show, displaying costumes, waking up the audience for the thrills to come." Instead—and here is the significant point—"*we* [my emphasis] have depended upon chuckles and laughs to put our friends in good humor for the scenes to come."

In truth, the choreographic ideas do not seem particularly novel, even for 1926—and especially following the dramaturgical use of dance in *Lido Lady*. Felix goes on to discuss the "Havana" number, for example, as a competition between the Cuban girls (with a tango-based dance style) and the American visitors (with a "Black Bottom" routine)—not much new there. But what is new for him is that he seems to have participated in collaborating on the show. This becomes most clear in his comments about the show's conclusion, which brings Peggy-Ann back to mundane reality as she wakes up. "I think I am proudest of the finale," he writes. "We cut the closing scene as much as we dared. Still we had no finale, in the conventional sense, for it would have been disastrous to lower the curtain on a dark, quiet scene. For a long time we ransacked our brains for an idea. At last it came. Why not a quiet dance finale? Why not a comedy finale?" What Felix expresses here with such delight is that the decision-making process of this show has been something in which he was involved, and that the show's ostensible "authors"—higher up the creative pecking order, so to speak—have welcomed his input.

Several differing versions of the libretto reveal the revisions to the ending, even if these innovations seem modest. The original script concludes with Peggy's final line, "Guy, I'm so glad you loved me," cueing nothing more than "FINALE by Entire Company."[32] Another version has the climactic race number cross-fading like a dream into the final scene with Peggy-Ann asleep:

They're off!
Gotta do the washing
Gotta do the washing.
Keep it up!
Gotta can the peaches.
Gotta can the peaches.[33]

The final redraft lays out the plan for the dramaturgically more interesting ending in which the music emerges from the play:

Music starts playing "Hello" very piano. GUY and PEGGY walk down stage, then two boys come on singing very piano, then MR. and MRS. FROST come on, MRS. FROST starts to sing very loud everybody says sh-sh, then FREDDY and PATRICIA come on, then ALICE comes on singing loud and COMPANY quiet her, then rest of the company come on and go down stage and start singing the theme number until Curtain.[34]

In fact, though the stage directions do not reveal as much, the final moment had the company tiptoeing to the footlights, and in a charming gesture of theatricality, blowing them out.

This is not integration as we know it from the Rodgers and Hammerstein period—on the contrary; this is a finale number bringing on the whole cast to sing a medley of already established song hits from elsewhere in the show. However, there is integration in a sense, since the ensemble song assumes a dynamic suited to the mood of the final scene. While the song itself is nothing more than a "number," it is integrated into the dramatic arc of atmosphere created through the play. Interruptions to the mood of calm offer comic moments, but the chorus conclude the show at a subdued level that is both unconventional and consistent with the dynamic of the drama.

This ending clearly comes from the same creative instinct we saw in *Lido Lady*, which concluded with Jack Hulbert's expressive rose dance—even if it is rather less sophisticated. Fresh from their work on the London show, Rodgers and Hart were obviously absorbing into their practice a sense of experimentation with the established musical comedy form, and this in no small part was enabled through working with collaborators. The idea of the family, it seems, was more than just a fond view of their creative team; it also articulated the team's creativity emerging from a shared process, from dialogue, and from a mutual respect between collaborators.

BETSY (1926)

Such respect was not so evident with the parallel project on which the boys were involved, a show called *Betsy* commissioned by the impresario Florenz Ziegfeld. It was a foolish commission to take on, given their workload; but under the circumstances, they were hardly going to refuse.

Florenz Ziegfeld had risen to become the greatest producer on Broadway. From 1907 he had staged his annual *Follies* revues, capitalizing on the American infatuation with all things French, and showcasing a melange of "sentimental love songs, topical numbers, social parodies, comic spectacles, and displays of beautiful women set to music."[35] He had been instrumental in forging the careers of several of Broadway's new writers: Irving Berlin was a regular collaborator on the *Follies*; George Gershwin had his first Broadway experience as rehearsal pianist for *Miss 1917* (1917); Jerome Kern had scored an enormous hit with *Sally* (1920), marking Ziegfeld's assertive step into musical comedy.

He was without doubt the most eminent producer in town, renowned for the scale and quality of his shows. If Rodgers and Hart were to rise to the highest echelons of success, Ziegfeld could offer the route-map. Compared to the "Great Glorifier," Lew Fields was small fry, struggling, hit and miss in his output, and under contract to the Shuberts. By contrast, Ziegfeld was at the height of his fame and busy overseeing the construction of his own Ziegfeld Theater. When it opened in early 1927 it bore his name beneath a façade of classical figures: "More than any of his shows, the theater would exhibit the great in The Great Ziegfeld," writes Marmorstein;[36] "if Dick and Larry . . . hadn't thought of themselves as having arrived, they did now."[37]

Ziegfeld's new show was a vehicle for vaudeville star Belle Baker, part of a two-show deal the boys would fulfill with *Simple Simon* (1930), headlining Ed Wynn. Ziegfeld had encountered Baker sailing back from the Continent and had been "bowled over"[38] by her star appeal. A diminutive figure from the Yiddish theater, "she knew how to put a song across, laughing and crying almost simultaneously and compelling an audience to listen."[39] She was the self-styled "Bernhardt of songs," using melody to create "pathos and drama,"[40] and her act was littered with ethnic caricatures of Irish, Italian, or Yiddish immigrants, drawn from the personalities among whom she had been raised. *Betsy* exploited this immigrant portrayal: responding to his previous success with *Sally*—about an Irish immigrant family—Ziegfeld proposed for Baker a show about a Jewish immigrant family.

Betsy is the eldest sister of a large household, whose sons are forbidden to marry until they have found her a suitable husband. Lining up the next-door pigeon trainer Archie, Betsy's brothers try all manner of stunts to unite the couple. In the end, Archie falls for Betsy's sister Ruth, and Betsy instead turns to a life on the stage and an opportunity to showcase a medley of Belle Baker standards.

Peggy-Ann and *Betsy* were slated to open on consecutive nights, December 27 and 28, 1926 (at one point it seemed they might open on the same night). Rodgers was rather blasé about this clash, perhaps seeing promotional mileage in it. "Just think of the fun that means," he wrote in a letter to Dorothy;[41] "I think it's a funny world. Don't you?"[42] Given the meteoric rise to success the boys had encountered in little over a year, they no doubt delighted in pressing this sentiment into song for the new Ziegfeld show: "This funny world / Makes fun of the things that you strive for," went Hart's lyrics; "If you're broke you shouldn't mind. / It's all a joke for you will find / This funny world is making fun of you."[43]

One can imagine Dick and Larry's mutual back-slaps over that little in-joke, though the production process of this new show was far from fun. Rodgers in particular found Ziegfeld testing, and their personalities seem to have clashed. In his letters to Dorothy he writes of the "three-hour battle" to sign contracts "with his lawyer and ours at each other's throats";[44] he reports Ziegfeld being "neglectful and not exactly proper in his dealings with me. . . . It makes me sick";[45] and he reveals that things came to a head in "a terrific blow-up" on December 3 when "Z. and the general manager bawled me out for not appearing at enough rehearsals. Z. said some rotten things and I told him I was 'through with his lousy show.' "[46] By the time the show opened for previews on December 22 in Washington, DC, Rodgers was through: "I don't like it at all. The book, if you can call it that, is terrible and the score has been such a source of extreme annoyance that I'm anxious only to have it all done with. . . . All I know is that I'm tired and I hate Ziegfeld."[47] The final straw came when Rodgers and Hart sat down for the New York opening of the show. Without their knowledge, Ziegfeld interpolated a song by Irving Berlin to assuage his leading lady. Not confident that "This Funny World" was the show hit she required, she had consulted her longtime friend Berlin, who dusted off a partially written song from his trunk. "Blue Skies" was an instant success, Baker was called back for no fewer than twenty-three encores, and Berlin received a rapturous ovation from the crowd. That had to smart: it was a flashback to *Poor Little Ritz Girl* when their music was replaced by Sigmund Romberg's, and a reminder to Rodgers and Hart of just how fickle Broadway was. Rodgers reportedly didn't talk to Berlin for almost ten years.

One might wonder why Ziegfeld did not turn to Berlin in the first place to write the show. Berlin had worked extensively with the impresario and had provided a number of popular successes. He was also Belle Baker's songster of choice. Instead, Rodgers reports Ziegfeld wooing him with a very personal invitation: "You two are the whiz kids of Broadway. . . . I wouldn't think of doing it with anyone else." As he asks in his autobiography, "How could I possibly refuse?"[48] Still, in characteristic Ziegfeld fashion, that was just a sales pitch, and however much he admired their work, he had no intention of creating the sort of book show Rodgers and Hart had created with Herb Fields for *Dearest Enemy, The Girl Friend,* and *Peggy-Ann.* Not only did *Betsy* include material scavenged indiscriminately from various sources (including specialty acts and songs by several writing teams), but Ziegfeld also trampled over everyone in pursuit of what he felt worked. The original writing team of Irving Caesar and David Freedman, for example, provided song material in an original script called *Buy Buy Betty*, but most of that was dismissed when Ziegfeld approached Rodgers and Hart. Even so, *Betsy* hardly became a full-blown Rodgers and Hart show: several numbers in the New Amsterdam program are credited to other writers—"Tales of Hoffman" and "Leave It to Levy" are by Caesar; "Follow On" by "the daughters of the Belles of New York"; specialty acts included a show-stealing rendition of Gershwin's "Rhapsody in Blue" by Borrah Minnevitch on the harmonica (see figure 6.2); and finally, Belle Baker finished off proceedings with a concert of her well-known songs, including her hit from the previous year, "My Kid" (by Al Dubin, Jimmie McHugh, and Irwin Dash). Frankly, as many of the reviewers reported, this was little more than "a pretty good two-a-day variety show";[49] or as the *Judge* put it, "a Keith vaudeville show dolled up for the expensive Broadway trade."[50]

In fact, this was formulaic Ziegfeld, whether he was producing revues or musical comedies. The storyline was "lost every now and then in a revue maze,"[51] leaving the whole show "disastrously betrayed by the wiles of a plot

Figure 6.2: Belle Baker as the title character of Betsy *with Borrah Minnevitch, leader of the Harmonica Symphony Orchestra. Photo by White Studio © Billy Rose Theatre Collection, The New York Public Library for the Performing Arts.*

that left it flat before the evening was half over."[52] Although in truth Ziegfeld had never pretended otherwise, this was a star vehicle whose narrative material was just so much fluff between appearances by Belle Baker and comic Jimmy Hussey. As we have seen, using musical comedy as a star vehicle for vaudeville headliners who would bring in the crowds had been the strategy of producers such as Ziegfeld and Dillingham since the mid-teens. Ziegfeld's *Follies* had already created many of these stars—Eddie Cantor, Fanny Brice, Marilyn Miller—and he turned increasingly to producing musical comedy vehicles tailored to their talents. *Sally* (1920) was Marilyn Miller's musical comedy debut; *Kid Boots* (1923) a showcase for Eddie Cantor; even *Show Boat* (1927)—the stalwart of integration that always seems somewhat incongruous within the Ziegfeld repertoire—was planned as a vehicle for Paul Robeson, its second act intended to be given over to a concert performance.

Caesar and Freedman's script for *Betsy* is scripted hokum at its finest, with scene after scene of comic banter, daft antics and carefully set up gags. These are all set pieces which score highly on laughs, but what suffers is the storyline. A lengthy scene on the beach in Act One, for example, has nothing to do with the plot, serving as an excuse to costume the girls in bathing suits and allow the comics some ridiculous business. This takes up twenty-nine pages of script (roughly a fifth of the show), confirming one critic's accusation that "after a preliminary skirmish with a plot . . . , the production discarded any further pretense . . . and became completely revue, even vaudeville."[53]

Musical comedy may have been on the billing, then, but this show had Ziegfeld's stamp of revue all over it. The first run out of town lasted well beyond one o'clock,[54] and after just a week of trials in Washington, DC—in a hastily rewritten form—it came straight into town. For all its virtues, *Betsy* just wasn't ready, and in that state it did no one any favors. Belle Baker was "hopelessly miscast"[55] in anything requiring her to act, opined some; "no ingenuity for stage effects, however opulent and spacious soever, could make Miss Belle Baker a musical comedy heroine,"[56] wrote one critic (though to be fair, Robert Coleman in the *Daily Mirror* thought her "splendid"). And Rodgers and Hart fared no better: Baker rendered their "smart tunes more than a little heavy and ponderous,"[57] according to the *Times*, though for the *Herald Tribune*, "[not even] the most gorgeous mise-en-scène or the most agile dancing by the most beautiful chorus [could] atone for the insufficiencies of Mr. Rodgers's music."[58] For Rodgers and Hart it was "not a highly successful evening,"[59] concluded the *Times* in something of an understatement. *Variety* called the whole thing "a butchered show" and put its judgment in no uncertain terms: "It's a waste of space to give this Ziegfeld production any attention."[60]

Still, it did have its virtues, even if these were chiefly demonstrated by the female chorus and the scenery. The girls were "typical Ziegfeld beauties, many of them getting their first touch at glorifying,"[61] wrote one early reviewer; "a pulchritudinous, vivacious and gorgeous bevy of beauties."[62] Ziegfeld was known for his girls, of course, and even if this show boasted a dramatic storyline (of sorts) and focused on the life of a small Jewish family, he still found room for "forty-odd bundles of sex appeal" on the stage.[63] Opinion was divided on quite how risqué Ziegfeld had made that appeal: some thought the show "bright and spotlessly clean,"[64] appearing slightly surprised that "all the girls wore stockings or tights" and that "there wasn't a bare leg to be seen";[65] others viewed the girls' apparel as "more scant, if possible, than any hitherto revealed."[66]

In terms of staging, the opening scene was particularly impressive—"a masterpiece of stage setting and effect,"[67] as one reviewer wrote, "with the lights of Brooklyn twinkling across the East River and the traffic moving on a nearby bridge."[68] One early draft script describes the scene, creating an evocative picture of the roof of an East Side settlement house at night. As strains of party music from a Jewish engagement party next door wane, an accordion player plays, and on the roof we see Archie, a pigeon trainer feeding his birds. "He guides them about in circles having them fly off and return, the pigeons flying occasionally to the foreground over the settlement roof." Caesar and Freedman imagine the scene not only visually but also as a soundscape:

> The fiddlers finish with a characteristic flourish. Applause within. For a moment nothing is audible but the accordion on the roof, R.C. Then the man and woman on roof R.C. stop dancing and the accordion stops. Again there is a moment's pause. ARCHIE is heard whistling to his birds. After his signals they all return to roost. Gradually ARCHIE's back is turned and when the action of the play begins he and his birds make a slow exit.[69]

If Hammerstein and Fields's unrealized rooftop denouement for *Winkle Town* showed dramaturgical brilliance in its staging of the city, this scene shows equal flair for creating stage atmosphere. One can imagine the transition in mood from the raucous energy of klezmer music and dancing to the lonely lament of the accordion and finally to the silence of the rooftop at night, punctuated by the intimate whistle of the bird trainer and the unusual sound of birds flocking to rest. Once again, it is an enchanting glimpse of the skyline at night that charms the audience, emphasizing the continued fascination of the Broadway musical with its locale and New York's evocative cityscape. Here, Caesar and Freedman show a real understanding of spectacle and an ability in their writing to capture and control the audience's focus, establishing Archie as the sympathetic central character around whom the drama turns (see Figure 6.3).

Figure 6.3: Drawing in the New York Times *on January 9, 1927, of the cast of* Betsy. *Notice the pigeon trainer Archie's dynamic position. Billy Rose Theatre Collection, The New York Public Library for the Performing Arts, Astor, Lenox and Tilden Foundations.*

One would imagine, too, that this opening sequence would offer Rodgers and Hart an opportunity to experiment with a use of music to dramaturgical effect, as they liked to do and as they had in *Winkle Town*, *The Melody Man*, *Dearest Enemy*, and *Lido Lady*—virtually all of the shows they had created. But for whatever reasons—a lack of time, an overwhelming workload, a less than collaborative production process—this was not to be the case. And with Ziegfeld they were at cross-purposes—he wanted hit songs for a star vehicle; they wanted integrity and a well-crafted musical comedy. For everyone, the conceit of mounting a formulaic show too quickly while focusing on other more personal projects (Ziegfeld's theater; Rodgers and Hart's *Peggy-Ann*) smacks of hubris.

Rodgers remained dismissive about this show and his whole relationship with Ziegfeld. Even fifty years later he continued to argue that Ziegfeld was "not a nice man."[70] In a candid interview he talked about his experiences on *Betsy*:

> [Ziegfeld] was awful. There was no relationship at all, except, oh, disagreeable encounters. Ziegfeld as far as I know was only good to the girls in his shows. He was very generous with them and very decent with them. But as far as I know, not with anyone else—certainly not with Larry and me.[71]

Quite why he was so upset at the interpolation of Berlin's "Blue Skies," though, is intriguing. The show was already a hotchpotch from at least five different writing teams (Rodgers and Hart; Caesar and Freedman; the Belles of New York; Gershwin; Dubin, McHugh, and Nash). It was hardly unusual for shows of this period to feature interpolations or to have scores put together like a patchwork quilt; this was a standard producing ploy to juggle the figures. And Rodgers and Hart were no strangers to this approach, having had their own material interpolated in many shows by other writers. "Did Rodgers really have no idea that 'Blue Skies' was going in?" asks Ethan Mordden; "*No one* in the production gave him a heads up?"[72]

Differing reports of *Betsy*'s opening night provide intriguing variations on the tale, some perhaps rather fanciful in their claims. Laurence Bergreen, for example, suggests that when Baker forgot the lyrics after numerous encores, "instantly, Berlin who was sitting in the first row, shot to his feet, shouted out the words, and sang the twenty-fourth encore of the song with her before the enraptured crowd."[73] Press reports from first night critics who were present are more circumspect: "Mr. Berlin sat out front and held out for eight minutes against Miss Baker's wheedling 'Aw, c'mon Irving.' Then he arose and bowed bashfully," reported the *Telegram*.[74] This has more plausibility—and *Variety*'s review of the first night concurs; "[Baker] called upon Irving to join in....Irving wouldn't sing but he did stand up to take a bow to still the clamor."[75] Still, Baker's partnership with Irving Berlin was well known, and Bergreen makes the claim that it was a convention of her vaudeville act that when he was watching her perform, she would "point to the audience, the spotlight following her finger until it alighted on the diminutive figure of Berlin himself, who would stand, receive the enraptured audience's tribute, and sing an extra verse or two, much to their delight";[76] perhaps it is not surprising that someone—Baker, Ziegfeld, maybe even Berlin himself—tried to interpolate this performative routine into *Betsy* as part of the performance of a vaudevillian introducing a new Berlin hit. "That was vaudeville, that free and easy big-time vaudeville," writes *Variety* rather witheringly of the stunt.[77]

Rodgers's nose was clearly put out of joint, even if one senses behind the animosity that something more may have been at stake. A year later when in the same manner Beatrice Lillie interpolated a number of her hits into *She's My Baby*, he hardly raised a brow—though one review would have come as something of a balm: the *Baltimore Evening Sun* praised his work, material "that transcends the meowing music and lumpy lyrics of Mr. Irving Berlin and others of the hack fraternity."[78] Payback at last, perhaps, for the "Blue Skies" slight. But perhaps his gripe was more a personal issue with Ziegfeld than with the show, brought to a head by the interpolation of the Berlin song. Perhaps he bristled at rushing through mediocre material; perhaps he resented missing rehearsals at which he could control how it was used; perhaps he felt left out of important production decisions such as which song hits were going to be interpolated; most of all, perhaps he envied the adoring accolades directed at a rival whose glittering career Rodgers was desperate to enjoy. *Betsy* was a wake-up call in many ways: aside from anything else, it reminded Dick and Larry that there was still a long way to go.

Betsy was generally perceived to have been a mess, and an expensive one at that. This was a $100,000 show that *Variety* was already shooing out the door just a week after it opened. Even with tickets priced at $4.40 ($60 in today's prices)—top end for 1926—the box office was only reporting a weekly gross of $23,000 on a capacity of $36,000.[79] That was hardly sustainable, and short of further drastic action, Ziegfeld had no option but to close after thirty-nine performances. "Perhaps if Ziggy had had his own money in it he would have given the thing some attention,"[80] chided *Variety*. Instead, it was his main backer, millionaire steel magnate J. Leonard Replogle, who bore the loss.

As *Betsy* came and went, *Peggy-Ann* settled in for a more sustained season, becoming Rodgers's favorite show of the 1920s. Following its Broadway run, it also had a reasonable afterlife, though one in which it diminished in public esteem. It was broadcast on WEAF radio on September 3, 1927, though this was not entirely successful, judging by the *New York World*'s comment that "when the actors were not screaming their lines, their voices were distant and indistinct and there was a great deal of attendant noise."[81] Later it was taken to London, where the comments suggested the same: "Everyone in it seems to have a high pitched voice and to keep it pitched high throughout the whole performance."[82] In the wake of *Lido Lady* and the veiled hostility of the British press, this reinforces the fact that British and American shows and their audiences were fundamentally different. "Even the most convinced admirer of the American tradition in musical comedy must have wished for just five minutes of some woman with a voice which is low and modulated, and for one tune which could forget trying to be clever and begin trying to be gentle," continued the reviewer for the *London Evening News*. The *Westminster Gazette* agreed, igniting a conversation topic that would escalate throughout 1927 in regard to the plugging of show tunes in the new American imports: "Why will American producers spoil what pleasure one might take in tunes by innumerable repetitions?"[83] the correspondent asked. What English papers didn't realize was what Rodgers and Hart were just learning: that the craft to their art was in juggling the integrity of their writing with the exigencies of scoring a commercial hit.

7

A COMMERCIAL SUCCESS
• • •
A CONNECTICUT YANKEE (1927)

Throughout the early part of 1927, as Dick and Larry whizzed around Europe, Rodgers was in regular communication with his new young sweetheart. It's surprising he found any time between social engagements, press interviews, business meetings, and opening nights to even think about his distant girlfriend, but the fact he did is testament to how much Dorothy Feiner meant to the successful young composer. In one letter, he confides that the whole European trip was funded by his royalties from just ten days of box office receipts;[1] in another, he claims that "in three weeks we received offers from every manager in London."[2] What a difference just a couple of years had made: "I keep thinking of eighteen months ago and have to laugh like Hell!"[3] These boys were big, their songs and shows coveted right across the world, and their interests now represented by the very brothers who had previously spurned their work: Max and Louis Dreyfus. These were not the only big names to reconsider the merit of Rodgers and Hart. After years of resisting the project, Lew Fields finally accepted the premise of *A Connecticut Yankee*.

A Connecticut Yankee in King Arthur's Court (1889) is a complex novel, characteristic of Mark Twain at his best. Even today its satire is poignant and amusing, but its strength is the social and cultural commentary framed in the disjunction between two contrasting worlds.

The novel is told in the first person and narrated by its protagonist, Hank Morgan. Early in the story he is surprised to find himself in sixth-century England, where his anachronistic clothes and manner quickly get him arrested and taken to the court of King Arthur. Here he is sentenced to be burned at the stake, but as luck would have it, he remembers that a solar eclipse is due to take place at exactly the time of his death. Hank convinces the crowd that he is an all-powerful sorcerer who can command the sun. After some impressive hocus-pocus, the sky goes black, and an awe-struck King

Arthur reprieves the condemned man. Thereafter, he is known as The Boss, and is revered as second only to the King himself.

This fanciful conceit takes place during the first few pages, establishing a scenario in which Twain can be playfully imaginative. As The Boss presides over the primitive society of Arthurian England, he introduces modern technologies and contemporary ways of thinking. Since he is the supervisor of a munitions factory back in Connecticut, Hank is able to use a knowledge of explosives to maintain his reputation for sorcery. Meanwhile, he introduces a printing press and daily newspaper, a telephone system, bicycles, factories producing soap and toothpaste, and a primitive advertising system using sandwich boards worn by knights as they tour the provinces. Many of these were important innovations introduced to the United States during Twain's lifetime and are in this context civilizing markers of nineteenth-century progress. Twain often introduces them in the book *en passant*, confident that readers will be familiar with the contemporary, giving him time to dwell on fairly detailed discussions of the historical beliefs, customs, and culture of this earlier society. Thus Hank encounters a penal system with no justice, a feudal system whose privileged dominate with impunity, a superstitious faith in sorcery, and a basic lack of common sense. Thanks to his more advanced knowledge, Hank maintains respect and status among the people: he mends a leaking well, for example, through practical know-how but dresses up this simple maintenance as another act of sorcery. Thus he belittles the bogus magic of Merlin, one of many points at which they clash. In the end, their ongoing feud leads to all-out war: Hank trains an army, barricades his forces inside a cave, and proceeds to electrocute thousands of Merlin's knights. With typical Twain irony, this endeavor backfires, leaving fields of rotting corpses that spread disease to The Boss and his men, now trapped within their protective enclave. The Connecticut Yankee ends his Arthurian odyssey in a coma, sleeping fitfully and nursed by his right-hand man Clarence.

Twain's novel was richly praised on publication and immediately gained the status of a literary classic. Its merit lies in the fact that beneath its playful adventure and colorful account of unfamiliar Arthurian life, the book's satire articulates the author's political views, challenging romanticized narratives of chivalry, critiquing the mythology of the frontier, and exposing the hypocrisies of slavery. Written in the wake of the American Civil War, the contexts of that war, particularly its relationship with the politics of slavery, can be keenly sensed. Although in *A Connecticut Yankee* he relocates his narrative to a different time and place, thereby distancing it from direct association with American attitudes (unlike other treatments of the same subject, such as *The Adventures of Huckleberry Finn*, 1884), this theme is writ large in the book. The Yankee encounters slavery wherever he goes, and Twain has no hesitation in expressing his disgust at the inhumanity of the slave trade. In the end, Hank and King Arthur fall victim to an unscrupulous slave trader when they decide to go incognito around the country to experience peasant life. Since no one recognizes them, and since the King keeps behaving inappropriately for a peasant, they are chased from one sticky situation to another, ending up in a slave chain, escaping, being condemned to death, and finally having to be rescued from the gallows by a fleet of troops on bicycles.

Eventually, Hank is able to abolish slavery and establish laws emulating the progressive nineteenth-century civilization with which he is familiar. As he rapidly imports nineteenth-century technologies and educates the people with contemporary attitudes to speed their journey to Enlightenment, it is tempting to see Hank as an avatar of Twain himself. But Twain's writing is more subtle, shackling Hank with a different set of—albeit more moderate—contradictions. Thus Hank becomes, in John Carlos Rowe's words, part "Yankee entrepreneur," part "Barnum-like promoter"[4] whose "theatrical displays and deadly force differ little from the church's enactment of miracles and terror: both are intended to control the workers."[5]

For all its hifalutin' literary merit, *A Connecticut Yankee* is a comedy, showing Twain the humorist at his best. Its fundamental humor is created by bringing contemporary American language, attitudes, and technology into the Arthurian setting: to undermine the pomposity of the knights-errant, Hank dispatches them as "Sandwich Men," who wander the kingdom advertising cosmetic products that don't yet exist; as a substitute for the deadly jousting tournaments he establishes a baseball league; and as a party trick he regularly flabbergasts audiences by predicting events that will happen years in their future. Much of the humor comes at the expense of the Britons, usually scoffed at for their archaic behavior or primitive understanding. Hank's romantic interest, Sandy, is just such a foil. When she christens their child "Hello Central," a common cry from Hank in the middle of the night which she takes to be the name of someone dear from his former life, Hank is blunt: "I didn't laugh—I am always thankful for that—but the strain ruptured every cartilage in me and for weeks afterward I could hear my bones clack when I walked."[6] Elsewhere, humor and satire combine, often at the most grotesque moments of black comedy: when the evil Queen Morgan Le Fay sentences a musician to hang because his music is so terrible, Hank begs a reprieve, listens to it again, then abruptly instructs her to hang the whole band;[7] when he finds himself cornered by the entire might of the round table he pulls out two revolvers and shoots nine of them dead.[8]

A CONNECTICUT YANKEE (1927)

It's easy to see why Rodgers, Hart, and Fields could have been so taken by the situation comedy of *A Connecticut Yankee* when they first encountered it in August 1921. Swinging into the Capitol Theater to view the recent Fox release directed by Emmett J. Flynn,[9] Dick and Herb were captivated. The film—an eight-reeler (c.100 minutes) which has largely now been lost—was rather remarkable: a special set had been built in the Santa Susana district outside Los Angeles, and the props list boasted "three freight cars full of antique and modern trappings, 700 suits of armor and 500 motorcycles."[10] The motorcycles were just one of the updates to the original Twain story, replacing the pedal cycles of 1889. A more contemporary slang was used on the title cards, and references to 1920s technologies and politics (such as the Volstead Act) were rife. The framing device of the novel was likewise adapted, adding romantic intrigue to the plot: in this version the Yankee is one Martin Cavendish, "a wealthy young man whose mother wants him to marry Lady Grey Gordon."[11] Cavendish, however, is in love with his mother's secretary, Betty. One night, he is knocked unconscious by a burglar and in a dream is transported back in time to Arthurian England.

The film was well received, though critics balanced their enjoyment of its humor with criticism of its rather free adaptation. This was "more of the art of Mack Sennett than that of Mark Twain," wrote one;[12] another described it as "Mark rent in Twain."[13] Central to the criticism was the fact that Flynn did away entirely with the social commentary of the novel. Instead, he presented a romantic comedy with swashbuckling overtones somewhat undertoned when Douglas Fairbanks turned down the lead. Instead, the Yankee was played by Harry B. Myers. Still, the film appealed to the boys' humor—it was irreverent, preposterous, and inventive. "We laughed for nearly two hours and walking home decided that there, by cracky, was the perfect idea for a musical comedy."[14] When Dick and Herb reported back to Larry, he too was taken by the idea. Before they could have second thoughts, Rodgers marched into the offices of Charles Tressler Lark, lawyer for the Mark Twain estate, and—at no cost—secured a six-month option on the stage rights. Unfortunately for the boys, this piece of good fortune was countered by the grim naysayers of reality. This was still 1921, and with no track record, the unknown writers had no producers. Their six-month option lapsed, and it was back to the drawing board for the *Connecticut Yankee* idea. Nevertheless, the seed had been sown, precipitating the team's long-running fascination with all things Camelot, and leading to *A Danish Yankee* (1923), "Idles of the King" (1926), "Progress" (1927), and "Make Hey! Hey!" (1927).

One can almost sense the nervous energy driving these Arthurian skits, and by 1927, with a string of successes under their belts, they finally managed to convince Lew Fields to produce the show. Even this was not without its challenges though. Fields was an extremely careful investor in ideas, with his own reputation at stake, and although the boys had proven with *Dearest Enemy* that a historical setting could work for musical comedy, "he preferred a contemporary setting." Besides, "there was no strong romance" in Herbert's first draft; in short, "he could see nothing in the book that would make a good musical."[15]

By coincidence, however, Fields traveled to London at the same time that Rodgers and Hart were working on *One Dam Thing after Another*. The success of *Peggy-Ann* in the United States had encouraged him to bring the show to London, where the boys were establishing a fine reputation. Since Lew was in rehearsal when *One Dam Thing* opened, it is likely he attended a performance shortly into its run. In "Progress" and "Make Hey! Hey!" the boys could show the old-timer how the conceit of *A Connecticut Yankee* might work, putting the contemporary idiom of jazz and the Charleston to comic effect in a historical setting. This sold the idea: "'It's my sort of show,'"[16] Fields admitted. He was hooked, quickly teaming up to co-produce with Lyle D. Andrews, owner of the Vanderbilt Theatre. Arrangements were made to try it out in Connecticut early in October before coming into town in November.

Herb's treatment of the novel uses it loosely and makes liberal cuts with its narrative. Apart from changing the Yankee's name (again) to Martin Barrett, the most significant alteration is to adapt the framing device (again) so that it rationalizes the narrative. Perhaps responding to Lew's reservations (and musical comedy lore), it also amplifies the romantic storyline. As with Flynn's film, the love interest Alice/Sandy is introduced far earlier than in the novel (where Alisande doesn't appear until Chapter 11), though even more than in the movie, she becomes the driving force of the plot.

The show begins with a prologue staging Martin's bachelor party in a Hartford hotel. Unexpectedly, his fiancée Fay Morgan (or Marvin, and later Merrill) turns up, followed by his former girlfriend Alice Carter (later Courtleigh). The name is significant, inverting Morgan le Fay, sister of King Arthur in the Camelot scenes who later kidnaps Sandy. Martin admits he is still in love with Alice and that his marriage to Fay is simply a convenience. Alice begs him to call the wedding off, and the couple sing a passionate duet. When Fay discovers Alice sitting on Martin's lap, she is furious and cracks him over the head with a bottle. He passes out, and by the time he is revived in the show's epi-logue, Fay has disappeared. Martin proposes to Alice and the show ends with the rightful couple reunited.

This contemporary, naturalistic premise—far removed from Twain's mys-terious meeting with a "curious stranger"[17] in Warwick Castle, and removed even from the plot device of the botched burglary in the film—enables a number of stylistic features, not least a contemporary musical style. We accept music at the wedding, and we accept songs of love in the air: two songs in the prologue itself set the tone. "A Ladies' Home Companion" (a reference to the popular magazine) establishes the engaged couple as rather jaded and presents a cynical vision of their future. "I've never any fun," sings Fay; "I feel so tired before my day's begun." This is not a young bride looking for a lover, but a disaffected urbanite seeking "Something that gets sleepy and turns off the light, / Something musical that snores all night." Perhaps she is joking when she refers to Martin as a "domestic animal" and "a monkey who wears trousers";[18] these are nevertheless unexpected terms of endearment for a bride on her wedding eve. So it is not surprising that Martin double-takes when the much younger Alice enters, lavishing him with affection.

By contrast to Fay's song, the duet Alice and Martin sing confirms musi-cally that they are in love and establishes the trajectory of the narrative. As Geoffrey Block asserts, "You're What I Need" "is a simple but engaging song that deserves to be better known."[19] It is well suited to this point in the show, both in plot and character development, so it is surprising to learn that it was replaced as the show headed toward Broadway. The song starts with Alice expressing her desire for Martin. "Long years through / I've been needing you," she sings in the verse, setting up a coy repetition of this idea throughout the refrain. Here, the music is built from a simple pattern repeated in varia-tions: "You're what I need," she murmurs over two notes, mots doux whose simplicity sounds sincere; "I mean, my need / Starts and ends with you."[20] These three phrases, repeated musically with slight rhythmical variation and then a pitch variation one tone lower, give both emphatic expression and confirmation to her initial comment, mimicking the variations in Hart's lyrics. The variations continue ("You've undone me, / I mean, won me…"), with two more short phrases and a final rising intonation on a question to end the first A-section: "Won't you give in, / I mean, live in / My home?" The refrain is structured in AABA form, so this sequence of variations is repeated again before the B section offers a change of thought. Here, Alice offers Martin a fantastical vision of their future, in which he becomes her "sky pilot," to "lead [her] to joy." These are still exciting, futuristic sentiments in 1927, linking love with flight as the writers did in *Fly with Me*. The music colors this sequence with a chromatic, rather exotic harmonic texture, evoking Alice's desire. Finally she returns to the A material, whose last phrase leaps up to the highest point of the song as if her exclamation "I love you so" really is a sigh of passion. It's a charming, lightly syncopated foxtrot that pairs Alice and Martin and distinguishes them from the less appealing Fay. Yet "You're What I Need" was not to last, appearing only briefly in the Connecticut tryout before being replaced by the tried and tested "My Heart Stood Still," from *One Dam Thing after Another*.

As we have seen, there was nothing new about recycling material in the 1920s, and Rodgers and Hart had few qualms about exploiting the commercial potential of their songs. Song hits were big business—this was an industry after all—and "My Heart Stood Still" was relatively unknown to American audiences who had not experienced *One Dam Thing*. It's possible that the decision to use it in *A Connecticut Yankee* was prompted by producer Charles Dillingham, who had been campaigning to have Beatrice Lillie sing it in one of his revues. Rodgers and Hart did not feel she had sufficient vocal ability to do the song justice. In any case, it was still wowing audiences in England, and their London producer Charles Cochran had bought outright permission. In order for the song to be performed at all in New York (even by Rodgers and Hart), someone would have to buy back the rights. Interest in the song soon escalated into a bidding war between producers, Nolan reports,[21] with Florenz Ziegfeld offering Cochran $10,000 to use the song in his next *Follies*. However, with the integrity for which he was recognized, Cochran agreed to sell the rights back to the writing team rather than to the highest bidder. According to his autobiography, he charged a fee of £2,000, then approximately $10,000, equivalent to $325,000 in today's money.[22] Rodgers and Hart's expensive gambit paid off; eventually, "My Heart Stood Still" went on to become one of the biggest selling hits of the era, eclipsing their other successes such as "Here in My Arms." It is one of just six Rodgers and Hart songs listed in *Variety*'s Golden 100 Tin Pan Alley Songs, and the earliest chronologically to hit that jackpot.[23] "My Heart Stood Still" replaced "You're What I Need" and became the hit of *A Connecticut Yankee*.

But this has so far just involved the prologue; Martin hasn't even arrived in Arthurian England where the main action takes place. To be fair, that conceit perhaps did need some setting up. Herb's solution to the bizarre "transposition of epochs—and bodies"[24] narrative was—like the film—to set Martin's Arthurian adventures as a dream that takes place while he is unconscious. As a dream narrative, *A Connecticut Yankee* therefore follows neatly the phantasmagoria of *Peggy-Ann*, and as with that story, any fantastical elements can be explained with a passing reference to Freud. When Martin awakes on the road to Camelot in the year AD 528, he encounters Alice—now Sandy—and again falls head over heels. Like Sandy, who seems vaguely familiar, many of the other characters resemble old acquaintances: his best man, the uncle of the bride, guests at the wedding, and eventually the bride herself. The first to accost him is a knight in shining armor, Sir Kay the Seneschal; and this is where the fun begins.

The main humor in Herb's script from this point—matched by Larry's lyrics—relies on the gimmick of old meets new. When Sir Kay threatens him in his vernacular ("Wit ye well. If ye do spit one flame of fire, I will hack thee limb from limb"), Martin responds using his own ("You've got the meanest way of putting things.... I won't spit fire, I'm on the wagon").[25] Such anachronistic banter would continue, prompting Ethan Mordden—like some of the show's original critics—to consider *A Connecticut Yankee* a one-gag wonder.[26] The idea was "rather transparent and labored," commented Brooks Atkinson in the *Times*,[27] with "too much of that sort of thing for comfort," according to the *Herald Tribune*.[28] Alexander Woollcott agreed: "By the time Merlin, infected by the Yankee's speech, has exclaimed 'Methinks yon damsel is a lovely broad,' and Sir Launcelot of the Lake has cried out 'Away, varlet, thou art full of the juice of the prune,' and Galahad has ejaculated 'Thou hast said a snootful,' the formula does begin to be just a trifle fatiguing."[29] Nevertheless, other reviewers embraced the fun: "Mark Twain hath been done in ye song and dance," cried the *Advocate*,[30] leading the positive notices. In town, the praise continued, if generally more muted: "Go thou sluggard and enjoy 'A Connecticut Yankee' and tell ye cocke-eyed worlde thou hast had ye heluva time."[31] Thanks to the weighty status of the show's source material—"far superior than ordinary musical comedy of current days"[32]—the boys had created a show whose book was "replete with delightful preposterousness,"[33] whose "dialogue really sparkle[d]," whose singing was "excellent," and whose dancing was "a revelation."[34]

The first opportunity for Arthurian song and dance—in the idiom of 1920s jazz, of course, though with lyrics that continued the old/new juxtaposition— was the song "Thou Swell." Although almost cut from the show, "with half the production staff believing the lyric was too complex for the audience to understand," "Thou Swell" has since become a classic.[35] Because of its complexity, Rodgers remembers fighting Lew Fields to keep the song in the score, though he was vindicated by the response it received on opening night. Rodgers took the conductor's baton and stationed himself in front of the audience, from where he could gauge how the audience was responding; though "My Heart Stood Still" "didn't produce the enthusiastic reception I had expected," "Thou Swell" elicited a response "so strong that it was like an actual blow." Rodgers recalls feeling the hairs on the back of his neck standing up with the "deafening"[36] applause at the end of the number.

The song occurs shortly after Martin has met Sandy outside Camelot and the two have fallen in love. It consolidates the feelings already expressed in "My Heart Stood Still" in a different style. This might be expected, given that the action has now decamped to Arthurian England. The style Rodgers and Hart choose, though, is completely anachronistic, establishing the fact that this Connecticut Yankee brings with him very modern, jazz-age sensibilities. "Thou Swell" positively oozes jazz, with its sharp syncopations and verbal somersaults, including the unique "Hear me holler / I choose a / Sweet lolla / Palooza / In thee."[37] After an opening verse that sets up the conceit with a nod to the Arthurian setting and a subtle gesture toward the theme of sorcery ("Babe, we are well met, as in a spell met"), the song kicks into its now familiar refrain, a simple melodic pattern laced over vibrant jazz rhythms.

"Thou Swell" is certainly a singular number, perhaps the most ambitious, even contrived composition in the Rodgers and Hart canon. Hart's fidelity to the old/new conceit of the show is methodical and thorough, right down to the title of the song. In the verses, this juxtaposition of period dialogues continues: Martin's first line, "Babe, we are well met," is followed by Sandy's reply, "Thy words are queer, Sir." Still, she listens to his strange vernacular, and in her second verse echoes his words from the first ("Sandy, thou art dandy"). The music also plays with patterns that sound alternately formal and modern, symbolizing different (if not authentic) musical idioms for the different periods: the first three measures offer a rising sequence in fairly straight meter ("straightlaced, upward-rising, mostly conjunct patterns,"[38] as Graham Wood describes them); the next five present a heavily syncopated retort to this, whose falling sixths ("wildly syncopated, downward-falling patterns with wild leaps")[39] descend in sequence, cutting across the barlines. This is challenging 1920s syncopation, following the ambitious lead set by George Gershwin in songs like "Fascinating Rhythm" (1924).[40] The meter becomes so abused that the sense of the regular beat feels lost. "*Thou Swell* provides ample demonstration of Richard Rodgers's rhythmic inventiveness," writes Allen Forte,[41] and it is perhaps because of this quality that jazz artists Fats Waller (1928), Bix Beiderbecke (1928), Artie Shaw (1936), Stan Getz (1951), Oscar Peterson (1952), and Bud Powell (1957) made it part of their repertoires. In these jazz recordings the song offers the musicians liberating material for their own interpretations. Art Tatum offers three ways of playing it on a single album (1952); Bing Crosby, apparently baffled by the rhythmical complexity of the refrain in one recording (1955) and the verse in another (1976), gives up.[42]

It is the effusive syncopation of "Thou Swell" that really makes the song stand out, a mixture of ragtime, Charleston, and foxtrot rhythms that sometimes vie for attention in the same phrase. Alec Wilder considers the syncopation, and noticing that the rhythmic leaps in the verse "fall in odd places just as a dancer might like them to," suggests that "Thou Swell" could have been "written for Fred Astaire."[43] This comment at first sounds flippant, though Astaire—a big star on Broadway at the time—had been the first to perform "Fascinating Rhythm" in *Lady, Be Good!* (1924) and would go on to make many other syncopated songs familiar standards.[44] Though he does not explain his comment, Wilder's remark suggests there is something in the rhythmic peculiarity of these heavily syncopated songs that lends itself to interpretation by dancers. Allen Forte supports this: the effect of composers attempting with their syncopation "to avoid metric 'squareness'"...is to enhance the regular metric pattern and to make the music more "danceable."[45] As such, qualities of song aside from lyric and character are seen to be equally significant to the writers, and this reminds us that for Lorenz Hart, the musicality of his lyrics is just as significant as the semantic meaning. Indeed, a lyric phrase like "Sandy; / You're just dandy. / For just this here lad" is revealed as semantically clumsy and almost illiterate; however, mapped against its musical phrase, the complex syncopated sequence we have been discussing, the lyrics resonate in a different way, as phonetic elements of the musical texture. Likewise, the infamous line "Hear me holler / I choose a / Sweet lolla / Palooza / In thee" works for its audacious combination of meaning and euphonics. Where the writers are striving to create a performative texture of song out of both music and words, they are additionally attempting, Wilder suggests, to create a performative texture of song in performance that implies the physicality and rhythmic energies of dance.

Such association of the music with dance is significant, not least because the choreographer for *A Connecticut Yankee* was the young Busby Berkeley, who was recognized for his innovative treatment of rhythm and who would be celebrated for his kaleidoscopic choreography in Hollywood films of the 1930s. In the light of Wilder's remarks—that "Thou Swell" seems written to be performed by a dancer—it is worth considering the role of dance within *A Connecticut Yankee* and the responses to Berkeley's choreography (see Figure 7.1).

Busby Berkeley William Enos was born into a theatrical family in 1895. He made his performing debut at the age of five but soon joined a military academy and was conscripted into the US forces in 1917. While serving in France he took drill practice, organizing the troops into precise configurations and geometric patterns, a precursor to the work he would later develop in Hollywood. Returning

Figure 7.1: Photo of the ensemble in A Connecticut Yankee. *Busby Berkeley's influence is evident. Photo by Vandamm Studio © Billy Rose Theatre Collection, The New York Public Library for the Performing Arts.*

to America and his stage upbringing in 1919, he played bit parts and then began choreographing for Broadway productions with the short-lived *Holka Polka* (1925), Friml and Hammerstein's *The Wild Rose* (1926), and the little-known *Lady Do* (1927) before joining the production team of *A Connecticut Yankee*.

Dancing was a notable feature of the show: it was almost universally praised by critics, with Berkeley and dancer Jack Thompson (Sir Galahad) being singled out. Berkeley's unusual cross-cutting of the physical movements with the musical rhythms—a bodily syncopation of dance with music—received particular attention. During his next collaboration with Rodgers and Hart, in *Present Arms* (1928), this approach was discussed in a series of articles by John Martin for the *New York Times*. Martin was taken by the way Berkeley unlocked the dancers' rhythmic expression from the authority of the music: "The dancers are required to execute contrary rhythms, and in one number they are called upon to perform simultaneously two rhythms counter to each other and also the music,"[46] he wrote. "From Martin's perspective," suggests dance scholar Allison Robbins, "dancers needed to distance themselves from the tyranny of music visualization. Berkeley's broken rhythms did just that."[47] If Berkeley's routines were recognized for the way they syncopated the dance with the music, it makes sense that his work should seem compatible with the new sounds of jazz. Although "Thou Swell" was by no means a dance number, its style is consistent with the other *Connecticut Yankee* numbers that were, "On a Desert Isle with Thee" and "I Feel at Home with You," performed by the second couple, Mistress Evelyn La Belle-Ans and Sir Galahad, and the opening ensemble of Act Two.

As we have seen, "Thou Swell" is a sophisticated example of songwriting for a number of different reasons, including its rhythmic complexity, its juxtaposition of old and new idioms, and its awareness of euphonics in the lyrics. Graham Wood also analyzes the song in terms of its structure and considers the difference this sets up dramatically between "Thou Swell" and "My Heart Stood Still." As we have seen from Wood's analysis of *Dearest Enemy*, Rodgers was very conscious of the structural possibilities of songs within the dramatic arc of a show. Here Wood notes that "My Heart Stood Still" is given a Lyric Binary Chorus (AABA), while "Thou Swell" has a Parallel Period Chorus (ABAB/C). This fundamental difference in the makeup of the songs was something with which Rodgers was experimenting in trying to establish different forms for different functions. Thus although "Thou Swell" may appear more playful than "My Heart Stood Still," the underlying structural composition of the chorus, Wood asserts, is read as "a structural pattern suggesting formality and restraint." Wood considers this pattern more suited to the situation not because of any link with the period but because of the way it colors the characters' dramatic situation. By contrast, "a lyric binary chorus at this dramatic moment...would have changed the musical syntax by suggesting the direct expression of youthful love," he suggests.[48]

If this confirms the careful songwriting technique the boys brought to their craft, Allen Forte's examination of the song supports such an observation. He notes how "Thou Swell" is tightly structured around a pentatonic palette—the gapped scale representative of American music. In particular, both the bass line and the melody of the refrain's first eight measures are organized in steps around a cycle of fifths, consolidating the harmonic structure of the passage and, in effect, allowing some of the otherwise unexpected elements (in particular the sixth of the scale) to fit in.[49] Unlike Wood, Forte does not critique his analysis or provide a commentary as to why such structuring might be significant. However, we can assert that the combination of these structural coherences in Rodgers's writing points to deliberate choices about compositional structure relating to dramaturgy, character, and musical idiom; this song, like others of this period, exemplifies the sort of integrational rigor that Broadway's new writers in the 1920s were bringing to their craft.

Having materialized in Arthurian England to the shock of Sir Kay, Martin is marched to the castle where his unseemly attire is a cause of great concern. In Camelot, we encounter the famous figures of the Arthurian tales: King Arthur and Queen Guinevere, his knights Launcelot and Galahad, the wily magician Merlin, and the King's evil sister, Morgan Le Fay. As in the novel, Guinevere barely features, and Launcelot plays only a cameo; however, Morgan Le Fay's role is greatly expanded so that she—rather than Merlin— becomes the main villain of the musical. This scene is set at the Round Table where the knights are breakfasting over an enormous banquet. They sing the first chorus number of the show, "At the Round Table," which introduces the pageantry and pomp of the court with the lyrics of a drinking song and the music of a march. The music is very distinct from the syncopated jazz we have heard from Martin and Sandy, signifying formality and gesturing toward a martial sound; on the other hand, this is clearly not Arthurian music, nor does it pretend to be. In characteristic style, Rodgers continues to work in a contemporary idiom, though he presents a different musical world for Arthur and his knights.[50]

On the other hand, the introduction of the secondary romantic couple, Evelyn and Galahad (two characters who barely feature in the novel), brings back the promise of jazz. Embarking on an illicit affair hidden from Galahad's father the King, they imagine a life away from the court—"On a Desert Isle with Thee." Much of the comedy suggests that Galahad is gay, or in the words of one reviewer, "something of a sissy."[51] Thus the gender expectations are reversed, sexualizing Evelyn and emasculating the bold knight. "I know not why I do weep for thee," remarks Evelyn, "thou art a most unsatisfactory lover." When she puckers her lips and asks him to kiss her, Galahad pecks her on the forehead and cries out "Oh! I am indeed a scarlet man! A fallen creature!" Evelyn makes her retort: "Prithee, fall a little lower."[52]

The juxtaposition of a central "straight" romantic couple with a secondary comic couple is a standard device, and although references to a character's homosexuality may during the 1920s have been implied rather than overt, the mugging of the comedy couple through subverting expected gender attitudes was common comic currency. Subverting gender stereotypes like this not only creates humor in the way it lampoons the stereotypes of romantic chivalry but also implies sexualities that audiences recognize but which society taboos. Rodgers and Hart had already anticipated such subversion in the portrayal of Galahad in "Idles of the King"; their show *Chee-Chee* the following year would push these boundaries further and result in a press drubbing. In *A Connecticut Yankee* they get the balance right, creating likeable characters with an unthreatening and ostensibly straight relationship. When innuendo appears it is easily interpreted as heterosexual, and the titillation of the most provocative lines is easily subsumed into the comedy of the number:

HE: I'll dress the way that Adam did
SHE: And I the way his Madam did.
BOTH: I'll see enough of thee![53]

One can imagine a juxtaposed lasciviousness (Evelyn) and horror (Galahad) in their expressions dissipating the salaciousness of this line and confirming Galahad's covert proclivity to comic effect.

When Martin is brought before the court, as in Twain's novel, Sir Kay weaves a fancy yarn about how he bravely captured his prisoner after having slaughtered thirteen barbarian knights. Martin is unsure how to escape but claims to be an all-powerful sorcerer, and he proceeds to perform parlor tricks that befuddle the court and trump Merlin's magic. At last, Martin is asked to prove his stature by predicting the future. In lieu of a crystal ball, he blows up a party balloon and reveals to King Arthur that Launcelot is having an affair with Guinevere. Unfortunately, the King sentences him to death for slander to the Queen, though when Martin remembers the impending eclipse, he is happy to be burned at the stake at three minutes past noon on June 21. With portentous weight, he issues his proclamation, taken straight from the pen of Mark Twain:[54]

> King, if you attempt to burn me, I will smother the whole world in blackness of midnight. I will blot out the sun, and he shall never shine again; the fruits of the earth shall rot for lack of light and warmth, and the people of the earth shall famish and die to the last man![55]

This sets the scene for the finale to the first act, which has stretched out the events of Twain's first six chapters to conclude with the *coup de théâtre* of Martin's wizardry over the sun. Now to music, Martin is tied to the stake, and a distraught Sandy and he sing a farewell reprise of "My Heart Stood Still." King Arthur orders the pyre to be lit, but Martin stops the proceedings and begins to command the elements with his incantation of nonsense. The finale is structured in typical ensemble form, with sections of underscored dialogue, passages of recitative, and a liberal use of melodramatic devices in chordal stings, tremolo accompaniments, and discordant modalities. Yet again this is reminiscent of the incantation sequence concluding *The Sorceror* (1877), though unlike in other shows, Rodgers does not borrow from the British collaborators explicitly. The sky goes dark, the people are dumbstruck, the King pardons Martin, and the Yankee lays out his terms: he is to be known as "The Boss," he is to preside as prime minister, and he is to take 1 percent commission on all the wealth he brings in.[56]

As the sun emerges, the people rejoice, and the act ends with an infectious gospel finale, "Rise and Shine,"[57] which gradually builds in volume, speed, and intensity as the people celebrate their salvation. It is a stirring end to the act, introducing yet another idiom of music to the score, on which it is interesting to comment.

A song called "Rise n' Shine" had been recorded in 1922 by the Harrod Jubilee Singers, a black gospel group led by Archie Harrod, who, like the Fiske Jubilee Singers, had gained an international reputation through extensive worldwide touring. These Jubilee groups were named for the year of Jubilee, 1861, in which the black population of the United States was symbolically released from slavery. Though a political and ideological evangelism guided their work, the Jubilee singers' profile was generally as gospel singers. "Rise n' Shine" was recorded to the melody of the traditional hymn "We Are Climbing Jacob's Ladder," and the Harrod version of the song with this melody was included in J. B. T. Marsh's 1892 anthology, *The Jubilee Singers and Their Songs*.

In extremely simple lyrics, the song solicits communities to "rise and shine" as soldiers for the year of Jubilee: "Don't you want to be a soldier?"/"Do you think I will make a soldier"/"Yes I think I will make a soldier."[58] This subtly conflates ideas of revolution and abolition that already blurred the political motivations of the Civil War, trading on militaristic language already used in relation to religion. The recording departs from the notation in Marsh's collection by including a call-and-response motif that was a characteristic feature of gospel, emphasizing both the lyrical content through repetition and the rhythmical off-beats of the music. Such a feature is written into the notation of a second "Rise n' Shine" song in Marsh's collection, "Rise, Shine, for Thy Light is A-coming," which more explicitly links the idea of emancipation and salvation with the metaphor of God's light.[59]

Theodore F. Seward's preface to the songs is interesting, not only because he historicizes this anthology as a clear example of Afro-Orientalism but also because he analyzes the musical idioms and comments about the physicality of the performers. He makes the observation that "more than half the melodies" are written "with the fourth and seventh tones omitted"—in other words, they feature heavily the pentatonic or gapped scale that we have established as a feature of American popular music. He also notes the typical rhythms of the songs, "often complicated, and sometimes strikingly original," generally avoiding "triple time, or three-part measure." Commenting on their performance, he notes the "beating of the foot and the swaying of the body which are such frequent accompaniments to the singing." Finally, he gestures toward the idea of syncopation in explaining how the physical performance is juxtaposed with the song's own rhythm: "These motions are in even measure, and in perfect time; and so it will be found that, however broken and seemingly irregular the movement of the music, it is always capable of the most exact measurement."[60]

Fields, Rodgers, and Hart's use of the "Rise n' Shine" motif is interesting on a number of levels.[61] As pastiche it substitutes the worship of God with the worship of the sun, playing on the primitivism of Arthurian society by referencing the religious values of ancient societies.[62] The words "rise and shine" are divested of the metaphorical currency of the gospel context and turned into literal invocations for the sun to rise and shine following the eclipse. As the sun appears, the music aids the crowd in working itself into a frenzy. The infectious rhythm of the gospel style encourages and is reinforced by hand-clapping on the off-beat; this, together with choreographed prayer gestures that alternate double-handed salutes to the sun with supine prostration to the ground, emulates traditional practice in gospel communities.

Seizing upon this style responds to the growing popularity of gospel-derived music on Broadway, in whose structure and performativity we see some of the black (as opposed to Jewish) origins of popular American music. Only six months previously, another Herb Fields show, *Hit the Deck*, had scored a gospel hit with "Hallelujah," also invoking imagery of the sun: "Satan lies a-waitin' and creatin' skies of grey / But hallelujah, hallelujah helps to shoo the clouds away." This trend indicates a subtle re-routing of the common "blue skies" metaphor, which hitherto—in Irving Berlin's "Blue Skies" (1926), for example—was linked more to Jewish-oriented music.[63] By the early thirties, the idiom had crossed over to a black Broadway sound, epitomized in yet another invitation to "Rise n' Shine" by Vincent Youmans and Buddy de Sylva, belted out by Ethel Merman as the Act One finale to *Take a Chance* (1932).

Beyond this though, the "Rise and Shine" incantation layers *A Connecticut Yankee* with other significant valences relating to popular song, race politics, and cultural value. It is sung by the Arthurian extras, who are depicted as primitive and unsophisticated throughout both the novel and the musical, a gesture that for Twain's purposes intended to valorize the technological sophistication of nineteenth-century America over the pre-Enlightenment values of the past. Associating these characters with music from black origins displaces the ideological commentary of Twain's novel and suggests a commentary on the primitivism of black culture. In his analysis of the Jubilee songs, Seward notes that they "are never 'composed' after the manner of ordinary music, but spring into life, ready-made, from the white heat of religious fervor during some protracted meeting in church or camp. They come from no musical cultivation whatever, but are the simple, ecstatic utterances of wholly untutored minds."[64] Like the "Make Hey!" sequence of *One Dam Thing after Another*, this finale trades on the idea of jazz stemming from a pre-articulate culture, exacerbating the potentially racist tones of the comedy. Where in *One Dam Thing* the gesture ultimately pointed to the inarticulacy of prehistoric populations (cavemen), thereby to some extent dissipating the implicit racism of that sketch, this song in *A Connecticut Yankee* is far more associated with black culture. Here, the pre-articulate language features in Martin's hoax spell, "Ibbidi bibbidi sibbidi sab," suggesting that the communicative expression of primitive, ancient, or non-white societies is unintelligible and rooted in deception. This attitude, a staple of minstrelsy, indicates that even if Fields, Rodgers, and Hart were oblivious to the problematic racial overtones of their work, their theater, like much of the period, was deeply entrenched and complicit in perpetuating the ideologies of the time.

Having framed the first act to dramatize just the opening events of the novel, Herb had the challenge of condensing chapters seven through sixty-four into Act Two. Naturally, he is compelled to cut much of the plot, including its satire. With these omissions, one can understand the griping of some reviewers that this show was not a faithful adaptation. Significant omissions are some of the further "miracles" Hank (Martin) performs (the destruction of Merlin's tower, the mending of a well), scenes in which he organizes a banquet for a poor charcoal-burner and then gives succor to a family dying from smallpox, a jousting duel in which he confronts the entire might of English knight-errantry, and the apocalyptic denouement in which he slays Merlin's army. Perhaps more important, and in common with Flynn's film, the social commentary Twain weaves throughout the novel is completely lost, in particular its insistent indictment of slavery. Instead, Act Two revels in the technological and infrastructural anachronisms Martin has introduced before it turns to a kidnapping plot that brings the show to a climax.

The Act Two opening, like a lot of the material, has been lost to the whimsies of time. Musical comedy of this period was an inconsequential activity, and once scripts, scores, and materials were no longer being used, there was little call to preserve them or archive them for future scholarship, a practice that is difficult to understand. Such problems are compounded in this show "because the placement of several known songs is unclear from the extant libretto."[65] We shall see in the following chapter how tricky it can be to reconstruct a musical whose material is so patchy; however, for scholars of *A Connecticut Yankee*, the gaps in our knowledge represent both a frustrating lacuna and a tantalizing invitation to speculate.

The opening number of Act Two is not clearly detailed in existing scripts from 1927,[66] though a stage direction indicates that it takes place in the factory at Camelot, performed by factory hands.[67] The Boss's factories are a feature of the novel: Hank's Connecticut life was spent at the Colt Arms Factory, where he was foreman, and once he gets to Camelot he quickly establishes factories producing commodities such as soap and matches and others providing training for skills in literacy, teaching, scientific principles, and modern warfare. The first scene in existing scripts shows the factory workers playing dice during a break and features the rather limp anachronism of Arthurian characters clocking-in for their shift; a "factory hands" opening number would certainly fit. On the other hand, Busby Berkeley's account of this opening suggests that it featured "Queen Guinevere's dancing school at the king's court," with the Queen "instruct[ing] her little subjects to arrange themselves in the first five classical positions of the dance."[68]

This discrepancy highlights the difficulties of reconstructing shows with any certainty: all three 1927 working scripts relating to the show are different, if only slightly, and, as can be seen from Figure 7.2, a running order of songs gleaned from various programs reveals at least four different versions of the show. In this, Bruce Kirle's central premise in *Unfinished Business* is corroborated: musicals are products not only of their writing but also of their development periods and subsequent rearticulations. Throughout the production process they change constantly, and it is nearly impossible to capture their definitive incarnation. Perhaps it matters little whether the opening number to Act Two was set in a factory or a dance class. If the former, it is likely the number emphasized masculine physicality; the latter would suggest a more feminine grace. The dance class option would hew close to the Act Two opening of *Lido Lady* with its "Exercise" class, and it is perfectly possible—though only a speculation—that this number or a version of it may have been inserted directly from the London show.

Stamford, CT, September 30, 1927.

Prologue
A Ladies' Home Companion (Fay, Ensemble)
You're What I Need (Martin, Sandy)

Act One
Thou Swell (Martin, Sandy)
At the Round Table (Arthur, Knights)
On a Desert Island With Thee (Galahad)

You're What I Need (reprise) (Martin, Sandy)
Finale (Company)

Act Two
Opening (Ensemble)
I Feel at Home With You (Galahad, Evelyn)
I Blush (Sandy)

The Sandwich Men (Knights)
Morgan Le Fay (Morgan, Knights)
Someone Should Tell Them (Martin, Morgan)
Finale (Company)

Philadelphia, October 24, 1927.

Prologue
A Ladies' Home Companion (Fay, Ensemble)
My Heart Stood Still (Martin, Sandy)

Act One
Thou Swell (Martin, Sandy)
At the Round Table (Arthur, Knights)
On a Desert Isle With Thee (Galahad, Evelyn)
Britain's Own Ambassadors (Company)
My Heart Stood Still (reprise) (Martin, Sandy)
Finale (Company)

Act Two
Opening (Ensemble)
I Feel at Home With You (Galahad, Evelyn)
I Blush (Sandy)
Dance (Alisande, Galahad)
The Sandwich Men (Knights)
Evelyn, What Do You Say? (Evelyn & Knights)
Someone Should Tell Them (Martin, Morgan)
Finale (Company)

New York, November 3, 1927.

Prologue
A Ladies' Home Companion (Fay, Ensemble)
My Heart Stood Still (Martin, Alice)

Act One
Thou Swell (Martin, Alisande)
At the Round Table (Ensemble)
On a Desert Island With Thee (Galahad, Evelyn)
My Heart Stood Still (reprise) (Martin, Alisande)

Act Two
Opening (Ensemble)
Nothing's Wrong (Alisande)
I Feel at Home With You (Galahad, Evelyn)
Dance (Galahad, Evelyn)
The Sandwich Men (Knights)
Evelyn, What Do You Say? (Evelyn & Knights)

Epilogue
Finale (Company)

London, November 11, 1929.

Prologue
A Ladies' Home Companion (Gerald, Ensemble)
I Don't Know Him (Martin, Alice) (Ellis / Carter)

Act One
Thou Swell (Martin, Sandy)
At the Round Table (Arthur, Knights)
On a Desert Island With Thee (Galahad, Evelyn)
I Don't Know Him (reprise) (Martin, Sandy)
Finale (Company)

Act Two
Opening (Ensemble) (Ellis / Carter)
Thou Swell (reprise) (Martin, Sandy)
Dance (Sandy, Galahad)
I Feel at Home With You (Galahad, Evelyn)

Evelyn, What Do You Say? (Evelyn & Chorus)

Finale (Company)

Figure 7.2: Four incarnations of A Connecticut Yankee: *Stamford, Philadelphia, Broadway, London.*

The second act is where Sandy's character really comes to the fore—at least, more than in the first, in which she has been simply a sap to the Yankee's charisma. Now she adopts nineteenth-century attitudes, becoming the self-appointed president of the League of Lucy Stone, named for the nineteenth-century women's rights campaigner (1818–1893) who was an inspirational force in women's suffrage and abolition. When we meet her she has been recruiting women's rights campaigners and is preparing to make a speech that evening: "Women of Britain, I do plead with ye to wake up! That we will hold fast to our birthright. Forget the fireside, forget marriage, love, and sufferance! Why should we lose our identity? Why should we give up our names to take those of men?"[69] This characterization is a departure from Sandy's depiction in the novel; for Rodgers, Hart, and Fields she becomes feistier, more independent, and vocally political. This is interesting for a number of reasons.

Lucy Stone, who is referenced a number of times in the script, is a personality from Twain's era rather than the 1920s. Nevertheless, great progress had by this time been made in women's rights, and Stone's legacy not only lived on for contemporary audiences but may arguably have been more iconic.

In reality, Sandy's political stature is short-lived: it is cut short when she is kidnapped by henchmen of Morgan Le Fay. Thereafter she is silenced and effectively becomes the damsel in distress, needing to be rescued by her chivalrous knight Martin in a complete reversal of the anti-romance satire that Twain intended. Moreover, the integrity of her political force is diminished thanks to a somewhat condescending tone in the libretto and Martin's virtual dismissal of her values. Furthermore—if Berkeley's assertion is correct—this scene directly follows a fairly gratuitous display of feminine pulchritude as Guinevere's "little subjects" are schooled in dance. But all this notwithstanding, the fact that Sandy is given any voice at all indicates that the collaborators had some respect for the values of women's rights.

This supports the impression that a recurring theme of Herb's libretti is his portrayal of strong women in empowering situations (somewhat undermined by a period condescension from the male characters and the gender humor of the day). If this sounds qualified, consider the usual portrayal of women on the stage in this period, particularly in revue. Rodgers, Hart, and Fields, by contrast, brought to the stage the revolutionary Betsy who rides through the night evading military forces to seek out the rebel commander (*Dearest Enemy*); Mollie, who stands up single-handedly to the corruption of sports promoters (*The Girl Friend*); and now Sandy, who embarks on a women's lib agenda (*A Connecticut Yankee*).

The contrast to Sandy is Evelyn, who represents another staple in the Rodgers, Hart, Fields shows: one half of a secondary couple who are as superficial as the leads are complex. We have already seen how this character's other half, Galahad, is painted in bold brush strokes as a comedy queen (surprising, isn't it, that the secondary couple is not Launcelot and Guinevere, who might have offered even more of an obvious counterbalance). Evelyn matches Galahad, to create like Jane and Harry in *Dearest Enemy*, Peaches and Bill in *Lido Lady*, and later, Dolores and Gus in *Babes in Arms*, a secondary comedy couple who are foils to the comedy itself. With superficial characterization, the emphasis moves to the material they perform, so it is in their songs that the writers' wit (particularly Hart's lyrics) stands out. Sure enough, the second act song for Evelyn and Galahad, "I Feel at Home with You," provides a classic Rodgers and Hart comedy duet in which these rather faceless characters exchange fond jibes with one another. Here the main feature is the lyric brilliance: "Your brain is dumber / Than that of a plumber," Evelyn sings, "That's why I feel at home with you." Later, "Your brain needs a tonic, / It's still embryonic," and "Our minds are featherweight, / Their together weight / Can't amount to much."[70] This is Hart at his Porteresque best—writing characters that don't really register to provide one-liners and multiple-liners that do.

Yet the character of Evelyn may well be double-voiced. As the show moved towards Broadway, she became more prominent when the second act song "Morgan, Morgan Le Fay" was re-titled "Evelyn, What Do You Say?"

BOYS: Evelyn, Evelyn, what do you say?
You have that cheery smile,
Good Morning Dearie smile.
EVELYN: By so many I'm led astray.
That's the reason, I suppose,
I am just a Wild, Wild Rose.
BOYS: Who Who Who made us that way?
If we could neck with you
We'd Hit the Deck with you.
ALL: That Certain Feeling
Comes a-stealing today...
Evelyn, what do you say![71]

This is littered with intertextual references to recent Broadway songs and shows: Jerome Kern's *Good Morning Dearie* (1921), "Sweet Lady" from *Tangerine* (1921), "That Certain Feeling" from Gershwin's *Tip Toes* (1925), "Who," from Kern's *Sunny* (1926), Friml's *The Wild Rose* (1926), and Vincent Youmans *Hit the Deck*, scripted by Herb Fields himself (1927). Thus the song speaks "beyond" the diegesis of *A Connecticut Yankee* and beyond the period of the action of the play. However, while it clearly shares a knowing awareness with the theatergoing public, I suspect the song also shares an in-joke with members of the company. Since it is featured in Morgan Le Fay's castle where Sandy is held captive after her kidnapping, it would make a lot of sense to include an "I am" song for Le Fay at this point; it makes far less sense to feature the character Evelyn, who is not associated with Le Fay or resident in her castle. However, as Jeffrey Spivak notes in his biography of the choreographer, Busby Berkeley had been having a show romance with actress Evelyn Ruh, who played the minor part of Angela, Le Fay's maid. "Less than a fortnight following the show's opening on November 3, Buzz announced that he and Evelyn would be married within the week," writes Spivak.[72] Is it possible that this retitled song is ribbing Berkeley about his whirlwind marriage proposal to Evelyn the chorus girl? Evelyn Ruh was certainly on stage, since a handwritten stage direction in the Broadway script indicates that "Le Fay enters & sits followed by Angela."[73] The coincidence of having both a character and a performer called Evelyn seems in this song to create a subtle double-voicing, reminding us that the significance of a show (the "work") is as much about its production context as it is about its script and score.

When Sandy is kidnapped, Martin pledges to rescue her and drags the King along, both of them disguised as commoners. To ensure speed, Martin unveils his "Leaping Lizzie," a car that in a spectacular effect in the original production suddenly assembled itself from a workbench. This recalls a section of the book in which "The Yankee and the King travel incognito" (Chapter 27), finding themselves in all sorts of scrapes because the King is unable to behave unlike a King. In the book their travels take them round the kingdom, resulting in their being captured as slaves and sentenced to death when Hank's escape plan goes wrong. Hank and the King are rescued only when he telegraphs Camelot to have his crack troops sent forth on bicycles. Thus two futuristic technologies—the telegraph and the bicycle—save the characters and offer Twain a humorous climax to this sequence. It was this scene that was updated in Flynn's movie version to feature the Yankee telephoning Camelot and the troops arriving on motorcycles. In the show, the technology is updated still further. When the knights are called, they arrive in a fleet of trucks, summoned by Martin's shortwave radio. The later television film of the show, from 1955, updates this sequence still further, unveiling a helicopter (albeit decidedly wooden and unimpressive). In both scenarios Martin and Arthur are left to walk the last few miles, allowing Herb to capture briefly some of the book's events and allowing Larry to have fun with another Twain invention, the Sandwich Men.

The Sandwich Men, wandering round the country with advertising boards strapped to their fronts and backs, are Hank's first ruse to undermine the status of the knights-errant. Though they take to their duties with the utmost sincerity, Hank's intention was that "by and by when they got to be numerous enough they would begin to look ridiculous; and then, even the steel-clad ass that *hadn't* any board would himself begin to look ridiculous because he was out of the fashion."[74] The Sandwich Men in the main carried boards advertising sanitary products ("Use Peterson's prophylactic tooth-brush—all the go"),[75] though the Yankee recognizes that this is by and large a pointless exercise in sales, since very few of the population could read and none were interested in hygiene. However, Twain has fun with the idea, and so too does Hart:

1ST KNIGHT: Brave Sir Launcelot
              Once would prance a lot;
              Now he's advertising the Victrola.
2ND KNIGHT: Bold Sir Bedevere
              Tramps ahead of here,
              Telling all the world of Coca-Cola![76]

Unfortunately, this is another song to which music is missing, though ac-cording to Ralph Holmes,[77] it took the melody of "Onward Christian Soldiers" in part; it certainly includes the line "Onward, gallant soldiers," and the middle section of the verse fits the hymn's tune. This is somewhat appropriate, since Twain's Hank refers to these Sandwich Men as his "missionaries," his wider purpose being to undermine the established church.

Finally, Martin and the King arrive at Le Fay's castle, having been arrested as madmen by Launcelot and the knights, who don't recognize them. Though Morgan realizes who they are, Merlin suggests that she could kill the King, seize the crown herself, and rule over the kingdom with Martin by her side. Merlin, of course, wants a prominent place at court, though Le Fay only has eyes for the Yankee. In an effort to beguile him, she mixes a love potion that will make him fall in love with the first person he sees. But Martin is no fool and he has seen this trick before—as he drinks, he pulls a curtain aside and reveals Sandy imprisoned in a cage with a noose around her neck. Pitting his Connecticut hero against the evil Queen in a finale aping Hollywood at its silent best, Fields makes of Le Fay's castle a macabre film studio. As she orches-trates the death of the heroine, Le Fay calls forth her slaves, named after film directors: De Mille, Goldwyn, Lubich (Lubitsch), and Laemmle (and in another script, Griffith).[78] First De Mille winds the crank that sets her torture appa-ratus in motion, pulling on the noose and beginning to hang the captive Sandy. As he turns the handle, it is not difficult to imagine him winding the crank of a silent movie camera, capturing the struggling damsel onto the permanence of celluloid. Yet before the apparatus can hang Sandy, Martin steps forward and shoots De Mille dead with a device of his own, "the enchanted Gat." Swiftly, Le Fay calls Lubich to the crank, only for him to be dispatched in the same way. It's a pastiche of memorable moments from various films: Fritz Lang's *Metropolis* (1927), Cecil B. De Mille's *Chicago* (1927), Josef von Sternberg's *Underworld* (1927), and Laemmle's Universal comic horror *The Cat and the Canary* (1927) (Sandy refers to herself as a "canary" while Martin relies on his "enchanted Gat"). But the Queen's forces are too much for the Yankee: slaves overpower him and he is made to drop the gun. Just as all looks desperate, in bursts Galahad with the troops. Merlin and Le Fay are captured and Martin rigs up explosives to blow the castle sky high.

The epilogue, in which Martin awakes back in Hartford and confirms his love for Alice rather than Fay, serves no further purpose than to balance the prologue and resolve the framing narrative. And so the show ends, a loose telling of the Twain original, to be sure, but for the boys a huge financial success, and for Hart in particular, a personal favorite.

As we have seen, the reviews were not unequivocally positive; there will always be detractors, and the *Evening Post*'s John Anderson was one: "They go at Twain's Arthurian legend with disastrous vehemence, as if impelled to be whimsical all evening at the tops of their voices. The book is embarrassingly feeble, and only the charming music by Mr. Rodgers, the radiant presence of Miss Constance Carpenter, and some expert foolishness by Mr. Gaxton saved anything for amusement."[79] On the other hand, many other reviewers considered this the work of a great team and their finest show to date. "There seem to be two divisions of musical comedy endeavor at present—the shows written by the Fields, Rodgers, and Hart combination, and all the others," suggested the reviewer for *Life*.[80] The *American* was equally impressed: "The Field[s] shows are always slightly different from the prevailing musical styles in musical comedies. Perhaps they are, rather, musical plays. Something unusual always occurs—you can bet on it—and in this latest there was a persistent drenching with the unusual."[81] As the *Philadelphia Public Ledger* put it, "Fields, Rodgers and Hart have done better here than in any of their previous hits."[82]

Although this version is by far the most celebrated musical telling of the tale, a 1949 Bing Crosby film with music by Victor Young is also much loved; it is surprising, coming only six years after their Broadway revival, that the film did not exploit any of the Rodgers and Hart material, though it did borrow some of the machinations of Herb's plot, including the magnified romance between the Yankee and Sandy, and the kidnapping of the heroine. Less well known is that Twain himself was reported to have written a libretto based on *A Connecticut Yankee*, to be set to music by M. W. Colwell.[83] This apparently never saw the light of day, though it suggests that Twain acknowledged the musical potential of his novel. Meanwhile in England the very similar tale *When Knights Were Bold* (originally written in 1907 by Charles Marlowe, though perhaps adapted from Robert Buchanan and Harriet Jay's *Good Old Times* from 1896) was eventually made into a musical in 1943, with music by Harry Parr Davies and starring *The Girl Friend*'s Sonnie Hale. This was surely capitalizing on the Rodgers and Hart revival of *A Connecticut Yankee* earlier that year, though since it folded after only ten performances it was hardly a threat to the Americans' success.

In 1929 *A Connecticut Yankee* came to England. Reborn, as the novel had been, as *A Yankee at the Court of King Arthur*, it opened at the King's Theatre in Southsea on September 30, before transferring to Daly's Theatre in the West End on October 10. Constance Carpenter reprised her role as Alice/Sandy, though the rest of the cast were new. Reviews in England unanimously panned the show, reminding us how different American and British attitudes to musical comedy were. To the *London Morning Post*, "most of the piece [was] the most puerile rubbish";[84] meanwhile, reviewer Alan Parsons wrote, "I cannot believe that [the book] is as dismally and steadfastly unfunny as the adaptation made by Mr. Herbert Fields."[85] "How much worse it would have been if no one had laughed," opined the *London Times*. "Then the play might have collapsed altogether, and we should have been denied the eclipse of the sun, which...was the brightest spot in the first act."[86]

It wasn't until another sixteen years had elapsed that the story would end. As Larry Hart slipped further into illness and their collaboration began to break apart, Rodgers offered him a sweetener with a revival of Hart's best-loved show. Hart responded, penning a further six songs for a partly new score, and *A Connecticut Yankee* opened in November 1943 for a successful revival. But Hart was too far gone. Just days after seeing the premiere of this revival, he was to collapse and die from complications relating to pneumonia.

8

CASTRATION AND INTEGRATION
• • •
CHEE-CHEE (1928)

Following the successes of *The Girl Friend*, *Peggy-Ann*, *A Connecticut Yankee*, and *Present Arms*,[1] the collaborators were riding high. Lew Fields had enjoyed a second wind as producer of this new writing triumvirate, and the boys had proved their worth with back-to-back successes, seizing momentum from the Princess team, and trumping the rather traditional approach of Kern and Hammerstein in the early twenties.

Their next project was identified by Larry and Herb.[2] Published in the United States in 1927, *The Son of the Grand Eunuch* was the first in a series of novels that received mild acclaim in the 1920s–30s. Its author, Charles Pettit (Henri Jules Marie Pettit, 1875–1948), was French but had lived in China, where he turned to writing salacious novels set in the Orient. *The Son of the Grand Eunuch* was "facetiously engaging," with "nothing to be found of insight into Chinese life";[3] *The Elegant Infidelities of Madame Li Pei Fou* (1928) was reviewed by Dorothy Parker for the *New Yorker*, where she concluded, "tripe is tripe,"[4] while *Petal-of-the-Rose* (1930), according to *Time* magazine, "[gave] about as realistic a picture of China as a musi-comedy does of life, [and] afford[ed] much the same kind of titillating entertainment."[5] An unlikely source of inspiration for the writing team, one might think—yet it appears to have tickled Hart's fancy, and he was quick to contact his collaborators about the prospect of turning *The Son of the Grand Eunuch* into a show.

According to Rodgers, Larry and Herb approached him with the idea while he was vacationing in Colorado Springs after the death of his grandfather. Rodgers claims to have been skeptical about the idea, and indeed the "tripe" in question seems more to the taste of Hart's impish wit and Fields's bawdy sense of humor than to Rodgers's conservative restraint. "This didn't strike me as a theatrically adaptable subject for the musical stage," Rodgers later recalled.[6] Despite this, it didn't take much convincing to persuade him: the Colorado trip took place in June, and they were ready to go into rehearsals "by early July."[7]

Previews began at the Forrest Theater in Philadelphia on September 4, and the New York run opened at the Mansfield Theatre on September 25.

As in the novel, *Chee-Chee* begins with the Grand Eunuch of China wishing to retire and hand over duties to his middle-aged son, Li Pi Tchou. Balking at the job's requirements—to forfeit his genitalia and wife—Tchou and Chti flee the palace, and the narrative traces their exploits on the road, pursued by the Grand Eunuch. Most of their adventures involve being attacked by gangs of marauding barbarians such as the Tartars and "Khonghouses," and having to bargain their way out of harm. When Tchou's diplomacy fails, Chti makes her own bargains with the barbarians: favors "in kind" that become increasingly evident through her growing collection of ornate jewelry gifts. Meanwhile, the Grand Eunuch's sixteen-year-old daughter Li Li Wee, desperate to become a concubine, follows her father round the country dressed as a coolie and in turn chased by the besotted Prince Tao Tee. Eventually, the Grand Eunuch catches up with Tchou and Chti and forces Tchou to accept the position and go through with the castration. Chti, for her indiscretions, is subjected to the Gallery of Torments, in which she is confronted by the seven deadly sins. One by one they accuse her, but when the final torment, Lust, approaches, Chti sees a way out of her dilemma. She makes a bargain, escaping eternal punishment and in the process saving Tchou from the chop. In the final processional scene, Chti and Tchou are reunited, and though it looks as if she may have been too late to save him from castration, Chti's fears are allayed when Tchou opens his mouth and a rich tenor voice sings the final refrain.[8]

A FAILURE

Most accounts of *Chee-Chee* source their information from the original reviews and Rodgers's testimony in *Musical Stages*. Thus a narrative has emerged that views the show as a critical failure,[9] supported by its run of just thirty-one performances. To be sure, often-quoted reviewers deemed the show "their most pretentious production and the least entertaining."[10] St. John Ervine, in a review entitled "Nasty! Nasty!," wrote "I did not believe that any act could possibly be duller than the first—until I saw the second!"[11] And Rodgers's distaste for the show is clear in interviews from his later years.[12] Yet his disapprobation of the show as an older man seems to clash with his fervent enthusiasm for it in his youth; and this contradiction—expressed in writings from 1928 and 1975—is useful to explore.

The most common criticism of the show centers on its distasteful subject matter. It "aches clumsily to be dirty and succeeds only in being tedious,"[13] cried the *Judge*, while to the *New York Daily News*, it "emanate[d] from the curbstones,"[14] star Helen Ford claimed that "it was a mistake right from the beginning,"[15] and in retrospect, Rodgers agreed: "No matter what we did to *Chee-Chee*, it was still a musical about castration, and you simply can't get an audience at a musical comedy to feel comfortable with such a theme."[16] This seems clear enough, and it's true that the comedy is a bit puerile. However, aside from the falsetto jokes and the odd comic reference in song ("Just a Little Thing"), castration isn't really a prominent focus in the storyline. What is prominent—and certainly problematic by today's standards—is the way in which the show finds humor in Chti's sexual commodification: the fact that she sells herself repeatedly for trinkets.

As Marybeth Hamilton notes, Broadway at that time "abounded in plays dealing with sexual relations, including prostitution":

> the 1925/26 theatre season, for example, featured such hits as *The Shanghai Gesture*, the story of China's most successful madam; and *Lulu Belle*, the tale of a mean, merciless, unrepentant mulatto hooker seducing black and white lovers from Harlem to Paris. Advertisements for [the Mae West show] *SEX*, with the title appearing in large, boldfaced capitals, [appeared] in every New York City newspaper; moreover, they did so alongside ads that more than outshone them in garish suggestiveness.[17]

As Broadway in various ways pushed at the boundaries of conservatism, the youthful and contemporary appeal of Rodgers, Hart, and Fields's shows traded on a casual—if provocative—sexualized content. Several songs in this early period had introduced the phrase "sex appeal" ("The Girl Friend" from *The Girl Friend*; "I Want a Man" from *Lido Lady*; "Je m'en fiche du sex appeal" from *Ever Green*); costumes were deliberately suggestive (Helen Ford's entrance wearing only a barrel in *Dearest Enemy*); and Herb Fields's scripts were notorious for their "randy subtext,"[18] "vulgar" humor,"[19] and "blue" material[20] which contrasted strikingly with the "Victorian morality"[21] of his father's shows. Yet this was par for the course—perhaps slightly naughty, but not exactly "Nasty! Nasty!"

However, as the *Stage* reviewer commented, with *Chee-Chee* it was not the offending words or even sexual innuendo of the story that "transgress[ed] the last boundaries of taste" but the "thoroughly objectionable hints of practices among the monks":[22] an undercurrent of homosexuality in coded language and references. The most obvious of these had in fact been removed from the show, though not until advance publicity alerted those in the know to the presence of a gay subtext. The show had originally been called *Violet Time*, a title that makes suggestive reference to the flower as a "symbol of homosexuality."[23] Both "pansy" and "violet" (a type of pansy) were common slang words referring to homosexuality in the 1920s, and by 1930 newspapers were referring to the "pansy craze" in New York and particularly around Times Square.[24] The word "violet" was more subtle than "pansy" and was associated more commonly with lesbianism, though it had been one of "the traditional colors of effeminacy" since Roman times.[25] A well-publicized reference to violets as homosexual symbols had been prominent in the previous year's hit play *The Captive*, and this set a precedent, causing "an association of this flower with lesbianism that lasted several decades."[26] Indeed, so provocative were the homosexual connotations now linked to the violet that, according to a 1934 *Harper's Bazaar* article, farmers in Dutchess County, New York, began "cursing this play as the knell of the violet industry."[27] *The Captive*, by French playwright Edouard Bourdet, had opened at the Empire Theatre on September 29, 1926, with Basil Rathbone and Helen Menken in the lead roles. Its storyline focused on a young lady (Menken) who marries her childhood friend (Rathbone) in order to disguise her clandestine relationship with another woman. The portrayal of a lesbian theme on the stage had "shocked the New York critics' sensibilities,"[28] though the play had been a runaway success with audiences. In his autobiography, Rathbone defends it:

> We were an immediate success and for seventeen weeks we played to standing room only at every performance. At no time was it ever suggested that we were salacious or sordid or seeking sensation.[29]

Indeed, *The Captive* was seen as quality playwriting, dealing sensitively with an important issue. Despite this, it fell victim to a clampdown on obscene productions brought about by the proposal by burlesque dancer and pornographer Mae West to stage a "homo-sexual comedy-drama" called *The Drag*.

The Drag was marketed as "A Male 'Captive,'"[30] and set up a parallel scenario: Rolly Kingsbury is married, though hiding behind this charade a flamboyant homosexual life. The show staged that flamboyant lifestyle, introducing Rolly's extravagant circle of friends, and offering a no-holds-barred drag burlesque in the third act. The play ends in tragedy—what some might see as "just desserts"—when Rolly is shot by his former lover.

West was already recognized as a threatening influence on middle-class society, and she already had one scandalous show on Broadway called, quite blatantly (and in capital letters), *SEX*, a show shut down by the district attorney's office on February 9, 1927.[31] That show had staged prostitution and featured West herself in the lead role of brothel-keeper Margy Lamont. However, *The Drag* threatened public decency in a more provocative way, in staging for the first time openly gay characters brandishing not only sexuality but *homo*sexuality brazenly.

The final act's sequence, the costumes, physicality, and even the language were laden with the posturing effeminacy of drag. As Marybeth Hamilton suggests, this was not entirely new to audiences, but its presentation in the classy environs of Broadway rather than in a burlesque hall on the Bowery was uncomfortable to middle-class crowds.

That said, the environs of Broadway were notorious haunts for New York's gay men, and a part of West's defense for staging these shows was her insistence that she was simply "staging 'real life.'"[32] She showcased on stage the gay culture of Greenwich Village and Times Square; and she populated the show with "a large supporting cast of flamboyantly expressive homosexual men recruited from New York's burgeoning gay underworld."[33]

George Chauncey Jr. describes the various kinds of gay activity common around Times Square in the 1920s, noting not only the well-known rooming houses and meeting places in which the gay community gathered socially, but also the "highly flamboyant, working-class street fairies"[34] and "well-dressed, 'mannered,' and gay-identified hustlers"[35] who worked as prostitutes in the area. Times Square—heart of the theater district—was a mecca for gay activity, and as Chauncey notes, the theater community was, generally speaking, tolerant and receptive of gay behavior, still at that time illicit.[36] Wider attitudes toward homosexuality were not so accepting, considering it an aberration that was to be punished or cured. Indeed, the perception that homosexuality was an illness was pervasive, serving to define strategies by which gay behavior could be brought into the mainstream. Thus Mae West's *The Drag* was framed within what Hamilton calls an "educational prolog":

> two brief scenes involving an enlightened physician who argues that homosexuals are not criminals but victims of a disease, deserving compassion and pity. Under cover of that preface, West posed *The Drag* as a vehicle of sex education. Through the story of Rolly Kingsbury and David Caldwell, she ostensibly illustrated the tragic consequences of society's cruel censure of what was in reality a curable sickness.[37]

To our twenty-first-century eyes, this apologia seems quaint and even offensive, though one senses that West's intentions—however provocative, self-serving, and counter-productive—were in their own way well-meaning and liberal. Regardless of this, West was locked up in April 1926 for ten days in the Women's Reformatory on Roosevelt Island on obscenity charges. The scandal clung to her reputation, though she managed to exploit her notoriety and turn it to her advantage as she became more successful in film.

Given the connotations of the word "violet," so forcibly brought to public attention amid the furor surrounding *The Drag*, we can speculate that the name-change from *Violet Town* to *Chee-Chee* during out-of-town tryouts in Philadelphia may have been a deliberate attempt to avoid gay associations. However, references in the script are clear enough, particularly in its opening scene: the Grand Eunuch's domain, the sacred citadel of the empress, is one which "none of the male gender may enter,"[38] yet which the audience sees to be inhabited exclusively by men—a chorus of eunuchs. This immediately queers gender, and the language of the eunuchs' first sung passage, presumably sung in falsetto to comic effect, consolidates the homosexual subtext with references to culturally encoded gay characteristics: "We're men of brains, endowed with tact! / We're muscular and neat!"[39] Later, a queering of the secondary romantic couple, Li Li Wee and Prince Tao Tee, complicates the gender subversion when she cross-dresses as a coolie because it is forbidden in Chinese imperial law for unmarried females to travel around China. Thus two ostensibly male characters are seen kissing and expressing affection for each other, sometimes with homo-erotic overtones:

> LI LI WEE: We'll go as two little married bonzlings...We'll pray all day...
> PRINCE: And the nights?
> LI LI WEE: The nights will take care of themselves...[40]

That these instances carry a homoerotic suggestion might not be surprising; though it was not characteristic of either to be explicit about their own practices, Herb and Larry clearly found resonances in cheeky allusions to a world they found fascinating. Hart's biographers talk about his late night wanderings to seedy joints and his relationship with several notorious characters, including the "'wild' and 'brazen'" Rocky Twins[41] and the unsavory Milton "Doc" Bender. As Nolan reports:

> What sexual adventures they got up to, no one knows, but since Doc made no attempt to conceal his proclivities, and it was widely rumoured that he was Hart's pimp, it was assumed these were as predatory as the ones indulged in by Cole Porter and his chum Monty Woolley, who spent many a happy evening cruising sleazy bars along the New York waterfront in Porter's Rolls, picking up sailors for what they called "fucking parties."[42]

More bizarrely, Nolan reports, "Larry often told [his friends] he was himself a Eunuch,"[43] and if this is true, it raises questions about Hart's choice of this novel as source material, not to mention the discomfort he felt about sexuality in general. Nolan goes on to suggest that "it takes no stretch of imagination to visualize him capering about, giggling and chortling over the verbal puns and double entendres he would be able to work into the show." While today's perspectives would scarcely conflate issues of homosexuality with the figure of the eunuch, it is easy to see how a less confident sexual discourse might find in one a clumsy metaphor for the other. Hart's treatment of a storyline involving eunuchs thus becomes an exercise in self-styled psychoanalytic transference through somewhat adolescent comedy.[44]

While the representation of gay characters may have been coded and clandestine, the sexualized representation of female characters could be overt, which to modern audiences, appears highly offensive. Early in their journey, Chti and Tchou encounter an Owl, representing an elderly spinster. In a late addition to the score ("The Owl Song"), the Owl chides them for kissing in public, and when Chti defends her honor, she is accused of being a "jezebel"[45] and a "hussy";[46] the Owl then issues a prophecy: "Your evil doom can be foretold in three words!...SEX! SEX! SEX!"[47] Whether this capitalized outcry is a reference to Mae West's play or not, Chti's identity in this narrative is reduced to both a figure of ignominy and a sexualized commodity.

The first sexual exchange occurs in scene three. The Grand Eunuch has asked a local Tartar Chief to pressure Tchou into returning to the Palace. The Chief does this by flirting with Chti in order to cause Tchou to doubt her purity. The Chief is paid by the Grand Eunuch to carry out this favor, and this is therefore the first transaction linked to the sexual services of a young woman. When the Chief meets Chti, his disrespect is evident, and the sequence is reminiscent of buying animals at a market. The Chief repeatedly pinches her (muttering, "Nice...very nice!")[48] and comments on her body parts (her fingers, her feet, her lips, her waist), before manhandling her off stage where, we later learn, he has his way with her. The animalizing effect is magnified in that we have already seen one animal character humanized (the Owl), while another animal (the Donkey) swaps places with a human, sitting in the cart alongside Chti while Tchou pulls them to the Inn. Thus *Chee-Chee* confuses boundaries of identity and expectations of behavior, all in a light-hearted manner, though with latent misogyny that is discomfiting to a modern audience.

A further troubling resonance recurs once the pattern of prostitution has been established. On the third occasion, by which time Chti is trying to get her badly beaten husband home, Chti's abuser is a Bonze (called "Radiance and Felicity"). He promises to transport the couple to the nearest refuge, but again the suggestion is that Chti must pay in kind for the favor. This time the suggestion is implicit but carries unsettling overtones when the Bonze "look[s] at her warmly" then asks "How old are you, my child?" (immediately before the blackout).[49] It is a question echoed by the torment Lust later in the act (again, immediately before the blackout),[50] and it adds further concern about the gender relations toyed with in this script. The other principal female character, Li Li Wee, desperate to become a concubine, is stated as being sixteen, which also problematizes the boundaries of adolescent sexual activity and the contemporary attitudes toward the sexualization of extremely young women.

In *Chee-Chee* the presentation of women as sexualized is no longer *simply* a celebration of beauty and a harmless indulgence of the male gaze, as might be a generalized judgment of other shows of the period. From the beginning, its comedic tone distracts us from the fact that a culture of prostitution pervades the narrative, explicitly staged in the early scenes, when the concubines parade in, line up, and hear the announcement that "He [the Emperor] has chosen number nineteen."[51] This puts a spin on the presentation of beauty— and specifically the *parading* of beauty—that is a traditional feature of musical theater (recall the similar parade in the beauty contest of *Ever Green*). Modern sensibilities undoubtedly magnify this issue, though the plot's subsequent casual flirtation with violent abuse, unwilling prostitution, and underage sexuality antagonize the notion that celebrating "girls" is a harmless entertainment.[52] The female chorus of concubines in this show are in one sense a balance to the male chorus of eunuchs—characters whom we have already seen to be rather complex; and one wonders whether the writing team consciously chose to complicate the audience's encounter with the traditional chorus of girls in offering this balance and in making explicit the Emperor's transaction.

Of course, our critique of a cultural attitude from over eighty years ago is inflected by a modern perspective, though this should not sanction the 1920s attitude toward gender. The way Chti coquettishly responds to her "duty" with dominant masculine bullies while her fey husband remains blithely unaware is indicative of a latent cultural misogyny, and the fact that this is barely mentioned by the press or by commentators on the show reveals such misogyny to be normalized in 1920s musical comedy. [53] The depictions of these scenes in the novel's detailed illustrations by Steele Savage (see Figures 8.1 and 8.2) are likewise romanticized (and orientalized), diluting the violence of the events into acceptable (even elegant) imagery. In fairness, the gender politics of the show's libretto seem fairly liberal in comparison to the grossly misogynist novel, whose tone is difficult for a twenty-first-century reader to stomach.

Chee-Chee was "objectionable" in its subject matter, then,[54] a quality that was blamed for its failure. After tryouts in Philadelphia, it transferred to New York for just thirty-one performances before Lew Fields chose to cut his losses.

THE MUSIC OF *CHEE-CHEE*

Nevertheless, a different spin on the tale reveals a somewhat different show. As Ethan Mordden observes,[55] reviews were in fact mixed, and many were far

Figure 8.1 (above) and 8.2 (opposite): Two of Steele Savage's salacious illustrations from The Son of the Grand Eunuch *(1927).*

more positive than accounts reveal: "At last a sophisticated musical show!," exclaimed *Billboard*; "Ultra-sophisticated song-and-dance fare," cried the *Daily Mirror*; "excellent entertainment," judged the *New York Telegram*. Most positive, the *New York Evening World* saw in *Chee-Chee*

> the most ambitious score in the whole series of Fields-Rodgers-Hart compositions; the most audacious libretto, the most sparkling lyrics...a thing of joy to the last of its melody...a rousing tale of stage adventure with a finale that was greeted by rousing cheers. And deserved them.[56]

At the time, Rodgers was also enthusiastic about *Chee-Chee*, at least in correspondence with Dorothy:

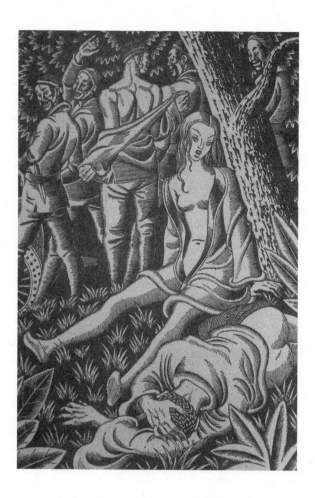

You're liable to get the idea that I'm raving about the show, but honestly, Dot, it all sounds marvellous. I never realized how deeply I'd gone into it from a musical standpoint until I heard the orchestrations.[57]

The show was "the best musical thing I've ever seen," he reported;[58] "we have managed to produce that difficult thing—a unit.... No matter what happens to us commercially we've accomplished what we've been after for years. We've produced a good show!"[59] Above all, one comment stands out: "we'll never be ashamed of it."[60] It is surprising then—and rather ironic—that this remains the one show in his output that Rodgers later wanted to disown.

By this time it is clear that to Rodgers "a good show" meant something that had musical integrity and a coherent score, one that avoids the interpolation of vaudeville material or hit songs for the star. His commentary on this show is particularly interesting in these terms. In *Musical Stages* he reflected in detail about the integration of the show's score, giving an authoritative perspective on the intentions of the writing team:

> To avoid the eternal problem of the story coming to a halt as the songs take over, we decided to use a number of short pieces of from four to sixteen bars each, with no more than six songs of traditional form and length in the entire score. In this way the music would be an essential part of the structure of the story rather than an appendage to the action.[61]

Jason Rubin goes further:

> the score was almost continuous, with songs, instrumental and sung fragments, leitmotifs and occasional reprises. Songs helped identify and describe characters, expand situations and forward the action, heighten emotions, or, in typical musical comedy fashion, highlight a particular bit of business. To some extent, the individual numbers could almost tell the story without the dialogue.[62]

Rodgers and Hart's approach to the music in *Chee-Chee*, then, suggests a prelude to the more formal tenets of integration epitomized by Rodgers's later collaboration with Oscar Hammerstein II, and commentators agree that it was a particularly important milestone in the development of the Rodgers and Hart approach to musical comedy. In terms of the ongoing integration project, it reveals a very interesting stylistic approach.

I have already considered how the scores of *Dearest Enemy* and *A Connecticut Yankee* became far more than simply collections of musically unrelated songs. With *Chee-Chee*, the original program for the show made this explicit:

> NOTE: The musical numbers, some of them very short, are so interwoven with the story that it would be confusing for the audience to peruse a complete list.[63]

There are only six songs as such in the show (see Figure 8.3),[64] yet as Rubin explains: "The authors used approximately twelve short forms from four to sixteen measures each, six of the standard form and length, and six longer sequences similar to those extended musical scenes in their previous musicals. With the addition of instrumental music and scene finalettos and entrance and exit songs, there were approximately 38 musical passages."[65] Kimball offers a probable list of these (see Figure 8.3), indicating how this show differs from conventional musical comedies. The first scene, for example, includes far more music than a typical scene of its length. Nevertheless, Kimball's list is a problematic reconstruction, and Rubin's precise breakdown of the musical fragments is also slightly confusing; neither correlate with existing

Act One
Scene one
1. Prelude
2. "We're Men of Brains" (Eunuch's Chorus)
3. "I am a Prince"
4. "In a Great Big Way"
5. "The Most Majestic of Domestic Officials" (Entrance of G.E)
6. "Holy of Holies" (Prayer)
7. "Her hair is black as licorice" (Food Solo)
8. **"Dear, oh Dear!"**
9. (Incidental Music)
10. "Await your Love" (Concubine's Song)
11. "Joy is Mine"
12. "I Wake at Morning"
13. "I Grovel to the Earth" (Chee Chee's First Entrance)
14. "Just a Little Thing"
15. "You are both Agreed" (Finaletto: Scene 1)

Scene Two
16. **"I Must Love You"**
17. "Owl Song" (Song of the Owl)
18. Change of Scene Music and "I Must Love You" reprise

Scene Three
19. "I Bow a Glad Good Day" (Tavern Opening)
20. **"Better Be Good to Me"**
21. **"The Tartar Song"**
22. "Chee Chee's Second Entrance"
23. "Finale Act I" inc. reprise of "I Must Love You"

Act Two
Scene One
24. (Instrumental?)
25. "Khonghouse Song"
26. "Sleep Weary Head"

Scene Two (?)
27. **"Singing a Love Song"**

Scene Three
28. "Monastery Opening"
29. "Chinese Dance"
30. "Living Buddha" "Impassive Buddha"
31. **"Moon of my Delight"**
32. "Grovel to your Cloth" (Chee Chee's 3rd Entrance)
33. Trio: Chti, Prince, Li Li Wee
34. "Bonze Entrance" (incidental music)
35. "I Must Love You" (reprise)

Scene Four
36. "We are the Horrors of Deadliest Woe"
          (Chorus of Torments)
Scene Five
37. "Oh Gala Day, Red-Letter Day"
38. "Farewell Oh Life" (Finale Act Two, inc. reprise of
          "I Must Love You")

Figure 8.3: Robert Kimball's list of musical passages from Chee-Chee, *with the six published songs in bold type.*

materials, and nor does Rubin's notion of an "almost continuous" score accurately describe the music. In this, the challenge of *Chee-Chee* is identified: a definitive set of materials no longer exists. The researcher's job becomes, in part, one of reconstruction, though attempts at this are confounded by the varying reliability of secondary sources.

Subsequent commentators offer differing synopses (as they do with the London shows), and Rodgers's own retrospective provides a selective and somewhat edited account. One script in the Dorothy Fields Papers of the Billy Rose Theatre Collection differs from another held by the Rodgers and Hammerstein Organization; archives at the Library of Congress, the New York Public Library, and the Rodgers and Hammerstein Organization include some draft material and orchestral parts. The common consensus, that the show was an unpalatable flop, means that less critical interest has been given to it, and in studies of the entire Rodgers and Hart oeuvre, this short-running show from 1928 warrants scant attention. Nevertheless, a 2002 attempt to stage the show was mounted by the off-Broadway production series *Musicals Tonight!* Producer Mel Miller and musical director James Stenborg's painstaking work on reconstructing the libretto and score resulted in a workable document which—although not validated as the authentic work of Rodgers and Hart—gives an indication of how the music may have worked. A table of the musical numbers (Figure 8.4) shows how short musical pieces contribute to

	"Overture"		a typical medley of tunes from the show.
1	"Opening (Act One)"	26 bars	instrumental passage modelled around material from the "Concubine's Song" (No.10).
2	"Eunuch's Chorus"	8 bars	Two phrases of melody harmonized in thirds to achieve a minor tone.
3	"I am a Prince"		Missing.
4	"In a Great Big Way"	2 x 20 bars	simple strophic form, repeating lyrics as well as music. Basic diatonic phrases over a tonic/dominant chordal pattern.
5	"Li Pi Siao's Entrance"	16 bars	AABA structure using a striking whole-tone motif, giving an oriental effect.
6	"Prayer (Holy of Holies)"	2 x 8 bars + 2 x 4 bars + 8 bars	an 8 bar phrase is repeated, followed by a four bar phrase in quasi-recitative that is repeated up a tone, and an 8 bar coda based on the material of the first 8 bars. Again makes use of whole tone cadences.
7	"Food Solo" (aka "Her hair is black as a licorice")	64 bars + 4 bars	conventional AABA form with a four bar coda. The melody involves distinctive passages of semitones.
[8]	"Dear, Oh Dear!"	16 + 32 bars	32 bar AABA form with a preliminary verse.
9	"Chatter Music"	8 bars	instrumental making use of a recurring chromatic chordal sequence often used for the concubines throughout the score.
10	"Concubine's Song"	71 bars	Recitative (soloists) alternates with rhythmical passages (concubine chorus).
10b	"Joy is Mine"	20 bars	Driven by the demands of character and plot situation rather than musical form.
11	"I Wake at Morning"	8 bars + 2 bars intro + 32 bars + 2 bars	32 bar AABA form preceded by 8 bars of "I Must Love You" over dialogue.
12	"Chti's first Entrance"	6 bars intro + 36 bars	ABAB form.
13	"Just a Little Thing"	16 bars + 12 bars + 24 bars dance repeated	strophic form, with a sung verse, a dance section and a second sung verse. Makes use of oriental devices including whole tone and modal sequences.
14	"Finaletto: Scene I Act 1 and Opening Scene II"	20 bars + 6 bars recitative + 8 bars intro + 14 bars then underscore	Binds together a lot of the material encountered in the score: extractsfrom "I Must Love You;" both chromatic scalar passages and modal sounding 4ths and 5ths; material between Li Pi Tchou and Chti that is at least reminiscent of their motif ("I love your face, for you're so dear"). Some recitative.
15	"I Must Love You"	24 bars + 32 bars etc.	AABA form.
15.5	"Donkey Music"	9 bars	scene-setting music already used in scene change into Scene II.
16	"I Must Love You"	32 bars (repeated)	Instrumental reprise
16.5	"Tavern Opening"	Various sections	Main theme makes use of a descending pattern of extensions found elsewhere in "I Wake at Morning" (No.11) and the "Concubine's Song" (No.10); the chromatic scales from "Chatter Music" (No.9) are given lyrics; the basic feature of the main theme finds variation later on, particularly in "Processional" (No.31).
17	"Better Be Good To Me"	24 bars + 29 bars etc.	AABA. A section unusual 7 bar phrase. The song itself consists of verse chorus verse chorus, then an instrumental piece (17a) reprises the refrain in modulating keys 4 times, with an additional two encores. (ie, a total of eight full renditions of the refrain)
17a	"Better Be Good To Me" (dance or alternate [sic] vocal)	29 bars etc.	
18	"The Tartar Song"	16 bars + 16 bars + 14 bars etc.	New material, stand-alone song, uses derivative rhythms and straight chord-based melody to present a characterizing element.
[19]	"The Tartar March"		Instrumental with final 8 bars reprise of "The Tartar Song." Note suggests this could be part of "Entr'acte."

20	"Finale Act I"	Various sections	Strangely, Li Pi Tchou's music ("Farewell, oh life") seems to use material from the "Food Solo" (No.7) and "Better be Good to Me" (No.17), neither of which are originally sung by Tchou; this material is directly repeated later in "Processional" (No.31). Li Li Wee's material comes from "Prayer (Holy of Holies)" (No.6), and therefore relates her to the domain of the Grand Eunuch through the repeated triple-time motif. Thereafter, the Finale becomes a (fairly haphazard) medley of songs from the first act (and one yet to be heard from the second). Odd sections of dialogue exist in the score between songs, though remaining libretto for this Finale missing.
21	"Entr'acte"	2 bars intro + 32 bar sections	reprises the two main songs from Act One: "Dear Oh Dear!" (No.8) and "I Must Love You" (No.15).
22	"Khonghouse Song"	Various sections	Most of its lyric material missing from score. Unrelated to other material, though derivative with a melody built up of basic chord patterns or repeated notes.
23	"Sleep Weary Head"	2 bars intro + 32 bars then extended underscoring	AABA. ¾ time. Followed by dance in 4 which introduces a syncopated rhythm used elsewhere.
[24]	"II – 24. Singing a Love Song"	8 bars intro + 20 bars + 32 bars etc.	AABA with preliminary verse. Initial song (verse chorus) succeeded by a reprise that includes three full renditions of the main refrain.
[24]	"II – 4. Singing a Love Song"	32 bars etc.	Another version? Main refrain without preliminary verse.
25	"Monastery Opening"	Various sections	Includes thematic material linked to the rest of the score in its use of seconds, perhaps part of Rodgers' representation of the East. Melody indicated but no lyrics survive.
25b	"Living Buddha" (aka "Chinese Dance")	Various sections	Picks up on syncopated rhythm of "Sleep Weary Head" (No.23). Uses repeated note motif previously heard in the "Concubine's Song" and "Prayer (Holy of Holies)" (one of Rodgers' musical devices for representing the East).
26	"Moon of my Delight"	16 bars + 26 bars etc.	ABA form. Features repeated notes throughout.
26(a)	"Moon of my Delight (Dance)"		12 repeats of the refrain in variation (the final repeat is unclear and could suggest even more).
27	"Chti's 3rd Entrance"	4 bars intro + 36 bars	Straight reprise of "Chti's First Entrance" (No.12).
28	"Bonze entrance"	2 bars + 20 bars + 4 bars	Straight reprise of "In a Great Big Way" (No.4), followed by a minor version of the fanfare theme ("I Must Love You"). Connects locations of the Grand Eunuch and the Monastery.
31	"Processional"	Various sections	New material ("Oh, Gala day, red letter day") associated with other choral scenes: notably the "Concubine's Song" (No.10) and the "Tavern Opening" (No.16.5). Use of material from elsewhere, in the manner of a finaletto. Begins with fanfare music ("I Must Love You") and the syncopated instrumental music of "Sleep Weary Head" (No.23) and "Living Buddha" (No.25b), all of which recurs throughout the number. "Li Pi Siao's Entrance" (No.5) used for Li Pi Siao's entrance. Number then reprises "I Wake at Morning" in its entirety. "I worship at thy shrine" is a variation of the "Concubine's Song" (No.10) / "Tavern Opening" (No. 16.5) material. "Farewell, oh life" has been heard before in the Act One Finale (No.20).
34	"Possibility for Finale Act 2"	Various sections	Reprised material: "Farewell, oh life" from No.20; the fanfare from "I Must Love You" and the syncopated material from "Sleep Weary Head" (No.23) and "Living Buddha" (No.25b); "Our holy man's chief minister" from "Concubine's Song" (No.10) / "Tavern Opening" (No. 16.5) material; finally, a straight reprise of "I Must Love You."

Figure 8.4: An indication of the musical structure of Chee-Chee, *compiled from material reconstructed by* Musicals Tonight! *(2002). (Herbert Fields,* Chee-Chee, *reconstructed piano-vocal score by James Stenborg, RHO, 1928.)*

the overall structure. Reviews of this 2002 production indicate twenty-first-century responses to the score, and it is worth quoting one to get a picture of the material in performance:

> It's hard to understand how critics or audiences—or Rodgers, for that matter—can have failed to appreciate the beauty and audacity of this score. It's a Rodgers and Hart work that sounds, and behaves, like no other. True, there are the expected and irresistible R&H charm ballads— the bubbly descending fourths of "Dear, Oh Dear," the lilt of "I Must Love You," and the showy Hart rhymes.... But convention goes out the window in "Better Be Good to Me," whose phrases are an unheard-of seven meas-ures long. Li-Pi-Tchou's "I Wake at Morning" is lush and ecstatic, more like Rodgers and Hammerstein of *Flower Drum Song* than the impudent Rodg-ers and Hart of the 1920s.... Most bizarrely, many of the 30-odd musical numbers are only a few bars long, the better to keep the action flowing and give the piece a through-composed feel. It's suitably exotic, too: Rodg-ers, while not striving for an authentic Oriental sound, does experimental [*sic*] with Ravel-like tone clusters and chord progressions.... Throughout the score, and however Rodgers may have disparaged *Chee-Chee* in later years, you can sense the joy with which he and Hart went about upending musical-comedy convention.[66]

THE LIBRETTO AND SCORE OF *CHEE-CHEE*

Scene one occupies fourteen pages of the libretto and includes fourteen mu-sical passages. At times, these follow one another almost continuously, as on page four of the libretto, which shows lyrics to "In a Great Big Way," "Most Majestic of Domestic Officials" and "Holy of Holies." Elsewhere, a more con-ventional arrangement is evident, in which passages of dialogue over several pages are periodically interrupted with song. Scene three, for example, is of a similar length (fifteen pages), yet includes only four suggested passages of music: the "Opening," a "Duet," a "Tartar number" and a fourth unnamed pas-sage indicated by a gap in the text between one stage direction and the next. According to Kimball's list, extra music was provided in the form of reprises and a finale to the first act. Thus the "Opening" (to scene three) becomes more clearly defined as "Tavern opening" ("I bow a glad good day"), the "Duet," Kim-ball suggests, is "Better Be Good to Me," the "Tartar number" is written as "The Tartar Song," and music is provided for "Chee Chee's Second Entrance" (reprising "I Grovel to the Earth" from scene one) before the extended finale, which includes a reprise of the show's main hit, "I Must Love You."

Several recurring features of the score bind it together, and Rodgers uses leit-motivic devices to represent characters, themes, and locations. "Chti's First Entrance" is structured in ABAB form, and makes use of two recurring elements: a melodic use of hollow fifths, a rather simplistic feature of Rodgers's easternization that picks up on the martial sound of the Grand Eunuch's processional music and becomes "I Must Love You" in due course (see Figure 8.9); and a short phrase of descending diminished chords over a chromatic bass line: vintage Rodgers and used as the romantic "sound" of Li Pi Tchou and Chti in "Dear, Oh Dear" and "I Wake at Morning." If Rodgers is deliberately appropriating techniques of operatic composition in this score—and he would be aware of such techniques following his training at the Institute of Musical Art and his familiarity with the operatic repertoire—it is in his use of leitmotif rather than any recourse to recitative or ensemble structuring.

There is some recitative, most apparent in the "Concubine's Song" from scene one, introducing the concubines in the imperial court. This involves rhythmically intoned dialogue interspersed with underscored speech, then several short melodic sections that either do not recur again ("Poor excited and benighted unrequited jades") or use material from elsewhere: "Each night it's just the same alone" from the "Prayer (Holy of Holies)" (No.6); "Ah, Lucky One! Ah, Fortunate!" related to the "Tavern Opening" (No.16.5) and "Processional" (No.31). At the very end of the show, the "Processional" itself ("Oh, Gala day, red letter day") also makes liberal use of thematic material from elsewhere, in the manner of a finaletto. It begins with fanfare music ("I Must Love You") and the syncopated instrumental music of "Sleep Weary Head" (No.23) and "Living Buddha" (No.25b), which recurs throughout the number. "Li Pi Siao's Entrance" (No.5) is reprised as "I Wake at Morning" in its entirety; "I worship at thy shrine" is a variation of the "Concubine's Song" (No.10)/"Tavern Opening" (No. 16.5), while "Farewell, Oh Life" has been heard before in the Act One Finale (No.20).

A use of modal-sounding music, with regular whole-tone scales and hollow fifths at times creates an ambiguous modality, particularly prevalent in the bass line of the piano score and another period signifier of the East. To represent Chinese-sounding music, he also uses either repeated note motifs (for example, in "Await Your Love," "Holy of Holies," and "Living Buddha") or rising and falling seconds. "Moon of My Delight" is built almost entirely on the first feature, while "In a Great Big Way" uses the second. These are techniques Rodgers defends:

> Obviously it would have been inappropriate for me to write typically "American" music, but equally obviously, even if I could have written "Chinese" music, Broadway audiences would have found it unattractive—to say nothing of the impossibility of Larry's finding the proper words to go with it.

The only solution was to compose my own kind of music but with an Oriental inflection, reproducing a style rather than creating a faithful imitation.[67]

Still, this close connection of character and theme with motif is not consistent throughout the score, as is clear in the Act One finale. Strangely, Tchou's music ("Farewell, oh life") (see Figure 8.5) exploits a descending chromatic chord cluster that is a feature of material from the "Food Solo" (No.7) and "Better Be Good to Me" (No.17), neither of which is originally sung by Tchou; a variation occurs later in the "Processional" (No.31), where it does mark Tchou's story-line, and a similar use of descending chromatic harmonies is found in "Sleep Weary Head" (No.23), Chti's lullaby to Tchou (see Figure 8.6). The prevalence

Figure 8.5–8.6: Descending chromatic chord clusters, a feature of the Chee-Chee score indiscriminately assigned to various characters. Reprinted by Permission of Hal Leonard Corporation

of this gesture in the score might be less a matter of leitmotif and more the habitual sound of early Rodgers.

Elsewhere, while Li Li Wee's material comes from "Prayer (Holy of Holies)" (No.6), and therefore relates her to the domain of the Grand Eunuch through a repeated triple-time motif (Figure 8.7), there seems to be little discrimination between the music representing the Grand Eunuch's domain in the Palace and that representing the Monastery of Celestial Clouds (Figure 8.8). Eventually, the

6. "Prayer" ("Holy of Holies"), mm.4-11

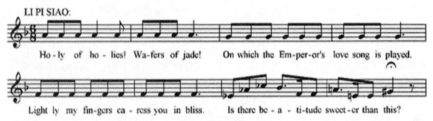

Figure 8.7: The triple time motif of the Grand Eunuch's music.
Reprinted by Permission of Hal Leonard Corporation

4. "In a Great Big Way"

25. "Monastery Opening"

Figure 8.8: Passages from "In a Great Big Way," set in the Grand Eunuch's palace, and "Monastery Opening," set in the Bonze's Monastery of the Celestial Clouds. Note how very similar patterns conflate the two locations.
Reprinted by Permission of Hal Leonard Corporation

Act One Finale becomes a typical Rodgers, Hart, and Fields finale of the period: a medley of songs from the first act (and at least one as yet unheard song from the second). In between these stitched-together songs, odd sections of dialogue occur, though unfortunately the remaining libretto for this Finale is missing.

Rodgers's commitment to the integrity of these leitmotivic devices is therefore admirable though somewhat undermined, and one wonders whether it was inexperience, the exigencies of production, the rush to develop the material, or the simple economy of the business that overwhelmed his attempts to fully integrate this score.

Ultimately, it remains an irony of even the most integrated musicals that they become marketed and commodified through a collection of "Take Home Tunes," which, as we have seen from the reception of "Here in my Arms" following its heavy-handed promotion during *Lido Lady*, often become prioritized above the artistic value of the shows.

Much has been made of the fact that only a handful of complete songs exist in the score of *Chee-Chee*: "Dear, Oh Dear," "I Must Love You," "Better Be Good to Me," "The Tartar Song," "Moon of My Delight" and an additional song written slightly later, "Singing a Love Song." These are certainly the six "Take Home Tunes" released as songsheets and the only material to be catalogued in the copyright archive of the Library of Congress. These are written in popular song form (mostly AABA), they have relatively dispensable introductory verses that locate them within the context of the show, and their catchy melodies are repeated inexorably to promote them as song-hits and sell the sheet music: "Better Be Good to Me" has eight reprises of its refrain in a row, and "Moon of My Delight" is followed with a dance reprise featuring the refrain at least twelve times in a row. A further four reprises of "I Must Love You" clearly make this the "theme song" of the show (as the libretto confirms), and its central themes are the most consistent binding material throughout the score.

"I Must Love You" is a standard song of the period. Its thirty-two-bar AABA' chorus is preceded by a twenty-four-bar AAB verse. Nevertheless, the harmonic relationship between the verse and chorus is unusual. The verse is established in F# minor, and the first twenty bars prepare us to expect a modulation into the relative A major; however, a displacement of the key in the final four bars shifts the expected F#, G#, E cadence to G, A, D, the dominant of G major. Once the chorus begins, it conforms to our expectations, and the repeated A section builds on material found elsewhere. The title phrase, "I Must Love You" is built around the fanfare that elsewhere heralds the Grand Eunuch (see Figure 8.9), thereby consolidating this as the heredity motif around which theme the whole story revolves.

"Overture," mm.3-4

14. "Finaletto, Act One, scene one," mm.44-47

CHEE-CHEE

I love him, I love him with ar - dor com - plete.

15. "I Must Love You," mm.26-29

LI PI TCHOU / CHEE-CHEE

I must love you while my heart is beat - ing.

*Figure 8.9: The repeated use of the "fanfare motif" throughout the
score of* Chee-Chee.
Reprinted by Permission of Hal Leonard Corporation

In fact, this fanfare has already been heard numerous times and, as can be seen, it is a theme extended elsewhere in the score.

The next two bars establish a second theme, related to Tchou and Chti and associated with their love. Again, this is material heard in slightly varied guises throughout the score (Figure 8.10), and is repeated in variation three times to complete the eight bars of the A section.

The B section offers two four-bar phrases of a syncopated descending motif, the second descending through almost the whole octave to return to the note D for the beginning of the final A section (see Figure 8.11).

Although this is the first introduction of the song "I Must Love You" in its entirety, all of this material has been heard before and is usually linked with Chti and Tchou's love. Most obviously, a barely disguised variation occurs at the end of scene one, where Tchou is banished from the palace and Chti opts to accompany him. Elsewhere, we might see it as the basis of the B section of "Dear, Oh Dear" (see Figure 8.12); sketchings in the Richard Rodgers collection at the Library of Congress include similar unspecified variations on this motif.

This use of material from "I Must Love You," both before and after its main refrain, establishes it as the main thematic material in the show; it also indicates a real understanding of character- and thematically driven musical integration. Indeed, the same can be said of some of the other "stand-alone" songs from the show. Although the precise placement of these numbers is often unspecified in the libretto, it is because of the way Rodgers and Hart have created character-based (integrated) numbers that their intended sequence can be established.

11. "I Wake at Morning," mm.31-34 (transposed)

14. "Finaletto, Act One, scene one," mm.16-17

15. "I Must Love You," mm.28-29

I-20. "Finale Act One," mm.13-14

[lyrics missing]

Figure 8.10: The "Chti and Tchou motif," as used throughout the score of Chee-Chee. Reprinted by Permission of Hal Leonard Corporation

15. "I Must Love You," mm.42-49

Figure 8.11: The B section of "I Must Love You," showing the descending diatonic scale. Reprinted by Permission of Hal Leonard Corporation

The first main number indicated, for example, occurs when Li Li Wee and Prince Tao Tee meet, at which point one might expect a conventional love song. These are the secondary, comic love interests of the show, she a mercenary trainee concubine who is seeking an affluent courtier for future prosperity, he a well-meaning friend of Tchou's who wants to find the escaped couple and resolve the problem. Their dialogue bristles with the sassy energy characteristic of Herb's scripts and defines two comically mismatched characters—the sappily romantic Prince and the urbane and sexually confident girl:

14. "Finaletto, Act One, scene one," mm.36-43

[8]. "Dear, Oh Dear," mm.35-42

Figure 8.12: Further uses of the descending motif.
Reprinted by Permission of Hal Leonard Corporation

LI LI WEE: Who are you?

PRINCE: I'm Prince Tao Tee. Son of the Holy man son of heaven.

LI LI WEE: Now I'm supposed to say, "Reverence to this!" Do you need any concubines to-day?

PRINCE: Are you a concubine?

LI LI WEE: No, but I'm apprentice to one.... Look, I have a jade tablet and everything.

PRINCE: Do you think you could fulfill the requirements?

LI LI WEE: I could if you don't mind large feet...

PRINCE: I don't mind...

DUET...[68]

In this case as elsewhere[69] the number does not appear in the libretto but instead is signaled "Duet," which has caused some confusion. According to the most accessible authoritative commentary, Dorothy Hart and Robert Kimball's *Complete Lyrics*, the original number used here was called "I'll Never Share You," or "If You Were My Concubine," but this was dropped in the out-of-town tryouts in Philadelphia and replaced—first by an untitled number that appears to have had no lyrics written, and subsequently by "Dear, Oh Dear!" However, aside from correspondence from Rodgers categorically stating that Helen Ford (Chti) and William Williams (Tchou) sing "Dear, Oh Dear!" in the second scene rather than here,[70] it seems unlikely to have occurred at this point for several reasons. First, "Dear, Oh Dear" is sung not by Li Li Wee and Prince Tao Tee who are on stage at this point, but by Tchou and Chti, who have not yet been introduced; second, the music to "Dear, Oh Dear" fits Tchou and Chti through the use of recurring musical motifs, a short phrase of descending diminished chords over a chromatic bass line: vintage Rodgers and used as part of the romantic "sound" of Tchou and Chti both here and in "I Wake at Morning"; and finally, the lyrics reflect sincerely on a relationship ("Dear oh dear, my darling, how I care for you! / I care for you alone," sings Tchou),[71] which suits their established marital situation rather than the mercenary negotiation of Li Li Wee with the Prince.

"Better Be Good to Me," on the other hand, is sung by Li Li Wee and the Prince, and its lyrics reflect the relationship established between them:

LI LI WEE: When a truly modest maid
        Is a lovely little jade,
        Then morality's an awful strain on appetite;
        I respect your stainless youth,
        But to speak the simple truth,
        I could put your form between my arms and wrap it tight.[72]

This, rather than "Dear, Oh Dear!" fits their conversation in scene one, and furthermore, the verse contains several phrases of repeated notes, a feature linked to their characters throughout the show. Their later song, "Moon of My Delight," uses the same device, and is strikingly different to the more melodic patterns representing Tchou and Chti. The way this repeated pattern is used works as a motif that is associated with the eunuchs and concubines (see Figure 8.13).

The jump to the fifth of the scale from the repeated third of the melody is extended to a sharpened fifth, creating a double tritone (the devil's chord) which not only characterizes the eunuchs and concubines but perhaps also represents a moralistic commentary by Rodgers on the culturally unfamiliar sexual relationships of the imperial Chinese court. Thus it seems likely that the song intended for this moment in the first scene was "Better Be Good to Me" rather than "Dear, Oh Dear!"

Elsewhere, "The Tartar Song" works as a stand-alone novelty number, though it clearly fits the point at which the Tartars appear, with a rather military sound and minor key somewhat suggestive of the renegade soldiers who sing the number.

In the second act, "Moon of My Delight" is built of repeated-note motifs as much of the concubines' musical material is, and employs Rodgers's orientalizing feature of the descending major second throughout. Again, however, there is no mention of this song in the libretto, and indeed no song is

Figure 8.13: *The Eunuch / Concubine motif, a repeated pattern followed by an extended fifth. The repeated pattern and interval of a minor third is also used in "Moon of My Delight."*
Reprinted by Permission of Hal Leonard Corporation

even anticipated at the point this most obviously appears in Act Two, scene three.[73]

The sixth main song from *Chee-Chee* is "Singing a Love Song." It is surprising that this number doesn't feature in the program's musical synopsis, given that Rodgers recognizes six conventional "songs" appearing in the show.[74] It was also published as a songsheet and later recycled as "I Still Believe in You" in *Simple Simon* (1930).[75] This is the least integrated song of all and the one that harks back most problematically to the typical 1920s interpolation of material. This number offered George Houston as the Tartar Chief an opportunity to engage his rich baritone, and it seems likely that its addition was a late development following press reviews praising Houston's voice. It is a musically and dramatically incongruous number, sung by a character from the first act in a second act scene that need not exist.

These six main songs, then, have interesting relationships with the libretto. As I have suggested, they are probably the most extractable numbers, and this renders them fairly interchangeable within it. Nevertheless, there are other "numbers": both Tchou's "I Wake at Morning" from Act One and Chti's "Sleep, Weary Head" from Act Two are written in standard AABA form and use elements of the motivic musical material that we have already encountered; "In a Great Big Way" and "Just a Little Thing," both from Act One, are in a simpler strophic form and use basic melodic and harmonic patterns, all of which fit in with the musical language given to Li Li Wee and Li Pi Siao,[76] as well as the eunuchs and concubines in their musical passages.

Just as Graham Wood discovered with *Dearest Enemy*, Rodgers appears to have used different song forms and different harmonic and melodic motifs for different characters. In this, he shows commitment to developing what would come to be termed "integration." One of the additional interesting features of Rodgers's musical characterizations in this show is that we sense an ideological commentary in the music. The traditional cultural expectations of the court characters are represented through music less advanced and more "ethnic"-sounding than the Westernized jazz harmonies that represent the ideology of love and marriage espoused by Tchou and Chti. Whereas Hart and Fields embraced the rather risqué material of the book with verve, Rodgers reveals an interesting ideological timidity in which he judges the characters through his music as much as he characterizes them.

In his memoirs, Rodgers's only fond memory of this score seems to be his witty insertion of a theme from Tschaikovsky's *Nutcracker Suite*. The insertion is hardly subtle, so anyone familiar with the ballet would undoubtedly have recognized the reference; Rodgers used similar intertextual quotations in other shows (such as Beethoven's Seventh Symphony in the Act One Finale of *Peggy-Ann*), so this is nothing new—it appears in the processional music at the denouement of the show, just as Tchou leaves to have, as it were, his nuts cracked. If nothing else, this musical joke at least uses humor consistent with the flippancy of this show, the Fields-Rodgers-Hart writing team in general, and 1920s musical comedy as a whole.

THE PRODUCTION

That *Chee-Chee* receives such a high profile in typical narratives of Rodgers and Hart *despite* its apparent failure is significant. Yet this is typical of the sort of dualities common to historiographies: shows are either huge successes or huge flops, and work viewed retrospectively is judged by today's standards and expectations. Many discussions of the show become distracted by the subject matter rather than its treatment; and in such examinations, commentators indulge existing mythologies rather than interrogating the cultural context in which they became established or noticing the developments in technique that challenge the dominant narratives. Of course, an instance of resounding failure in the otherwise celebrated career of Richard Rodgers offers a dramatic punch to anyone telling his story; and it is difficult to see beyond the very short run this show enjoyed on Broadway, the handful of particularly acerbic reviews, and the unlikely pairing of musical theater with castration—a subject that easily becomes a target of scorn.

Very few writers mention, however, that this show was produced by Lew Fields, and it is worth considering how his decision to close the show may have been due to his own concerns and self-image than to the reception or quality of the show itself. Fields's reputation for providing clean, family entertainment had been carefully maintained for half a century, and as part of an older generation he was uncomfortable with the assertive, sexualized behavior of the jazz age. As his family biographers note, the Weber and Fields brand established a "wholesome image," maintaining "rigid standards of propriety" and a "Victorian code of gentility."[77] This was against all odds: the sort of vaudeville and burlesque in which he worked had grown notoriously distasteful in its sexual references, states of undress, and use of language. Other big name producers such as Florenz Ziegfeld, Al Woods, and particularly Earl Carroll were pushing boundaries both on stage and off, with scandalous promotional events flouting standards of decorum and taste. Even Fields's own brother Solly had been charged with indecency for producing what amounted to a striptease show at the Chelsea Theatre in 1926. In this climate, the censorship lobby was striving to be heard, and as we have seen, authorities were beginning to clamp down on the prurient entertainments that were endemic to the jazz era.

The visible force with which District Attorney Joab H. Banton closed down offending productions in early 1926 followed a steady increase in complaints from the moral right. Initially, Banton's response was informal, establishing a panel of 300 citizens to comment on the moral acceptability of theatrical material, and a jury to pass judgment. However, when the first report of the citizens' jury—advising the closure of the Gene Lockhart revue *Bunk of 1926*—was overturned by a real courtroom decision, the mayor of New York, James J. Walker, enacted more punitive legislation that led to the closure of *SEX*, *The Captive*, and *The Virgin Man* on February 9. A formal bill, the Wales Act, or informally the "Wales Padlock Bill," was passed by the New York State legislature in April 1927 "to protect audiences against lewd, obscene and degenerate subject matters."[78]

The initial response to these events, and the Wales Act in particular, was for Broadway to scoff at the authorities. This took its most obvious form in the Billy Rose/Shubert revue *Padlocks of 1927*, a satirical swipe that opened on July 5, 1927, and starred aging nightclub icon Texas Guinan whose own venue had been the victim of similar legislation. Why almost a year's delay occurred between the institution of the Wales Act and its first invocation to shut down a production is unclear, though the protracted saga of these events is undoubtedly connected to Governor Alfred E. Smith's ambitions for the US presidency and the need to show the electorate that something was being done to curb degenerate entertainment in New York. As Burton W. Peretti reports, the press took a cynical stance, with the left campaigning for freedom of speech and the right accusing politicians of hypocrisy and bluster.[79]

The first production shut down under the act (almost a year later) was the Shuberts' *Maya*, an English translation of the French play by Simon Gantil- lon, which had opened on February 21, 1928, at the Comedy Theatre for just fifteen performances. The raid was a surprise, and as Laurence Senelick sug- gests, "neither the critics nor the producer Lee Shubert found anything of- fensive" in *Maya*.[80] Shubert was angered by what he viewed as inconsistent policies regarding the law and the financial implications of shutting down a production ahead of schedule.[81] However, his agreement to shut down the production acknowledged a clause in the act that held producers responsible, and threatened to revoke their theater licenses for a year should they breach court decisions. This was significant in Lew Fields's response to the criticism of *Chee-Chee*. As John H. Houchin suggests,

> The District Attorney and the Police Commissioner had now established themselves as unofficial censors. They only had to intimate that a show was obscene to persuade frightened theatre owners to evict troublesome tenants. The state had not instituted an official censor, but it had clearly established a censorship mechanism.[82]

Indeed, as the *World* commented, the act "so terrorizes the owner of the the- atre with its threat of a year's padlock that he does not dare take the risk of letting the case be taken to court."[83]

Just as *Chee-Chee*'s reviews were coming out, Mae West hit the headlines yet again, with a production called *The Pleasure Man*. This "blended *The Drag* with the sordid story of a heterosexual lothario,"[84] and although "the homo- sexual characters were secondary to the plot [t]he major objections to *The Pleasure Man* came from the play's suggestive dialogue and provocative ho- mosexual slang."[85] As Watts reports, "The DA had acted against several other productions in the weeks preceding the *Pleasure Man* raid, and rumors circu- lated just before its Manhattan debut that the authorities planned to stop it."[86] *The Pleasure Man* opened on October 1, 1928, at the Biltmore Theatre for just two performances before it was closed under the orders of the Wales Padlock Bill. Lew Fields's production of *Chee-Chee* had opened in the Mansfield Theatre—literally right opposite the Biltmore—only the previous week.

The cumulative distaste generated by the scandalous *Pleasure Man* and the mixed reviews of *Chee-Chee* prompted at least one newspaper to label West 47th Street "the theatrical red light district."[87] Is it surprising that a producer in any case uncertain about the show, as Fields was, would want to protect his reputation, if even a minority of reviews expressed any negativity? Fields could not risk either the press outrage or the financial stress of a raid, and in the end, perhaps it was this "castration anxiety" that caused a promising, if dubious, show to close.

So what about Rodgers's subsequent disenchantment with *Chee-Chee*? It certainly marked a turning point for him, both in his personal life (announcing his engagement to Dorothy Feiner within the year) and in his professional life (which suddenly hit the doldrums). Aside from the London shows and the Dillingham commissions, all of Rodgers and Hart's output between 1925 and 1928 involved some or all of the "family." Herb Fields, already a firm friend and collaborator, worked on all seven, Lew Fields produced five, Roy Webb musically directed four,[88] Alexander Leftwich directed three and went on to work on *Spring Is Here* the following year, and Helen Ford starred in *Dearest Enemy, Peggy-Ann,* and *Chee-Chee*. Now things were moving on, and perhaps with the experience of *Chee-Chee* the boys took stock, realizing they were just cogs in the cultural machine, recognizing they were growing up. The close-knit "family" that had worked together for more than three years and on several shows was beginning to break apart, and a newly thoughtful Rodgers and Hart would begin to seek a way to move into the next phase in their lives and careers. Leaving the 1920s behind was also leaving their youth behind; perhaps Rodgers's later rejection of *Chee-Chee* can be rationalized as the growing up of a boy into a man.

9

COPING WITH THE CRASH

• • •

The premature closure of *Chee-Chee* surprised many critics, who continued to write of "Rodger's [*sic*] best score to date,"[1] one that had brought "at least three irresistible melodies into a season which sadly needed them."[2] And it seemed to knock Rodgers and Hart's confidence. For more than three years they had enjoyed uninterrupted success in New York and London. Following *Chee-Chee*, plans were put on hold as the team retrenched.

Lew had been bruised by *Chee-Chee* as much as the writers, and with the sense of a family closing ranks, he put straight into the Mansfield a new show by a replacement writing team, effectively dismissing Rodgers and Hart. *Hello Daddy* was another adaptation of a former Fields success, *The High Cost of Loving* (1914). Herb wrote the book, Dorothy the lyrics, and Jimmy McHugh, Dorothy's writing partner, wrote the music. Alexander Leftwich was kept on to direct, and Busby Berkeley was called back for choreography. Although Rodgers would deny that his own team had split in the aftermath of *Chee-Chee*,[3] this was the Rodgers and Hart show that never happened, and his words have a somewhat hollow ring. Indeed, the continued success of Herb Fields while his former writing partners floundered begs questions of whether it was he as much as Rodgers and Hart who had driven the team's success, as one correspondent to *New York Amusements* suggested.[4] Although often sidelined in narratives of Rodgers and Hart, and although his contribution often received criticism, one wonders whether his flossy, farcical humor was the glue holding Rodgers and Hart's shows together. Fields, Rodgers, and Hart would work together again, but for now they went their separate ways.

Larry might be excused for floundering in October 1928. Not only did *Chee-Chee* close unceremoniously, but his ailing father also passed away, swiftly followed by his uncle. Hart was not exactly close to his father, though in many ways they were similar characters. Max's health had been deteriorating for some time, and as it did, Larry was reminded of his extrovert character as various creditors emerged from a shady past. Lawyers worked hard to stall their demands, but Larry had to pay up. Larry's loss may have caused

Dick to take stock; his cherished grandfather Jacob Levy had also died in April, while Rodgers was characteristically run off his feet—their new show *Present Arms* was opening at the Mansfield on April 26. At the time, Rodgers took compassionate leave to Colorado Springs, but that was in the context of a hectic schedule. It may not have been until *Chee-Chee* forced a period of reflection on him—particularly if Max Hart's death served as a reminder—that he could really grieve. "It hit me terribly hard," he wrote years later; "I adored the old man."[5] Meanwhile, his relationship with Dorothy was strained, and long, separate trips to the Continent did not help. Meryle Secrest's biography of Rodgers perhaps over-dramatizes the situation, though through the words of Dorothy she tells a poignant story:

> When he was on the high seas returning from his Mediterranean trip in March of 1928, Rodgers sent a radiogram saying "Hello"—"just 'Hello,' she said. And I didn't know that was meant to be the beginning of a conversation." So she sent another one-word radiogram back. It said, "Goodbye."[6]

To be sure, the last couple of theater seasons had been exhausting. Even though the boys had taken regular vacations and led a privileged transatlantic life between New York, London, and Paris, they had worked solidly. Between the opening of the *Garrick Gaieties* on June 8, 1925, and the closures of *Chee-Chee* and *A Connecticut Yankee* within a week of one another (October 20 and October 27, 1928), there had only been twenty-five nights on Broadway without a Rodgers and Hart production. Now they would go five months without an opening, and although they couldn't know it at this stage, it would be years before their next bona fide hit. In this context, it is easy to see *Chee-Chee* as a huge setback, and it is not surprising that Rodgers's later reflections would view it as such a failure. Yet he hadn't really been thrown by the similar failure of *Betsy* (39 performances to *Chee-Chee*'s 31), even if he didn't enjoy the experience; nor had he worried about the short run of *She's My Baby* (71 performances) earlier in the year. Now Dick and Larry were treading water. "Larry and I are tired and want to sit back and let the other fellows do the shows for a time," Rodgers told one reporter; "right now we're in need of a rest."[7] The press treated that remark with typical hyperbole: The *Sun* headlined its article "Temporary retirement for Rodgers and Hart"—though perhaps this wasn't too far off the mark.

SPRING IS HERE (1929)

Nevertheless, just before the end of the year, the *New York Times* reported that producers Aarons and Freedley would be mounting the next Rodgers and Hart show, a musical based on the Owen Davis play *Loving Ann*. Davis was a Pulitzer Prize–winning playwright known for melodrama but not musical comedy,[8] though his play *The Nervous Wreck* had been adapted to create the Eddie Cantor smash hit *Whoopee!*, and another play, *Easy Come, Easy Go*, was to open as *Lady Fingers* in January 1929. Steeled by this, Davis turned his attention to writing a libretto. His show, renamed *Spring Is Here*, would open at the Alvin on March 11.

Rodgers remembers a convivial experience, "far more rewarding for the congeniality of the company than for any creative accomplishments of our run-of-the-mill show."[9] The company mood was respectful and friendly, and work stopped every day at 5 P.M. for cocktails and leisurely dinner dates. If the show that resulted was mediocre ("Competent but unoriginal" is Nolan's verdict;[10] "a throwback to the nineteenth-century comedy-melodrama," suggests Marmorstein[11]), it was at least more favorably treated than *Chee-Chee*, and even hostile critics found little at which to gripe. "The music isn't quite up to that of *Chee-Chee*," suggested the *New Yorker*[12] (indeed, Rodgers's score was considered by the *Judge* to be "the poorest he has turned out in a long while");[13] but the *Herald Tribune* disagreed, hearing in *Spring Is Here* "the finest score and the most expert lyrics that the oncoming team of Richard Rodgers and Lorenz Hart has yet provided."[14] The *Evening Public Ledger* summed things up: "While realizing it is not a grand explosion of musical comedy brilliance, [one] manages to have a pretty good time all the way through."[15]

Betty Braley is besotted with cad Stacy Haydon, though her father Peter is set on her marrying the much more reliable Terry Clayton. A date is fixed—without any agreement from Betty—and though Terry tries to woo her, she has been captivated by Stacy's charm. When Terry seeks advice from an older, married woman, he is told to play away from home (with her) to make himself more desirable. He goes out with a bevy of girls and returns steaming drunk. At this—and catching Betty with Stacy—the furious Mr. Braley cancels the wedding. Stacy and Betty plan to elope, though in the confusion of their moonlight escape, Mr. Braley gets shot accidentally by Terry. In the second act we find that he has made great efforts to change, becoming more assertive. Struck by his devotion, Betty shows pity. When Stacy climbs in a window to steal her away again, Terry—evading Mr. Braley and the police—throws him over the balcony and wins Betty's undying respect. The tables have turned: Stacy proposes, though she is now smitten with Terry.

The script makes good use of Owen Davis's stock-in-trade skills. The end of Act One, for example, is an extended farce in the garden at night. Stacy climbs over the wall to escort Betty down from her balcony so they can run away;

Terry climbs over to try to meet her; another character, Steve, climbs over for a tryst with sister Mary Jane. Ladders go up and down, crashes and bangs awake the family, Steve and Terry keep climbing trees or ducking behind bushes, and all of these shenanigans disturb Braley who puts the incompetent Slade on guard duty. Various farcical gags lead to Betty meeting Terry instead of Stacy; Terry then reports the imminent escape to Braley who tells him to load a gun with rock salt pellets. Finally, Stacy and Betty escape, chased by Braley whom Terry then shoots. This is pure farce, and despite acknowledging its hackneyed conventions, most reviewers acceded that it was hilariously funny. Another farcical scene in Act Two continues the hilarity, with Braley and the police chasing Terry up ladders and through trap doors in the barn but suffering accident after accident and ending up covered in oats.

Many of the reviews singled out Charles Ruggles ("just about our most accomplished farceur") for his performance as Peter Braley.[16] Aside from him, the critics were taken with Inez Courtney as Mary Jane, and specialty dancer Cy Landry, "one of the best of the jelly dancers,"[17] as Burns Mantle put it. He "plays astonishingly simple tricks with his anatomy," wrote Brooks Atkinson. "His arms swing like a pendulum. His feet move in all directions. But best of all, he can shift from one idea to an idea completely foreign through the most logical pantomime transitions."[18]

The leading man was an interesting choice—matinee idol Glenn Hunter couldn't sing. Though this seems a ridiculous mistake to have made (even if "it would be futile, of course, to expect much in the way of singing in a piece like this," as one reporter wrote),[19] Rodgers and Hart turned it to their advantage. They bookended the character development of the painfully shy Terry with two renditions of the same song, "Yours Sincerely." Dramaturgically, this represented a letter the tongue-tied suitor read out to woo his girl, and the lyrics were spoken over the orchestral accompaniment. "[Glenn Hunter's] part in 'Yours Sincerely' is the basis of what will probably turn out to be the best hit of the show," wrote one reviewer. Spoken though it was, this song was labeled Rodgers's "finest melody to date."[20] Whether or not it was the melody that impressed critics (almost unanimously), the review of the *Philadelphia Inquirer* suggested something else: "Rodgers and Hart have written a new kind of song," raved The Callboy, "breaking away from the stereotyped numbers that were part and parcel of the musical comedies of the old days. They apparently endeavor to express the spirit of the book, to carry on for the librettist, so to speak."[21] In this—however much by happenstance—Rodgers and Hart created another example of integration; so although, as Geoffrey Block notes, "most musical theatre historians share the view that Rodgers became less artistically ambitious after *Chee-Chee* . . . [and that] *Spring Is Here*

(1929) reflects some creative backtracking," there are certainly in this show vestiges of their progressive musical theater craft.[22]

Nevertheless, *Spring Is Here* was hardly "groundbreaking musical theater,"[23] and it ran for only 104 performances, which following *Chee-Chee* must have been another disappointment. The heady excitement of their first flush of success was beginning to falter, and in taking stock, hitting a new decade, and—perhaps—maturing a little, it is now that one senses a crisis of confidence.

Among the ephemera and press coverage from this period are numerous accounts of Rodgers's activities away from the stage. His social appointments were closely scrutinized, and though often guarded with the press, he spoke regularly and, occasionally, candidly to interviewers; in his ongoing correspondence with Dorothy he includes news about himself; and in his autobiography—however carefully scripted—he projects an image that, despite careful editing and selective recall, often reveals more than it masks. During this period of withdrawal in 1928–29, it is very interesting to follow both his affairs and his remarks.

After the opening of *Spring Is Here* he traveled to Europe for a trip that, he later claims, was made rather whimsically: "the fact that I agreed to cross the Atlantic just to go to one party gives a pretty good idea of the kind of life I was leading in those days," he wrote.[24] Indeed, there was a party on April 23, thrown in his honor by Cartier magnate Jules Glaenzer and his wife, and attended by "an eye-popping guest list" of "theatrical royalty and real royalty."[25] A second party equally as lavish was hosted on April 29 by Katherine and Esther Leslie;[26] following a brief trip to Cannes, he returned the compliment by hosting his own party at the Ritz on May 7.[27]

During the trip he was interviewed by the *Paris Herald* and confirmed that he was on vacation: "'I think I'll go to Gibraltar or some nice quiet place like that,'" he said; "'The people here are lovely, but—. Well, I want some rest.'"[28] In the article, the reporter asked him a revealing question, "'What's new in America, musically?'" His reply—in two parts—is tantalizing: "'Nothing, since Toscanini left'"; and then, "'You meant real music, didn't you?'"[29]

Quite what Rodgers meant by this quip is obscured in the ambiguity of his tone and the complexity of its context. The Italian conductor Arturo Toscanini had been a prominent character on the New York classical music scene for years, first as director of the Metropolitan Opera (1908–15), and then as guest conductor and music director of the New York Philharmonic (from 1926). Typically, the Philharmonic season would end in April, so Toscanini would have only recently left New York. He was known for introducing new repertory to New York audiences, so in one sense Rodgers's first comment is a flippant, superficial remark about the music scene. However, it is the second part of his reply that is ambiguous: " 'You meant real music, didn't you?' " Known as a popular songwriter (and largely only interested in this vocation), Rodgers would have been acutely aware of the cultural value accorded to various repertoires, represented here by Toscanini and himself. But drawing attention to the perceptual gulf between these worlds suggests an insecurity in how he valued his own work. Here in Paris he was feted because of his popular profile and asked to perform his music for the great and the good: "The guests weren't content merely to meet Mr. Rodgers," reported the *Sun*; "They insisted upon hearing his compositions, upon having him play them and sing them."[30] Still, one gets the impression that he felt somehow unworthy, as if undervalued at what mattered to him most.

Like his contemporaries, Rodgers showed ambivalence at his artistic standing as a songwriter rather than a composer of distinction. His attempts to elevate the Broadway musical were as much attempts to be recognized as a composer as they were concerned with the form. The conflict between classical and popular music was significant—both cultures rubbed shoulders in New York, and as Seldes's *The Seven Lively Arts* had shown, an ongoing debate was attempting to distinguish one from the other in terms of value and artistic difference. In America's quest for its own artistic voice, both classical and popular composers turned to jazz, so many of the perceived "differences" were shared similarities that blurred boundaries between high and low and exacerbated attempts of artists to self-identify within one camp or another.

One other phrase in the *Paris Herald* article catches attention. Here, as elsewhere, Rodgers is referred to as "the second Gershwin."[31] We can only speculate how that comparison made him feel, though he reflected on this in his autobiography. "I suppose what bothered me most," he wrote, "was that my most celebrated contemporaries...had gone on to even greater achievements."[32] He and Gershwin moved in the same circles, plied the same trade, and to an extent, enjoyed comparable success. But Rodgers was always second fiddle, and in one crucial respect he had not achieved what Gershwin had: recognition as a serious composer.

Rodgers's remark looked back some years, to 1924. Even then, Gershwin was the talk of the town, with *Lady, Be Good!* on Broadway (for 330 performances) and "Rhapsody in Blue" giving him credibility as a serious composer. Originally titled "An American Rhapsody," this had been commissioned by bandmaster Paul Whiteman, one of several pieces presented at a February 1924 concert at the Aeolian Hall to "determine what constituted American music."[33] It publicly launched Gershwin's career as a classical composer and concert pianist, establishing his sound as new and American. To Deems

Taylor the "Rhapsody" "hinted at something new, something that had hitherto not been said in music."[34] In July Gershwin had appeared on the cover of *Life* magazine, the youngest person ever to be featured.

By 1928, Rodgers would have been acutely aware of the furor surrounding Gershwin. His run of hit musicals—*Lady, Be Good!* (1924); *Tip-Toes* (1925); *Oh, Kay!* (1926), and *Funny Face* (1927)—had consolidated his success, and their slew of hit songs ("Swanee," "Fascinating Rhythm," "Someone to Watch over Me," "'S Wonderful") were popular beyond the stage. But it was Gershwin's increasing forays into concert music that set him a class apart. "Of all those writing the music of today," wrote one commentator, "he alone actually expresses us."[35]

With two prestigious successes and a catalogue of minor classical pieces, Gershwin took time in writing his most ambitious work yet, "An American in Paris" (1928). Characteristically, he prevaricated and sought training in composition from a number of composers; these may have been cursory flirtations as Joan Peyser suggests, but he sought advice from Nadia Boulanger, Alexander Glazunov, Maurice Ravel, Igor Stravinsky, Alban Berg, and Henry Cowell. By the summer of 1928, a two-piano version of the score was ready, and it was this he first performed for the guests of Jules and Kendall Glaenzer—including Richard Rodgers—at their Westchester beach house. In his autobiography Rodgers is effusive: "Like everyone else I was captivated by the vividly evocative work," he wrote.[36] One wonders whether such gracious recognition of Gershwin's talent was his immediate response.

That summer (1928) Rodgers had been riding high, with *A Connecticut Yankee* still going strong, *Present Arms* playing at the Mansfield, and the exciting *Chee-Chee* in development. But just four months later when "An American in Paris" publicly premiered on December 13, the ever-reflective Rodgers was in a different situation. How bittersweet it must have been to hear the critical response: though not universally accepted, Gershwin's composition did receive public acclaim, and this elevated the status of the precocious pianist even further.

Rodgers's response to the success of his rival may have been as benevolent as his memoirs recall. Even in that recollection, though, his tone is odd. He reports a conversation with Gershwin, seizing on a spiky retort from the composer: "When I told George how much I admired it, he looked surprised and said, 'I didn't know you were like that.' 'Like what?'" (replied Rodgers); "'I didn't think you'd like anybody's music but your own.'"[37] This is a curious anecdote to relate, portraying a petulant Gershwin dismissing Rodgers's charm; but what purpose does the story serve? To me, Rodgers's report bristles with significance, and it is interesting to trace the subsequent events.

First, he takes a leaf out of Gershwin's book and seeks musical tuition. He does not make it public, but in letters to Dorothy it is clear he is trying to develop technique: "What with a fair amount of practice and a will to learn it now looks as though my music course has brought permanent results," he wrote on August 7;[38] he even visited his old music teacher "to tell him of a recent and overwhelming improvement."[39] The music teacher may have been Frank Damrosch, brother of Walter who had commissioned Gershwin's "Concerto" and set up a school in Paris with Nadia Boulanger; and Rodgers's trips to Paris may therefore have had more motive than being just vacations or whimsical party romps. Was he discreetly trying to improve musically in order to elevate his credibility like Gershwin?

Second, he jumps at the chance to work with Gershwin's producers Aarons and Freedley, and for *Spring Is Here* he adopts the Gershwinian device of two pianos in the pit. Perhaps he hoped in this to inherit some of the production team's success—though if he is concerned about playing second fiddle, it seems strange to copycat the master step for step.

Finally, Rodgers throws a lavish party, just days after the December 13 premiere of "An American in Paris." This may be entirely unrelated, but the timing seems significant: while Gershwin very visibly basks in publicity, Rodgers has been out of the spotlight. If nothing else, this event reminds the press who he is, seizing focus away from Gershwin (who was a guest) and asserting his presence to a Broadway set looking the other way. The dinner and dance was held at the Park Lane Hotel on December 17, 1928. The guest list was published in the *American*, the *Sun*, and the *Herald Tribune* the following day.

It is of course mere speculation that Rodgers envied his rival and sought to gain status through self-publicity, and credibility through self-improvement. Doing this in part by emulating Gershwin is ironic; but one wonders what he made of the view of the *Telegram* that his music was "too near-Gershwinian for its own good."[40] Rodgers was just as much as Hart a sucker for language. They would turn casual expressions into songs at the drop of a hat ("My Heart Stood Still," "This Funny World"); they were well versed in the subcultural euphemisms of New York ("The Violet Town," "Winkle Town," "Sky City"); and they reveled in throwing references to all manner of things into their material, musically and lyrically ("It May Rain"). Rodgers's ear was absolutely tuned to double meaning, insinuation, and spin. Furthermore, the wider circle of critics and commentators also relished language, whether it was in their poetic use of metaphor ("nutty fudge brought in hot from the kitchen") or their biting putdowns ("tripe is tripe"). He would undoubtedly have interpreted comments like "the second Gershwin" or "too near-Gershwinian" in leading ways, and for good or ill would have incorporated that into his sense of self.

Although few commentators recognized the milestone, the boys had now been together for ten years, and it is interesting to read comments written from a distance about their early projects, some of which were patently ridiculous: "When *Garrick Gaieties* first broke," wrote one reviewer, "it was the general opinion that Master Rodgers was just an incubus about the neck of Hart."[41] That's not a comment that chimes with anything else, but it does add to the impression—perhaps manufactured—that the boys had creatively matured. "A couple of boys they were four years ago," recalled Percy Stone in the *Herald Tribune*, adding, "fourteen plays and they are grown up." Stone had high hopes for their future too, and rather prescient ones: "Fourteen more, if the love of money doesn't get them, and they'll be doing something far better than they have done as yet."[42]

The maturing we have seen in Rodgers's creative ambitions was balanced by changes in his personal life. In July 1929, he moved out of his parents' house to take a nineteenth-floor apartment in the Hotel Lombardy, south of Central Park. A few weeks later one of his letters to Dorothy points out how much he has grown up: "I've become quite even-tempered, and, I believe, less vague. I'm so anxious to see you because, among other things, you will be the one to know if I've changed and if for the better."[43] If this self-reflection was to impress Dorothy it worked; on December 7 they announced their engagement, celebrated with another party at the Park Lane Hotel on January 12; and in a quiet ceremony at the Feiner home on March 5, 1930, the couple were married. The boy had very definitely grown up.

One would suppose that the fruits of this maturity would be evident in his work. He even asserts as much in newspaper interviews relating to their next show *Heads Up!*: "convention alone dictates the rigid 4-4, 32-bar popular song," he stated; "but in 'Heads Up',...two of our outstanding numbers are of irregular form." He goes on to explain how "A Ship without a Sail" is written in an innovative 12-8-12 (ABA) structure, while "Why Do You Suppose" comes in at just twenty-four measures in length. "Convention has been defied and the heavens have not fallen," he concludes, rather over-emphasizing innovations that would hardly worry the Gods.[44]

Actually, *Heads Up!* was hardly groundbreaking in any sense, even if it was enjoyable and generally well received. "Whatever the show might lack in high spots, or however short it might be of greatness, it is spirited in action, gifted with good music, and has a full measure of jovial, chuckly humor,"[45] wrote the *Philadelphia Evening Public Ledger*. "Not the best of the town's shows," concurred the *Evening Journal*, "but comfortably wedged in the middle."[46]

The show started life as *You for Me*, and with the same production team as *Spring Is Here*: Aarons and Freedley, Rodgers and Hart, and Owen Davis on book. By the end of summer, the show was ready for tryouts in Detroit (as *Me for You*), but the book simply didn't work, and worse, audiences could not relate to one of their favorite personalities, Victor Moore, being cast against type. Moore played the aristocrat Egbert Peasley, an illicit bootlegger. When his daughter Janet returns from finishing school with the District Attorney Rodney Stoddard (or Rodman Stoddart) on her arm, Peasley panics and sends her immediately to sea with his accomplice Gil Stark. With the DA out of the way, Peasley can continue his racket undetected. On board the yacht, Janet falls for the charms of her guardian.

As Rodgers recalls, "audiences simply would not accept lovable Victor Moore in the unlovable role of a smuggler" (though he had played the bootlegger Shorty McGee in the Gershwins' *Oh, Kay* (1926), also an Aarons and Freedley show); "nor did they care much for a story that ended with the heroine ditching a district attorney to marry a lawbreaker. What to do?"[47] he asks, then fancifully imagines a salvage operation in which the show is turned from turkey to golden goose in the manner of a Hollywood summer stock movie (a premise remarkably similar to that of *Babes in Arms* just a few years later). This is not exactly what happened, though they did turn the show around.

The decision to rewrite the show following its Detroit tryouts threw the entire production into a state of emergency. Davis was dismissed, and script doctors Jack McGowan and Paul Gerard Smith set to work, completing a new book in ten days, which went immediately into rehearsal. Davis would later dismiss musical comedy himself, calling it "the least interesting and the most difficult" type of writing (and, marvelously, likening it to "putting peas up your nostrils"; "not at all impossible, but why do it?").[48] Ten more days and the new show opened as *Heads Up!*, rewritten to feature—according to the *New York Times*—just five of its original nineteen numbers.[49] In fact, only four of the songs survived: "My Man Is on the Make," "A Ship without a Sail," "It Must Be Heaven" and "Me for You."[50]

In the revision, the storyline was markedly different, and Victor Moore played the more likable character of good-hearted ship's cook Skippy Dugan. Captain Denny is using the luxury yacht of high-class Martha Trumbell to run a bootlegging racket. He has press-ganged Skippy—a reformed convict and amateur inventor—to abet him. But detective Larry White has got wind of the racket. Just as they finish loading a delivery of the contraband, Larry turns up to quiz Skippy, who blusters and gives the game away. Meanwhile, handsome cadet Jack Mason and Mary Trumbell have fallen head over heels.

She is leaving that evening and tries to convince him to join them. He promises to meet her later in the summer, but stows away on the lifeboat just as the yacht sails. They continue their affair in secret, though Captain Denny and jealous suitor Rex Cutting find out and Jack is arrested. Back on shore, he is recruited by Larry to crack the booze smuggling racket. They board the yacht with the help of Skippy, but Captain Denny blows the yacht up. While some of the passengers make it safely back to shore, Skippy gets marooned on a desert island with comedy character Betty. Eventually, he gets her bloomers off to use as a distress flag, and by the time they make it home he discovers that one of his inventions has been sold, making him a millionaire. Since the boat went down with all of the contraband, no one is charged with smuggling, and Captain Denny—now a reformed character—takes a new job as Skippy's faithful chauffeur.

While it may seem odd that a storyline from the Prohibition period might hinge so much on alcohol, quips about drinking pepper the scripts of many of the team's 1920s shows, from the drunken denouement of *The Girl Friend* to the bootlegging plotline of this show. Liquor may have been out of sight but it was certainly not out of mind: "What do you think of prohibition?" asks one character in *The Girl Friend*; "It's better than no liquor at all!" Mollie replies.

One of the most engaging anecdotes relating to the rewrite concerns the creation of "Why Do You Suppose?," which became the show's hit song along with "A Ship without a Sail." The story was publicly aired by Larry,[51] who suggested that, during tryouts, the producers had requested a new number to serve as a hit. Rodgers and Hart decided to recycle a trunk song cut from *She's My Baby*, "How Was I to Know?" The first set of new lyrics (about the all-new talking pictures craze: "They Sing! They Dance! They Speak!") was quickly rejected in favor of "Why Do You Suppose." With one further day of tryouts the team were keen to test the song, so it was rushed through the preparation process and included in the matinee performance the following day. Quite how rushed this process was is the subject of a *Herald Tribune* article.[52] Here the author queries Rodgers and Hart's apparent claim that it was written in twenty minutes, but then conducts a forensic examination of the time available between the Friday night show finishing and the Saturday matinee beginning. According to this article, the team had no more than an hour between the Friday curtain and the departure of the 12.15 from Philadelphia's Broad Street station. They wrote the song, which was couriered to New York—about two hours away—for Robert Russell Bennett to orchestrate. Rodgers and Hart coached the performers Jack Whiting and Barbara Newberry the following morning. By noon the now fully orchestrated song parts were back on a train to Philadelphia, where they arrived at 2.00 P.M. in time for the 2.30 performance. By 2.17 the parts reached the theater, though with no time to rehearse with the orchestra.

> The problem was solved simply. The overture was dispensed with that day and the new number, "Why Do You Suppose?" was played instead. Played and played and played. When Mr. Whiting and Miss Newberry sang the number a few minutes later, the coordination between orchestra and performers may have been somewhat less than perfect, but it got by.[53]

Rodgers identified "A Ship without a Sail" and "Why Do You Suppose" as the most innovative of the songs in the score, and they are both engaging. "Why Do You Suppose?" did indeed become the hit, although critics in England dismissed its lyrics for their "quite unsurpassable silliness."[54] However, these innovations were minor intrigues in a score that otherwise adhered to typical musical comedy fare, with little evidence of the progressive techniques they displayed in *Chee-Chee*.

Both versions of the show begin with (different) opening numbers in the style of Gilbert and Sullivan. *Me for You*'s "Jazz Reception" pastiches the parade of peers in *Iolanthe*: "Kindly nullify your fears. / Ta-ra-ta-ra! / Ta-ra-ta-ra! / For we are not British Peers. / Ta-ra-ta-ra! / Ta-ra-ta-ra-ta-ra!"[55] *Heads Up!*'s stand-alone opening, "You've Got to Surrender," pastiches the opening of *Patience*: "Thirty-three lovesick maidens, we, / Twenty and a baker's dozen."[56] Beyond this, much of the material has been lost, though it is clear from the casting that there are plenty of comedy numbers in the score: "jelly dancer" Cy Landry reappeared, this time with "rubber-legs" Ray Bolger in one of his first featured roles.[57] Their numbers "The Three Bears" and "We're an English Ship" (aka "The Bootleggers Chantey") capitalized on their "exceptional trick dancing."[58] Meanwhile, "My Man is on the Make," one of the songs that survived through to New York, was performed as a stand-alone number by Peggy and the tap-dancing specialty act Atlas and LaMarr (to great acclaim). Peggy was also given another stand-alone song with Ray Bolger: "Knees" is entirely gratuitous, speculating whether Rudyard Kipling was responsible for the 1920s popularity of rhythmic dancing.

In terms of more romantic fare, it is Hart who springs to the fore, with lyrics that by now show less extrovert rhyme-schemes than his earlier work and more sensitive emotional content. Isaac Goldberg's judgment is assertive: "if words are being listened to once again in the musical playhouse, Hart is among those who recaptured the straying ear."[59] In this show, the lyrics speak for themselves: "Sweetheart, You Make Me Laugh," for example, sung early in *Me for You* by Janet and Gil, establishes their shared senses of humor: "We'll stand at the altar / Like silly giraffes; / Our Rock of Gibraltar / Is founded on laughs."[60] The quirky imagery is engaging. Later, the couple sing the equally charming "I Can Do Wonders with You," in which she entreats him, "Let me fix your cap, / It's over your eye. / Do you think your map / Is helped by that tie?"[61] As with the best examples of Hart's less "pyrotechnic" writing, he presents tender images in the vernacular of his characters, reminding us in lyrics like this of other enchanting couples like Tom and Edith in *Winkle Town*, Lenny and Mollie in *The Girl Friend*, and Harry and Fay in *Lido Lady*.

Although Hart has left less than Rodgers by way of commentary, his occasional interviews offer insights into his songwriting approach. Around this time he spoke to the *Boston Herald*, for example, and while his philosophy was somewhat sketchy, what he said provides an interesting perspective.

> The romantic scene at the piano used to play an important part in courtships. Then girls didn't have "sex appeal"; they had "allure," and they all knew this allure could be displayed to the best advantage at the piano. When the beau called on Sunday night and presented his bouquet or box of bonbons, the girl spoke of a new song which was "simply divine." . . . The songwriters of the day had that little scene in mind as they wrote their stuff. They built everything around the boy and girl at the piano, and the thrill when their eyes met while singing of love. The songwriters had to change their tactics, for Henry Ford came along and the pianos remained silent while the girls went out riding. You can't sing "Kiss Me Again" to the tune of a slapping tire-chain. . . . Now the direct declaration of love in a song is passé. That's because the scene of the big emotional moment in the lives of young people has changed. If the girl plays the piano, she plays jazz. The piano tête-à-tête has gone, and there is a crowd dancing. . . . Words must have a lighter ring to them, but must appeal to the emotions of the dancing couple.[62]

As if to confirm this, his lyrics to *Me for You*—especially in those songs carried through to *Heads Up!*—offer the lightness to which he alludes. The title song itself ends with the fabulous entreaty, "When you sail your ship, / Please promise on each trip / To disappoint each girl."[63] Meanwhile, "It must be Heaven" comes across, as one reviewer put it, "quite delightfully":[64]

It must be Heaven
Coming home at seven
Just to find you there;
Oh, how exquisite!
Nothing's missing, is it,

In the home we share;
You can't cook,
But that won't hurt;
One sweet look
Is my dessert;
And at eleven
I will go to Heaven
Just to find you there.[65]

The maturing Rodgers and Hart are showing a more sophisticated approach not only in their lives and attitudes but also in the way they create their work. This is not altogether successful yet; nor is it altogether new—we have seen how *Chee-Chee* aspired to a form of musical theater that integrated words and music more coherently than usual. However, in developing technique, both Rodgers and Hart show an interesting progression. In another interview, Hart articulated this:

> In his agile mind there has evolved the plan for a new form of musical show on Broadway. "It will not be a musical comedy." And about this he was emphatic. "And it will not be an operetta." And about this he was equally emphatic. "It's going to be something entirely new. Something the likes of which has never been done on Broadway. There is going to be no moment when the tag line of a lyric is the cue for the prima donna to break forth into song. The songs are going to be a definite, essential part of the progress of the piece. Not extraneous interludes without rime or reason."[66]

Meanwhile, Rodgers's riposte to Gershwin came in an interview of January 12: "Dmitri Tiomkin," he announced, "is to play my 'Little Africa,' a free jazz development in program music, on his impending transcontinental concert tour."[67] Tiomkin was a Russian classical pianist who had come to the United States in 1925. Already passionate about popular American music, he was to champion American jazz as classical repertoire before the Wall Street crash cut short his concert tour schedule. In 1928 he gave the European premiere of Gershwin's "Concerto in F" in a program that also featured "Rhapsody in Blue"; Rodgers would find no better way to emulate Gershwin than having Tiomkin premiere his music. Everything was arranged, and Tiomkin's promoters issued pre-publicity to announce the first program: "Debussy and Modern Jazz, Gershwin, Dick Rodgers, Dimitri Tiomkin, Emil Gerstenberger, etc."[68] The tour was announced again on February 7 in the *New York Sun*, which claimed that it would begin "in San Francisco next week" and end "in New York next month"; "'Little Africa' appears on the same program with Stravinsky, Ravel, Milhaud, and others of the modernist school whom Tiomkin interprets."[69] Yet even though Rodgers and Tiomkin were pictured together in the *Hollywood News* on February 24,[70] this was the last news of any tour. Tiomkin—like an increasing number of artists—found Hollywood an enticing consolation, and with that, Rodgers's aspirations to succeed in serious music may well have been shelved. It would be years before he returned to that ambition, with a handful of concert and ballet pieces—"Slaughter on Tenth Avenue" (1936), "All Points West" (1936), the "Nursery Ballet" (1938), and "Ghost Town" (1939). By then Gershwin had passed away, and thereafter Rodgers's desire to compose serious music seemed to wane.

SIMPLE SIMON (1930)

The crash came just days after the *Heads Up!* tryouts in Philadelphia. The 1920s party was over, though it didn't stop Aarons and Freedley continuing with plans to move into town. They had their own theater, after all—the Alvin, named for the first parts of their names, Alex and Vinton. Perhaps surprisingly, and buoyed by the press's overwhelming praise for Victor Moore, the show sustained a reasonable run. But Rodgers and Hart also had other plans; back in July they had been reminded by Florenz Ziegfeld of an outstanding show he had contracted at the time of *Betsy*.[71] This must have struck them as ironic, given the painful experience of that show; but they were obliged.

Simple Simon was a simple affair, a star vehicle for comic Ed Wynn with a book by Guy Bolton; and in true Ziegfeld fashion it was managed from the top. According to rumors in the press,[72] Wynn's idea—originally pitched to William Anthony Maguire—was pilfered to feature as Maguire's Rip Van Winkle show *Ripples* at the New Amsterdam. There are indeed similarities, not least in the Hunting scene opening Act Two; but *Simple Simon* was never really threatened by *Ripples*. This, agreed the critics, was a "wholesome, beautiful, fanciful extravaganza, 'Babes in the Woods' brought up to date and embellished a hundred-fold."[73] It was lavish and sumptuous, with exquisite Joseph Urban designs and beautiful chorus girls who had critics swooning. Compared in reviews to extravaganzas of the previous generation—*Fantasma* (1884, 1889), *Superba* (1892), *Babes in Toyland* (1903), and *The Pearl and the Pumpkin* (1905)[74]—this was a feast for the eyes, though it perhaps found more influence from British pantomime.

Wynn is Simon Eyes, a cheeky Coney Island shopkeeper who works on Ferryman Street. (His name derives from the popular car wax product, Simoniz). Surrounded by colorful characters, he gives authority the runaround but generally means well and becomes everyone's confidant. One of his friends, Ella, has been promised to shady mobster Bert Blue, who is planning a jewelry heist. But she has fallen for charming Tony Prince, the son of her father's long-term adversary. When she promises to go to the charity ball with Tony instead of Bert, she is threatened by the mob and runs to Simon for protection. One day Simon falls asleep and in his dreams finds himself in Fairytale Street, on the border between two warring kingdoms. Gayleria, land of "Wine, Women and Song" is ruled by Old King Cole; Dullna is a puritan kingdom ruled by King Otto. Otto has captured Cole and his followers, though they have escaped to the magical wood. In the wood, Simon discovers an old lamp with magical powers; when he rubs it a genie appears who will grant him three wishes. Bluebeard kidnaps Cinderella and allies himself to King Otto; Otto's son Prince Charming joins King Cole's forces in the forest. They must break into the walled city to save Cinderella, so they build a Trojan Horse which Otto mistakes for a peace offering. As Cole's troops storm the city, Simon awakes again in Ferryman Street where he foils the jewelry heist and has Bert arrested. Tony can take Ella to the ball, and all ends happily ever after.

It's a chaotic jumble of fairy tales, with recognizable characters and fantastical events. Simon is the happy-go-lucky jack-the-lad, the comic character-type of the British pantomime (known as Buttons in *Cinderella*, and Wishee Washee in *Aladdin*). Even with some hackneyed jokes, and despite its "pretty stupid"[75] book, critics found Wynn's comedy infectious, and Wynn stole the highest praise in every review. Against this, nothing could compare, though the dancing was favorably reviewed and the music, though "nothing to boast of," was considered "at least passable."[76] But the many set pieces delighted audiences: an opening scene in which Wynn apprehends a balloon-seller and gets carried up to the rafters by the balloons; a much-lauded hunting scene with real horses riding across the stage; a separate hunting ballet staged by Seymour Felix with a corps of sixty dancers and celebrated soloist Harriet Hoctor; a giant bullfrog played by vaudeville contortionist William J. Ferry; a giant head that appeared in the woods to consume an entire picnic in one gulp; a "piano-velocipede"[77] which Wynn rode to accompany Ruth Etting singing "Ten Cents a Dance"; a Trojan horse bringing the troops of King Otto's army into the city; and a finale that attempted—if not entirely successfully—a magical dove reveal.

The score veered, perhaps appropriately, from typical late-1920s jazz in the real-world scenes to operetta choruses and ensembles in Gayleria. The *Vagabond King* pastiche of the Hunting sequence recalls similar scenes in *Chee-Chee* and the *Garrick Gaieties*, and while "its songs are not the best that Richard Rodgers and Lorenz Hart have ever done,"[78] critics noted several:

"Send for Me" was recognized as "I Must Love You" from *Chee-Chee*, and most approved the decision to "rescue" it: "[it] is given you over and over again until you go home with it curling like silvery cigarette smoke through your memory,"[79] wrote Gilbert Gabriel. Meanwhile, "I Can Do Wonders with You" was another interpolation from the tryouts of *Me for You*. "After hearing this latter number one can scarcely blame Mr. Rodgers and Mr. Hart for wanting to retrieve it."[80] If these were the highlights, though, gleaned from other shows, it hardly speaks highly of the score itself, "Rodgers and Hart in pleasant, but not inspiring form,"[81] as Burns Mantle wrote. The only other song that "went" was the oddly placed "Ten Cents a Dance." According to Nolan, it was a late addition following familiar criticism—this time from Ziegfeld—that the show had no hits. Again Rodgers and Hart scurried away, and this time returned with what is now a recognized classic. It was "rushed into rehearsal just as soon as the ink was dry,"[82] but on its original outing, singer Lee Morse came on stage drunk and was promptly sacked. As luck would have it the ideal performer emerged. Ruth Etting, herself a hit in Ziegfeld's *Whoopee*, took over at a day's notice, and with the gimmick of Ed Wynn wheeling her in and accompanying her on his piano-velocipede, the song "went" indeed, even if its story of a jaded taxi-dancer had nothing to do with the plot.

That sort of mismatch didn't bother Ziegfeld. Money talked, and he attracted that by stamping his own idiosyncratic mark: "I never have been able to tell just what it is he does to a show to make it, however simple or sappy it may be in book, always a kind of adventure in playgoing,"[83] wrote one mystified reviewer, expressing the admiration many people seem to have had. His shows were always spectacle first, but in *Simple Simon* he seems to have trumped them all. Characteristically, Ziegfeld showed his temperament, not least in berating Rodgers and Hart for their mediocre material, and unceremoniously (though understandably) firing Morse without a second thought. This time he also mounted a battle with the press. Ziegfeld recognized that disposable income was stretched—he, after all, had been hit badly by the Crash. He negotiated with ticket agencies to secure a capped brokers' fee of 75 cents per ticket, a deal that required him to cap his own prices at $5. The press then accused the producer of trying to mask what was just a cheap show. In response, Flo came out fighting: "Salary list, $18,655; total expenses, $33,000 weekly; production, $210,000. Be good."[84] Unfortunately, that instruction was not one he would follow himself. For the second time, Rodgers and Hart's experiences with the impresario would leave a sour taste when he failed to pay them. They would never work with this producer again.

In jobbing for Ziegfeld and in scoring for a star vehicle, Rodgers and Hart's writing really did play second fiddle. Despite their many meditations on technique and the development of the form, there is little evidence in *Simple Simon* of their craft at its best. Three shows in a row now had seen the team treading water, and the one thing they had in common was the absence of Herb Fields. With his libretti, they seemed to flourish; and even if there were setbacks, as there had been with *Chee-Chee*, the material seemed collaborative, guided by one directive and written in a single voice—the specter of Herbert Richard Lorenz. As the new decade began, the whisper began to be heard: "We would like to see these three working together again."[85] By mid-summer, it was the talk of the town: the *Evening Post* published a retrospective;[86] the *World* reported a new show;[87] but it was the writers themselves who fed the marketing machine. On August 20 the *New York Telegram* reported from the dockside as Larry boarded the S.S. *Europa* en route to London for the opening of *Ever Green*. Here, flanked by his collaborators, he gushed enthusiastically about new horizons. And central to these was the reconciliation of the old family.

AND SO TO HOLLYWOOD

A new chapter began, closing the page on the 1920s and opening to a world shaken by economic collapse, family losses, and new beginnings. For Dick and Larry there were opportunities, but it was, in a sense, time for the lonely gypsies to go back to the open road. "For the first time in many years my telephone was not jangling with offers from producers to write new shows,"[88] Rodgers recalled. "Before I was married I'd had one show after another on Broadway; now that I had a wife at home there didn't seem to be any work for me nearer than three thousand miles in either direction."[89] This was only half in jest: the options were either England in one direction or Hollywood in the other.

Hollywood in 1930 was not quite the shantytown the first film crews had established twenty years previously; nor was it quite an enclave of "illiterate immigrants," "self-made merchants and nickelodeon owners...who had created a new world of entertainment."[90] By now, studios were up and running, a national distribution network had been formed, and an established industry was in place. Nevertheless, it was remote—a five-day train journey through the sweltering Midwest heat. This was not Broadway, and it was not New York.

Neither was the film industry yet the center of glamour and cultural value it became. Sure, its products were popular, and its meteoric expansion of movie houses across the country showed vitality. But Hollywood was a far cry from the cultural refinement of the concert hall and a long way from the modest respectability of Broadway. "'We had all sorts of ominous warnings [about Hollywood],'" Rodgers told one reporter. "'We were good and scared.'"[91] Still, there was work, and that was enticement enough for many creative individuals who had been hit by economic collapse.

Of course, the allure of film had not registered at all with the musical theater crowd since until 1927 it had been a resolutely silent art. But with *The Jazz Singer* (1927), things changed, and Hollywood moguls began bringing composers and lyricists into town. Rights were bought, contracts issued, and film versions thrown into production with only an eye for the bottom line. The year 1930 saw *Spring Is Here* (First National), *Present Arms* (RKO, as *Leathernecking*) and *Heads Up!* (Paramount) made into films; and Rodgers and Hart were commissioned to provide material for other movies such as *Follow Thru* (Paramount), overseen by its original Broadway scriptwriters Frank Mandel and Lawrence Schwab. Before long they had signed a three-picture deal with Warner Bros.: the studio promised security, huge offices on the Burbank lot, a secretary for their personal affairs, and a writing partner with whose work they were already familiar: Herb Fields. His script for *The Hot Heiress* would be their first original Hollywood venture.

The story was an age-old yarn with an up-to-the-minute twist: Hap Harrigan is a Sky Boy, one of the riveters on a Manhattan high-rise. When a hot rivet is thrown through an open window, Hap falls in love with the rich heiress Juliette Hunter who owns the apartment. Introduced to the affluent trappings of society, Harrigan feels out of place and returns to his roots. But she follows him, rents an apartment by his new construction site, and clambers out onto the scaffolding to bring him a romantic lunch. It's *Cinderella* in reverse, set in a contemporary milieu.

Larry and Herb trekked out to Los Angeles as the advance party, with Dick arriving on June 23. The following day *The Hot Heiress* started production, with leading couple Ben Lyon and Ona Munson shooting dialogue scenes while the writers worked on the six commissioned songs. Very soon, six became five, and by the time the film was released, just three songs remained: "Nobody Loves a Riveter," "Like Ordinary People Do," and "You're the Cats." Still, this was material of which Rodgers and Hart seemed proud. Hart at least was effusive about his new conception of songwriting for the movies:

> The point is not that they be logically "planted." The very planting of a number is false.... Most important in songs for the screen is their *relevance*. We are not making them numerous. They are seldom reprised. And they are all definitely connected with the story—pertinent to the actors and the action. We ease into them in the dialogue so that before you know

it, you realize that the characters are speaking lyrics and their gradual entry into the song appears very logical.[92]

This, in the December 1930 edition of *Cinema*, emphasizes their commitment to developing song craft. And interviewer Margaret Reid is clearly convinced by that ambition: "in these six expert hands the cinema musical comedy as an independent medium will be evolved."[93]

Certainly the placement of the opening song, "Nobody Loves a Riveter," seems commensurate with this integration. After an opening montage of the skyscraper under construction, the city streets way below, and Sky Boys clambering over the skeletal structure, we encounter Hap Harrigan and his colleague Bill Dugan. Bill throws the rivets to be caught by Hap, and the action sets up a rhythmic exchange:

BILL: Get me?
HAP: Gotcha!
BILL: Get me?
HAP: Gotcha!

Then the characters speak a rhythmical *Sprechgesang* over the instrumentation, before the scene cuts to local residents disturbed by the noise of construction. Their dialogue is almost obscured by the cacophony of construction noise and busy orchestration. Finally, Hap begins the song proper, a simple AABA refrain with a repetitive motif reflecting the monotony of work.

But in announcing his intentions, Hart had raised the bar. Reviewers were invited to scoff, and they did: "this may not be musical comedy convention— but it is certainly not screen realism,"[94] whined the *Sun*. Nor was it groundbreaking.[95] The film received lukewarm notices in a season flooded with movie musicals. However innovative their technique, the developments were perhaps too subtle to be noticed.

Still, they were more than enthusiastic. "'It is a step in the right direction,'" Hart told one reporter.[96] And Rodgers in his letters to Dorothy gushes about the film: "The pitcher looks very good...and people are very enthusiastic about the ditties";[97] "The talk around the studio is that we have a great picture."[98] He reflects on the performances of the leading couple, remarking that "Ben Lyon and Ona Munson sing the songs very well indeed"[99]—a claim supported by the press,[100] who lamented the lack of songs in the film.[101]

More than this, though, working in the movies was exciting, exhilarating, and stimulating: "Working conditions are so much better than I ever dared hope for," he told Dorothy,[102] "and people are increasingly nice to us."[103] They were allocated an enormous office and given a surprising degree of creative control: "'Our supervisor never interferes and we have almost *carte blanche,'*" they reported to the press. "'They gave us the cast we wanted, they've put every facility at our disposal, [and] given us intelligent cooperation.'" Interviewer Margaret Reid continues: "Fields supervised every detail of production, from directing the dialogue to selecting the costumes, and Rodgers and Hart were given completely free rein on the arrangement of the musical numbers."[104] "'Never have we come so close to having everything precisely as we wanted it,'" Rodgers said.[105] And to Dorothy, he admitted "I can't get over the surprise of liking the racket"; "I know you'll love it."[106] Larry Hart already did, if Marmorstein's account is anything to go by: "'I want to stay forever!'"[107] Indeed, "so pleased were they with Hollywood and life as it is lived there," the *New York World* later wrote, "that they are spreading unsolicited indorsements [*sic*] of the picture capital."[108]

Despite this clear enthusiasm, a mythology has arisen around their Hollywood experiences, giving an interesting example of how events can be differently represented over time. Although Rodgers's and Hart's contemporary reports show nothing but excitement and enthusiasm about the experience, others disagree: "It was an unpleasant experience," comment Marx and Clayton with little evidence,[109] while Marmorstein suggests that Rodgers found it a bore and that it left them with a "jaundiced view of picture-making."[110] Nolan's account makes the claim that "not only could their leading man not sing worth a damn, [but] Ona Munson's range was as limited as her voice was insipid."[111] What are we to make of these remarks? The team returned to New York on August 11 and crossed the Atlantic to honor their commitment to *Ever Green*. But six months later, they were headed back out West to start production on their second Warner picture, *Love of Michael*. That was to be a reunion with the same stars, Ben Lyon and Ona Munson, though in the end, and to the writing team's disappointment, the project was shelved.

America's Sweetheart (1931)

Their film experiences gave Rodgers, Hart, and Fields plenty of material to work with, and they turned their creative energies to a ribbing of Hollywood. Using the silent era's hackneyed title-card phrase *Came the Dawn* as its title, and featuring a leading character called Dawn Monroe, the team returned to the theater with a new show lampooning the talkies.

Michael and Gerry are a young couple who hitch-hike to Tinseltown. Pretty soon Gerry is spotted, and she quickly rises to become a star. But with success, she snubs Michael and leaves him for her glamorous life. Then comes the dawn of the talking picture, when star quality requires a voice as well as looks. With her lisp, Gerry's charm fades, while the tables turn and Michael rockets to success. Feted by the crowd at the premiere of his latest movie, he spots her, whisks her up onto the stage with him, and pledges his undying love.

This wasn't the first time they had lampooned Hollywood and its ways. Cicely Courtneidge's character in *Lido Lady* was an absolute fool, suffering countless slapstick indignities in scenes staging typical silent set pieces. In "Camera Shoot," Hart's lyrics give the industry characteristically sardonic treatment: "I know a man who writes the stories for the picture / And when he learns to spell he'll write the captions too."[112] That song was cut, though, like many of the songs from *Lido Lady*, it reappeared in *She's My Baby* (1928). The following year it was the talkies he ribbed, in an unused song "They Sing! They Dance! They Speak!" from *Me for You*. These lyrics offered a dress rehearsal for *America's Sweetheart*: "Now Clara Bow can squeak!" they josh; while Romeo betrays his working-class Brooklyn origins in a vocabulary of "'dem's' and 'dose's.'"[113] Not surprisingly, it found its way into the score of *America's Sweetheart* as the Act Two opening number, introducing the world of sound.[114]

The script to *America's Sweetheart*—a nickname of silent star Mary Pickford whose success was fading with the advent of talkies—offered ample opportunity to pursue this humor. The opening scene in the studio cafeteria throws together an anomalous collection of characters from various movies: coolies, wise men, a deep-sea diver, some Keystone Kops, Bill Sykes from *Oliver Twist* (who speaks in a high-pitched voice), and a Court lady from a period drama (who speaks in a Hard Whiskey voice). Then a scene in a boardroom has executives discussing *Othello*: first they change the storyline to give it a happy ending; then they decide the plot will work better with audiences if they make Othello white; finally, they decide to change the title to *Hot Lips*. This scene had reviewers in stitches with its irreverent yet intellectual humor. The final scene staged a premiere at the famous Grauman's Chinese Theater, where the cast imitated a host of stars: Clara Bow, Claudette Colbert, Douglas Fairbanks, and Nancy Carroll (who was played by her own sister Terry).

But their timing was once again out of sync. Playwrights George S. Kaufman and Moss Hart had beaten them to it with a very successful stage play, *Once in a Lifetime* (1930). As a result, critics saw *America's Sweetheart* as a pale imitation. "It is one of these Hollywood dingleberries recently become the vogue," wrote the *Washington Daily News*;[115] "sounds a good deal like a set of discarded cues from 'Once in a Lifetime' set to music."[116]

The show opened for tryouts in Pittsburgh and moved to Washington, DC, and Newark before arriving in New York. Strangely, the reviewers from out of town barely mentioned the involvement of Rodgers, Hart, and Fields. Instead they referred to *America's Sweetheart* as "Schwab and Mandel's new musicomedy,"[117] the latest in a run of hits including *Desert Song* (1926), *Good News* (1927), *New Moon* (1928) and *Follow Thru* (1929). Some rated the new show as Schwab and Mandel's best yet;[118] in reality it was not in the same league.[119]

Typical reviews were moderate: this was "a good, workmanlike job of its kind, without startling brilliance";[120] "everything one might wish for in musical comedy, with the possible exception of breath-taking inspiration."[121] But reviewers used their writing to exercise the cutthroat wit that was de rigueur in the society press: Brooks Atkinson wrote of the "many excellent items" in the show, which "have a dispiriting habit of tumbling out of the story."[122] Dorothy Parker called Rodgers and Hart "extraordinarily over-rated young men," and referred to Hart's rhyme schemes as "less internal than colonic."[123] Scathing though these one-liners may have been, they are worth revisiting for the brilliance of their acerbic putdowns. "The wit is clumsy, much of the humor is foul, and the book goes to a great deal of trouble to make both ends meet,"[124] concluded Atkinson. As much as Fields, Rodgers, and Hart, many of these reviewers were demonstrating panache in their craft; stage reviews of the period that showed a community of witty, literate, and erudite intellectuals.

Once again, reviewers didn't appreciate vulgarity, so while "The chief strength of the show [lay] in Richard Rodgers's exceedingly attractive music," as the *London Stage* put it, "the chief weakness [lay] in Herbert Fields's far from distinguished and all-too-often smutty book."[125] "More than occasionally it rambles verbally in and out of the smoker,"[126] wrote another critic, not the only observer to recall the masculine environment of the Transcontinental smoking cars; Jennings was resolute: "The smut, I suppose, must be borne."[127]

On the other hand, one of the hits ("The real joy of the evening") was a vocal trio called the Forman Sisters, "one of those doleful feminine trios who sing nasal laments in harmony so close that it melts into agony."[128] Their country singing style ("wierdly harmonious"[129] "hillbilly crooning"[130]) was clearly striking, with "queer barbed-wire harmonies that were quite entrancing and [that] justly brought down the house."[131] Others were less generous, and those acerbic one-liners came back out: "Even adenoids have their charm," sneered the *Evening World*.[132]

Rodgers's draft music sketches point to a style influenced by his encounter with Hollywood. Unusually—with the exception of the opening number—all of these sketches are written in the same key, D major, giving the sense that he is producing a tonally coherent body of songs.[133] While D major itself was a common enough key (one of his preferred keys) for jotting thoughts down, his sketches before this point demonstrate no real tonal consistency for songs within a single show. Those for *Heads Up!*, for example, use different keys apparently indiscriminately for each individual song. Although *Dearest Enemy*,

Chee-Chee, and to some extent *Ever Green* showed serious attempts to conceive their musical material as a score, this marks the most sustained score-based approach in Rodgers's writing to this point, even if the glue binding the score together seems rather simplistic. Nevertheless, Rodgers strengthens its consistency with repeated patterns and motifs, most notably a mixolydian nuance that captures the spirit of Tinseltown.

The mixolydian mode was a common feature of Ukrainian music, and one that therefore figures prominently in the work of Dimitri Tiomkin. Indeed, it came to epitomize his music for Westerns some years later (*Duel in the Sun*, 1946; *High Noon*, 1952); even by 1930, thanks to his influence, we can see this as idiomatic of Hollywood—musically suggestive of films. Through Rodgers's friendship with the Ukrainian, he may have absorbed some compositional flavors.

In this mode, the seventh of the scale is flattened, producing a tonality that is unfamiliar to our diatonically accustomed ears. Harmonically, this allows the composer to pitch in this case a C-major chord (the seventh) against a D-major chord (the tonic), which both "My Sweet" and "Movies" do, establishing solid diatonic writing in the first few measures before inviting in this foreign mode (see Figure 9.1). Another untitled sketch in D major introduces a similar modality; the sketch for "Innocent Chorus Girls" also introduces a C natural in an otherwise fluid D major scale beginning on the lower C#; meanwhile, the untitled sketch for "A Lady Must Live," also in D, features a flattened seventh in the melody (though this is more of a blues note than a modality). At the very least, conspicuous gestures toward this mixolydian coloring make it a real feature of the score.

"My Sweet"

"Movies"

Untitled sketch

Figure 9.1: Rodgers's use of the mixolydian mode in America's Sweetheart.
Reprinted by Permission of Hal Leonard Corporation

But compositional integrity or not, *America's Sweetheart* did not make great waves, though it sustained a modest run (135 performances) and garnered generally positive reviews. The depression was beginning to bite, and whereas previously a popular show could sustain a lengthy run, the Broadway climate in 1931 simply did not support such longevity.

Perhaps surprisingly, the same was true in Hollywood, though reportedly for different reasons. By 1931, audiences had grown tired of the deluge of movie musicals churned out since the advent of talkies. Studios had been quick to jump on the bandwagon two years previously; now they excised songs from films under production and jettisoned house composers to produce non-musical material. In this light, reviewers saw *America's Sweetheart* not as a fond pastiche of Hollywood but as an attack: "If the screen serves no other purpose," sniffed Brooks Atkinson (he referred to it as "the art of squeaks and incorporated hokum"), "it is a good subject for ridicule on the stage."[134] The *Sun* was more forthright: "When even the musicals turn against it..., it becomes evident that nobody loves the movies any more."[135]

With so many Broadway personalities transferring stage techniques to film, one assumption must have been that talkies simply offered a parallel art in which to copycat the stage. The very first encounters of music with film, as most commentators observe, were insistently wedded to the exclusive use of diegetic music: song heard when the jazz singer sings, as it were. However, Rodgers and Hart's use of rhythmic dialogue and *Sprechgesang* in *The Hot Heiress* seems to counter that insistence, suggesting instead that film could offer a new medium for incorporating music into the telling of a story. "Nobody Loves a Riveter" magnifies the diegetic soundscape of what is viewed by the camera; the underscoring emphasizes the rhythms of construction noise and formalizes the sounds of the city into musical patterns. Hap and Bill's rhythmic dialogue stems from the contours of their speech to guide the listener into the artificiality of song. These techniques would be developed in Rodgers and Hart's next few films—notably in *Love Me Tonight* (1932)[136] and *Hallelujah, I'm a Bum* (1933), in which, as Stanley Green observes,[137] diegetically rhythmic sound (a ticking watch) is emphasized in rhythmic speech leading into full-blown song.[138] In this pursuit, the already existing aesthetic of film music underscoring was significant, adopted from melodrama and confirmed by composer Erno Rapée in his definitive reference book, *Motion Picture Moods for Pianists and Organists* (1924). As silence moved to sound, though, Hollywood developed other ways of using music. Both American jazz (Alfred Newman) and European classical music (Dimitri Tiomkin) were exploited, though the innovations had less to do with style than with the way music interacted with the medium. In the process of developing this new sound, Hollywood began to create a musical aesthetic, and in finding that voice, film music would become distinct from the Broadway sound on which the transition to talkies had so relied.

With that influence came a different sound for both screen and stage, guided by some of the "'godfathers' of the film-music art"[139] with whom Rodgers and Hart had intimate links: Alfred Newman had been musical director for both *Spring Is Here* and *Heads Up!* in 1929;[140] Dimitri Tiomkin had been slated to tour "Little Africa" in 1930; Erno Rapée served as musical director on *The Hot Heiress* that same year. Each of these connections would influence the ongoing development of the composite craft, and Rodgers and Hart, ever receptive to the new, absorbed it all.

Certainly, Rodgers had developed stylistically by the time he emerged from his Hollywood sojourn in the mid-1930s, as Felix Cox notes;[141] and he himself referred to his writing having taken "a faltering step in a basically right direction."[142] This new direction reinforced the drive toward integration, but in an idiom that incorporated the sounds of cinema as much as the sounds of jazz. By the 1930s that new sound world had captured exactly what Rodgers and Hart had wanted: a sound of America, and the twentieth century.

EPILOGUE

• • •

THE END OF AN ERA

The year 1931 marks a significant point in the collaboration of Rodgers and Hart, and marks a point in this story to pause. With *America's Sweetheart*, it brought to an end the first productive period of their Broadway career—they would not work in theater again until 1935; and with *The Hot Heiress*, it began a short but intensive foray into musical film. It seems likely that this change in direction offered a chance to reflect, emerging four years later with a new-found strength. While they take a break on their working holiday in Holly-wood, I will pause to reflect on the boys from Manhattan.

Throughout this book I have been considering three main themes: how Rodgers and Hart worked together to develop the way in which music and words unite; how a part of that creativity was guided by the exigencies of the industry; and how their own sense of self both informed and grew from their work. The material they developed over this period speaks volumes, espe-cially when framed by an ever-present critical voice; the constant companion-ship of the press gives texture to the understanding of their work, and at times, Rodgers and Hart's own contributions to that reflective voice have re-vealed their aspirations, defended their position, and constructed their my-thology in ways that both reveal and disguise.

In terms of developing their craft, we can see clear trends. There's the push toward integration, using techniques that after twelve years were still unsure but growing; there's a confidence in jazz, which they underpin with classical technique; and there's a real sense of dramaturgical insight, understanding the different ele-ments of performance like design, atmosphere, lighting, and especially dance, and understanding the dynamics of performance like mood, reception, entertainment, and pathos. All of these were helped by the overlooked third figure in the Rodgers and Hart team: Herbert Fields, whose role was fundamental and inspirational.

As they developed, they were guided by the Broadway machine, in ways that at times constrained but just as often let them fly. Growing to understand the demands of the business enabled them to work but also instructed them in how their craft was part of a landscape. The tastes of the public, outbursts of the critics, and whims of producers are not sent to shackle creativity but to nourish it, molding the terrain in which those with ideas can chance to play. While some of the industry demands and production decisions may have seemed stifling, many breakthroughs came from reading that landscape and collaborating within it.

Finally, the boys had grown up. Gone was the naivety of youth and the reckless pursuit of desires, but in their place was a surety of themselves and an understanding of who they were. We see this in particular in how they learned to present themselves—something that would continue and which, for Rodgers at least, would offer the chance to re-present a vision of himself that fashioned him as Broadway grand-père. In writing his own history, he literally rewrote his life, especially through the powerful voice of his memoirs. The story of this book seeks to peer through that re-presentation to understand the boy from which it emerged. Some of the most compelling insights we have encountered on our journey have been those moments that strip away his later account to give an intimate view: of Dick, Larry, and Herb before they became consolidated as Rodgers and Hart (Figure 10.1).

Figure 10.1: Fields, Rodgers, and Hart, ca. 1927.

NOTES

INTRODUCTION

Epigraph: Dorothy Hart and Robert Kimball, eds., *The Complete Lyrics of Lorenz Hart* (New York: Harper and Row, 1976), 33.

1. Richard Rodgers, *Musical Stages: An Autobiography* (New York: Da Capo Press, 2002), 36.

2. Arnold Aronson, *Architect of Dreams: The Theatrical Vision of Joseph Urban*. Online catalogue for "Joseph Urban and the Great American Revue" exhibition, Columbia University Library, July 2–August 27, 2012. http://www.columbia.edu/cu/lweb/eresources/archives/rbml/urban/architectOfDreams/index.html. Accessed August 27, 2012.

3. Urban would design exactly this sort of cityscape scene for De Sylva, Brown, and Henderson's *Flying High* (1930); his designs for the *Ziegfeld Follies of 1917* also show extremely detailed images of cityscapes.

4. Frederick Nolan, *Lorenz Hart: A Poet on Broadway* (New York: Oxford University Press, 1994), 22.

5. Nolan, *Lorenz Hart*, 22.

6. Samuel Marx and Jan Clayton, *Rodgers and Hart: Bewitched, Bothered and Bedevilled* (London: W. H. Allen, 1977), 9.

7. Meryle Secrest, *Somewhere for Me: A Biography of Richard Rodgers* (New York: Alfred A. Knopf, 2001), 3.

8. Dorothy Rodgers, quoted in Secrest, *Somewhere for Me*, 12.

9. Morris B. Holbrook, *Music, Movies, Meanings and Markets: Cinemajazzamatazz* (London: Routledge, 2012), 103.

10. Hammerstein in Geoffrey Block, *The Richard Rodgers Reader* (New York: Oxford University Press, 2002), 79.

11. Marx and Clayton, *Bewitched*, 55.

12. Meryle Secrest, *Shoot the Widow: Adventures of a Biographer in Search of Her Subject* (New York: Alfred A. Knopf, 2007), n.p.

13. Quoted in Robert Russell Bennett, *The Broadway Sound*, ed. George Ferencz (Rochester, NY: University of Rochester Press, 1999), 251.

14. Lahr in Rodgers, *Musical Stages*, 333.

15. Jesse Green, "A Complicated Gift," *New York Times*, July 6, 2003.

16. Bennett, *The Broadway Sound*, 252.

17. Rodgers, *Musical Stages*, 21.

18. Dorothy Hart, ed., *Thou Swell, Thou Witty: The Complete Lyrics of Lorenz Hart* (New York: Harper and Row, 1976), 16.

19. Nolan, *Lorenz Hart*, 12.

20. Rodgers, *Musical Stages*, 8.

21. Kenneth Leish, "Interview with Mr. Richard Rodgers: December 19, 1967," transcript of Oral History Project interviews with Rodgers, 1967–8 in NYPL for the performing arts, RRP, TMS-1987-006, Series III, Box 9, 40–84.

22. Armond Fields and L. Marc Fields, *From the Bowery to Broadway: Lew Fields and the Roots of American Popular Theatre* (New York: Oxford University Press, 1993), 337.

23. *Very Good Eddie* had a libretto and lyrics by Schuyler Greene and Philip Bartholomae. Kern, Bolton, and Wodehouse came together for *Have a Heart* (1917). Although neither of these was produced by Comstock and Marbury or staged at the Princess Theatre, the formula took, and the Comstock/Marbury third outing, *Oh, Boy!* (1917) sealed the legacy, with *Leave It to Jane* (1917), *Miss 1917* (1917), and *Oh, Lady! Lady!* (1918) following and works by other writing teams adopting the pattern in *Oh! My Dear* (Guy Bolton, P. G. Wodehouse, Louis A. Hirsch, 1918) and *Kissing Time* (George V. Hobart and Ivan Caryll, 1920).

24. Leish, "Interview," December 19, 1967, 52.

25. Nolan, *Lorenz Hart*, 18. "Gems from *Nobody Home*" by the Victor Light Opera Company was released as Matrix C-16055 in May 1915; "Gems from *Very Good Eddie*" was released as Matrix C-17126 in February 1916; a second selection from *Very Good Eddie* on Matrix B-19604 was released the following year.

26. Fields and Fields, *From the Bowery*, 338.

27. Joseph Kaye, *Victor Herbert: The Biography of America's Greatest Composer of Romantic Music* (New York: Crown, 1931), 237.

28. Kaye, *Victor Herbert*, 235.

29. "The cause of an American national literature in independence of English literature, and the cause of American contemporary ideas as against the ideas of the last generation": Edmund Wilson, cited in Michael Kammen, *The Lively Arts: Gilbert Seldes and the Transformation of Cultural Criticism in the United States* (New York: Oxford University Press, 1996), 101.

30. Kaye, *Victor Herbert*, 238–39.

31. Kaye, *Victor Herbert*, 7.

32. Edward Marshall, "We Have No Distinctive American Music—Damrosch," *New York Times*, June 18, 1911, SM8.

33. Marshall, "We Have No Distinctive American Music," SM8. Sadly, these high pretensions remain culturally elite pretensions and, with a European set of values that never strays far from being overt and obvious, Damrosch rather undermines his own argument with a total rejection of popular culture, cited in the same article: "A household which hears nothing but songs from our cheap American musical comedies is likely to develop musical predilections of the very lowest. Such songs may easily kill really good musical taste in children, and that is a cruel thing."

34. Charles Hamm, *Music in the New World* (New York: W. W. Norton, 1983), 410–59.

35. Raymond Knapp, *The American Musical and the Formation of National Identity* (Princeton, NJ: Princeton University Press, 2005), 103.

36. J. Ellen Gainor, "Introduction," in *Performing America: Cultural Nationalism in American Theater*, ed. Jeffrey D. Mason and J. Ellen Gainor (Ann Arbor: University of Michigan Press, 1999), 9.

37. Gainor, "Introduction," 3.

38. Leish, "Interview," December 19, 1967, 52.

39. Block, *Reader*, 296.

40. Alec Wilder, *American Popular Song: The Great Innovators 1900–1950* (New York: Oxford University Press, 1972), 31.

41. Stephen Banfield, *Jerome Kern* (New Haven, CT: Yale University Press, 2006), 17.

42. Gerald Bordman, *Jerome Kern: His Life and Music* (New York: Oxford University Press, 1980), 90.

43. Gerald Bordman, *American Musical Comedy: From Adonis to Dreamgirls* (New York: Oxford University Press, 1982), 123.

44. David Savran, *Highbrow/Lowdown: Theater, Jazz, and the Making of the New Middle Class* (Ann Arbor: University of Michigan Press, 2009), 28–29.

45. Knapp, *National Identity*, 83.

46. Knapp, *National Identity*, 74. In fact, Richard Rodgers is one of the few commentators to reflect on the unqualified remark that the musical is a "distinctly American art form": "That is true up to a point," he wrote in a 1964 article for the *New York Times*, but he goes on to acknowledge the heavy European influence on the form. He concludes by equating the Americanization of musical theater with the drive toward integration, identifying "a genuine attempt to make the music and lyrics flow smoothly as part of the stories" as the defining "American" quality in the shows: "They were far from being realistic, but they made sense both musically and dramatically" (Block, *Reader*, 296). However useful this commentary is, it is nevertheless a rather self-serving case of spin that strengthens the integration myth and enables his work—particularly *Oklahoma!*—to be seen as the definitive example of the form.

47. Raymond Knapp and Mitchell Morris, "Tin Pan Alley Songs on Stage and Screen before World War II," in *The Oxford Handbook to the American Musical*, ed. Raymond Knapp, Mitchell Morris, and Stacy Wolf (New York: Oxford University Press, 2011), 88.

48. Knapp and Morris, "Tin Pan Alley Songs," 88.

49. Graham Wood, "The Development of Song Forms in the Broadway and Hollywood Musicals of Richard Rodgers, 1919–1943" (PhD diss., University of Minnesota, 2000).

50. Rodgers, *Musical Stages*, 20.

51. Savran, *Highbrow*, 47.

52. Van Wyck Brooks, *America's Coming of Age* (New York: B. W. Huebsch, 1915), 9.

53. Brooks, *America's Coming of Age*, 7–8.

54. Cited in Carol Oja, *Making Music Modern: New York in the 1920s* (New York: Oxford University Press, 2000), 304.

55. Oja, *Making Music Modern*.

56. Oja, *Making Music Modern*, 301.

57. Jeffrey Magee, *Irving Berlin's American Musical Theater* (New York: Oxford University Press, 2012), 76.

58. Magee, *Irving Berlin's American Musical Theater*, 26.

59. Magee, *Irving Berlin's American Musical Theater*, 16.

60. Alexander Woollcott, *The Story of Irving Berlin* (New York: G. P. Putnam, 1925), 215.

61. Robert Wyatt and John A. Johnson, eds., *The George Gershwin Reader* (New York: Oxford University Press, 2004), 116.

62. Savran, *Highbrow*, 71.

63. Savran, *Highbrow*, 22–35.

64. Gilbert Seldes, "Jazz and Ballad," *New Republic* 43 (August 5, 1925): 293. Seldes was one of the most significant contributors to the highbrow/lowbrow debate with his publication in 1924 of *The Seven Lively Arts*. Here he offered the most sustained consideration yet of popular culture, giving it the attention usually reserved for highbrow art and thereby elevating it in cultural status. Seldes's case studies were varied: from slapstick to circus, comic strips to revue. He later explained his thinking: "the circumstance that our popular arts are home-grown, without the prestige of Europe and of the past, had thrown upon them a shadow of vulgarity, as if they were the products of ignorance and intellectual bad manners" (Gilbert Seldes, *The Seven Lively Arts* [New York: Sagamore Press, 1957], 81). Above all, in his analysis of Irving Berlin, he championed jazz, ragtime, and popular song as "our characteristic expression"; "the expected, and wonderful arrival of America at a point of creative intensity" (Seldes, *The Seven Lively Arts*, 83–84). Subsequently he would confirm this view, calling jazz "the musical counterpart to some of our physical and perhaps some of our mental, or spiritual rhythms" (Seldes, *Jazz and Ballad*, 293).

65. Savran, *Highbrow*, 37.

66. Knockabout double acts involved a pair of mismatched characters who would trade physical and verbal banter with varying degrees of brutality. In the case of Weber and Fields (respectively, Mike and Meyer), the towering Meyer would often try to swindle the diminutive but far more astute Mike, a verbal battle that usually led to blows being exchanged. In the manner of the time, much of Mike and Meyer's language was also botched to comic effect, signifying their immigrant status and their handling of the idiosyncrasies of English. These acts were known as "Dutch" acts, the "Dutch" deriving from "Deutsch": German.

67. Fields and Fields, *From the Bowery*, 203.

68. Fields and Fields, *From the Bowery*, 231.

69. Fields and Fields, *From the Bowery*, 207.

70. Fields and Fields, *From the Bowery*, 177.

71. Rodgers, *Musical Stages*, 91.

72. Fields and Fields, *From the Bowery*, 164.

73. Fields and Fields, *From the Bowery*, 214.

74. Fields and Fields, *From the Bowery*, 242, 263.

75. Baldwin Sloane also provided the music for *Tillie's Nightmare* (1910), which was to be reworked in 1926 by Rodgers, Hart, and Herbert Fields to become *Peggy-Ann*.

76. Fields and Fields, *From the Bowery*, 225.

77. Rodgers, *Musical Stages*, 26.

78. Hart and Kimball, *Complete Lyrics*, 33.

79. Rodgers, *Musical Stages*, 51.

CHAPTER 1

1. Leavitt in Hart, *Thou Swell*, 30. It was through his friendship with Mort Rodgers at the Akron Club that Leavitt was first introduced to Dick. Serendipitously, his parents also rented a house next to the summer home of Lew Fields. Through Herb, Leavitt met Hart. Having introduced the two, he proceeded to get Fields into the mix. Yet talent scout though he may have been, Leavitt eschewed a Broadway career for the paint industry.

2. Rodgers in Block, *Reader*, 262.

3. Leavitt in Hart, *Thou Swell*, 30.

4. Rodgers, *Musical Stages*, 27.

5. Rodgers, *Musical Stages*.

6. Rodgers in Block, *Reader*, 262.

7. Richard Rodgers, "A Score of Years and One," *New York Times*, May 5, 1940, 156.

8. Rodgers in Block, *Reader*, 262.

9. *A Lonely Romeo* had opened on June 10 at the Shubert Theatre but moved on July 28 to the Casino, which is where Rodgers places it at the time of the Fields audition; Geoffrey Block pinpoints the meeting in early August: *Richard Rodgers* (New Haven, CT: Yale University Press, 2003), 18.

10. Fields and Fields, *From the Bowery*, 380.

11. Although the account of Rodgers auditioning for Lew Fields in front of the assembled family is verified in several sources, it is also challenged by Herb Fields in the *Evening Graphic*, in an interview that Frederick Nolan cites. According to Herb, "one of his favourite memories" was of himself, Larry, and Dick "serenading Pop Fields with 'Any Old Place with You' nightly outside his dressing room until in disgust, to keep us quiet, he put it in a show" (Nolan, *Lorenz Hart*, 26). The discrepancy between these accounts points to the shaky reliability of personal testimony, which can be at best misremembered and at worst deliberately fabricated. Various differing perspectives in the biographical testimonies relating to Rodgers and Hart suggest that a good deal of rose tinting and spin doctoring has taken place over the years, making a reliable account unlikely.

12. Rodgers, *Musical Stages*, 30.

13. Rodgers and Leavitt remember this detail differently, though Rubin corroborates Rodgers's report (Jason Rubin, "Lew Fields and the Development of the Broadway Musical," PhD diss., New York University, 1991, 344).

14. Again, reports of the precise date on which "Any Old Place with You" was first performed in *A Lonely Romeo* differ. The additional confusion presented by the Actors' Equity strike, then hitting theaters, makes it difficult to ascertain more precise information.

15. Marx and Clayton, *Bewitched*, 26.

16. Rodgers, *Musical Stages*, 9.

17. Rodgers, *Musical Stages*, 17.

18. Beth Levin Siegel, "Richard Rodgers—One of America's Foremost Composers of Musical Comedy," *Detroit Jewish Chronicle*, August 9, 1929. Lack of technique limited his ability, and in fact this lack of technical skill was something Rodgers would come to regret; as his career progressed he became increasingly self-conscious—particularly, as we shall see, in comparison to Gershwin. Eventually he would seek tuition, and as late as 1941, he finally took piano lessons. Rodgers, *Musical Stages*, 202.

19. Marx and Clayton, *Bewitched*, 30.

20. Marx and Clayton, *Bewitched*.

21. Block, *Richard Rodgers*, 8–46.

22. H. W. Gibson, *Camping for Boys* (New York: Association Press, 1911), 7.

23. In Hart, *Thou Swell*, 17.

24. Indeed, summer camps were something of a training ground for Jewish Broadway talent; not only did these camps ferment the collaboration of Rodgers, Hart, and Fields but some years later Leonard Bernstein and Adolph Green would meet at Camp Onata in Pittsfield.

25. Phil Brown, *Catskill Culture: A Mountain Rat's Memories of the Great Jewish Resort Area* (Philadelphia: Temple University Press, 1998), 11.

26. Myrna Katz Frommer and Harvey Frommer, *It Happened in the Catskills: An Oral History in the Words of Busboys, Bellhops, Guests, Proprietors, Comedians, Agents and Others Who Lived it* (Albany: State University of New York Press, 1991), x.

27. Sig Herzig in Hart and Kimball, *Thou Swell*, 17–18.

28. Gary Marmorstein, *A Ship without a Sail* (New York: Simon and Schuster, 2012), 24–27.

29. Rodgers, *Musical Stages*, 19.

30. Block, *Richard Rodgers*, 9.

31. "Amateur Night, July 11th," *Paradoxian* 11, no.1, August 1920, 14.

32. "The Faculty Song," *Paradoxian* 11, no 2, November 1920, 2.

33. "When Taps Have Blown," *Paradoxian* 11, no. 2, November 1920, 27.

34. Untitled article, *Paradoxian* 16, no.1, August 1925, 6.

35. "A Worthy Revival: August 2," *Paradoxian* 16, no. 1, August 1925, 11.

36. "Music and the Camper," *Paradoxian* 11, no. 2, November 1920, 17.

37. Block, *Richard Rodgers*, 13.

38. Rodgers, *Musical Stages*, 24.

39. Rodgers, *Musical Stages*, 35.

40. Hart and Kimball, *Complete Lyrics*, 13.

41. Lyrics reprinted in the *Baton* 1, no. 6, June 1922, 8.

42. Hart and Kimball, *Complete Lyrics*, 22.

43. Hart and Kimball, *Complete Lyrics*, 22.

44. Rodgers, *Musical Stages*, 21.

45. This remarks on the fascination at the time with air travel, and perhaps the previous year's first transatlantic crossing by John Alcock and Arthur Brown. Alcock and Brown piloted their Vickers-Vimy plane from Newfoundland in Canada

to County Galway in Ireland, winning the *Daily Mail*'s prize of £10,000, which was presented by British Secretary of State for Air Winston Churchill.

46. Milton Kroopf and Phillip Leavitt, *Fly with Me*, libretto, the Columbia Varsity Show of 1920, adapted by Michael Numark under the supervision of Andrew B. Harris for the Columbia Varsity Show of 1980, with music and lyrics by Richard Rodgers, Lorenz Hart, Oscar Hammerstein II, LOC ML50.R67 F7, 1982, 27.

47. S. Jay Kaufman, "Round the Town," *Globe*, March 25, 1920.

48. "Columbia Boys Give Show," *Evening World*, March 25, 1920.

49. S. R. W., "Catchy Music Is Strong Point of Varsity Show, Says Reviewer," *Columbia Spectator*, March 26, 1920.

50. Thomas J. Vinciguerra, "Sing a Song of Morningside," in Paul Gelinas, *The Varsity Show: A Celebration* (New York: Columbia, 2004), 28.

51. "Columbia Actors Present a Snappy Play, 'Fly with Me,'" *Sun and Herald*, March 25, 1920.

52. Vinciguerra in Gelinas, *The Varsity Show*, 42.

53. "Fly with Me—a brief history," program note, *Fly with Me* program, the Columbia University Varsity Show 1980, np. CU—VSR Box 16, Folder 17.

54. Hammerstein, Oscar II, "Always Room for One More," *Fly with Me*, lyrics transcribed in *Fly with Me* program, the Columbia University Varsity Show 1920, np. CU—VSR Box 10, Folder 2, np.

55. "Fly with Me—a brief history." Despite this, it is worth noting the *Tribune*'s remark that "A professional flavor was given to the performance by a two weeks' course of study in feminine graces which the students underwent at some of the vaudeville houses" ("College Boys in Girl Roles," *Tribune*, March 25, 1920).

56. The first of these is from "Another Melody in F," the second from "Gone Are the Days." Hart and Kimball, *Complete Lyrics*, 14.

57. Originally used in *You'd Be Surprised*.

58. Hart and Kimball, *Complete Lyrics*, 13.

59. Hart and Kimball, *Complete Lyrics*, 15.

60. Hart and Kimball, *Complete Lyrics*, 16.

61. "Columbia's Play Bright," *Times*, March 25, 1920; "Columbia Actors Present a Snappy Play, 'Fly with Me,'" *Sun and Herald*, March 25, 1920.

62. Although it had been Rodgers's intention to double these two motifs using a divided chorus, one report explains that the chorus could not cope with singing in harmony. "In desparation [*sic*], he asked [Leonard] Manheim [playing the role of Mrs. Houghton] to sing Rubinstein's melody as a solo against the chorus": "Fly with Me—a brief history."

63. Hart and Kimball, *Complete Lyrics*, 15.

64. Hart and Kimball, *Complete Lyrics*, 17.

65. Hammerstein is credited as the lyricist of "Always Room for One More," the Pony Girl number, and "Weaknesses."

66. "Choose 'Fly with Me' as New Varsity Show," *Columbia Spectator*, Columbia College, March 19, 1920.

67. "Rodgers to conduct orchestra himself," *Columbia Spectator*, March 19, 1920. Rodgers actually complained to the *Spectator* about his name being misspelled: "'Why

don't you tell 'em about me?' inquired Richard C. Rodgers, who wrote the beautiful music of *Fly with Me*. 'And why don't *Spec* spell my name with a 'd' in it. You're a _____' (here he used all the 'd's that *Spec* omitted)" (*Columbia Spectator*, March 22, 1920).

68. "Varsity Show Is Up to Date," *Globe*, March 23, 1920.

69. "'Fly with Me,' by Columbia Students, Has Pleasant Echoes of Broadway," *Evening Telegram*, March 25, 1920.

70. "Lew Fields Believes Youth a Greater Asset than Too Much Stage Experience," *New York Tribune*, September 5, 1920.

71. "Don't Love Me like Othello" from *You'd Be Surprised* was rewritten as "You Can't Fool Your Dreams"; "The Princess of the Willow Tree" became "Will You Forgive Me?"; "Dreaming True" from *Fly with Me* turned into "Love Will Call"; "Inspiration" became "All You Need to Be a Star"; and "Peek in Pekin'" was adapted into "Love's Intense in Tents."

72. As a program note details, "The Entire Action of the Play takes place in the Apartment" (*Poor Little Ritz Girl* program, Wilbur Theatre, Boston, 1920. NYPL—RRS JPH 85-5, Book 1), giving the impression—as one reviewer would remark—that the *Ritz Girl* scenes were in effect flashbacks, or dream sequences. (C. P. S., "Poor Little Ritz Girl," *New York Post*, July 29, 1920). The quick changes between completely different scenes were achieved using a cleverly designed contraption that swung the apartment open to reveal the stage of the Frivolity Theatre; although the first night reviews in Boston indicate that this technology had yet to be mastered by stagehands, it subsequently became such a feature of the show that the stagehands were given their own curtain calls in New York.

73. Hart and Kimball, *Complete Lyrics*, 18.

74. Philip Hale, "Musical Show at the Wilbur," *Boston Morning Herald*, May 30, 1920.

75. Fields and Fields, *From the Bowery*, 389–90.

76. Hart and Kimball, *Complete Lyrics*, 20. Several reviewers observe the Freudian suggestion of this scene, and it is interesting to see this as a precursor to *Peggy-Ann* some six years later. If that show in turn is often overlooked in discussions about the Moss Hart/Ira Gershwin/Kurt Weill show *Lady in the Dark* (1941), whose conceit is to stage its musical numbers as three dream sequences during the lead character's therapy sessions, this even earlier flirtation with psychoanalysis receives barely any attention in the literature. One reviewer describes it in a way that makes its structure seem intriguingly similar to *Lady in the Dark*: "There is only one set, an apartment, but there are four 'dream scenes,' cleverly manipulated." C. P. S., "Poor Little Ritz Girl."

77. Hart and Kimball, *Complete Lyrics*, 21.

78. F. H. Cushman, "Little Ritz Girl Has Premier at Wilbur Theatre," *Boston Record*, May 30, 1920.

79. Hale, "Musical Show at the Wilbur."

80. Fields and Fields, *From the Bowery*, 392; Block, *Richard Rodgers*, 20.

81. In one extended interview, Fields is particularly defensive on this subject: "I want to say, in view of certain comments upon the alleged similarity between my

play and another legitimate comedy now running in New York, that I have had the script of 'Poor Little Ritz Girl' in my possession over five years and it is entirely original." Given the circumstances, it is difficult to see how this can be anything but untrue. Colgate Baker, "Lew Fields Tells Secret of 'Poor Little Ritz Girl's' Success," *New York Review*, August 7, 1920.

82. William A. Everett, *Sigmund Romberg* (New Haven, CT: Yale University Press, 2007), 73.

83. Heywood Broun, "Jokes at Last Have a Place in Musical Shows," *New York Tribune*, July 29, 1920.

84. Kenneth MacGowan, "The New Play," *New York Globe*, July 29, 1920.

85. Baker, "Lew Fields Tells Secret."

86. Baker, "Lew Fields Tells Secret."

87. Rodgers, *Musical Stages*, 39.

88. Notably, this included Percy Goetschius, whose influence on Rodgers is considered by Geoffrey Block in *Richard Rodgers*, 30–33.

89. William B. Chase, "'Say It with Jazz,'" from *New York Times*, June 5, 1921; reprinted in the *Baton* 1, no. 4, April 1922, 16.

90. "The Three B's" reappeared in the song "Questions and Answers" from *On Your Toes* (1936), a schoolroom pastiche in which pupils are quizzed about the classical composers.

91. "Say It with Jazz," 16.

92. "Dick" Rodgers and "Herb" Fields, "In Payment of Two Cups of Tea and Twelve Sandwiches!" in the *Baton* 1, no. 6, June 1922, 7. Both Rodgers and Fields contributed extensively to the *Baton* for the next two years. The newspaper was edited by Dorothy Crowthers, who also scripted the IMA shows.

93. Rodgers, *Musical Stages*, 47.

94. Block, *Richard Rodgers*, 32.

95. Herbert Fields's review of the production in the *Baton* gives a lengthy paraphrase of this impersonation, showing language play very similar to that used by his father throughout his career: I. B. Anonymous, "Jazz a La Carte! A Review," in the *Baton* 1, no. 6, June 1922, 5.

96. See Marmorstein, *A Ship*, 76–77; Nolan, *Lorenz Hart*, 36; Hart and Kimball, *Thou Swell*, 28, Marx and Clayton, *Bewitched*, 33–34.

97. Rodgers, *Musical Stages*, 46.

98. This was a popular frame of reference for students of the Institute. Just one month previously, the college newspaper the *Baton* had published a poem by Maurice Popkin, "3000 Years B.C.," and a satirical cartoon depicting an Egyptian frieze showing Tutankhamen attending the Institute and struggling with ear-training and music theory: Beatrice Kluenter, "Interpretation," *Baton* 2, no. 8, May 1923, 12.

99. "'Jazz Show' Given at Musical Institute; Burlesque on King Tut and His Court Presented by Students in Claremont Avenue Hall," *New York Times*, June 1, 1923.

100. I. Witness, "The Play's the Thing," *Baton*, 2, no. 9, June, 1923, 5.

101. *Baton* 3, no. 5, February 1924, 6.

102. *Baton* 4, no. 7, April 1925, 5.

103. London's Gaiety Theatre enjoyed a string of burlesques throughout the 1890s, including *Faust Up to Date* (1888), *Carmen Up to Date* (1890) and *Cinder-Ellen Up Too Late* (1891).

104. Mel Schauer in Nolan, *Lorenz Hart*, 10.

105. Marx and Clayton, *Bewitched*, 54–55.

106. Rodgers, *Musical Stages*, 52.

107. Untitled article, *The New York World*, February 3, 1924.

108. V. K. Richards, "Innovation in Comedies Disclosed in Auditorium," *Toledo Blade*, March 29, 1924.

109. Ashton Stevens, "Every Act Is a Different Play, says Stevens," *Chicago Herald and Examiner*, April 21, 1924.

110. "Lew Fields Monday," *Zit*, May 9, 1924; Arthur Pollock, " 'The Melody Man,' " *Brooklyn Daily Eagle*, May 14, 1924; " 'Melody Man' Libel on Composers," *Clipper*, May 15, 1924; " 'The Melody Man,' " *New York Times*, May 18, 1924; Blythe Sherwood, "Round the Town," *Telegram and Mail*, May 31, 1924; untitled article, *Herald Tribune*, June 1, 1924. The Institute of Musical Theatre's newsletter, the *Baton*, was also privy to the real facts: untitled article, *Baton*, May 24, 1924.

111. Untitled article, *American Hebrew*, May 23, 1924; Metcalfe, "Rather a Stab at Jazz," *Wall Street Journal*, May 14, 1924.

112. Richard C. Rodgers, Lorenz M. Hart, and Herbert Fields, *The Jazz King*, libretto, LOC—Man D64166, 1923, Act One, 19.

113. "Henky" is the fond nickname given to Lew Fields's character Franz Henkel in the play. However, it is interesting to see how quick-fire newspaper coverage of this play's name-change misreported the new title as "Henky Shop" (*New York News*, April 24, 1924) and "Hinky Stop" (*New York World*, April 25, 1924).

114. "Lew Fields in a Striking Production," *Bethlehem Times*, March 24, 1924.

115. " 'The Jazz King' a Clever Play," *Bethlehem Globe*, March 25, 1924.

116. Len G. Shaw, "Lew Fields Experiments with Unusual End to Play," *Detroit Free Press*, April 6, 1924. The *Detroit Evening Times* expressed a similar view, "for all of which, three large, loud cheers!" "Jazz King Is Good," *Detroit Evening Times*, March 31, 1924.

117. "Jazz King Is Good."

118. William F. McDermott, "Lew Fields, like Warfield, Plays Role of Music Master," *Cleveland Plaindealer*, April 8, 1924.

119. " 'Henky' at Shubert," *Brooklyn Daily Times*, May 6, 1924.

120. " 'The Melody Man,' " *New York Times*, May 18, 1924.

121. Percy Hammond, "Mr. Lew Fields Is Good in a Comedy that Is Otherwise," *New York Herald and Tribune*, May 14, 1924.

122. "Lew Fields in 'Henky' at LaSalle," *Chicago Daily News*, April 21, 1924.

123. Rodgers, Hart, and Fields, *The Jazz King*, 4–5.

124. Rodgers, Hart, and Fields, *The Jazz King*, 18.

125. Rodgers, Hart, and Fields, *The Jazz King*, 20.

126. Rodgers, Hart, and Fields, *The Jazz King*, 23.

127. Fields and Fields, *From the Bowery*, 419.

128. *The Melody Man* program, 49th Street Theatre, 1924. NYPL T-PRG.

CHAPTER 2

1. Rodgers, *Musical Stages*, 57.
2. Rodgers, *Musical Stages*, 57.
3. Margery Darrell, "Garrick Gaieties," in Rodgers, *Song Book*, 10.
4. Rodgers, *Musical Stages*, 58.
5. Theresa Helburn, *A Wayward Quest* (Toronto: Little, Brown, 1960), 215.
6. Edith Meiser, "As It Was in the Beginning," *Garrick Gaieties* program (1925), Garrick Theatre, 1925. NYPL—RRS JPH 85–5, Book 2, 3.
7. Helburn, *Wayward Quest*, 216.
8. Darrell, "Garrick Gaieties," 9.
9. E. W. Osborn, untitled review, *Evening World*, May 18, 1925.
10. Osborn, untitled review.
11. Untitled article, *Variety*, May 13, 1925.
12. The *Ziegfeld Follies of 1925* and the *Garrick Gaieties* were already running at the start of the theatrical season; *The Grand Street Follies* would open on June 18, *George White's Scandals* on June 22, *Artists and Models* on June 24, *Earl Carroll's Vanities* on July 6, and *Gay Paree*, slightly later on August 18.
13. Osborn, untitled review.
14. M. L. "'Garrick Gaieties' Spoofs Mamma Guild," *Daily News*, May 19, 1925.
15. Gilbert W. Gabriel, "Gayly at the Garrick," *Evening Telegram*, May 19, 1925.
16. Such pastiche was also the material of *The Grand Street Follies*, whose 1925 offering included sketches called "They Knew What They Wanted under the Elms," "Mr. and Mrs. Guardsman (illustrating the difficulties of keeping in the character when one is playing en famille)," and "What Price Morning-Glories," which quipped the Maxwell Anderson/Laurence Stallings war drama, *What Price Glory* (1924).
17. R. W. Jr., "'The Garrick Gaieties' Will Perform Nightly," *Herald Tribune*, June 9, 1925.
18. The *Evening Post* reviewer considered this sketch "in very bad taste," though Joseph Wood Krutch writes in an ironic tone when he calls it "as intimately and disrespectfully personal as a revue should be": "Guild Gaieties at the Garrick Theatre," *Evening Post*, May 18, 1925; Joseph Wood Krutch, "Two Revues," *Nation*, July 8, 1925.
19. Hart and Kimball, *Complete Lyrics*, 53.
20. "'Rancho Mexicano' in Gaieties," *Garrick Gaieties* program (1925), 7.
21. Richard C. Norton, *A Chronology of American Musical Theater*, Volume 2: 1912–1952 (Oxford: Oxford University Press, 2002), 403.
22. Marmorstein, *A Ship*, 37.
23. This clearly references the Mason-Dixon Line, the symbolic border between Northeastern states and the South, or Dixie, though in this context Hart imagines a different symbolic boundary between Macy's and Gimbel's department stores around 34th Street.
24. Frank Sullivan, untitled article, *World*, July 14, 1925. Alexander Woollcott also criticized the lyrics: "rich in sprightly, elaborate rhymes, and suffering only from the not unimportant qualification that they do not sing well": Alexander Woollcott, "The Guild's Offspring Cut Up," *Sun*, May 18, 1925.

25. Rodgers, *Musical Stages*, 27.

26. Hart and Kimball, *Complete Lyrics*, 51.

27. Hart and Kimball, *Complete Lyrics*, 51–52.

28. "Youth Is at the Prow, though Pleasure May Be Distant from the Helm," *Herald Tribune*, July 24, 1925.

29. Frank Vreeland, "Flaunting Youth," *Evening Telegram*, June 12, 1925.

30. Leon Blumenfeld, "Garrick Gaieties," *Herald Tribune*, July 5, 1925.

31. John Howard Lawson, letter to the dramatic editor, *Herald*, August 17, 1925.

32. Woollcott, "Guild's Offspring."

33. Rodgers, *Musical Stages*, 27.

34. After Hart's death, Rodgers increasingly reported on the fact that Hart was unreliable and that he (Rodgers) was the driving force in their collaboration. His 1967 account in "A Composer Looks at His Lyricists" is typical: "He had to be literally trapped into putting pen to paper—and then only after hearing a melody that stimulated him." In Otis L. Guernsey Jr., ed., *Playwrights, Lyricists, Composers on Theatre* (New York: Dodd, Mead, 1974), 98–102.

35. Margaret Case Harriman, "Words and Music: Rodgers and Hart," *New Yorker*, May 28, 1938, 19.

36. Block, *Richard Rodgers*, 26.

37. "Cleverest of Our Lyricists Are Seldom Big Hit Writers," *New York-Herald Tribune*, May 31, 1925.

38. Arthur Schwartz in Hart and Kimball, *Complete Lyrics*, 36.

39. "Cleverest of Our Lyricists."

40. "Cleverest of Our Lyricists."

41. Untitled article, *Morning Telegraph*, July 26, 1925.

42. Hart and Kimball, *Complete Lyrics*, 53.

43. "The Garrick Gaieties Acquire the Dignity of Night Performances," *Evening Post*, June 9, 1925.

44. Hart and Kimball, *Complete Lyrics*, 48.

45. Richard Rodgers and Lorenz Hart, "On with the Dance," from the *Garrick Gaieties*, published sheet music (New York: Edward B. Marks Music Co., 1925).

46. Hart and Kimball, *Complete Lyrics*, 32.

47. Hart and Kimball, *Complete Lyrics*, 48.

48. Bernard Simon, "Guild Juniors Sport Gleefully," *Morning Telegraph*, May 18, 1925.

49. Sisk, "Garrick Gaieties," *Variety*, May 27, 1925.

50. "Guild 'Gaieties' a Dandy Revue," *Zits*, May 23, 1925.

51. Woollcott, "Guild's Offspring."

52. Hart and Kimball, *Complete Lyrics*, 48.

53. Hart and Kimball, *Complete Lyrics*, 54.

54. Sisk, "Garrick Gaieties."

55. "The Garrick Gaieties," *Evening Graphic*, May 18, 1925.

56. Nolan, *Lorenz Hart*, 72.

57. Nolan, *Lorenz Hart*, 71–72.

58. Marx and Clayton, *Bewitched*, 55.

59. Nolan, *Lorenz Hart*, 49.

60. Rodgers, *Musical Stages*, 78; Nolan, *Lorenz Hart*, 51.

61. Burton W. Peretti, *Nightclub City: Politics and Amusement in Manhattan* (Philadelphia: University of Pennsylvania Press, 2007), 193.

62. Abel, "5th Ave. Club," *Variety*, February 3, 1926.

63. *The Fifth Avenue Follies* program, Fifth Avenue Club, 1926. NYPL—RRS JPH 85–5, Book 2.

64. Gerald Bordman, *American Musical Revue: From the Passing Show to Sugar Babies* (New York: Oxford University Press, 1985), 56.

65. Abel, "5th Ave. Club."

66. Winchell, "Fifth Avenue Follies."

67. Abel, "5th Ave. Club."

68. "Supper Club Pays Royalty," *Variety*, February 3, 1926.

69. Romney Brent, "The Theatre Guild Studio," *Garrick Gaieties* program (1926), Guild Theatre, 1926. NYPL—MWEZ+nc 7745, 3.

70. Percy Hammond, "'The Garrick Gaieties,' Smart, Youthful, Worldly and Just a Bit Awkward," *Herald Tribune*, May 11, 1926.

71. Gilbert W. Gabriel, "Spring Revels by the Juniors of the Guild Repeating All in All the Jollities of Yore," *Sun*, May 11, 1926.

72. Rodgers, *Musical Stages*, 81.

73. John Forbes, "Children's Hour at the Garrick," *Morning Telegraph*, May 11, 1926.

74. John Anderson, untitled article, *Evening Post*, May 11, 1926.

75. "The Garrick Gaieties," *Brooklyn Standard Union*, May 11, 1926.

76. J. Brooks Atkinson, "Theatre Guild Cut-Ups," *Times*, May 11, 1926.

77. Atkinson, "Theatre Guild Cut-Ups."

78. Frank Vreeland, "When We Were Very Young," *Evening Telegram*, May 11, 1926.

79. Two more successful sketches were added: "Washington and the Spy" and "Crossing the Avenue," and a new song, "Allez-Up."

80. Rodgers *Musical Stages*, 82.

81. Gabriel, "Spring Revels."

82. Alexander Woollcott, untitled article, *World*, May 11, 1926.

83. Alexander Woollcott, untitled article, *World*, May 11, 1926.

84. Atkinson, "Theatre Guild Cut-Ups."

85. Rodgers, *Musical Stages*, 82.

86. Hart and Kimball, *Complete Lyrics*, 73.

87. Rodgers's piano roll recordings are available commercially and have been collected on the CD *Richard Rodgers: Command Performance* (Rodgers 2008).

88. Philip Loeb, "Interview," *Garrick Gaieties* program (1926), 14.

89. Hart and Kimball, *Complete Lyrics*, 74

90. Nolan, *Lorenz Hart*, 238.

91. Marx and Clayton, *Bewitched*, 74.

92. Marx and Clayton, *Bewitched*, 74.

93. Hart and Kimball, *Complete Lyrics*, 75.

94. E. W. Osborn, untitled article, *Evening World*, May 11, 1926.

95. Woollcott, untitled article.

96. Woollcott, untitled article.

97. Untitled article, *Women's Wear*, May 11, 1926.

98. The *Garrick Gaieties* opened on May 10, 1926; *Dearest Enemy*'s last performance was on May 22. *The Vagabond King* played until December 4.

99. Hart and Kimball, *Complete Lyrics*, 73.

100. "The Three Musketeers," *Garrick Gaieties* program (1926), 5.

101. Rodgers points directly to this reference to "The Love Nest" from the 1920 show *Mary*, by Louis A. Hirsch and Otto Harbach: "The Three Musketeers," *Garrick Gaieties* program (1926), 5.

102. Woollcott, untitled article.

103. "Robinson Crusoe" was written by Sam M. Lewis, Joe Young, and George Meyer. It was first sung in the hit show *Robinson Crusoe, Jr.* (1916) by Al Jolson.

104. Hart and Kimball, *Complete Lyrics*, 72.

105. John Anderson, untitled article, *Evening Post*, May 29, 1926.

106. John Anderson, untitled article.

107. Hart and Kimball, *Complete Lyrics*, 75.

108. Magee, *Irving Berlin*, 20.

109. Untitled article, *Evening World*, May 15, 1926.

110. Lincoln Barnett, *Writing on Life: Sixteen Close-Ups* (New York: William Sloane Associates, 1951), 312.

111. Hart and Kimball, *Complete Lyrics*, 76. "A Little Souvenir" can be heard performed by Elaine Stritch on Ben Bagley's *Rodgers and Hart Revisited IV*.

112. Lorenz Hart, "Lyrics Made to Order," *Garrick Gaieties* program (1926), 12.

113. Richard Rodgers, "How Music Is Not Written," *Garrick Gaieties* program (1926), 12. The two articles cited in notes 112 and 113 are on the same page(12) of the souvenir program.

CHAPTER 3

1. "Richard Rodgers Composer of Many Musical Comedies," *Long Beach Life*, August 15, 1925.

2. *Dear Enemy* was the title of a popular 1915 novel by Jean Webster. There is no similarity between the plots of this novel and the musical, though the writing team undoubtedly borrowed the title for marketing purposes.

3. Nolan, *Lorenz Hart*, 60.

4. Lahr in Rodgers, *Musical Stages*, 333.

5. Michael Feinstein, *The Gershwins and Me: A Personal History in Twelve Songs* (New York: Simon and Schuster, 2012), 190.

6. Meryle Secrest, *Somewhere for Me: A Biography of Richard Rodgers* (New York: Alfred A. Knopf, 2001), 54.

7. Rodgers, *Musical Stages*, 44.

8. Rodgers, *Musical Stages*, 68.

9. Herbert Fields, *Sweet Rebel*, libretto, LOC—Man D69211, 1924, Act One, 3.

10. Herbert Fields, *Dearest Enemy*, libretto, RHO, 1925, Act One, 36.

11. Fields, *Sweet Rebel*, Act Two, 26.

12. Fields, *Sweet Rebel*, Act Two, 13–14.

13. Fields, *Dearest Enemy*, Epilogue, 5.

14. Alan Dale, "'Dearest Enemy' Agreeably Odd," *American*, September 19, 1925.

15. Frank Vreeland, "'Dearest Enemy,'" *Telegram*, September 19, 1925.

16. Untitled article, *Evening World*, September 26, 1925.

17. Untitled article, *Evening Post*, September 19, 1925.

18. Untitled article, *Evening Telegram*, September 26, 1925.

19. Untitled article, *Women's Wear*, September 21, 1925.

20. Norman Clark, "Ford's Is Off on Another Season," *Baltimore News*, September 8, 1925.

21. Untitled article, *Times*, September 19, 1925.

22. Clark, "Ford's Is Off."

23. Nolan, *Lorenz Hart*, 60.

24. Fields, *Dearest Enemy*, Act One, 4.

25. Fields, *Dearest Enemy*, Act One, 10–11.

26. Robert Garland, untitled article, *Baltimore American*, September 8, 1925.

27. Gilbert W. Gabriel, "'Dearest Enemy' of 1776," *Sun*, September 19, 1925.

28. Amy Leslie, "'Dearest Enemy' Is Praised by Critic," *Chicago Daily News*, September 6, 1925.

29. Untitled article, *Times*, September 19, 1925.

30. Max Wilk, *They're Playing Our Song: Conversations with America's Classic Songwriters* (New York: Da Capo Press, 1997), 63

31. Earl F. Bargainnier, "W. S. Gilbert and American Musical Theatre," *Journal of Popular Culture* 12, no. 3 (1978): 450.

32. Marmorstein, *A Ship*, 22.

33. Untitled article, *Brooklyn Daily Eagle*, September 19, 1925.

34. Hart and Kimball, *Complete Lyrics*, 56.

35. Hart and Kimball, *Complete Lyrics*, 31.

36. Hart and Kimball, *Complete Lyrics*, 58.

37. W. S. Gilbert and Arthur Sullivan, *The Complete Works of Gilbert and Sullivan* (New York: W. W. Norton, 1976), 189.

38. Hart and Kimball, *Complete Lyrics*, 57.

39. Hart and Kimball, *Complete Lyrics*, 59.

40. Hart and Kimball, *Complete Lyrics*, 59.

41. Knapp, *National Identity*, 83.

42. Knapp, *National Identity*, 85.

43. Knapp, *National Identity*, 103.

44. E. W. Osborn, "'Dearest Enemy,'" *Evening World*, September 19, 1925. Osborn doesn't quite get all of his facts right, noting that the music is written by a "Richard Hodges."

45. Metcalfe, "General George Washington in Person," *Wall Street Journal*, September 19, 1925.

46. Henry P. Johnston, *The Campaign of 1776 around New York and Brooklyn* (Brooklyn: Long Island Historical Society, 1878), 233.

47. Johnston, *The Campaign of 1776*, 237, fn.185.

48. Johnston, *The Campaign of 1776*, 239.

49. Alan Axelrod, *The Real History of the American Revolution: A New Look at the Past* (New York: Sterling, 2007), 171.

50. Johnston, *The Campaign of 1776*, 240.

51. Untitled article, *American Hebrew*, October 16, 1925.

52. Wood, "Song Forms," 196.

53. Wood, "Song Forms," 181.

54. Wood, "Song Forms," 136.

55. Wood, "Song Forms," 185.

56. Wood, "Song Forms," 188.

57. Wood, "Song Forms," 190.

58. Wood, "Song Forms," 191–92.

59. Hart and Kimball, *Complete Lyrics*, 57.

60. Gabriel, "Dearest Enemy."

61. Gabriel, "Dearest Enemy."

CHAPTER 4

1. Fields and Fields, *From the Bowery*, 94. For a succinct description of this process, see Mona Rebecca Brooks, "The Development of American Theatre Management Practices between 1830 and 1896" (PhD diss., Texas Tech University, 1981), 4–5.

2. Fields and Fields, *From the Bowery*, 403.

3. Magee, *Irving Berlin*, 39.

4. Margaret Knapp, "'Watch Your Step': Irving Berlin's 1914 Musical," in Benjamin Sears, ed., *The Irving Berlin Reader* (New York: Oxford University Press, 1981), 59.

5. Knapp, "'Watch Your Step,'" 58.

6. Magee, *Irving Berlin*, 43.

7. Harold Phillips, "What They Liked in the Lillie Show," *Washington Times*, December 13, 1927.

8. John J. Daly, "Dillingham Offers Hit of His Career in 'She's My Baby,'" *Washington Post*, December 13, 1927.

9. Playgoer "Dillingham Production Brings Out the Comic Qualities of Overseas Star," *Star-Eagle*, December 27, 1927.

10. Untitled article, *Herald Tribune*, January 4, 1928.

11. Ralph D. Palmer, untitled article, *Washington Daily News*, December 13, 1927.

12. Untitled article, *Times*, January 4, 1928.

13. Magee, *Irving Berlin*, 35.

14. "Lew Fields' Play at the Vanderbilt Is a Riotous Success," *Journal of Commerce*, March 18, 1926.

15. Untitled article, *Evening Graphic*, March 18, 1926.

16. "Sam White and Eva Puck Star in 'The Girl Friend,'" *Women's Wear*, March 18, 1926.

17. Untitled article, *Evening Graphic*, March 18, 1926.

18. "'Dr. Fix-It' Creates the Musical Comedy Hits," *Sun*, August 12, 1926.

19. Gilbert W. Gabriel, "Song, Dance and a Girl Friend," *Sun*, March 18, 1926.

20. Rubin, *Lew Fields*, 171.

21. Rubin, *Lew Fields*, 239.

22. Foster Hirsch, *The Boys from Syracuse: The Shuberts' Theatrical Empire* (Carbondale: Southern Illinois University Press, 1998), 82.

23. Fields and Fields, *From the Bowery*, 246.

24. Rubin, *Lew Fields*, 166.

25. Rubin, *Lew Fields*, 255.

26. Marx and Clayton, *Rodgers and Hart*, 99.

27. Fields and Fields, *From the Bowery*, 449.

28. Charlotte Greenspan, *Pick Yourself Up: Dorothy Fields and the American Musical* (New York: Oxford University Press, 2010), 30.

29. "Fields Departs from Precedent in New Show," *Sun*, March 4, 1926.

30. Richard Rodgers, *The Girl Friend* (1926), reconstructed piano-conductor score by James Stenborg, RHO, 11.

31. Hart and Kimball, *Complete Lyrics*, 64.

32. Untitled article, *Morning Telegraph*, May 10, 1926.

33. Harry Hirschfield, "'Girl Friend' Is Gem of Comedy, Says Abie," *Evening Journal*, April 14, 1926.

34. Untitled article, *Evening Graphic*, March 18, 1926.

35. E. F. Smith, "'The Girl Friend' Needs Grooming," *Atlantic City Evening Union*, March 9, 1926.

36. "'Dr. Fix-It' Creates the Musical Comedy Hits," *Sun*, August 12, 1926.

37. Fields and Fields, *From the Bowery*, 443.

38. "Lew Fields' Remarkable Youth Serves Him as Stage Director," *Herald Tribune*, March 1, 1926.

39. "How 'Peggy-Ann' Came Close to Tragedy," *New York Telegraph*, January 6, 1927.

40. Fields and Fields, *From the Bowery*, 442–43.

41. Rubin, *Lew Fields*, 421–22.

42. Untitled article, *Evening Post*, March 18, 1926.

43. Fields and Fields, *From the Bowery*, 442.

44. Rubin, *Lew Fields*, 423.

45. Abel, untitled article, *Variety*, March 20, 1926.

46. Untitled article, *Evening Post*, March 18, 1926.

47. Untitled article, *Variety*, October 6, 1926; untitled article, *Variety*, October 20, 1926.

48. Untitled article, *Variety*, April 28, 1926.

49. Untitled article, *Variety*, May 26, 1926.

CHAPTER 5

1. Chester B. Bahn, "Will Rogers Will Erect Costly Home: Herald Humorist Will Spend $100,000 on Coast Mansion," *Syracuse Herald*, January 22, 1927, 4.

2. Jack Hulbert, *The Little Woman's Always Right* (London: W. H. Allen, 1975), 122.

3. Rodgers, *Musical Stages*, 26.

4. Rodgers, *Musical Stages*, 51.

5. "Today's Gossip: News and Views about Men, Women and Affairs in General," *Daily Mirror*, April 16, 1926, 9.

6. "4,000 First Nighters Crowded Out: New Play with Music by George Gershwin," *Daily Express*, April 15, 1926, 9.

7. Carados, untitled article, *Referee*, September 5, 1926. The word "lyrists" was often used as an alternative to "lyricists" during this period.

8. H. S., "Song Broadcast in a Theatre: American Idea at the Gaiety: 'Lido Lady,'" *Daily Express*, December 2, 1926.

9. Harris Deans, "The Stage of the Day," *Illustrated Sporting and Dramatic News*, December 11, 1926, 256.

10. "The Gaiety: 'Lido Lady,'" *Stage*, December 9, 1926.

11. Rodgers, *Musical Stages*, 89.

12. Ronald Jeans, *Lido Lady*, libretto, BL—LCP 1926/39, no.7155, 1926, 12/LC15. Playscripts held in the Lord Chamberlain's collection have been paginated during the process of censorship. Where this has occurred I have indicated both the original author's pagination and the Lord Chamberlain's pagination.

13. *Telegraph*, December 2, 1926. In some reports of Guy Bolton's involvement, his writing team is indicated as Bert Kalmar and Harry Ruby, though whether their involvement was significant is not clear. They were also credited as co-writers of *The Ramblers*, while P. G. Wodehouse assisted in writing the libretto for *Oh, Kay!* Of course, given Bolton's hectic schedule, it is possible that they in fact served as ghostwriters, writing the script but giving it his name. See Lee Davis, *Bolton and Wodehouse and Kern: The Men Who Made Musical Comedy* (New York: James H. Heineman, 1993), 287–91.

14. Rodgers, *Musical Stages*, 89.

15. "The Passing Shows: 'Lido Lady' at the Gaiety Theatre," *Tatler* 1329, December 15, 1926.

16. Not so the reviewer of the *Sunday Pictorial*: "I think I'd rather have a tooth out myself, but it takes all sorts to make an audience." Untitled article, *Sunday Pictorial*, December 5, 1926.

17. Crescendo, "Gaiety Theatre: Jack Hulbert, Cicely Courtneidge and Phyllis Dare In 'Lido Lady,'" *Star*, December 2, 1926.

18. Untitled review, *Stage*, October 7, 1926.

19. Jeans, *Lido Lady*, Act One, 20/LC48.

20. Block, *Richard Rodgers*, 27.

21. Jeans, *Lido Lady*, Act Two, 3–5a/LC151.

22. Jeans, *Lido Lady*, Act Two, 3–5a/LC151.

23. Rodgers, *Musical Stages*, 89.

24. Nolan, *Lorenz Hart*, 82.

25. Nolan, *Lorenz Hart*, 83.

26. Jeans, *Lido Lady*, 3/LC6. The connection between diet and nationalism is not such an unlikely link. A popular notion celebrating the national dish suggests that

it was a diet of fish and chips that helped Britain win the First World War. See John K. Walton, *Fish and Chips and the British Working Class, 1870–1940* (London: Leicester University Press, 1992).

27. Gilbert and Sullivan, *Complete Works*, 20. This is also reminiscent of the "kettle of fish" chorus in *Iolanthe* (228–29), in which Gilbert's use of familiar though ridiculous phrases in excessive repetition by angry members of the House of Lords creates a farcical impression.

28. Nolan, *Lorenz Hart*, 82.

29. In this respect, Rodgers and Hart are no less culturally imperialistic than Rodgers and Hammerstein would later be in *The King and I* or *South Pacific*.

30. "It seems to have worried neither Mr. Rodgers nor Mr. Hammerstein very much that the behaviour of war-torn Pacific islanders and nineteenth-century Siamese might be slightly different from that of Chinese residents of present-day California," wrote Tynan. "Perhaps as a riposte to Joshua Logan's 'The World of Suzie Wong,' Rodgers and Hammerstein have given us what, if I had any self control at all, I would refrain from describing as a world of woozy song." Kenneth Tynan, "The Theatre: Tiny Chinese Minds," *New Yorker*, December 13, 1958, 104–9.

31. Gershwin's *Oh, Kay!*, also from 1926, includes a similar song, "Clap Yo' Hands," so incongruous to the plot that, in Howard Pollack's words, "Bolton and Wodehouse framed the song with a plea from the ensemble not to have to hear this cheerful 'mammy song'": see *George Gershwin: His Life and Work* (Berkeley: University of California Press, 2006), 384. Although the near-simultaneous development of *Lido Lady* and *Oh, Kay!* on different sides of the Atlantic makes it unlikely that there was any direct reference of one by the other, the similarity testifies to the popularity of this trope. One senses that Rodgers and Hart were aware of the extent to which such numbers stretch the credibility of dramatic integrity; "Queen of Sheba Pageant" surely pastiches and even celebrates the ridiculous incongruities that musical comedy indulged.

32. Jeans, *Lido Lady*, Act Two, 18/LC82.

33. Jeans, *Lido Lady*, Act Two, LC145.

34. In common with other songs of the period with the word "blues" in the title, this is by no means a blues song and bears no similarities to the musical structures of the blues such as the twelve-measure form.

35. Links with "Try Again To-morrow" may be tenuous, though the B sections of both songs move to the subdominant, where they emphasize the sixth note of the scale, which is a feature Alec Wilder recognizes of American music. The main refrain of "Try Again To-morrow" also uses melodic ingredients from the verse of "Here in My Arms" (see excerpts from "The Girl Friend" and "I'd Rather Charleston"), though as has already been noted, a suggestion of Gershwin's "Fascinating Rhythm" is more apparent.

36. Wood, "Song Forms," 181fn.

37. "The Gaiety: 'Lido Lady,'" *Stage*, December 9, 1926.

38. "A Bright New Revue: 'One Dam Thing after Another,'" *Daily Mail*, May 21, 1927.

39. J. T. G., "Ever Green" at the Adelphi," unlabeled clipping, December 17, 1930.

40. Troupes of American minstrels such as the Fiske Jubilee Singers were touring the UK as early as the 1870s; *Variety* magazine notes ragtime's "big wave of popularity in England" in 1913; and the New York (or Southern) Syncopated Orchestra were the toast of the town in 1919 before a tragic accident at sea in which several musicians drowned. Karl Koenig, *Jazz in Print (1856–1929): An Anthology of Selected Early Readings in Jazz History* (Hillsdale, NY: Pendragon Press, 2002), 92, 140.

41. The song is more commonly known as "Berkeley Square and Kew." This theme has been explored by Jeffrey Magee in his paper "From Flatbush to the Sea: The Broadway Musical's Cozy Cottage Trope, 1910s–1970s," Harvard-Princeton Forum on Musical Theater, Harvard University, April 15, 2011.

42. A time line of events only consolidates the impression that "I'd Rather Charleston" responds to "The Girl Friend": the Rodgers and Hart show opened on March 17, 1926, and Gershwin left New York around March 27 for the London rehearsals of *Lady, Be Good!*, for which "I'd Rather Charleston" was written. *Lady, Be Good!* opened in London on April 14. See Joan Peyser, *The Memory of All That: The Life of George Gershwin* (New York: Billboard Books, 1998), 119.

43. Phillida, "Ladies Mirror: The New Dance—Parties and Presents," *Daily Mirror*, July 20, 1925, 17.

44. The Chaperon, "Round the Ballrooms: What Really Killed the Charleston?" *Daily Mirror*, October 31, 1925, 4.

45. The Chaperon, "Round the Ballrooms: Pleasant Club Classes—'Wallflower' Revival," January 30, 1926, 4.

46. "Ladies Mirror: Season Opens with Dress-Shows and Tango Teas," *Daily Mirror*, September 28, 1925, 18.

47. "'Lido Lady': Miss Phyllis Dare's Return: Clever Cast in New Musical Comedy," *Daily Mail*, December 2, 1926.

48. "Today's Gossip: News and Views about Men, Women and Affairs in General," *Daily Mirror*, October 1, 1925, 9.

49. H. S, "Song Broadcast in a Theatre."

50. Untitled review, *Sunday Pictorial*, December 5, 1926. The second of these "Big Tunes" appears to have been "Not To-Day" ("Lido Lady," *Sporting Times*, December 4, 1926; "Lido Lady at the Gaiety," *Era*, December 8, 1926).

51. "'Lido Lady': Phyllis Dare's Happy Return," *Westminster Gazette*, December 2, 1926; similar sentiments are expressed in "'Lido Lady': A Great Gaiety Success of Acting and Dancing," *Referee*, December 5, 1926.

52. Untitled article, *Stage*, October 7, 1926.

53. "That Song!" *Sunday News*, December 5, 1926.

54. Untitled review, *Sunday Express*, December 5, 1926; Edith Shackleton, "'Ricey Man' Steps on the Stage: First Nights Hectic and Hilarious," *Queen*, December 8, 1926.

55. "'Lido Lady,'" *Sunday Times*, December 5, 1926.

56. Unfortunately, recordings of 1920s American artistes singing this song are not available, though recordings by, for example, popular singer Jane Green demonstrate a markedly different tessitura and a more relaxed style. A recording of Helen Ford singing "Here in My Arms" on a radio broadcast of 1934 is available as an additional

track on the soundtrack recording to the 1955 television broadcast. Her vocal manner on this version is, like Phyllis Dare's, somewhat formal and discomfiting, unlike the relaxed crooning of Anne Jeffreys and—particularly—Robert Sterling in the 1955 version.

57. Nolan, *Lorenz Hart*, 82.

58. Unlabeled article, *Daily Mail*, October 6, 1926.

59. Hulbert, *Little Woman*, 128.

60. Rodgers, *Musical Stages*, 90.

61. Nolan, *Lorenz Hart*, 83.

62. Nolan, *Lorenz Hart*, 82.

63. P. P., "The 'Lido Lady' Comes to Stay," *Evening Standard*, December 2, 1926.

64. Crescendo, "Gaiety Theatre."

65. H. H., "Gaiety. 'Lido Lady.' Written by Ronald Jeans. Music by Richard Rodgers," *Observer*, December 5, 1926.

66. "Today's Gossip: News and Views about Men, Women and Affairs in General," *Daily Mirror*, December 20, 1926, 9.

67. Rodgers, *Musical Stages*, 88.

68. Rodgers, *Musical Stages*, 88.

69. Rodgers, *Musical Stages*, 89.

70. Richard Rodgers, letter, Tuesday March 15, 1927, from correspondence with Dorothy Rodgers, 1927, in NYPL—RRP TMS-1987-006, Series III, Box 6, Folder 12.

71. Rodgers, *Musical Stages*, 103.

72. Nolan, *Lorenz Hart*, 99.

73. The Stoll and Moss companies were two of the biggest theater-owning chains in the UK throughout this period; they were originally created by Oswald Stoll (1866–1942) and Edward Moss (1852–1912) and were committed to music hall and variety entertainment. The companies merged to form Stoll-Moss Theatres, which was bought out by Andrew Lloyd Webber's Really Useful Group in 2000.

74. Jeans, *One Dam Thing*, 1/LC3.

75. Indeed, this was "Mr. Cochran's fourth, fifth or sixth retraction of his annually announced decision to present no more revnes [sic] for the sophisticated section of London," Alan Bott, "Drama," *Tatler*, June 4, 1927.

76. E. W. B., "London Pavilion: The Prince Becomes a First Nighter: London Review [sic] in 23 Scenes. Mr. Cochran at his Best," *Westminster Gazette*, May 21, 1927; "Plays of the Week," *People*, May 22, 1927; "Mr. Cochran's New Revue," *Liverpool Post*, May 21, 1927. A number of these opening night scenes may have been dropped soon into the run: the *Era* from May 25 and the *Jewish Graphic* from June 3 report just "twenty-one dam things." Dramaticus, "Amusement Notes: London Pavilion: 'One Dam Thing after Another,'" *Jewish Graphic*, June 3, 1927; "'One Dam Thing after Another' at the London Pavilion," *Era*, May 25, 1927. *Tatler* from June 15 reports that by then, "The Lady in the Lake" and "Lost Souls" had been replaced: Trinculo, "The Passing Shows: 'One Dam Thing after Another' at the London Pavilion," *Tatler* 1355, June 15, 1927, 484–85.

77. S. T. H., "'One Dam Thing aAfter Another'," *Theatre World*, May 20, 1927.

78. Jeans, *One Dam Thing*, LC29.

79. "London Pavilion: 'One Dam Thing Aafter Another,'" *Stage*, May 26, 1927.

80. L. E. F., "The Prince at a First Night: Clever Revue at the Pavilion," *Morning Post*, May 21, 1927.

81. H. Chance Newton, "New Plays of the Week: 'One Dam Thing after Another' at the London Pavilion," *Referee*, May 22, 1927.

82. S. T. H., "One Dam Thing."

83. I. B., "Mr. Cochran's New Revue," *Manchester Guardian*, May 21, 1927.

84. Untitled review, *Queen*, June 1, 1927.

85. J. T. G., "'One Dam Thing after Another' at the London Pavilion," *Sketch*, June 1, 1927.

86. "New Cochran Revue: Wit, Beauty and Burlesque at London Pavilion: Prince at First Night," *Daily Mirror*, May 21, 1927.

87. Sir Topaz, "Second Thoughts on First Nights: 'One Dam Thing after Another'—London Pavilion," *Eve*, June 1, 1927, 493.

88. "London Pavilion: 'One Dam Thing after Another': A Revue. By Ronald Jeans," *Sunday Times*, May 20, 1927.

89. O. S., "At the Play: 'One Dam Thing after Another' (London Pavilion)," *Punch, or the London Charivari*, June 1, 1927, 610.

90. Ronald Jeans, *One Dam Thing after Another*, libretto, BL—LCP 1927/19, no.7641, 1927, LC50-51.

91. Ronald Jeans, *One Dam Thing after Another*, libretto, 7/LC44.

92. "London Pavilion: 'One Dam Thing after Another'," *Telegraph*, May 21, 1927.

93. "Mr. Cochran's New Revue: Production at the Pavilion," *Times*, May 21, 1927.

94. "London Pavilion: 'One Dam Thing after Another,'" *Telegraph*, May 21, 1927.

95. "Mr Cochran's 'Not Quite' Revue: 'One Dam Thing after Another': And Not All Good," *Evening News*, May 21, 1927.

96. Rodgers, *Musical Stages*, 101.

97. Block, *Richard Rodgers*, 36–39; *Reader*, 19–30.

98. Hart and Kimball, *Thou Swell*, 55.

99. Rodgers, *Musical Stages*, 130.

100. The Lord Chamberlain's libretto calls this the "Casino de la Folie" throughout. Benn W. Levy (unattributed), *Ever Green*, libretto, BL—LCP 1930/43, no.9944, 1930.

101. Levy, *Ever Green*, libretto, Act One, 2. This unusual rhyme is also used in "The Three B's" from *On Your Toes* (1936). See Hart and Kimball, 221.

102. Levy, *Ever Green*, Act One, 12. In the script, "Harlemania" is sung by contest entrant Miss Lindfield, Sussex, though in the program Madeline Gibson, playing the part of Miss Cheltenham, is credited as the singer.

103. At around the same time, Bradley was working closely with Busby Berkeley on the New York revue circuit; in some accounts, it is Bradley's influence that made what has become known as the Busby Berkeley style so characteristic. Certainly, the film *Evergreen* (1934), which Bradley choreographed, shows innovative choreographic ideas that at least rival the Berkeley films of the same period.

104. Susan Rusinko, *The Plays of Benn Levy: Between Shaw and Coward* (London: Associated University Presses, 1994), 30.

105. Nevertheless, both the trouser gag and another heavily censored scene, one of the revue sketches set in a Parisian brothel, are mentioned in press reviews, which causes us to ask how closely the Lord Chamberlain's regulations were followed.

106. Sheridan Morley, *Spread a Little Happiness: The First Hundred Years of the British Musical* (London: Thames and Hudson, 1987), 67.

107. Ivor Brown, "The Week's Theatres: Adelphi: 'Ever Green,'" unattributed clipping, December 7, 1930.

108. "Charles B. Cochran's Production *Ever Green*: A Musical Show, Royal Adelphi Theatre," promotional flyer, *Ever Green* production file, VA, 1930.

109. "'Ever Green' at the Adelphi Theatre," *Play Pictorial* 346, no. 58, January 1931, v.

110. "Charles B. Cochran's Production," 1930.

111. Charles B. Cochran, *Cock-a-doodle-do* (London: J. M. Dent, 1941), 155.

112. "'Ever Green,'" *Play Pictorial*, v.

113. I am grateful to Bruce Pomahac of the Rodgers and Hammerstein Organization for further details on the fairground scene. *Carousel*'s opening music was first sketched out for the Al Jolson film *Hallelujah, I'm a Bum* (1933), though never used in that context. A holograph sketch in the Library of Congress shows the melody of a waltz we now know as "The Carousel Waltz." Written only three years later, it is very likely that the fairground scene in *Ever Green* was in Rodgers's mind as he worked on the Jolson score, though it didn't surface until 1945.

114. James Agate, "'Ever Green,'" unattributed clipping, December 3, 1930.

115. E. K., "'Ever Green'—Some New Features," unattributed clipping, April 22, 1931.

116. "Diseuse" is a term coined by the press, seemingly to describe singers of the new American style of jazz, in which, as the critics see it, the songs were not so much sung as shouted over music. The masculine "diseur" is found elsewhere in reviews, for example, Ivor Brown, "The Theatre: Is Revue Damned?" *Saturday Review*, May 28, 1927, 823–24.

117. "What 'J. G. B.' said about 'Ever Green' in *The Evening News*," in "Mr. Cochran Excels Himself," promotional flyer, *Ever Green* production file, VA, 1930.

118. "Mr. Leon Morton, a Welcome Prodigal, Exquisite in the Dryness of His French Humour" (J. T. G. "'Ever Green'"); "Somebody had the exquisite inspiration of engaging for the star's mother, masquerading as daughter, not one of your rough-and-tumble 'ugly sister' viragoes, but that impeccable artist, Miss Jean Cadell" (Agate, "'Ever Green'").

119. Agate, "'Ever Green.'"

120. Agate, "'Ever Green.'"

121. "'Ever Green,'" *Play Pictorial*, v.

122. Levy, *Ever Green*, Act One, 23.

123. Levy, *Ever Green* , Act One, 59–60.

124. Benn Levy was an outspoken advocate for socialist ideals. Later in his career, he became the Labour Member of Parliament for Eton and Slough and served as a backbench member of the Attlee government from 1945 to 1950.

125. Levy, *Ever Green*, Act One, 20–21.

126. Levy, *Ever Green*, Act One, 18.

127. Levy, *Ever Green*, Act One, 43.

128. Hart and Kimball, *Complete Lyrics*, 161. These lyrics differ slightly from those originally presented to the Lord Chamberlain, where Eric sings: "I shall not be vain; / Very clearly I see / You're a little bit insane / For you love me" (Levy, *Ever Green*, Act Two, 44).

129. Levy, *Ever Green*, Act Two, 45.

130. Levy, *Ever Green*, Act Two, 6–7.

131. As Hart and Kimball report (*Complete Lyrics*, 137), this song went through a number of slight rewrites as it migrated through no less than four shows: *Spring Is Here* (1929), *Me for You* (1929), *Heads Up!* (1929), and finally *Ever Green* (1930). Which lyrics ended up being sung in the production of *Ever Green* is unclear, though a studio recording from 2004 includes this third verse (James Stiepan, *Rodgers and Hart's Ever Green*, Bygone records CD BG-1002, 2004).

132. Jeans, *Lido Lady*, 3–23/LC192.

133. "The Story of 'Ever Green,'" *Ever Green* program, Adelphi Theatre, 1930, *Ever Green* production file, VA.

134. Levy, *Ever Green*, Act Two, pp. 39–40.

135. This is by no means the only example of song faltering at a moment of heightened emotional intensity. I am reminded of the compelling measure of silence in Monteverdi's *Orfeo* in which Orfeo is struck dumb by the weight of his passion; Rose's breakdown in *Gypsy* is also discussed earlier. I am grateful to Geoffrey Block for further examples such as the dramatic use of silence in Debussy's *Pelléas et Mélisande*, and the interruption of music by Maria's speech in *West Side Story*.

136. See, for example, D. A. Miller, *Place for Us: Essay on the Broadway Musical* (Cambridge, MA: Harvard University Press, 1998); Jason Fitzgerald, "'I Had a Dream': 'Rose's Turn,' Musical Theatre and the Star Effigy," *Studies in Musical Theatre* 3, no. 3 (December 2009): 285–91.

CHAPTER 6

1. Rodgers, *Musical Stages*, 90.

2. *Tillie's Punctured Romance* (1914) was the first, which is often considered to be an adaptation of *Tillie's Nightmare*, though it is quite different. Nevertheless, *Tillie's Punctured Romance* is notable both as the first feature-length comedy and as the last film to feature Charlie Chaplin before Chaplin began writing and directing his own movies. Subsequently, Dressler went on to star in *Tillie's Tomato Surprise* (1915) and *Tillie Wakes Up* (1917).

3. Matthew Kennedy, *Marie Dressler: A Biography* (New York: McFarland, 1999), 64.

4. Kennedy, *Marie Dressler*, 65.

5. Kennedy, *Marie Dressler*, 61.

6. Untitled article, *Sun*, December 28, 1926.

7. "'Peggy-Ann' Is Here Bright and Fantastic," *Times*, December 28, 1926.

8. Untitled article, *American*, December 28, 1926.

9. Rowland L. Field, untitled article, *Brooklyn Daily Times*, December 28, 1926.

10. "'Peggy-Ann' Scores Hit with 'Wise Ones,' Lobby Gossip Shows," *Herald Tribune*, December 28, 1926.

11. "'Peggy-Ann' Is a Breathless Musical Comedy," *Telegram*, December 28, 1926.

12. "The Walnut – 'Peggy.'" *Philadelphia Evening Bulletin*, December 14, 1926.

13. Waters, "Peggy-Ann," *Variety*, December 22, 1926.

14. "Peggy at the Walnut Has First Performance," *Philadelphia Record*, December 14, 1926.

15. "Helen Ford Has Leading Role in New Musical Show," *Philadelphia Public Ledger*, December 14, 1926.

16. Woollcott, Alexander, "*Peggy-Ann*," *World*, February 27, 1927.

17. Mardi Valgemae, *Accelerated Grimace: Expressionism in the American Drama of the 1920s* (Carbondale: Southern Illinois University Press, 1972), 2.

18. Valgemae, *Accelerated Grimace*, 2–3.

19. Peter Moruzzi, *Havana before Castro: When Cuba Was a Tropical Playground* (Layton, UT: Gibbs Smith, 2008), 39.

20. Herbert Fields, *Peggy-Ann*, libretto, RHO, 1926, 1-2a-29.

21. The setting is far more glamorous, though a precursor for this department store scenario is clearly "The Joy Spreader" from the *Garrick Gaieties* (1925).

22. Hart and Kimball, *Complete Lyrics*, 89.

23. Nolan, *Poet*, 88; Rodgers, *Musical Stages*, 91–92.

24. Later he goes to see *Twinkle Twinkle*, "mainly to see Ona Munson. She wasn't awfully good, but the show – Ouch! You can't imagine anything worse." Richard Rodgers, *Letters to Dorothy (1926–1937)*, edited by William W. Appleton (New York: New York Public Library, 1988), 12.

25. Rodgers, *Letters*, 11.

26. Rodgers, *Letters*, 11.

27. Rodgers, *Letters*, 16.

28. Seymour Felix, "Novelty Dances Were Developed for 'Peggy-Ann' at Vanderbilt," *Herald Tribune*, January 16, 1927.

29. Alan Dale, "'Peggy-Ann,' Musical Play, Throws Dale into Ecstasy," *American*, January 8, 1927.

30. "'Peggy-Ann,' at Vanderbilt, Scores Strenuously for Tired Business Man," *Women's Wear*, December 28, 1926.

31. Untitled article, *Telegram*, January 18, 1927.

32. Herbert Fields, *Peggy-Ann*, libretto, LOC—Man D78188, 1926.

33. Hart and Kimball, *Complete Lyrics*, 92.

34. Herbert Fields, *Peggy-Ann*, libretto, RHO, 1926.

35. Ann Ommen van der Merwe, *The Ziegfeld Follies: A History in Song* (New York: Scarecrow Press, 2009), 72.

36. Marmorstein, *Ship*, 120.

37. Marmorstein, *Ship*, 117.

38. Rodgers, *Musical Stages*, 92.

39. Laurence Bergreen, *As Thousands Cheer: The Life of Irving Berlin* (London: Hodder & Stoughton 1990), 119.

40. Bergreen, *Thousands*, 191.

41. Rodgers, *Letters*, 16.

42. Rodgers, *Letters*, 13.

43. Hart, *Complete Lyrics*, 97.

44. Rodgers, *Letters*, 5.

45. Rodgers, *Letters*, 7–8.

46. Rodgers, *Letters*, 16–17.

47. Rodgers, *Letters*, 19.

48. Rodgers, *Musical Stages*, 93.

49. Walter Winchell, untitled article, *Evening Graphic*, December 29, 1926.

50. Untitled article, *Judge*, January 27, 1927.

51. Bide Dudley, untitled article, *Evening World*, December 29, 1926.

52. Untitled article, *New Yorker*, January 8, 1927.

53. J. H., "Ziegfeld Unveils 'Betsy,'" *World*, December 29, 1926.

54. Ph. J., "New National—'Betsy,'" *Washington Evening Star*, December 22, 1926.

55. Untitled article, *Journal of Commerce*, December 29, 1926.

56. George Goldsmith, "Ziegfeld 'Glorifies' 'Betsy,' New Comedy at the Amsterdam," *Herald Tribune*, December 29, 1926.

57. "'Betsy' Presented; Elaborately Staged," *Times*, December 29, 1926.

58. Goldsmith, "Ziegfeld 'Glorifies,'"

59. "'Betsy' Presented."

60. Sime, untitled article, *Variety*, January 5, 1927.

61. Lee Somers, "Ziegfeld's Latest Proves Marathon," *Washington Herald*, December 22, 1926.

62. Robert Coleman, "'Betsy' a Family Show," *Daily Mirror*, December 29, 1926.

63. Nathan Zatkin, untitled article, *Morning Telegraph*, December 29, 1926.

64. Coleman, "'Betsy' a Family Show."

65. J. H., "Ziegfeld Unveils."

66. Ph. J., "New National."

67. John J. Daly, "Ziegfeld's 'Betsy' Looks Good in Capital Premiere," *Washington Post*, December 22, 1926.

68. Stephen Rathbun, untitled article, *Sun*, December 29, 1926.

69. Irving Caesar and David Freedman, *Buy Buy Betty*, libretto, NYPL—FZ T-Mss 1987–010, series 1, Box 1, Folder 6, 1926.

70. Rodgers, *Musical Stages*, 96.

71. Kenneth Leish, "Interview with Mr. Richard Rodgers: February 21, 1968," transcript of Oral History Project interviews with Rodgers, 1967–8, in NYPL—RRP TMS-1987-006, Series III, Box 9, Folder 4, 112.

72. Ethan Mordden, *Ziegfeld: The Man Who Invented Show Business* (New York: St. Martin's Press, 2008), 235.

73. Bergreen, *Thousands*, 277.

74. Untitled article, *Telegram*, December 29, 1926.

75. Sime, untitled article, *Variety*, January 5, 1927.

76. Bergreen, *Thousands*, 119.

77. Untitled article, *Variety*, January 12, 1927.

78. Gilbert Kanour, "'She's My Baby' Has Pep, Charm," *Baltimore Evening Sun*, December 21, 1927.

79. Untitled article, *Variety*, January 12, 1927.

80. Sime, untitled article, *Variety*, January 5, 1927.

81. Untitled article, *New York World*, September 11, 1927.

82. "The Shrill Tone of 'Peggy-Ann,'" *London Evening News*, July 28, 1927.

83. "Musical Play with a Plot," *Westminster Gazette*, July 28, 1927.

CHAPTER 7

1. Rodgers, *Letters*, 24.

2. Rodgers, *Letters*, 29.

3. Rodgers, *Letters*, 29.

4. John Carlos Rowe, *Literary Culture and US Imperialism: From the Revolution to World War II* (Oxford: Oxford University Press, 2000), 129.

5. Rowe, *Literary Culture*, 134.

6. Twain, *Connecticut Yankee*, 244. Perhaps only a coincidence, Hart wrote the libretto for an operetta titled *Hello Central* in 1917.

7. Twain, *Connecticut Yankee*, 85.

8. Twain, *Connecticut Yankee*, 236.

9. The movie opened at the Selwyn Theater but transferred after ten weeks first to the Central and subsequently to the Capitol, where Rodgers recollects having seen it. Richard Rodgers, "Mr. Rodgers' Yankee," *New York Times*, November 21, 1943, X1; Aubrey Solomon, *Fox Film Corporation, 1915–1935: A History and Filmography* (Jefferson, NC: McFarland, 2011), 56; "The Screen," *New York Times*, August 8, 1921.

10. "Fox Offers New Twain Picture Based on Story of 'Connecticut Yankee,'" *New York Tribune*, March 13, 1921, 4.

11. Kevin J. Harty, *Cinema Arthuriana: Twenty Essays* (Jefferson, NC: McFarland, 2002), 11.

12. Solomon, *Fox Film*, 56.

13. "New Dunsany Play and Mark Twain Picture Capture London," *New York Tribune*, June 19, 1921, 2.

14. "Mr. Rodgers' Yankee," *New York Times*, November 21, 1943.

15. Fields and Fields, *From the Bowery*, 463–64.

16. Fields and Fields, *From the Bowery*, 464.

17. Twain, *Connecticut Yankee*, 1.

18. Hart and Kimball, *Complete Lyrics*, 107.

19. Block, *Richard Rodgers*, 52.

20. Hart and Kimball, *Complete Lyrics*, 111.

21. Nolan, *Lorenz Hart*, 107.

22. Cochran, *Cock-a-doodle-do*, 132.

23. The others are "With a Song in My Heart" from *Spring Is Here* (1929), "Lover"

from the film *Love Me Tonight* (1932), "Blue Moon" (originally written as "Prayer" but unused in the film *Hollywood Party* (1934), then rewritten as both "Manhattan Melodrama" and "The Bad in Every Man" for *Manhattan Melodrama* (1934), before becoming a hit with its now familiar title), "My Funny Valentine" from *Babes in Arms* (1937), and "Bewitched" from *Pal Joey* (1940). Rodgers also features in the list with a further three songs from his first collaborations with Oscar Hammerstein II: "You'll Never Walk Alone" from *Carousel* (1945), "It Might as Well Be Spring" from *State Fair* (1945), and "Some Enchanted Evening" from *South Pacific* (1949). This gives him a tally of nine of the top 100 songs, compared to Berlin's nine, Arlen's seven, Gershwin's six, Porter's six, and Kern's four. The list is included as Appendix 6 of Hamm, *Yesterdays*, 489–92. This list claims to show the top 100 songs from 1918 to 1935, though as is clear, the latter date must be wrong, and more likely to be 1950. As Hamm acknowledges (xxi), there is no indication as to how this list had been drawn up, so its statistics should be treated with some hesitation; nevertheless, as Block suggests, "My Heart Stood Still" is undoubtedly "one of the most popular songs of its era": Block, *Richard Rodgers*, 36.

24. Twain, *Connecticut Yankee*, 1.

25. Herbert Fields, *A Connecticut Yankee*, libretto, RHO, 1-2-19.

26. Ethan Mordden, *Make Believe: The Broadway Musical in the 1920s* (New York: Oxford University Press, 1997), 199.

27. J. Brooks Atkinson, "Mark Twain to Music," *Times*, November 4, 1927.

28. Percy Hammond, "'The Connecticut Yankee,' a Rich Song and Dance Thing with a Dubious Libretto," *Herald Tribune*, November 4, 1927.

29. Alexander Woollcott, "The Successor to Peggy-Ann," *World*, November 4, 1927.

30. Untitled article, *Advocate*, October 1, 1927.

31. Frank Vreeland, "Give This Little Round Table a Big Round Hand," *Telegram*, November 4, 1927.

32. Untitled article, *Advocate*, October 1, 1927.

33. J. F., "Twain's Yankee Set to Music at the Walnut," *Philadelphia Public Ledger*, October 4, 1927.

34. "Mark Twain's Tale a Musical Comedy," *Philadelphia Enquirer*, October 4, 1927. One context for *A Connecticut Yankee*'s reception, both in the press and by audiences, was a trend on Broadway for contemporized historical dramas throughout 1927. The instigator of this had been Robert Sherwood's play *The Road to Rome*, which opened at the Playhouse Theatre on January 31, 1927. The success on Broadway of a number of plays in this vein caused reviewers of *A Connecticut Yankee* to draw comparisons.

35. Marmorstein, *A Ship*, 136.

36. Rodgers, *Musical Stages*, 108.

37. Hart and Kimball, *Complete Lyrics*, 108.

38. Wood, "Song Forms," 204.

39. Wood, "Song Forms," 204.

40. Deena Rosenberg writes of "Fascinating Rhythm" that "from the moment the song begins, the 'fascinating rhythm' of the title seems to bewitch the music and lyrics themselves. In the refrain, it is difficult to beat a steady pulse. The lyric, in turn,

comes out sounding as breathless as the music; the syllables seem to stumble and fall over one another, the music to actually 'quiver'"; "Fascinating Rhythms," sleevenotes to *Lady, Be Good!*, Elektra Nonesuch 7559-79308-2, 28–29.

41. Allen Forte, *The American Popular Ballad of the Golden Era: 1924–1950* (Princeton, NJ: Princeton University Press, 1995), 182.

42. Crosby's earlier version of "Thou Swell" (1955) can be found at the Internet Archive http://archive.org/details/BingCrosby-500-510. The second recording, from *At My Time of Life* (United Artists, 1976), can be found on the album *The Complete United Artists Sessions* (1997), EMI 7243 8 59808 2 4.

43. Wilder, *American Popular Song*, 175.

44. One of Astaire's most famous hits, Irving Berlin's "Top Hat, White Tie and Tails" (1935), is a good example, abusing the barlines in its verse in a similar way as "Thou Swell" ("Nothing now could take the wind out of my sails").

45. Forte, *American Popular Ballad*, 21.

46. John Martin, "The Dance: New Musical Comedy Talent," *New York Times*, July 22, 1928.

47. Allison Robbins, "Busby Berkeley, Broken Rhythms, and Dance Direction on the Stage and Screen," *Studies in Musical Theatre* 7, no.1 (2013): 79.

48. Wood, "Song Forms," 204.

49. Forte, *American Popular Ballad*, 180–81.

50. It is also worth noting, as many commentators have, that the dated dialogue of the script approximates Elizabethan dialogue far more than Arthurian: none of the team were interested so much in accuracy as in effect, and it is reasonable to say that a theater audience would be more familiar with language associated with, for example, Shakespeare, than they would with the language of the Dark Ages.

51. Waters, "Connecticut Yankee," *Variety*, October 12, 1927.

52. Fields, *Connecticut Yankee*, 1-3-36/7.

53. Fields, *Connecticut Yankee*, 1-3-38.

54. Twain, *Connecticut Yankee*, 26.

55. Fields, *Connecticut Yankee*, 1-3-52.

56. Fields, *Connecticut Yankee*, 1-3-61.

57. This is the final section of the Act One Finale, which Kimball refers to as "Ibbidi Bibbidi Sibbidi Sab" in *Complete Lyrics*, 109.

58. J. B. T. Marsh, *The Jubilee Singers and Their Songs* (Mineola, NY: Dover, 2003), 251.

59. Marsh, *Jubilee Singers*, 296.

60. Seward in Marsh, *Jubilee Singers*, 156.

61. One staging of the song can be seen in the 1955 telecast of the show, directed by Max Liebman and available on DVD.

62. The Egyptians worshipped the sun, reminding us that an earlier Rodgers, Hart, and Fields take on Twain's novel had been *A Danish Yankee in King Tut's Court* (1923); Rimsky-Korsakov's opera *Le Coq d'Or*, which was the inspiration for *Say It with Jazz* (1921), includes a "Hymn to the Sun."

63. Berlin's "Blue Skies," whose performance history has been meticulously traced by Jeffrey Magee, is a particularly interesting example, since its interpolation in Rodgers and Hart's *Betsy* (1926) had been so contentious.

64. Seward in Marsh, *Jubilee Singers*, 155.

65. Block, *Richard Rodgers*, 56.

66. The Rodgers and Hammerstein Organization has two slightly different drafts of the script, both dated 1927; the Lord Chamberlain's Plays collection at the British Library has a third prepared for the London production with only slight amendments that target topical references at an English audience.

67. Fields, *Connecticut Yankee* (1927a), 2-1-1; Fields, *Connecticut Yankee* (1927b), 2-1-1.

68. Jeffrey Spivak, *Buzz: The Life and Art of Busby Berkeley* (Lexington: University Press of Kentucky, 2011), 34.

69. Fields, *Connecticut Yankee* (1927a), p.2-1-6.

70. Hart and Kimball, *Complete Lyrics*, 109–10.

71. Hart and Kimball, *Complete Lyrics*, 110. Hart and Kimball maintain that the song changed simply in terms of its title and its references to Morgan (i.e., the line "Evelyn, Evelyn, what do you say?" was formerly "Morgan, Morgan, Morgan Le Fay").

72. Spivak, *Buzz*, 34.

73. Fields, *Connecticut Yankee* (1927b), 2-3-22.

74. Twain, *Connecticut Yankee*, 78.

75. Twain, *Connecticut Yankee*, 101.

76. Hart and Kimball, *Complete Lyrics*, 110.

77. Ralph Holmes, untitled article, *Detroit Evening Times*, July 30, 1929.

78. By 1927, Cecil B. de Mille had directed, among many other films, *The Ten Commandments* (1923) and *The King of Kings* (1927); Samuel Goldwyn produced *Potash and Perlmutter* (1923) and had set up the Samuel Goldwyn Company by 1924; Ernst Lubitsch emigrated to America in 1922 and directed for Warner Bros. and then MGM; and Karl Laemmle was one of the founders of Universal Studios in 1912.

79. John Anderson, untitled article, *Evening Post*, November 4, 1927.

80. Untitled article, *Life*, November 24, 1927.

81. Alan Dale, "Dale Finds Much to Praise in Play from Twain Novel," *American*, November 4, 1927.

82. J. F., "Twain's Yankee Set to Music at the Walnut," *Philadelphia Public Ledger*, October 4, 1927.

83. Prompter, "The Lorgnette," *Observer* 29, no. 48 (August 14, 1909): 6.

84. S. R. L., "Mark Twain Set to Music," *London Morning Post*, October 11, 1929.

85. Alan Parsons, "Mark Twain Musical Play," unattributed clipping, October 11, 1929.

86. Untitled article, *London Times*, October 11, 1929.

CHAPTER 8

1. *Present Arms* managed a solid 155 performances, which at the time Rodgers referred to as "a flop": Rodgers, *Letters*, 63.

2. Nolan claims that it was Lorenz Hart who first discovered *The Son of the Grand Eunuch* (*Lorenz Hart*, 118); Fields and Fields suggest it was Herbert Fields (*From the Bowery*, 484). What all agree on is that Rodgers was approached later by his other two collaborators.

3. "Chinese Life: The Son of the Grand Eunuch," *New York Times Book Review*, July 31, 1927, 18.

4. Dorothy Parker (as Constant Reader), "Reading and Writing: Far from Well," *New Yorker*, October 20, 1928, 99.

5. "Books: Lickerish Lacquer," *Time Magazine*, May 12, 1930. Other books in the series included *The Woman Who Commanded 500,000,000 Men* (1929) and *The Impotent General* (1931).

6. Rodgers, *Musical Stages*, 117.

7. Nolan, *Lorenz Hart*, 119.

8. Versions of the show's ending differ: this version is given in Fields and Fields, *From the Bowery*, 487; some commentaries suggest that Tchou's brother-in-law Prince Tao Tee swaps places with the surgeon to conduct a fake operation—see, for example, Nolan, *Lorenz Hart*, 118; Gerald Bordman, *American Musical Theatre: A Chronicle* (third edition) (Oxford: Oxford University Press, 2001), 492; Stanley Green, *Rodgers and Hammerstein Fact Book: A Record of Their Work Together and with Other Collaborators* (New York: Lynn Farnol Group, 1980), 94–95. Rubin suggests that the two different versions come from different libretti: one incomplete script held in the Dorothy Fields papers of the Billy Rose Theatre Collection in NYPL, and an apparently later script held by the Rodgers and Hammerstein Organization. "The Rodgers and Hammerstein Theatre Library script appears to be a later version because it clarifies the plot where it is ambiguous and inconsistent in the other version" (Rubin, "Lew Fields," 522n). It is the second of these scripts on which my research has focused.

9. Secrest, *Somewhere for Me*; Marx and Clayton, *Bewitched*; Nolan, *Lorenz Hart*.

10. Brooks Atkinson, untitled review, *New York Times*, September 26, 1928.

11. St. John Ervine, "Nasty! Nasty!," *New York World*, September 26, 1928.

12. Mel Gussow, "It's Always 'Rodgers &' Musical Time," *New York Times*, August 5, 1975, 21.

13. George John Nathan, untitled review, *Judge*, October 20, 1928;

14. Burns Mantle, "Music Most Salable Feature of the New Mansfield Effusion," *New York Daily News*, September 26, 1928.

15. Marx and Clayton, *Rodgers and Hart*, 129.

16. Rodgers, *Musical Stages*, 119.

17. Marybeth Hamilton, "Mae West Live: 'Sex, the Drag, and 1920s Broadway,'" *Drama Review* 36, no. 4 (Winter, 1992): 86.

18. Of *Betsy* (1926): Fields and Fields, *From the Bowery*, 434.

19. Of *Present Arms* (1928): Fields and Fields, *From the Bowery*, 476.

20. Fields and Fields, *From the Bowery*, 483.

21. Fields and Fields, *From the Bowery*, 422.

22. Untitled article, *Stage*, October 18, 1928.

23. Fields and Fields, *From the Bowery*, 486.

24. See George Chauncey, *Gay New York: Gender, Urban Culture, and the Making of the Gay Male World, 1890–1940* (New York: Basic Books, 1994), 327 and elsewhere.

25. Wayne R. Dynes, *The Encyclopedia of Homosexuality* (New York: Garland, 1990), 249.

26. Dynes, *The Encyclopedia of Homosexuality*, 411.

27. "The Story of Violets," *Harper's Bazaar*, November 1934. Cited in Norma Bered-jiklian, "The Violets of Dutchess County," *Violet Gazette*, 2000, V1-4, 3. Prior to this, the violet had been universally popular, and Beredjiklian even writes of "violet-mania" breaking out in early 1900s New York. This earlier love affair with the violet prompted both Yale University and New York University to link the flower to their sports teams, an association that—in the guise of the NYU Violets and with no ostensible homosexual overtones—exists to this day.

28. J. R. Couch, "Are These Queer Times? Gay Male Representation on the American Stage in the 1920's and 1990's" (MA diss., University of Kentucky, 2003), 16.

29. Basil Rathbone, *In and Out of Character* (New York: Doubleday, 1956), 101–2.

30. Hamilton, "Mae West Live," 90.

31. A third production, William Francis Dugan's *The Virgin Man*, was also raided by police on the same night.

32. Hamilton, "Mae West Live," 97.

33. Hamilton, "Mae West Live," 92.

34. George Chauncey Jr., "The Policed: Gay Men's Strategies of Everyday Resist-ance," in William R. Taylor, ed., *Inventing Times Square: Commerce and Culture at the Crossroads of the World* (Baltimore: Johns Hopkins University Press, 1996), 320.

35. Chauncey, "The Policed," 321.

36. Chauncey, "The Policed," 317–18.

37. Hamilton, "Mae West Live," 90.

38. Fields, *Chee-Chee*, 1.

39. Fields, *Chee-Chee*, 2. The Eunuchs quickly slip into rather conventional musical comedy ensemble figures—comedic, characterless ciphers that act as stooges for the principal characters. At times, they resemble the male chorus from a Gilbert and Sullivan operetta (there is more than a whiff of *The Mikado* throughout the show), and—as expected—Rodgers and Hart employ lyrical and musical patterns that are recognizably Gilbert and Sullivan-esque ("We bow our heads in reverence / Lest we would feel their severance": Fields, *Chee-Chee*, 4).

40. Of course, cross-dressing has been a staple part of theatrical comedy for cen-turies, and this minor comic conceit does not queer the play to anything like the extent that, say, the cross-dressing of *Twelfth Night* or *As You Like It* does.

41. Nolan, *Lorenz Hart*, 192.

42. Nolan, *Lorenz Hart*, 238.

43. Nolan, *Lorenz Hart*, 118.

44. Fields and Fields suggest another psychoanalytical reading of Herb Fields's attraction to the show, noting that his relation with his father and his inheritance of Lew Fields's career path bears some resemblance to the father-son relationship in *Chee-Chee*: Fields and Fields, *From the Bowery*, 485.

45. In the Owl's song, a hastily handwritten insertion to the libretto. Fields, *Chee-Chee*, n.p.

46. Fields, *Chee-Chee*, Act One, 4.

47. Fields, *Chee-Chee*, Act One, 4–5.

48. Fields, *Chee-Chee*, Act One, 11.

49. Fields, *Chee-Chee*, Act Two, i.7.

50. Fields, *Chee-Chee*, Act Two, iv.3.

51. Fields, *Chee-Chee*, Act One, i.8.

52. Among the many discussions of gender, sexuality, and the chorus line, I find Siegfried Kracauer's Marxist essay "The Mass Ornament" (written in 1927, the year before *Chee-Chee*) to be particularly interesting: in Siegfried Kracauer, *The Mass Ornament: Weimar Essays*, ed. Thomas Y. Levin (Cambridge, MA: Harvard University Press, 1995), 75–87.

53. Cultural attitudes were indeed extremely different in the 1920s, as can be seen in this flippant review of *Lido Lady* by self-proclaimed "serious critic" Harris Deans: "Let us be seriously, even perhaps painfully, serious for a moment. Just oblige me by concentrating—mentally—on Girls. Which is the most popular girl you know? Oh, tut-tut-tut-tut, I wasn't asking was her name Bobby, or Bunnie, or Bee, or Binks, or whatever it is you modern lads call the girl of your heart; what I am trying to get at is what sort of a wench is she?" Harris Deans, "The Stage of the Day," *Illustrated Sporting and Dramatic News*, December 11, 1926, 256.

54. Fields and Fields, *From the Bowery*, 489.

55. "It got five pans, two half-and-halfs, and six raves": Mordden, *Make Believe*, 199.

56. E. W. Osborn, *New York Evening World*, September 26, 1928.

57. Rodgers, *Letters*, 63.

58. Rodgers, *Letters*, 65.

59. Rodgers, *Letters*, 64.

60. Rodgers, *Letters*, 63.

61. Rodgers, *Musical Stages*, 118.

62. Rubin, "Lew Fields," 518.

63. *Chee-Chee* program, AS, 1928, 37. Rodgers also references this in *Musical Stages*, 118.

64. Five of these songs ("Dear, Oh Dear," "Moon of My Delight," "Singing a Love Song," "I Must Love You," and "Better Be Good to Me") were recorded by Betty Comden on her 1963 album, *Remember These: Songs from "Treasure Girl" and "Chee Chee,"* Ava Records A-26.

65. Rubin, "Lew Fields," 519.

66. Marc Miller, "Chee-Chee," online review at *Theatre Mania.com*, November 18, 2002. http://www.theatermania.com/new-york/reviews/11-2002/cheechee_2798.html. Accessed February 26, 2011.

67. Rodgers, *Musical Stages*, 118.

68. Fields, *Chee-Chee*, Act One, i,7.

69. Several other points in the libretto have similar indicators, though apparently no corresponding numbers exist. In some cases, a gap in the layout of the page indicates some intention for a song to be featured, though no material exists.

70. Copyright for "Dear, Oh Dear!" was filed at the Library of Congress some three weeks later than the rest of the songs from the score, which supports Rodgers's claim that it was a last-minute addition: see Block, *Reader*, 42.

71. Hart and Kimball, Complete Lyrics, 125.

72. Hart and Kimball, Complete Lyrics, 127.

73. Act Two, scene three, is the point suggested by Hart and Kimball for this number.

74. Rodgers, *Musical Stages*, 118. The same number of songs is acknowledged by Bordman (*Chronicle*, 493) and, as we have seen, Rubin ("Lew Fields," 519). Rodgers does not identify the six songs, though the program lists "I Must Love You," "Dear, Oh, Dear," "Moon of My Delight," "Better Be Good to Me," and "The Tartar Song."

75. Passages from "I Must Love You" were also recycled in "Send for Me" from *Simple Simon* (1930); meanwhile, rewritten lyrics to "Moon of My Delight" date from around 1931–32 in a song called "Thank You in Advance." As Block suggests, "when Rodgers gave up on a show (for example, *Betsy, She's My Baby, Chee-Chee*) he felt no compunction about reusing songs from these shows, with or without new titles and lyrics": Block, *Richard Rodgers*, 63.

76. Chti joins in with "Just a Little Thing" in response to Li Pi Siao; given the more simplistic musical material it seems more likely that this was intended for the court character Li Pi Siao (with Chti) rather than for Tchou and Chti, to whom Hart and Kimball attribute this song.

77. Fields and Fields, *From the Bowery*, 231, 247, 409, 480.

78. Couch, "Queer Times?," 18; see also Atkinson, *Broadway*, 248, and Rubin, "Lew Fields," 516.

79. Peretti, *Nightclub City*, 63.

80. Laurence Senelick, "Private Parts in Public Places," in Taylor, *Inventing*, 329–53, 334.

81. Shubert retaliated, clearly making a point with a call for productions of two highly regarded plays to be shut down—Ben Jonson's *Volpone* and Eugene O'Neill's *Strange Interlude*.

82. John H. Houchin, *Censorship of the American Theatre in the Twentieth Century* (Cambridge: Cambridge University Press, 2003), 106.

83. Quoted in Houchin, *Censorship*, 106.

84. Jill Watts, *Mae West: An Icon in Black and White* (Oxford: Oxford University Press, 2001), 111.

85. Couch, "Queer Times?," 19.

86. Watts, *Mae West*, 114.

87. *Variety*, October 3, 1928. Reviews in Green, *Fact Book*, 94–95.

88. Rodgers's letters to Dorothy not only reveal an animosity toward Helen Ford but also suggest that he had by this time fallen out with musical director Roy Webb: "It seems that Roy sort of fell apart on us and there were so many complaints that something had to be done" (Block, *Reader*, 42). Webb was removed from the show and Rodgers himself took over the musical direction of the orchestra.

CHAPTER 9

1. "The Matter of Song Hits," *Times*, October 21, 1928.

2. Untitled clipping, *New York World*, September 30, 1928.

3. Rodgers, *Musical Stages*, 120.

4. Samuel Marx, "Now That I Come to Think of It," *New York Amusements*, October 21, 1929.

5. Rodgers, *Musical Stages*, 117.

6. Secrest, *Richard Rodgers*, 110–11.

7. Ward Morehouse, "Temporary Retirement for Rodgers and Hart—7 Plays Next Week—Mrs. Selwyn Signed," *Sun*, October 17, 1928.

8. "Preparing 'Loving Ann,'" *New York Times*, December 17, 1928.

9. Rodgers, *Musical Stages*, 124.

10. Nolan, *Lorenz Hart*, 125.

11. Marmorstein, *A Ship*, 152–53.

12. Untitled article, *New Yorker*, March 23 1929.

13. Untitled article, *Judge*, April 6, 1929.

14. Richard Watts Jr., untitled article, *Herald Tribune*, July 22, 1929.

15. H.T.M., "'Spring Is Here' Proves Likable Show at Shubert," *Evening Public Ledger*, February 26, 1929.

16. Bide Dudley, untitled article, *Evening World*, March 12, 1929.

17. Burns Mantle, untitled article, *Daily News*, March 12, 1929.

18. J. Brooks Atkinson, untitled article, *Times*, March 12, 1929.

19. "An Athletic Musical Comedy with a Strong Flavor of Vaudeville," *Philadelphia Inquirer*, February 26, 1929.

20. Untitled article, *New York Amusements*, March 18, 1929.

21. The Callboy, untitled article, *Philadelphia Inquirer*, March 3, 1929.

22. Block, *Richard Rodgers*, 42.

23. Marmorstein, *A Ship*, 155.

24. Rodgers, *Musical Stages*, 124.

25. Rodgers, *Musical Stages*, 125. Guests were listed in the *Paris Herald* on April 24, 1929.

26. Guests were listed in the *Paris Herald* on April 30, 1929.

27. Guests were listed in the *Paris Herald* on May 8, 1929.

28. "Richard Rodgers Considers Opera to Dodge Comedy," *Paris Herald*, April 29, 1929.

29. "Richard Rodgers Considers Opera."

30. Untitled article, *Sun*, May 13, 1929.

31. "Richard Rodgers Considers Opera."

32. Rodgers, *Musical Stages*, 56. This was a reference to Gershwin having beaten Rodgers to his first Broadway hit show, even though "Any Old Place with You" predated any individual song by Gershwin on Broadway.

33. Peyser, *The Memory*, 74.

34. Deems Taylor, "Music," *New York World*, February 17, 1924.

35. Samuel Chotzinoff, "New York Symphony at Carnegie Hall," *New York World*, December 4, 1925.

36. Rodgers, *Musical Stages*, 121.

37. Rodgers, *Musical Stages*, 121.

38. Rodgers, *Letters*, 77.

39. Rodgers, *Letters*, 76.

40. Untitled article, *Telegram*, March 14, 1929.

41. "Fields, Rodgers & Hart, Inc.," *Screenland*, October, 1928.

42. Percy N. Stone, "The Pair that Broke Broadway of Its 'Love' and 'Dove' Habit," *Herald Tribune*, March 24, 1929.

43. Rodgers, *Letters*, 77.

44. Lew Levenson, "Jazz Is Moaning Low the 'Left Alone Blues,'" *New York World*, January 12, 1930.

45. Henry T. Murdock, untitled article, *Philadelphia Evening Public Ledger*, October 26, 1929.

46. W. A. U., "'Heads Up,' Musical Comedy. Lively, Gay, Tuneful," *Evening Journal*, November 12, 1929.

47. Rodgers, *Musical Stages*, 127.

48. Owen Davis, *I'd Like to Do It Again* (New York: Farrar and Rinehart, 1931), 205.

49. "Re-Vamp till Ready," *New York Times*, December 29, 1929. Marx and Clayton erroneously report that "Dick and Larry were not involved in the rescue effort—no new lyrics needed to be rewritten; no additional melodies composed." *Bewitched*, 134.

50. Hart and Kimball, *Complete Lyrics*, 140–43.

51. Lorenz, Hart, "A Lesson in Song Writing: How We Wrote the Hit Song of 'Heads Up!'" *New York World*, December 1, 1929. This article is reprinted in Hart and Kimball, *Complete Lyrics*, 145.

52. "'Heads Up' Song Hit Really Was Written in Less than an Hour," *Herald Tribune*, January 5, 1930.

53. "'Heads Up' Song Hit Really Was Written."

54. E. K., "'Heads Up!' at the Palace," *Daily Telegraph*, May 1930; similar sentiments are expressed by H. S., "Sydney Howard's Best Yet," *Daily Express*, May 2, 1930.

55. Hart and Kimball, *Complete Lyrics*, 140.

56. Hart and Kimball, *Complete Lyrics*, 44.

57. J. H. Keen, untitled article, *Philadelphia Daily News*, October 26, 1929.

58. Frank Smith, "'Me for You' Makes Its Bow—and Looms as Another Hit," *Detroit Daily News*, September 16, 1929.

59. Isaac Goldberg, "Men of Notes, of Parts and Tuneful Puns," *Boston Evening Transcript*, February 1, 1930.

60. Hart and Kimball, *Complete Lyrics*, 141.

61. Hart and Kimball, *Complete Lyrics*, 142.

62. H. F. Manchester, untitled article, *Boston Herald*, November 3, 1929.

63. Hart and Kimball, *Complete Lyrics*, p.143.

64. Russell McLaughlin, "Lots of Tunes, Plenty Talent," *Detroit News*, September 16, 1929.

65. Hart and Kimball, *Complete Lyrics*, 142.

66. Ben Washer, "Lorenz Hart Visions New Type of Musical Show in Broadway," *New York Telegram*, August 20, 1930.

67. Levenson, "Jazz Is Moaning."

68. "Dimitri Tiomkin the Great Russian Pianist," promotional material, New York: Bogue Laberge, 1930.

69. "Rodgers Becomes Ambitious," *New York Sun*, February 7, 1930.

70. "Writing the Hits," *Hollywood News*, February 24, 1930.

71. In *Musical Stages* Rodgers implies that this offer came far later, and at least after the crash: "in the closing days of 1929 it was not the time to refuse any reasonable proposal" (*Musical Stages*, 131); in fact, as he reports to Dorothy, the offer was made around July 19 and the contract signed around August 14 (*Letters*, 75, 78).

72. Libben, untitled article, *Variety*, February 5, 1930.

73. W. E. G., "Colonial Theatre: Simple Simon," *Boston Herald*, January 28, 1930.

74. Libben, untitled article.

75. Arthur Pollock, "Ed Wynn Comes to the Ziegfeld Theater in One of Mr. Ziegfeld's Handsome Entertainments Called 'Simple Simon,'" *Brooklyn Daily Eagle*, February 19, 1930.

76. S. L. P., untitled article, *New York Wall Street News*, February 25, 1930.

77. Arthur Ruhl, untitled article, *Herald Tribune*, February 19, 1930.

78. Pollock, "Ed Wynn."

79. Gilbert W. Gabriel, "Ed Wynn's Back Again!," *New York American*, February 19, 1930.

80. Untitled article, *New York Telegraph*, February 20, 1930.

81. Burns Mantle, untitled article, *Daily News*, February 19, 1930.

82. Rodgers, *Musical Stages*, 132.

83. Burns Mantle, untitled article.

84. F. P. Dunne Jr., "Mr. Z., the Glorifier, Steps to Bat for 'Simple Simon' as a 5 Buck Show," *New York World*, February 7, 1930.

85. "Those Hart-Rodgers-Fields Boys," *Bnai Brith Magazine*, January 1930.

86. "Fields, Rodgers and Hart," *New York Evening Post*, August 16, 1930.

87. James Gow, "Fields, Rodgers and Hart to Begin Work on New Musical Show," *New York World*, August 19, 1930.

88. Rodgers, *Musical Stages*, 143.

89. Rodgers, *Musical Stages*, 142.

90. Rodgers, *Musical Stages*, 138.

91. Margaret Reid, "Three Young Men of Manhattan," *Cinema* (December, 1930): 23, 58.

92. Reid, "Three Young Men of Manhattan."

93. Reid, "Three Young Men of Manhattan."

94. "At the Warner Strand," *New York Sun*, March 14, 1931.

95. It's also a topical theme, and one that others would also touch on: around the same time, the Gershwins also came out west to work on their first original film, *Delicious* (1931), which featured "Rhapsody in Rivets," later the basis of Gershwin's "Second Rhapsody."

96. Washer, "Lorenz Hart Visions."

97. Rodgers, *Letters*, 94.

98. Rodgers, *Letters*, 97.

99. Rodgers, *Letters*, 93.

100. "Fast Farce on View," *American*, March 14, 1931.

101. "At the Warner Strand," *New York Sun*, March 14, 1931; W. B., "Musical Comedy at Strand Suffers from Lack of Songs," *World Telegram*, March 14, 1931.

102. Rodgers, *Letters*, 93.

103. Rodgers, *Letters*, 97.

104. Rodgers, *Letters*, 97.

105. James Gow, "A Confidential Report on Hollywood Life from Messrs. Rodgers and Fields," *New York World*, August 24, 1930.

106. Rodgers, *Letters*, 91.

107. Marmorstein, *A Ship*, 177.

108. Gow, "A Confidential Report."

109. Marx and Clayton, *Bewitched*, 143.

110. Marmorstein, *A Ship*, 177, 196.

111. Nolan, *Lorenz Hart*, 144.

112. Hart and Kimball, *Complete Lyrics*, 83.

113. Hart and Kimball, *Complete Lyrics*, 143.

114. The advent of talking pictures marked a challenge for many a silent screen star, some of whom—like Marion Davies, or John Barrymore's wife Dolores Costello—really did suffer from speech impediments that were highlighted by the microphones. The theme of sound pictures revealing unexpected vocal character traits has become somewhat romanticized, with both *Singin' in the Rain* (1952) and *The Artist* (2011) hingeing on this plot-twist. In 1931, of course, it was fairly new material.

115. Mabelle Jennings, "We Get a New Musical Comedy, and Lean More towards the Lyrics than the Lines . . . But 'America's Sweetheart' Is a Pretty, Peppy Gal, All the Same," *Washington Daily News*, January 27, 1931.

116. John Anderson, untitled article, *Evening Journal*, February 11, 1931.

117. Harvey Gaul, "American Premiere of 'America's Sweetheart' Is Genuine Smash Hit," *Pittsburgh Post-Gazette*, January 20, 1931.

118. Gaul, "American Premiere."

119. Cohen, "'America's Sweetheart.'"

120. Arthur Ruhl, "Schwab and Mandel Present Fields-Rodgers-Hart Musical at the Broadhurst," *Herald Tribune*, February 11, 1931.

121. Lockridge, "'America's Sweetheart,'"

122. J. Brooks Atkinson, "Lampooning the Screen," *New York Times*, February 11, 1931.

123. Dorothy Parker, untitled article, *New Yorker*, February 21, 1931.

124. Atkinson, "Lampooning the Screen."

125. "'America's Sweetheart,'" *London Stage*, March, 1931.

126. Jennings, "We Get a New Musical Comedy."

127. Jennings, "We Get a New Musical Comedy."

128. Atkinson, "Lampooning the Screen."

129. Vandamm, picture caption, *Theatre Magazine*, April 1931.

130. Robert Coleman, "New Musical Show at the Broadhurst Here for Long Run," *Daily Mirror*, February 11, 1931.

131. Robert Littell, "Fun in the Film Studios," *New York World*, February 11, 1931.

132. Charles Darnton, untitled article, *Evening World*, February 11, 1931.

133. The verse to "I've Got Five Dollars" is given a key signature of three sharps, to imply that it is in A major; actually, it is really just an extended articulation of the dominant leading into the tonic D of the refrain. On publication, "I've Got Five Dollars" and "A Lady Must Live" were published in E-flat major; "There's So Much More" and "I Want a Man," imported from other shows, are both in F (though again, the sketches for "I Want a Man" are written in D.

134. Atkinson, "Lampooning the Screen."

135. Richard Lockridge, "'America's Sweetheart,'" *New York Sun*, February 11, 1931.

136. Rodgers, *Musical Stages*, 148.

137. Stanley Green in Block, *Reader*, 73.

138. Rodgers and Hammerstein also make use of rhythmic speech patterns in several songs, including "It's a Scandal! It's a Outrage!" from *Oklahoma!* (1943) and the Bench Scene from *Carousel* (1945).

139. Laurence E. MacDonald, *The Invisible Art of Film Music: A Comprehensive History* (second edition) (Lanham, MD: Scarecrow Press, 2013), 23.

140. With a far more "American" sound than either Steiner or Tiomkin, Newman can perhaps be said to have brought Broadway to Hollywood rather than forging a new quasi-European aesthetic for the screen.

141. Felix Cox, "'A Faltering Step in a Basically Right Direction': Richard Rodgers and *All Points West*," *American Music* 23, no.3 (Autumn 2005): 355–76.

142. Rodgers, *Musical Stages*, 180.

BIBLIOGRAPHY

Reference to newspaper articles throughout the book come from a variety of sources in various archives. Many clippings were collected by Richard Rodgers in his scrapbooks, now housed at the New York Public Library (NYPL-RRS).

AS	Alvah Sulloway Sheet Music and Theater Program Collection, University of New Hampshire
BL-LC	Lord Chamberlain's Collection, British Library, London
CU-VSR	Varsity Show Records, University Archives, Rare Book and Manuscript Library, Columbia University Library, New York
LOC-Man	Manuscript Division, Library of Congress, Washington, DC
LOC-RRC	Richard Rodgers Collection, Music Division, Library of Congress, Washington, DC
NYPL-FZ	Flo Ziegfeld–Billie Burke Papers, 1907–1984, Theatre Division, Billy Rose Theatre Collection, New York Public Library for the Performing Arts, Dorothy and Lewis B. Cullman Center, New York
NYPL-RRP	Richard Rodgers Papers, Billy Rose Theatre Collection, New York Public Library for the Performing Arts, Dorothy and Lewis B. Cullman Center, New York
NYPL-RRS	Richard Rodgers Scrapbooks, Music Division, New York Public Library for the Performing Arts, Dorothy and Lewis B. Cullman Center, New York
RHO	Rodgers and Hammerstein Organization, New York
VA-RJ	Ronald Jeans Scrapbooks, Theatre Museum Collection, Victoria and Albert Museum, London
YU	Beinecke Manuscripts Library, Yale University, New Haven, CT

MUSICAL SCORES BY RICHARD RODGERS

Rodgers, Richard. *A Connecticut Yankee* (1927). Reconstructed piano-conductor score by Wayne A. Blood and Bruce Pomahac. RHO.

Rodgers, Richard. *Dearest Enemy* (1925). Reconstructed piano-conductor score. Edited by Larry Moore. RHO.

Rodgers, Richard. *The Girl Friend* (1926). Reconstructed piano-conductor score by James Stenborg. RHO.

Rodgers, Richard. *Peggy-Ann* (1926). Piano-vocal score. RHO.

Rodgers, Richard, and Lorenz Hart. "Lady Raffles Behave." From *Poor Little Ritz Girl*. Published sheet music. New York: Jerome H. Remick, 1920.

Rodgers, Richard, and Lorenz Hart. "On with the Dance." From the *Garrick Gaieties*. Published sheet music. New York: Edward B. Marks Music Co., 1925.

LIBRETTOS AND SCRIPTS

Caesar, Irving, and David Freedman. *Betsy*. Libretto. NYPL–FZ T-Mss 1987-010. Series 1, Box 1, Folder 5, 1926.

Caesar, Irving, and David Freedman. *Buy Buy Betty*. Libretto. NYPL–FZ T-Mss 1987-010. Series 1, Box 1, Folder 6, 1926.

Davis, Owen. *Spring Is Here*. Libretto. LOC–Man D87693, 1929.

Fields, Herbert. *A Connecticut Yankee*. Libretto. RHO, 1927.

Fields, Herbert. *Dearest Enemy*. Libretto. RHO, 1925.

Fields, Herbert. *Peggy-Ann*. Libretto. LOC–Man D78188, 1926.

Fields, Herbert. *Peggy-Ann*. Libretto. RHO, 1926.

Fields, Herbert. *Present Arms*. Libretto. LOC–Man D82957, 1928.

Fields, Herbert. *Sweet Rebel*. Libretto. LOC–Man D69211, 1924.

Jeans, Ronald. *Lido Lady*. Libretto. BL–LCP 1926/39, no.7155, 1926.

Jeans, Ronald. *One Dam Thing after Another*. Libretto. BL–LCP 1927/19, no.7641, 1927.

Kroopf, Milton, and Phillip Leavitt. *Fly with Me*. Libretto. The Columbia Varsity Show of 1920. Adapted by Michael Numark under the supervision of Andrew B. Harris for The Columbia Varsity Show of 1980. With music and lyrics by Richard Rodgers, Lorenz Hart, and Oscar Hammerstein II. LOC ML50.R67 F7, 1982.

Levy, Benn W. (unattributed). *Ever Green*. Libretto. BL–LCP 1930/43, no.9944, 1930.

McGowan, John, and Paul Gerard Smith. *Heads Up!* Libretto. LOC–Man D3974, 1930.

Rodgers, Richard C., Lorenz M. Hart, and Herbert Fields. *The Jazz King*. Libretto. LOC–Man D64166, 1923.

Wynn, Ed. *Simple Simon*. Libretto. LOC–Man D4544, 1930.

PROGRAMS

America's Sweetheart. Broadhurst Theatre (1931). NYPL–RRS JPH 85-5, Book 5.

Chee-Chee. Mansfield Theatre (1928). AS.

Connecticut Yankee, A. Vanderbilt Theatre (1927). NYPL T-PRG.

Ever Green. Adelphi Theatre (1930). *Ever Green* production file. VA.

Fifth Avenue Follies, The. Fifth Avenue Club (1926). NYPL–RRS JPH 85-5, Book 2.

Fly with Me. The Columbia University Varsity Show (1920). CU–VSR Box 10, Folder 2.

Fly with Me. The Columbia University Varsity Show (1980). CU–VSR Box 16, Folder 17.

Garrick Gaieties. Garrick Theatre (1925). NYPL–RRS JPH 85-5, Book 2.

Garrick Gaieties. Guild Theatre (1926). NYPL–MWEZ+nc 7745.

Girl Friend, The. Vanderbilt Theatre (1926). NYPL T-PRG.

Heads Up! Alvin Theatre (1929). NYPL T-PRG.

Lido Lady. Gaiety Theatre, London. (1926). VA–RJ, Scrapbook 16, File 9.

Me for You. Shubert Detroit Opera House (1929). NYPL–MWEZ+nc 21333.

Melody Man, The. 49th Street Theatre (1924). NYPL T-PRG.

One Dam Thing after Another. Pavilion Theatre, London. 1927. VA–RJ, Scrapbook 17 S.186-1988.

Peggy-Ann. Vanderbilt Theatre (1926). NYPL–MWEZ+nc 5990.

Poor Little Ritz Girl, The. Wilbur Theatre, Boston (1920). NYPL–RRS JPH 85-5, Book 1.

Present Arms. Mansfield Theatre (1928). NYPL T-PRG.

She's My Baby. Globe Theatre (1928). NYPL–MWEZ+nc 29092.

Simple Simon. Ziegfeld Theatre (1930). NYPL–RRS JPH 85-5, Book 5.

Spring Is Here. Alvin Theatre (1929). NYPL T-PRG.

BOOKS AND ARTICLES

Aronson, Arnold. *Architect of Dreams: The Theatrical Vision of Joseph Urban*. Online catalogue for "Joseph Urban and the Great American Revue" exhibition. Columbia University Library, July 2–August 27, 2012. http://www.columbia. edu/cu/lweb/eresources/archives/rbml/urban/architectOfDreams/index.html. Accessed August 27, 2012.

Axelrod, Alan. *The Real History of the American Revolution: A New Look at the Past*. New York: Sterling, 2007.

Banfield, Stephen. *Jerome Kern*. New Haven, CT: Yale University Press, 2006.

Banfield, Stephen. *Sondheim's Broadway Musicals*. Ann Arbor: University of Michigan Press, 1994.

Bargainnier, Earl F. "W. S. Gilbert and American Musical Theatre." *Journal of Popular Culture* 12, no. 3 (1978): 446–58.

Barnett, Lincoln. *Writing on Life: Sixteen Close-Ups*. New York: William Sloane Associates, 1951.

Bennett, Robert Russell. *The Broadway Sound*. Edited by George Ferencz. Rochester, NY: University of Rochester Press, 1999.

Bergreen, Laurence. *As Thousands Cheer: The Life of Irving Berlin*. London: Hodder & Stoughton, 1990.

Block, Geoffrey. *The Richard Rodgers Reader*. New York: Oxford University Press, 2002.

Block, Geoffrey. *Richard Rodgers*. New Haven, CT: Yale University Press, 2003.

Bordman, Gerald. *American Musical Comedy: From* Adonis *to* Dreamgirls. New York: Oxford University Press, 1982.

Bordman, Gerald. *American Musical Revue: From* The Passing Show *to* Sugar Babies. New York: Oxford University Press, 1985.

Bordman, Gerald. *American Musical Theatre: A Chronicle* (third edition). New York: Oxford University Press, 2001.

Bordman, Gerald. *Jerome Kern: His Life and Music*. New York: Oxford University Press, 1980.

Brooks, Mona Rebecca. "The Development of American Theatre Management Practices between 1830 and 1896." PhD diss., Texas Tech University, 1981.

Brooks, Van Wyck. *America's Coming of Age*. New York: B. W. Huebsch, 1915.

Brown, Phil. *Catskill Culture: A Mountain Rat's Memories of the Great Jewish Resort Area*. Philadelphia: Temple University Press, 1998.

Chauncey, George. *Gay New York: Gender, Urban Culture, and the Making of the Gay Male World, 1890–1940*. New York: Basic Books, 1994.

Cochran, Charles B. *Cock-a-doodle-do*. London: J. M. Dent and Sons, 1941.

Couch, J. R. "Are These Queer Times? Gay Male Representation on the American Stage in the 1920's and 1990's." MA diss., University of Kentucky, 2003.

Cox, Felix. "'A Faltering Step in a Basically Right Direction': Richard Rodgers and *All Points West*." *American Music* 23, no. 3 (Autumn 2005): 355–76.

Davis, Lee. *Bolton and Wodehouse and Kern: The Men Who Made Musical Comedy*. New York: James H. Heineman, 1993.

Davis, Owen. *I'd Like to Do It Again*. New York: Farrar and Rinehart, 1931.

Dynes, Wayne R. *The Encyclopedia of Homosexuality*. New York: Garland, 1990.

Everett, William A. *Sigmund Romberg*. New Haven, CT: Yale University Press, 2007.

Fields, Armond, and L. Marc Fields. *From the Bowery to Broadway: Lew Fields and the Roots of American Popular Theatre*. New York: Oxford University Press, 1993.

Fitzgerald, Jason. "'I Had a Dream': 'Rose's Turn,' Musical Theatre and the Star Effigy." *Studies in Musical Theatre* 3, no. 3 (December 2009): 285–91.

Forte, Allen. *The American Popular Ballad of the Golden Era: 1924–1950*. Princeton, NJ: Princeton University Press, 1995.

Frommer, Myrna Katz, and Harvey Frommer. *It Happened in the Catskills: An Oral History in the Words of Busboys, Bellhops, Guests, Proprietors, Comedians, Agents and Others Who Lived it*. Albany: State University of New York Press, 1991.

Gelinas, Paul. *The Varsity Show: A Celebration*. New York: Columbia University Press, 2004.

Gibson, H. W. *Camping for Boys*. New York: Association Press, 1911.

Gilbert, W. S., and Arthur Sullivan. *The Complete Works of Gilbert and Sullivan*. New York: W. W. Norton, 1976.

Green, Stanley. *Rodgers and Hammerstein Fact Book: A Record of Their Work Together and with Other Collaborators*. New York: Lynn Farnol Group, 1980.

Greenspan, Charlotte. *Pick Yourself Up: Dorothy Fields and the American Musical*. New York: Oxford University Press, 2010.

Guernsey, Otis L. Jr., ed. *Playwrights, Lyricists, Composers on Theatre*. New York: Dodd, Mead, 1974.

Hamilton, Marybeth. "Mae West Live: 'Sex, the Drag, and 1920s Broadway.'" *Drama Review* 36, no. 4 (Winter, 1992): 82–100.

Hamm, Charles. *Music in the New World*. New York: W. W. Norton, 1983.

Hamm, Charles, *Yesterdays: Popular Song in America*. New York: W. W. Norton, 1983.

Hart, Dorothy, ed. *Thou Swell, Thou Witty: The Life and Lyrics of Lorenz Hart*. New York: Harper and Row, 1976.

Hart, Dorothy, and Robert Kimball, eds. *The Complete Lyrics of Lorenz Hart*. New York: Da Capo Press, 1995.

Harty, Kevin J. *Cinema Arthuriana: Twenty Essays*. Jefferson, NC: McFarland, 2002.

Helburn, Theresa. *A Wayward Quest*. Toronto: Little, Brown, 1960.

Hirsch, Foster. *The Boys from Syracuse: The Shuberts' Theatrical Empire*. Carbondale: Southern Illinois University Press, 1998.

Holbrook, Morris B. *Music, Movies, Meanings and Markets: Cinemajazzamatazz*. London: Routledge, 2012.

Houchin, John H. *Censorship of the American Theatre in the Twentieth Century*. Cambridge: Cambridge University Press, 2003.

Hulbert, Jack. *The Little Woman's Always Right*. London: W. H. Allen, 1975.

Hyland, William G. *Richard Rodgers*. New Haven, CT: Yale University Press, 1998.

Johnston, Henry P. *The Campaign of 1776 around New York and Brooklyn*. Brooklyn, NY: Long Island Historical Society, 1878.

Kammen, Michael. *The Lively Arts: Gilbert Seldes and the Transformation of Cultural Criticism in the United States*. New York: Oxford University Press, 1996.

Kaye, Joseph. *Victor Herbert: The Biography of America's Greatest Composer of Romantic Music*. New York: Crown, 1931.

Kennedy, Matthew. *Marie Dressler: A Biography*. New York: McFarland, 1999.

Kirle, Bruce. *Unfinished Show Business: Broadway Musicals as Works-in-Process*. Carbondale: Southern Illinois University Press, 2005.

Knapp, Raymond. *The American Musical and the Formation of National Identity*. Princeton, NJ: Princeton University Press, 2005.

Knapp, Raymond, Mitchell Morris, and Stacy Wolf, eds. *The Oxford Handbook to the American Musical*. New York: Oxford University Press, 2011.

Koenig, Karl. *Jazz in Print (1856–1929): An Anthology of Selected Early Readings in Jazz History*. Hillsdale, NY: Pendragon Press, 2002.

Kolb, Eva. *The Evolution of New York City's Multiculturalism: Melting Pot or Salad Bowl? Immigrants in New York from the 19th Century to the End of the Gilded Age*. Norderstedt: Books on Demand, 2009.

Kracauer, Siegfried. *The Mass Ornament: Weimar Essays*. Edited by Thomas Y. Levin. Cambridge, MA: Harvard University Press, 1995.

MacDonald, Laurence E. *The Invisible Art of Film Music: A Comprehensive History* (second edition). Lanham, MD: Scarecrow Press, 2013.

Magee, Jeffrey. *Irving Berlin's American Musical Theater*. New York: Oxford University Press, 2012.

Marmorstein, Gary. *A Ship without a Sail*. New York: Simon and Schuster, 2012.

Marsh, J. B. T. *The Jubilee Singers and Their Songs*. Mineola, NY: Dover, 2003.

Marx, Samuel, and Jan Clayton. *Rodgers and Hart: Bewitched, Bothered and Bedevilled*. London: W. H. Allen, 1977.

Mason, Jeffrey D., and J. Ellen Gainor. *Performing America: Cultural Nationalism in American Theater*. Ann Arbor: University of Michigan Press, 1999.

Melnick, Jeffrey. *A Right to Sing the Blues: African Americans, Jews, and American Popular Song*. Cambridge, MA: Harvard University Press, 1999.

Miller, D. A. *Place for Us: Essay on the Broadway Musical*. Cambridge, MA: Harvard University Press, 1998.

Mordden, Ethan. *Broadway Babies: The People Who Made the American Musical*. New York: Oxford University Press, 1983.

Mordden, Ethan. *Make Believe: The Broadway Musical in the 1920s*. New York: Oxford University Press, 1997.

Mordden, Ethan. *Ziegfeld: The Man Who Invented Show Business*. New York: St. Martin's Press, 2008.

Morley, Sheridan. *Spread a Little Happiness: The First Hundred Years of the British Musical*. London: Thames and Hudson, 1987.

Morrissey, Will. *On a Shoestring: The Autobiography to End All Theatrical Biographies*. New York: W. Paul, 1955.

Moruzzi, Peter. *Havana before Castro: When Cuba Was a Tropical Playground*. Layton, UT: Gibbs Smith, 2008.

Nolan, Frederick. *Lorenz Hart: A Poet on Broadway*. New York: Oxford University Press, 1994.

Norton, Richard C. *A Chronology of American Musical Theater*, Volume 2: *1912–1952*. New York: Oxford University Press, 2002.

Oja, Carol. *Making Music Modern: New York in the 1920s*. New York: Oxford University Press, 2000.

Ommen van der Merwe, Ann. *The Ziegfeld Follies: A History in Song*. New York: Scarecrow Press, 2009.

Peretti, Burton W. *Nightclub City: Politics and Amusement in Manhattan*. Philadelphia: University of Pennsylvania Press, 2007.

Peyser, Joan. *The Memory of All That: The Life of George Gershwin*. New York: Billboard Books, 1998.

Pollack, Howard. *George Gershwin: His Life and Work*. Berkeley: University of California Press, 2006.

Rapée, Erno. *Motion Picture Moods for Pianists and Organists, a Rapid Reference Collection of Selected Pieces Adapted to Fifty-two Moods and Situations*. New York: Schirmer, 1924.

Rathbone, Basil. *In and Out of Character*. New York: Doubleday, 1956.

Robbins, Allison. "Busby Berkeley, Broken Rhythms, and Dance Direction on the Stage and Screen." *Studies in Musical Theatre* 7, no.1 (2013): 75–93.

Rodgers, Richard. *Letters to Dorothy (1926–1937)*. Edited by William W. Appleton. New York: New York Public Library, 1988.

Rodgers, Richard. *Musical Stages: An Autobiography*. New York: Da Capo Press, 2002.

Rodgers, Richard, ed. *The Rodgers and Hart Song Book*. New York: Simon and Schuster, 1951.

Rodgers, Richard, and Oscar Hammerstein II. *Six Plays by Rodgers and Hammerstein*. New York: Modern Library, n.d.

Rowe, John Carlos. *Literary Culture and US Imperialism: From the Revolution to World War II*. Oxford: Oxford University Press, 2000.

Rubin, Jason. "Lew Fields and the Development of the Broadway Musical." PhD diss., New York University, 1991.

Rusinko, Susan. *The Plays of Benn Levy: Between Shaw and Coward*. London: Associated University Presses, 1994.

Savran, David. *Highbrow/Lowdown: Theater, Jazz, and the Making of the New Middle Class*. Ann Arbor: University of Michigan Press, 2009.

Sears, Benjamin, ed. *The Irving Berlin Reader*. New York: Oxford University Press, 1981.

Secrest, Meryle. *Shoot the Widow: Adventures of a Biographer in Search of Her Subject*. New York: Alfred A. Knopf, 2007.

Secrest, Meryle. *Somewhere for Me: A Biography of Richard Rodgers*. New York: Alfred A. Knopf, 2001.

Seldes, Gilbert. "Jazz and Ballad." *New Republic* 43 (August 5, 1925): 293–94.

Seldes, Gilbert. *The Seven Lively Arts*. New York: Sagamore Press, 1957.

Sheed, Wilfrid. *The House That George Built*. New York: Random House, 2007.

Solomon, Aubrey. *The Fox Film Corporation, 1915–1935: A History and Filmography*. Jefferson, NC: McFarland, 2011.

Spivak, Jeffrey. *Buzz: The Life and Art of Busby Berkeley*. Lexington: University Press of Kentucky.

Tawa, Nicholas. *The Way to Tin Pan Alley: American Popular Song, 1866–1910*. London: Schirmer Books, 1990.

Taylor, William R., ed. *Inventing Times Square: Commerce and Culture at the Crossroads of the World*. Baltimore, MD: Johns Hopkins University Press, 1996.

Valgemae, Mardi. *Accelerated Grimace: Expressionism in the American Drama of the 1920s*. Carbondale: Southern Illinois University Press, 1972.

Walton, John K. *Fish and Chips and the British Working Class, 1870–1940*. London: Leicester University Press, 1992.

Watts, Jill. *Mae West: An Icon in Black and White*. New York: Oxford University Press, 2001.

Wilder, Alec. *American Popular Song: The Great Innovators 1900–1950*. New York: Oxford University Press, 1972.

Wilk, Max. *They're Playing Our Song: Conversations with America's Classic Songwriters*. New York: Da Capo Press, 1997.

Wood, Graham. "The Development of Song Forms in the Broadway and Hollywood Musicals of Richard Rodgers, 1919–1943." PhD diss., University of Minnesota, 2000.

Woollcott, Alexander. *The Story of Irving Berlin*. New York: G. P. Putnam, 1925.

Wyatt, Robert, and John A. Johnson, eds. *The George Gershwin Reader*. New York: Oxford University Press, 2004.

DISCOGRAPHY

Comden, Betty, and Richard Lewine. *Remember These: Songs from "Treasure Girl" and "Chee Chee."* Ava Records A-26, 1963.

Crosby, Bing. *The Complete United Artists Sessions*. EMI 7243 8 59808 2 4, 1997.

Gershwin, George, and Ira Gershwin. *Lady, Be Good!*, Elektra Nonesuch 7559-79308-2, 1992.

Rodgers, Richard. *Richard Rodgers: Command Performance*. Harbinger Records HCD2501, 2008.

Rodgers, Richard, and Lorenz Hart. *Ben Bagley's Rodgers and Hart Revisited III*. Painted Smiles Records PSCD-106, 1989.

Rodgers, Richard, and Lorenz Hart. *Ben Bagley's Rodgers and Hart Revisited IV*. Painted Smiles Records PSCD-126, 1991.

Rodgers, Richard, and Lorenz Hart. *Ben Bagley's Rodgers and Hart Revisited II*. Painted Smiles Records PSCD-139, 1992.

Rodgers, Richard, and Lorenz Hart. *Ben Bagley's Rodgers and Hart Revisited V.* Painted Smiles Records PSCD-140, 1992.

Rodgers, Richard, and Lorenz Hart. *Rodgers and Hart's Ever Green.* Bygone Records CD BG-1002, 2004.

Rodgers, Richard, and Lorenz Hart. *Rodgers and Hart Revisited.* Painted Smiles Records PSCD-116, 1990.

Various. *Gems from Nobody Home.* Matrix C-16055, 1915.

Various. *Gems from Very Good Eddie.* Matrix C-17126, 1916.

Various. *Selection from Very Good Eddie.* Matrix B-19604, 1917.

Whyte, Ronnie, and Travis Hudson. *The Songs of Rodgers and Hart.* Audiophile ACD-57, 1998.

FILMOGRAPHY

Max Liebman Presents Rodgers and Hart: A Connecticut Yankee. Video Artists International DVD Video 4541, 2011.

Max Liebman Presents Rodgers and Hart: Dearest Enemy. Video Artists International DVD Video 4550, 2012.

CREDITS

The following songs and musical examples are excerpted with permission.

Figure 5.1: Recurring melodic features of the *Lido Lady* score

Figure 5.2: Motivic connections between Rodgers's "A Tiny Little Flat in Soho" and Gershwin's "I'll Have a House in Berkeley Square"

Figure 5.3: Motivic connections between Rodgers's "Try Again To-morrow" and Gershwin's "Fascinating Rhythm"

Figure 5.4: motivic connections between Rodgers's "The Girl Friend" and Gershwin's "I'd Rather Charleston"

Figure 5.6: An early draft of "My Heart Stood Still"

Figure 5.7: Recurring use of dropped phrasing in Rodgers's score to *Ever Green*

Figure 5.8: Use of cross-rhythm in "The Color of Her Eyes"

Figure 8.5–8.6: Descending chromatic chord clusters, a feature of the *Chee-Chee* score

Figure 8.7: The triple time motif of the Grand Eunuch's music in *Chee-Chee*

Figure 8.8: Passages from "In a Great Big Way," and "Monastery Opening," both from *Chee-Chee*

Figure 8.9: The "fanfare motif" throughout the score of *Chee-Chee*

Figure 8.10: The "Chti and Tchou motif," as used throughout the score of *Chee-Chee*

Figure 8.11: The B section of "I Must Love You"

Copyright Renewed and assigned to Imagem CV and WB Music Corp for the United States and British Reversionary Territories.
International Copyright Secured. All Rights Reserved

Figure 8.12: Further uses of the descending motif
Copyright © 1928 Chappell & Co. Inc.
Copyright Renewed and assigned to Imagem CV and WB Music Corp for the United States and British Reversionary Territories.
International Copyright Secured. All Rights Reserved

Figure 8.13: The Eunuch / Concubine motif, also used in "Moon of My Delight"
Copyright © 1928 Chappell & Co. Inc.
Copyright Renewed and assigned to Imagem CV and WB Music Corp for the United States and British Reversionary Territories.
International Copyright Secured. All Rights Reserved

Figure 9.1: Rodgers's use of the mixolydian mode in *America's Sweetheart*
Copyright © 1931 Chappell & Co. Inc.
Copyright Renewed and assigned to Imagem CV and WB Music Corp for the United States and British Reversionary Territories.
International Copyright Secured. All Rights Reserved

IMAGEM CV

Mary Queen of Scots (lyrics by Herbert Fields, *You'd Be Surprised*, 1920)
© 1920 by Imagem CV / © 1920 (Renewed) Warner Bros. Inc.
Used by Permission of Williamson Music, A Division of Rodgers & Hammerstein: An Imagem Company

Lady Raffles Behave (*Poor Little Ritz Girl*, 1920)
© 1920 by Imagem CV / © 1920 (Renewed) Warner Bros. Inc.
Used by Permission of Williamson Music, A Division of Rodgers & Hammerstein: An Imagem Company

You Can't Fool Your Dreams (*Poor Little Ritz Girl*, 1920)
© 1920 by Imagem CV / © 1920 (Renewed) Warner Bros. Inc.
Used by Permission of Williamson Music, A Division of Rodgers & Hammerstein: An Imagem Company

All You Need to Be a Star (*Poor Little Ritz Girl*, 1920)
© 1920 by Imagem CV / © 1920 (Renewed) Warner Bros. Inc.
Used by Permission of Williamson Music, A Division of Rodgers & Hammerstein: An Imagem Company

Watch Yourself (*Say Mama*, 1921)
© 1921 by Imagem CV
Used by Permission of Williamson Music, A Division of Rodgers & Hammerstein: An Imagem Company

Chorus Girl Blues (*Say Mama*, 1921)
© 1921 by Imagem CV
Used by Permission of Williamson Music, A Division of Rodgers & Hammerstein: An Imagem Company

Since I Remember You (*Winkle Town*, 1922)
© 1986 by Imagem CV / © Warner Bros. Inc.
Used by Permission of Williamson Music, A Division of Rodgers & Hammerstein: An Imagem Company

And Thereby Hangs a Tail (*The Garrick Gaieties*, 1925)
Copyright © 1986 by Estate of Richard Rodgers and Estate of Lorenz Hart
Used by Permission of Williamson Music, A Division of Rodgers & Hammerstein: An Imagem Company

Bye and Bye (*Dearest Enemy*, 1925)
© 1925 by Imagem CV / © Warner Bros. Inc.
Used by Permission of Williamson Music, A Division of Rodgers & Hammerstein: An Imagem Company

Camera Shoot (*Lido Lady*, 1926)
© 1986 by Imagem CV / © Warner Bros. Inc.
Used by Permission of Williamson Music, A Division of Rodgers & Hammerstein: An Imagem Company

I Want a Man (*Lido Lady*, 1926)
© 1986 by Imagem CV / © Warner Bros. Inc.
Used by Permission of Williamson Music, A Division of Rodgers & Hammerstein: An Imagem Company

Queen of Sheba; aka My Heart Is Sheba Bound (*Lido Lady*, 1926)
© 1926 by Imagem CV / © Warner Bros. Inc.
Used by Permission of Williamson Music, A Division of Rodgers & Hammerstein: An Imagem Company

Four Little Song Pluggers (*The Garrick Gaieties*, 1926)
© 1986 by Imagem CV / © Warner Bros. Inc. Used by Permission of Williamson Music, A Division of Rodgers & Hammerstein: An Imagem Company

Idles of the King (*One Dam Thing after Another*, 1927)
© 1927 by Imagem CV / © Warner Bros. Inc. Used by Permission of Williamson Music, A Division of Rodgers & Hammerstein: An Imagem Company

Make Hey (*One Dam Thing After Another*, 1927)
© 1927 by Imagem CV / © Warner Bros. Inc. Used by Permission of Williamson Music, A Division of Rodgers & Hammerstein: An Imagem Company

You're What I Need (*A Connecticut Yankee*, 1927)
© 1927 by Imagem CV / © Warner Bros. Inc. Used by Permission of Williamson Music, A Division of Rodgers & Hammerstein: An Imagem Company

I Feel at Home with You (*A Connecticut Yankee*, 1927)
©.1927 by Imagem CV / © Warner Bros. Inc. Used by Permission of Williamson Music, A Division of Rodgers & Hammerstein: An Imagem Company

Evelyn, What Do You Say? (*A Connecticut Yankee*, 1927)
© 1986 by Imagem CV / © Warner Bros. Inc. Used by Permission of Williamson Music, A Division of Rodgers & Hammerstein: An Imagem Company

The Sandwich Men (*A Connecticut Yankee*, 1927)
© 1986 by Imagem CV / © Warner Bros. Inc. Used by Permission of Williamson Music, A Division of Rodgers & Hammerstein: An Imagem Company

Better be Good to Me (*Chee-Chee*, 1928)
© 1928 by Imagem CV / © Warner Bros. Inc. Used by Permission of Williamson Music, A Division of Rodgers & Hammerstein: An Imagem Company

The Beauty Contest (Opening for *Ever Green*, 1930)
© 1986 by Imagem CV / © Warner Bros. Inc. Used by Permission of Williamson Music, A Division of Rodgers & Hammerstein: An Imagem Company

Harlemania (*Ever Green*, 1930)
© 1930 by Imagem CV / © Warner Bros. Inc. Used by Permission of Williamson Music, A Division of Rodgers & Hammerstein: An Imagem Company

Doing a Little Clog Dance (*Ever Green*, 1930)
© 1986 by Imagem CV / © Warner Bros. Inc. Used by Permission of Williamson Music, A Division of Rodgers & Hammerstein: An Imagem Company

Waiting for the Leaves to Fall (*Ever Green*, 1930)
© 1986 by Imagem CV / © Warner Bros. Inc. Used by Permission of Williamson Music, A Division of Rodgers & Hammerstein: An Imagem Company

If I Give In to You (*Ever Green*, 1930)
© 1930 by Imagem CV / © Warner Bros. Inc. Used by Permission of Williamson Music, A Division of Rodgers & Hammerstein: An Imagem Company

The Color of Her Eyes (*Ever Green,* 1930)
© 1930 by Imagem CV / © Warner Bros. Inc. Used by Permission of Williamson Music, A Division of Rodgers & Hammerstein: An Imagem Company

I Wish I Were in Love (*Babes in Arms*, 1937)
© 1937 by Imagem CV / © Warner Bros. Inc. Used by Permission of Williamson Music, A Division of Rodgers & Hammerstein: An Imagem Company

The Girlfriend (1926)
© 1926 by Imagem CV / © Warner Bros. Inc. Used by Permission of Williamson Music, A Division of Rodgers & Hammerstein: An Imagem Company

Goodbye Lenny (1926)
© 1986 by Imagem CV / © Warner Bros. Inc. Used by Permission of Williamson Music, A Division of Rodgers & Hammerstein: An Imagem Company

This Funny World (1926)
© 1926 by Imagem CV / © Warner Bros. Inc. Used by Permission of Williamson Music, A Division of Rodgers & Hammerstein: An Imagem Company

It Must Be Heaven (1929)
© 1929 by Imagem CV / © Warner Bros. Inc. Used by Permission of Williamson Music, A Division of Rodgers & Hammerstein: An Imagem Company

Manhattan
Imagem CV / © Warner Bros. Inc.
Used by Permission of Williamson Music, A
Division of Rodgers & Hammerstein: An Imagem
Company

Heigh-Ho, Lackaday
Imagem CV / © Warner Bros. Inc.
Used by Permission of Williamson Music, A
Division of Rodgers & Hammerstein: An Imagem
Company

The Hermits
Imagem CV / © Warner Bros. Inc.
Used by Permission of Williamson Music, A Division
of Rodgers & Hammerstein: An Imagem Company

Tho' We've No Authentic Reason Imagem CV /
© Warner Bros. Inc.
Used by Permission of Williamson Music, A
Division of Rodgers & Hammerstein: An Imagem
Company

Full Blown Roses
Imagem CV / © Warner Bros. Inc.
Used by Permission of Williamson Music, A
Division of Rodgers & Hammerstein: An Imagem
Company

Here in My Arms
Imagem CV / © Warner Bros. Inc.
Used by Permission of Williamson Music, A Division
of Rodgers & Hammerstein: An Imagem Company

WARNER/CHAPPELL MUSIC LIMITED

Mary Queen of Scots (Music: Richard Rodgers;
   Lyrics: Lorenz Hart)
Lady Raffles Behave (Note: Composer and
   Lyricist the Same for All Songs)
You Can't Fool Your Dreams
All You Need to Be a Star
Since I Remember You
And Thereby Hangs a Tail
Dearest Enemy
Camera Shoot
I Want a Man
Four Little Song Pluggers
You're What I Need
I Feel At Home with You
Evelyn, What Do You Say?

Sandwich Men
Better Be Good to Me
The Beauty Contest
Harlemania
Doing a Little Clog Dance
Waiting for the Leaves To Fall
If I Give In to You
The Color of Her Eyes
I Wish I Were in Love Again
The Girl Friend
Goodbye, Lenny
This Funny World
It Must Be Heaven
Bye and Bye
Manhattan

INDEX

and Richard Rodgers (*see* Rodgers and
    Hammerstein)
Winkle Town (1922), 4–7, 27, 72, 112–13,
    181–82, 245, 250
Hammerstein, William, 10
Harms, T. B., 27, 124
Hart, Frieda, 9–10, 35
Hart, Lorenz
    and Billy Rose, 75
    and homosexuality, 7, 81–82
    attitude to theater, 68, 83
    "Elliot's Plagiarism," 35
    If I Were King (1923), 39–40, 63, 83
        "Band of the Ne-er-Do-Wells," 40
        "If I Were King," 40
    on euphonics, 70, 85, 194, 196
    on lyric writing, 70, 256–57
    On Your Way (1915), 40
    Shakespeares of 1922 (1922), 53–54, 59
Hart, Max, 9–10, 35, 55, 238–39
Hart, Moss, 173, 259, 274n76
    Lady in the Dark (1941), 173, 274n76
    Once in a Lifetime (1930), 259
Hart, Theodore (Teddy), 10, 35
Helburn, Theresa, 65
Henderson, Ray, 143, 148
Herbert, Richard Lorenz, 56–58, 61, 255
Herbert, Victor, 4, 11–12, 23, 37, 43, 110, 125
highbrow, 13, 18–19, 73, 83, 268n33,
    270n64
Holloway, Sterling, 65–7, 80, 83, 85
Hollywood, xv, xvii, 3, 5, 26, 38, 69, 113,
    154, 165, 170, 194, 207, 247, 252,
    255–63
homosexuality, 82, 197–98, 212–16, 236,
    298n27
    Hart and, 7, 81–82
Hubbell, Raymond, 16, 23, 43, 110
Hulbert, Jack, xviii, 124, 126–27, 133, 135,
    138–39, 176
Hunter, Glenn, 241

"I Am" Song, 206
"I Want" Song, 172

Institute of Musical Art (IMA), 33, 51–53,
    225, 275n92
    Baton, The, 51–53, 275n92, 275n95,
        275n98, 276n110
integration, 14, 22, 25, 33, 46, 48, 50, 61,
    108, 116, 121–22, 164, 176, 180,
    197, 220, 228–29, 233–34, 241, 251,
    256–57, 263, 264, 269n46
    dialogic writing, 47, 61

jazz, 15–17, 19–22, 24, 32–33, 44, 47, 51–52,
    56, 59, 61–62, 70–73, 95, 97,
    107, 114, 118–19, 122, 124, 129,
    132–33, 136, 143–45, 150–51, 189,
    192–93, 196–97, 201, 234, 243,
    250–51, 253, 262–64, 270n64,
    289n116
    Jazz Age, the, 31, 43, 58–59, 193, 235
    jazz opera, 72–73
Jazz Singer, The (1927), 256
Jeans, Ronald, 125–26, 141
    Lido Lady (1926), xiv, 44, 124–40, 146,
        156, 158–59, 162, 165–66, 174–75,
        182, 184, 202, 205, 212, 228, 250,
        259, 284n13, 299n53
    One Dam Thing After Another (1927),
        xiv, 81, 124, 133, 136, 139–48, 156,
        165–66, 189, 191, 201, 287n76
Jolson, Al, 54, 84, 122, 289n113

Kaufman, George S., 170, 259
    Beggar on Horseback (1924), 170
    Once in a Lifetime (1930), 259
Kaye, Benjamin, 64–67
Kerker, Gustave, 4
Kern, Jerome, 4, 12, 15, 19–22, 24, 84,
    110, 125, 134, 177, 205, 268n23,
    293–94n23
    Good Morning Dearie (1921), 205
    Oh, Boy! (1917): "Till the Clouds Roll
        By," 83–84
    Sunny (1926): "Who," 205
    Swing Time (1936): "Way You Look
        Tonight, The," 118